*Deception at Work*

# Deception at Work

Investigating and Countering Lies
and Fraud Strategies

MICHAEL J. COMER and
TIMOTHY E. STEPHENS
Cobasco Group Limited

Routledge
Taylor & Francis Group

LONDON AND NEW YORK

First published 2004 by Gower Publishing

2 Park Square, Milton Park, Abingdon, Oxon OX14 4RN
711 Third Avenue, New York, NY 10017, USA

*Routledge is an imprint of the Taylor & Francis Group, an informa business*

First issued in paperback 2017

Mind Maps® is a Registered Trade Mark of The Buzan Organization and is used with enthusiastic permission. Original concept supplied by Buzan Centres Ltd, 54 Parkstone Road, Poole, Dorset BH15 2PG.

All Mind Maps in this book were drawn on Mindjet. A trial version can be downloaded from www.mindjet.com

**British Library Cataloguing in Publication Data**
Comer, Michael J.
    Deception at work: investigating and countering lies and fraud strategies
    1. Deception 2. Employee crimes 3. Fraud investigation
    I. Title II. Stephens, Timothy E.
    658.4'73

ISBN 978-0-566-08636-6 (hbk)
ISBN 978-1-138-25622-4 (pbk)

**Library of Congress Cataloging-in-Publication Data**
Comer, Michael J.
    Deception at work : investigating and countering lies and fraud strategies / Michael J. Comer and Timothy E. Stephens.
        p. cm.
    Includes index.
    ISBN 0-566-08636-0
        1. Fraud. 2. Fraud investigation. I. Stephens, Timothy E. II. Title.

HV6691.C663 2004
363.25'963--dc22

2004053923

Typeset by Sparks, Oxford, UK – www.sparks.co.uk

# Contents

'IT DEPENDS WHETHER YOU WANT TO DO IT TEN TIMES A NIGHT,
OR JUST SAY YOU HAVE'

# List of Figures

# List of Tables

# List of Mind Maps®

THE DANGERS OF LATIN

# *Foreword*

## by Spot the dog

## Every dog has its day

It is the ultimate irony that towards the close of his career, when the few faculties he ever had have long since evaporated, that my master – Mike Comer – should be coming into vogue. It really is a funny old world and proves that you should never have thrown out your purple flared trousers and yellow Hush Puppies because every dog has its day and what goes round, comes round. If Mr Comer can come into fashion, anything can.

## The dangers of Latin

At a recent fraud conference, George Staple QC, a very distinguished man and a top lawyer in a leading City firm, former head of both the Fraud Panel and the Serious Fraud Office, introduced Mr Comer as 'the international doyen of fraud specialists' or words to that effect. Mr Comer suspects anything in Latin and was thus unsure what 'doyen' meant. He crawled to his feet and was about to give the distinguished QC a kick in the pants when someone pointed out that what Mr Staple had said was a compliment and wasn't even remotely Latin. Mr Comer, being unaccustomed to compliments, took time to regain his *compos mentis* before delivering an hour's tirade on the devastating impact that Latin has on the lives of ordinary folk. He never gives up, especially when he is wrong.[1]

## Putting it in writing

For those of you who have cleverly avoided having to read Mr Comer's stuff or listen to him drone on at seminars, I should explain how I, a simple spotted mutt, ended up writing a foreword to what is supposed to be a serious textbook for humans. The truth is that no human (and especially Mr Staple) would agree to having their names associated in print with the author. It is one thing saying something fleetingly nice about the geriatric guru at a fraud conference and quite another committing it to paper. In short, I got the job because no one else would do it. *Stercus accidit*: or as they say, 'shit happens'.

---

[1]  I don't think I was wrong. Just see how many times Latin phrases appear in this book

## The geriatric devil child

Through some baffling quirk of nature, Mr Comer has always seemed able to get people to tell him the truth, or at least most of it, and to do things that they would rather not do. I am sure that the people at Gower never wanted to commission him to write this book, but somehow here it is. You may be familiar with films and books on Damian, the fiendish child, and Chuckie, the devilish doll. Mr Comer is the geriatric equivalent.

## Making things happen

Things just seem to happen when Mr Comer is around. For example, the other day we were just sauntering along Victoria Street in London, minding our own business. I was hallucinating about nice juicy bones and lamp-posts and Mr Comer about his increasing band of grandchildren and his new Scotty Cameron putter when – all of a sudden – our paths were crossed by a couple of young heavies who rudely asked for 50 pence for a cup of tea. They obviously did not appreciate the dangers of interrupting the ex-guru when he is deep in thought and, after a two hour interrogation – held on the pavement in the pouring rain and in front of a growing crowd of Japanese tourists who thought they were on *Candid Camera* – the heavies confessed to three bank robberies and, worse still in Mr Comer's eyes, to being supporters of Birmingham City Football Club. Instead of getting 50 pence, the heavies face five years in the cooler. The first lesson from this is that you can always get humans and humanoids to tell the truth, providing you have a cunning plan. The second is never ask Mr Comer for money.

## Commendations and condemnations

Over the past 40 years Mr Comer has interviewed many hundreds, if not thousands, of people: appearing in all shapes and sizes, nationalities and sexes in all parts of the world and in cases of varying complexities. In some he has cleared people wrongly under suspicion, but in the majority he has exposed guilty secrets by using the cunning plan described in this book. On a few occasions he has failed to get anywhere, but in a painfully extended career as an investigator and as a witness in criminal and civil courts he has been commended more times than his ass has been kicked. This is not a bad record for an investigator trapped in a time capsule in a lawyer's world.

## Learning from mistakes

As will become obvious, Mr Comer is not a qualified psychologist, accountant or even an estate agent but he has built on his GCE 'O' level certificates in scripture, woodwork and geometrical drawing to become a keen interpreter of human behaviour, learning what works and what doesn't. This book is the result of mistakes made over 40 years as a practitioner and, in a very narrow way, as an academic.[2]

---

[2]    Mr Comer served as a Visiting Professor at Cranfield Institute of Technology and is currently a Visiting Fellow at the Scarman Centre, University of Leicester. He is also Past President of the European Chapter of Certified Fraud Examiners and, believe it or believe it not, a member of MENSA

## The most important lessons

In a rare burst of lucidity, Mr Comer told me that the most important lesson he has learned is that people too quickly dismiss their instincts that something is wrong. He says if something does not look or sound right, the chances are it is iffy and must be dealt with. In short, if something is too good to be true, it is. Secondly, problems do not get better by themselves and unresolved suspicions of deception leave a cloud hanging over innocent people while evil escapes unscathed. This is a very bad scene.

We dogs are totally different and if we don't like someone, we just bite them. This is a natural animal instinct but humans try to consciously control everything and would rather be deceived than face the truth. Just ask yourself: 'When did I last bite someone in anger?'

## Acknowledgements

Mr Comer has asked me to thank Mike Williams, who drew the cartoons for this book. I have never met Mr Williams although I have corresponded with him and spoken to him on the telephone. He seems a pleasant sort of bloke even though his accent is difficult to understand, the more so since he had his National Health dentures fitted. Mike Williams is what is known as a 'Scouser' and lives in the Wirral, which is perilously north of civilization, bordering even on Scotland, with all that entails. A sense of humour is essential to survive in such extremes and Mike Williams has a good one. He too is a keen interpreter of human behaviour, particularly in pubs, bars, bingo halls and bookmakers' shops which he seems to frequent a lot. He claims he only goes in them to stimulate the right hemisphere of his brain and to get ideas for cartoons, but I think he may be dissembling the truth and is really a voyeur. Anyway, if you don't like the words, I am sure you will appreciate the cartoons.

I have also been instructed to thank Patrick M. Ardis, of the Woolf Ardis law firm in Memphis, Tennessee, and David H. Price of Ealing, who were dragged in by Mr Comer to co-author *Bad Lies in Business*, which was also about deception and is fortunately out of print except for the Thai and Brazilian editions. It is to their credit that Mr Ardis and Mr Price have managed to disassociate themselves from this book, although it does contain many of the ideas they developed together.

Mr Comer also acknowledges some good work by Don Rabon of the North Carolina Justice Academy and Avinoan Sapir of LSI in Phoenix, Arizona, on the analysis of written statements. He is especially grateful to Tim Stephens on whom most of the techniques in this book have been tried and tested *ad nauseam*. However, his family seems to like him and so do dogs of the more intelligent variety.

Enjoy the book; I guarantee it will make you a happier person and far more effective in dealing with deception. It will also give you a good insight into the twisted mind of a fraud investigator, but you can pick out the good bits and ignore the rest.

Best wishes,
Spot

HE WAS DETERMINED NOT TO BE CAUGHT IN A LIE

# Prologue: The Advantages of Finding the Truth

## Monkey waves

In the summer of 1999, Herman Snooks, a sandal-wearing, ginger-haired research scientist from Newbury, Berkshire – in a moment of extraordinary genius – invented an electronic device which was about the size of a ballpoint pen and emitted what he called 'monkey waves'. These invisible and silent surges concatenated, reversed and redirected the brain's alpha and beta waves, thereby compelling human targets to tell the truth, the whole truth and nothing but the truth, regardless of the consequences.

## Revealing the truth

It was an extraordinary invention that gave new meaning to the phrase 'to get on the same wavelength as someone else'. Victims who were enveloped by the waves had an unfailing reaction: they blinked hard four times, scratched their noses twice and then exploded with the truth. There was no stopping them and honesty would pour out like a raging torrent. Once removed from the beams, the victims reverted to deceptive normality but, as if in their worst nightmare, they remembered every word they had said while under the influence. The way they tried to recover and explain away their eruptions of unexpurgated truth was pitiable and the panic-ridden aftermath was the most disturbing of all. Grown men turned into blubbering imbeciles.

*The truth really hurts, especially when you had no intention of telling it*

Herman tested the device on his neighbours, friends and family with astonishing results. His wife pleaded guilty to voting for New Labour and is now in a mental home, his teenage kids admitted to being multimillionaire drug pushers with massive real estate investments in Highgate and his mother-in-law confessed that she was undergoing sex change therapy and planned to become a professional wrestler. This last disclosure did not surprise Herman, but the others were shocking.

## Clever investments

Other successes followed quickly, including sudden, unexplained bursts of honesty by car salesmen, pension advisers, social security claimants and, to everyone's total amazement, even estate agents and accountants. People could not stop themselves from telling the truth and Herman soon became very wealthy by making astute investments in all manner of honest enterprises. He thus avoided telecoms shares. His device changed his world by guaranteeing he only reacted to the truth. He could do no wrong and every decision was a winner.

*Knowing the truth makes life easy*

## The bubble bursts

But it was all too good to be true and Herman became overconfident and went one step too far. He should have known the bubble had to burst and when it did it was in the most spectacular way imaginable. The downfall started when Herman beamed the gadget at the judge, defendants, witnesses and lawyers in a high-profile televised court case, much like the OJ Simpson trial. The tumult that followed, when justice collapsed under the unacceptable burden of the deep truth, does not bear repeating. The bottom line was that Herman was pilloried and the device seized, classified as 'top secret' and sent to the Pentagon for analysis amid great judicial and political rumblings of 'anarchy', 'communistic-inspired revolution' and 'black magic'. A few people said the device was an al-Qaeda plot to bring down Western economies by compelling accountants to tell the truth: others said the Martians were behind it. But they all thought that Herman had stockpiled better and more powerful weapons of mass detection and was a permanent danger.

## Politicians close ranks

Politicians everywhere could see the implications, were the device to become generally available. 'If we are made to tell the truth and cannot spin,' some said, 'our world, as we know it, will come to an end. This is an intolerable attack on democracy: it must be banned forthwith or even quicker.' Laboratories were commissioned to develop antidotes to the diabolical beams; pills were invented and one enterprising scientist designed a wave-proof helmet and mouth guard – much like that worn by Hannibal Lecter in *The Silence of the Lambs*. This worked well, but politicians who tested the prototype were not convinced that it conveyed the right image.

They said: 'Aren't we admitting, if we wear it, that we need it and, if we need it, aren't we acknowledging that we tell lies? What the heck shall we do? This is scandalous. It gives us no room for manoeuvre and a world without spin is not worth living in.'

Political enemies, who had agreed on nothing for decades, became as one in swearing themselves to secrecy and condemning Herman's invention. 'It's a monkey on our back', they moaned. Parliament was put into indefinite recess and some MPs went on permanent sick leave, while others disappeared on world cruises.

## London abandoned

Travel agents in London SW1 and Islington could not figure out why there was such a sudden rush of last-minute bookings for sponsored political fact-finding trips to the Himalayas and the Upper Volta. Haunts used by politicians and journalists, such as steam baths, bingo halls, massage parlours and expensive restaurants, were deserted and for the first time in over 30 years, table one at Langan's restaurant in the West End of London was available to non-politicians. It really was that bad!

Paranoia ran wild, and people who thought they had been beamed but hadn't confessed to everything imaginable and to lots of things that weren't. Stock markets collapsed when at annual general meetings directors, who had heard secret rumours about the device and were fearful they might be beamed midway through presenting their annual results, took the safe course and told the truth about the shocking state of their businesses. Staff working in Buckingham Palace resigned in droves, but did not think even once of speaking to Max Clifford or tabloid journalists. It was that bad, it really was.

## Academia

Universities, research centres, laboratories and other repositories for academics shut their doors, forcing their occupants to seek meaningful employment as plumbers and butchers or, in one case, even as an investigator. Scientists quickly recalibrated the results of widely accepted research projects, admitting that smoking was extremely healthy, that Big Macs were highly nutritional, and that Viagra had previously hidden side effects such as multiple slipped discs and inflamed knees. Sales plunged.

But the most embarrassing scientific turnaround was from NASA, which admitted that it had never landed a rocket on the moon and that the photographs of the astronauts jumping about with flags and golf clubs had been staged in a disused warehouse in the Bronx. It really was that bad, it was. And all because of Herman.

## Authors

Gurus who had written management texts stood in queues outside bookshops to buy up entire stocks of their own works so they could be burned. Amazon.com sold out overnight. Tom Peters reissued his landmark book with the new title *In Search of Flatulence* and *The One Minute Manager* was changed to *Late is Better Than Never.* It was bad. Really bad. Fear that the truth might strike anyone down at any time created pre-emptive panic and the effect was universal. No one was safe.

## The closure

Very serious consideration, at the highest levels,[1] was given to having Herman assassinated. But in the end, as is often the case, common sense based on bribery prevailed and under an oath of absolute secrecy Herman was given $50 million to destroy his invention and all plans, specifications and prototypes which, being an honest man, he did. This is probably why you have never heard of the device before now.

For readers who are interested in the ending to this story, Herman changed his name and is now living happily in Mexico with his sixth wife, Bernard. His beard has gone and he is heavily

---

[1]   i.e. Alistair Campbell

into designer clothes, Cartier watches, polo shirts, Volvos, crocodile shoes, dark glasses and silk socks. He is sometimes mistaken for a fraud investigator and this irritates him.

## At it again

While technically in semi-retirement Herman invented an electronic collar that translates barks, mews and other sounds made by dogs, cats, rabbits and other furry and feathery creatures into plain English, Japanese and Yiddish. Don't ask why he included English and Japanese, but that's just the way it was. The beta version is working well and Herman has spent many happy hours discussing the works of Van Gogh and Rembrandt with his gerbil, Basil.

Sadly, Herman knows that the device can never be marketed commercially. *Entre nous,* the drawback is that most domestic pets are totally obsessed with their genitalia and bowel movements. Worse still, apparently innocent barks, mews, grunts and squeaks decode into awfully bad language and pets are not up to snuff on either political correctness or discretion. They are also sexually indiscriminate and spend most of their waking hours figuring out how to roger their colleagues.[2] To release the contraption on the open market – thereby empowering billions of pets to swear at and inform on their owners – would cause an international uproar of unparalleled proportions. And just think what the taxman would do if he could turn all domestic pets into whistle blowers; the mind boggles at the thought.

## The latest invention

You have to admit that Herman, although a brilliant inventor, is more than a tad unlucky in his selection of commercially viable ideas. He has said if he ever gets over the problems with his animal invention, he will release an even more advanced computer that will enable people to communicate effectively with their teenage kids and elderly parents. As we speak, this contraption requires the processing power of 200 paralleled Cray computers and is about the size of ten London buses. Herman is confident, given the advances in microtechnology, it can be miniaturized to fit into a pen. The truth is that most things can if you make them small enough.

This book won't fit into a pen, but it will make you almost as effective as Herman, and without the downside.

---

[2]  To that extent they are much like politicians

# PART 1

# The Problem of Deception

'THAT'S IT, POTTER, YOU'LL MAKE A GREAT ACCOUNTANT'

# **1** *Introduction*

*Lies are the truth to people who don't know better*

## Lies in business

Most days of your life you are deceived. *Think about it!* No, please, really think about it. Take it on board at a conscious level: look upwards and to your left.[1] *Deception is a really bad scene.*

*The cheque is in the post*

---

### A TYPICAL DAY?

You got out of bed, read lots of lies in the newspaper; watched the breakfast show, with people pretending to be happy early in the morning; walked to the station with your neighbour who told you he had just been promoted, when you know he had been fired; caught the train, but could not get a first-class seat because the compartments were full of fare dodgers; came into the office, spoke to your colleagues who said your new employee was doing fine, when you know he is not; received a call from Bill Smith saying that he could not come to work today as he was ill; attended meetings; approved a bunch of purchase invoices for payment; signed a few expense statements, some of which looked a bit dodgy; telephoned a customer who promised you the cheque was in the post; called your banker, but his PA told you he was in a meeting and would call you back; had lunch with a job candidate and then lost to him at golf because he cheated. You then returned home; spoke to the kids, who told you they had no homework and were going to a disco; watched television, read your emails and responded to them and then clambered into bed, pretending you had a bad migraine.

How many lies were you told during this very ordinary day? Did you do anything about them? Were any of them really important?

---

*The fact is that most people would prefer to be deceived than be perceived as being distrustful*

In the majority of cases, the lies you are told are insignificant, but sometimes they have very serious consequences. In his book *Rogue Trader*, Nicholas Leeson said:

---

[1]   We will explain later the reason for this

## BUYING TIME

'I put the phone down. These conversations were always the same with Mary [Mary Walz was his functional manager whose career was seriously damaged by Mr Leeson's dishonesty]. She tried to give me some kind of tough instruction, but I always deflected her so she ended with the promise of another chat tomorrow. This was fine by me. Each tomorrow I passed was another day … I just needed to buy time.'

When Tony Railton, an auditor from Baring's head office, was sent to Singapore to sort out the trading positions, Mr Leeson said:

## INCREDIBLE EXPLANATION

'I wondered what Tony Railton had uncovered. My list of deceit was too long … it could have been anything from the Balance Sheet to the Citibank account or to the 88888 account. I waited for him. Then the penny dropped and then the millions dropped. I realised Railton was asking me a question rather than accusing me of fraud … and wrestling me to the ground in a citizen's arrest. If he was asking a question he might not know the answer.

'"It's a consolidation account we use, something like the gross account reporting we do for you," I said airily. This was all gobbledegook. He couldn't possibly swallow this one. I put one hand out of sight below my desk and pinched my thigh to stop myself from laughing at my own idiocy. My explanation made no sense, but it was the best I could come up with on the spot and he believed it.'

*For every credibility gap, there is a gullibility fill …*

Fortunately you may never be confronted with someone quite like Mr Leeson but, just the same, there are hundreds of occasions every year when it would be to your advantage to extract the truth from people who don't want to tell it. Whatever job you do, your success ultimately depends on your ability to sort out the good from the bad and to deal, effectively and politely, with deception.

## Economic advantages of the truth

### COST OF LIES IN FRAUD

Fraud in the UK costs taxpayers billions each year. Banks write off over £20 billion annually on loans they thought were good; credit card companies lose 4 per cent of turnover through card abuse, identity theft and skimming; the cost of recovering from a bad employee is around £50000 per instance, and there are tens of thousands of them every year; companies lose between 2 and 5 per cent of turnover as a result of fraud, and even more by relying on inaccurate information. So what?

*Principle: Never tell a lie, unless lying is one of your principles*

## COST OF LIES AND PERSONAL LIABILITIES

Increasingly managers are being held personally liable for their alleged errors and omissions at work. Despite everything, Barings, like many victims of catastrophic fraud, was a very good company. Many good managers lost their jobs and, in another banking case, the Head of Compliance – who was an honest, hard-working man – was banned from his profession for life. True, the good managers who lost their jobs did not ask the questions they should have, but it is easy to be wise after the event. So what?

## COST OF LIES TO ACCOUNTING FIRMS

Nearly every large accounting firm is now embroiled in legal action for alleged negligence in not recognizing the symptoms of fraud. The average claim per case is over $480 million. Arthur Andersen was put out of business with the loss of hundreds of jobs and many personal disasters. So what?

During 2002, following multiple scandals and false reporting by leading companies, stock exchanges throughout the world collapsed. One observer pointed out that accountants did far more damage to confidence in the financial markets than Al Qaeda. Pension funds have collapsed under the weight of false reporting, leaving an aging population exposed to poverty. So what?

## COST OF POLITICAL LIES

Never has the public had such little confidence in our political leaders. The idea that truth can be 'spun' to mislead has become the norm and blatancy the benchmark. Case after case – of political leaders with their hands in the cookie jar – merely scratch the surface of corruption at the highest levels. This happens while the poorest members of society suffer.

Frauds in and against government bodies, such as the European Union, the Benefits Agency, and the Department of Health are totally out of control, despite endless 'initiatives' and spinning to the contrary. So what?

## COST OF LIES IN CIVIL LITIGATION

The cost of civil litigation in the UK resulting from alleged breaches of contract, failure and misunderstandings runs into billions of pounds each year. Most are the result of someone being deceived. The idea that every citizen should have equal access to justice is a very sick joke. The legal aid system is woefully ineffective and the litigant with the most money usually wins. So what?

## COST OF LIES TO LAW ENFORCEMENT

For law enforcement agencies, the cost of contested cases is staggering. It is estimated that the majority of a detective's working day is wasted on administrative and support duties rather than on chasing down crooks and questioning suspects. Many cases reported for prosecution are dropped before trial and if a contested case goes forward, the time spent preparing for hearings, waiting around for proceedings to start and attending them is beyond belief. Even if the villain is convicted, the penalties are usually more derisory than a deterrent, with one judge recently saying that he could not impose a custodial sentence because the jails were overcrowded. So what?

## COST OF MALINGERING

Malingering, by people claiming to be ill when they are not, or wasting time at work, is unquantified in the UK but in the USA amounts to $40 billion per annum. It was recently reported that, on any given day, up to 10 per cent of the UK police force is absent through sickness. On average, public servants take 17 days off a year, supposedly through sickness, whereas employees in the private sector take around 7. In some companies, extended and unjustified sick leave is considered part of the employment package. So what?

## THE ANSWER TO 'SO WHAT?'

The answer to the question is obvious, isn't it? Most of these costs and problems could have been avoided if honest people had asked the right questions at the right time and had exposed the deep truth. But the unfortunate fact is that managerial training – even in our best universities – makes no mention of dishonesty and deception at work. On the contrary, the smelly socks of this world, politicians and legislators, place the greatest emphasis on the human rights of villains to the extent that they invariably prevail over the well-being of victims. It is, therefore, no wonder that businesses are woefully unprepared and unwilling to deal with deception. For every credibility gap, there is a gullibility fill.

# The quest for truth over time

## GOOD AND BAD IDEAS

Through the centuries, civilizations (and France) have tried different ways of finding the truth. To say that some methods have been bizarre would be an understatement, but others have had reasonably sound foundations.
   For example:

- The ancient Hindus would ask people suspected of wrongdoing to chew mouthfuls of dry rice or bread. The person with the most clogged-up mouth was judged to be guilty.
- Some Arab nations would require suspects to lick a hot iron: the person whose tongue was the most charred was in serious trouble.
- In some parts of China a hanging bell was placed in a closed room. Suspects were told that they were to enter the room and place their hands firmly on the bell and that if they were guilty and nervous their hands would tremble and the bell would ring. What they were not told was that the bell was covered in black soot, which would cling to the hands of anyone touching it.
- Jews tried the same thing with a donkey with a soot-covered tail. The accused would be placed in a darkened room with the donkey and told to pull its tail. He was told that if the animal brayed he was guilty.

The first two methods were based on the fact that liars tend to have dry mouths and the third and fourth on the belief that the liar would not risk touching the bell or pulling the donkey's tail. Thus his hands would not be covered in soot.

Among others, J. Baptiste de la Porte (1535–1615) and Cesare Lombrosso (1836–1909) were supporters of the 'science' of physiognomy, which postulated that a person's appearance, especially the face, reveals his or her personality. They were suspicious of people with narrow faces, wide chests, larger waists and big forearms. Bartholomew Cocles in the sixteenth century stated that people with snub noses were 'vain, untruthful, unstable and seducers.'

Franz Joseph Gall (1758–1828) and his pupil John Gaspar Spurzheim (1776–1832) were supporters of phrenology, the theory that personality could be determined by bumps on a person's head. This is not a particularly practical method in business unless the subject is bald.

Personology came into and went out of fashion. It was developed in the 1930s by a Los Angeles judge who cannily noticed that the wretches and criminals who appeared before him seemed to share common facial and other characteristics. Having set his mind to his theory, he then reinforced it by further observations and, if human nature is anything to go by, dismissing anything that did not fit.

*All lies in jest, till the man hears what he wants to hear and disregards the rest[2]*

## CURRENTLY USED METHODS

In the USA, reliance is sometimes placed on polygraph machines (or lie detectors), and this equipment still causes much controversy. There are basically two types. The first, the conventional polygraph requires subjects to be attached to it by wires and sensors that monitor heart rate, galvanic skin resistance (sweating) and other physical characteristics mainly driven by the limbic system and brainstem. The subject is asked a number of control questions and his response plotted on a graph. He is also asked relevant questions, stressful responses identified and he is confronted with them for an explanation. Experience shows that conventional polygraph machines are effective, but they are rarely used in Europe mainly because they are heavily disliked by members of the sandal-wearing fraternity.

### AL-QAEDA

The *Encyclopaedia of Jihad*, part 1 (see www.Ketab25.com) deals with security and intelligence and states: 'Lie detectors are nothing more than a myth to trick the accused. To the extent that the accused does not believe in its effectiveness, it will not be effective against him.' This, as we will see later is a clever bit of neurolinguistic programming.

The second type of lie detector is called the Voice Stress Analyser (VSA) or Psychological Stress Evaluator (PSE). These devices are based on the theory that under stress, micro-tremors in the laryngeal muscles in the range of 8–12 Hz are distorted (see also page 125). The machines operate without any physical connection to the subject and can be applied to a real-time conversation, telephone line or tape recorder.

---

2   Paul Simon, *The Boxer*

## THE DEMONSTRATION

At a London conference on deception, a vendor of PSE equipment was invited to give a demonstration. He had planned to connect the device to a telephone extension in the conference room and to ask participants – at random – to speak to any colleague whom they believed might be deceptive. The vendor connected the PSE to a projector displaying Microsoft PowerPoint slides, and explained how the device would display the results.

The first participant tried, but failed, to connect to his colleague and the vendor explained to the enthralled audience how the device would have worked. The only problem was that he forgot to turn off the projector and as he was extolling the device's virtues the screen was flashing 'Unsure', 'Possible Deception'. It took a few minutes for the vendor to appreciate why the audience was laughing. Then the penny dropped.

The bottom line is that polygraph and other machines are not acceptable in most business situations. However, they do draw out confessions because they bring some liars to the Pivotal Point where anxiety causes them to lose confidence in their ability to succeed.

## THE LYING WITNESS

During a police investigation a witness was shown photographs and asked to pick the villain who shot the bartender during a drugs related robbery. Her response, which took just over a second, was captured on a VSA and subsequently examined. When she was confronted with the findings (which were to the effect that her response was 92.5 per cent certain to be deceptive), she changed her story and admitted that she was trying to cover for a friend who was the real murderer.

The effective interviewer can do this just as well without a polygraph machine, providing he has a cunning plan.

## The cunning plan

This book explains how and why lies are told and how you can deal with them whatever job you do. There are two main sorts of lies. The first is the achievement lie, which is told in order to lead you down the garden path so that you give a job to a bad candidate, part with your money or do something else that is against your interest. The second sort is the exculpatory lie, used to hide wrongdoing and normally told after the event, such as in a disciplinary interview or when someone is challenged for doing something wrong.

But either way, the fact is that the clues to deception are overwhelming, providing you register them at a conscious level. Once you have done this, the initiative swings in your favour. You must decide what your objectives are: do you want to deal with the lie or let it pass? If you decide to expose it you must plan and rehearse your approach and then execute it in a clinical and low-key way (see Mind Map 1). And the more you practice, the better you will become.

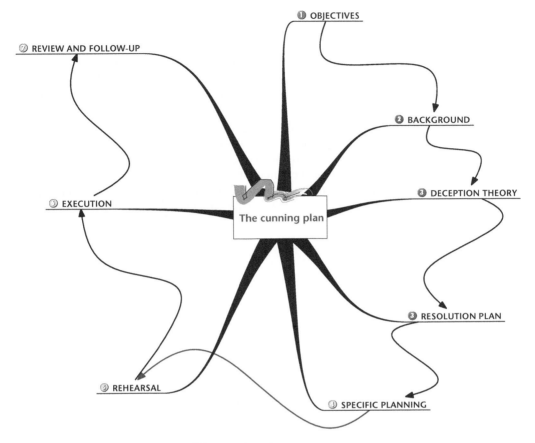

**Mind Map® 1**    The seven stages of the cunning plan

*The plan works largely through careful planning and rehearsal*

By working through this book, you should become almost as successful as Herman in dealing with hot air and deception in business. If you want, you will also be able to develop non-verbal methods of communicating with your pets, other humans and humanoids who don't understand plain language.

*Deception at Work* is intended as a practical guide for anyone who has to expose and deal with bad lies and serious deception, including investigators, auditors, lawyers, regulators and senior line managers.

Good lies you can still continue to enjoy as they will do you no harm. Some of the techniques suggested in Chapters 5, 6 and 7 are only appropriate for really tough interviews where gross deception is suspected and where the stakes are really high. The chances are that in the sorts of interviews you have to conduct you will not have to use these, but it is important that you should know about them so that you can use diluted versions in your day-to-day work.

*If you think telling the truth is difficult, try lying*

## Buying this book

If you are reading these words in a bookshop and considering whether to buy the book, remember that even if you don't plan to read it, you can still benefit greatly from buying it. The reason it has a gaudy cover and big letters is so that you can leave it on your desk or take it with you into meetings instead of your Filofax or mobile telephone. Just let everyone see it and you will have improved your chances of not being deceived by 75.876 per cent.

Better still why not buy three copies: one for the office, one for your personal use and keep the last on your golf trolley. Do this and you will increase your chances of finding the truth simply by letting people know that you are aware of the possibilities that they might try to deceive you. If you want to improve your chances of finding the truth to 98.617 per cent you should open the book in meetings, flick through the pages, look at the person you suspect might be dissembling the truth and say: 'Aaaah … that's it. I knew it was in there somewhere.' This will unnerve most liars.

## Structure of the book

### GENERAL

This book covers lies in all shapes and sizes, and the situations in which they most commonly occur (Figure 1.1).

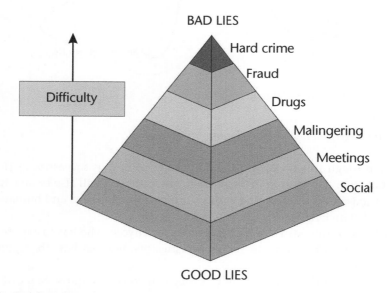

**Figure 1.1**   Tough and easy interviews

Figure 1.1 shows the hierarchy of interviews, and that those where the potential punishment is greatest (and the level of remorse insignificant) are usually the most difficult to resolve. But there are exceptions.

The book is written in a modular, mildly progressive format, in four main parts:

- Part 1 (Chapters 1 to 4) covers the *problems* of deception, both oral and written.

- Part 2 (Chapters 5 to 9) deals with *countermeasures*, from generic questions through to the policies and procedures needed to assure an honest workforce, a personal manifesto to make sure you do not go the way of the Enron directors, and how to interview people suspected of fraud.
- Part 3 (Chapter 10) is absolutely essential, because it applies to the rare but very important cases when you may be called to give evidence in court or at an employment tribunal.
- Part 4 (Chapter 11) is, perhaps, even more important because it deals with the risks of deception on a golf course. This is really important.

## MIND MAPS® AND DIAGRAMS

Humans absorb information in different ways. Some prefer visual stimulation, others auditory, sensory or emotional channels. Mind Maps, which were invented by Tony Buzan (former editor of the *Mensa International Journal*, coach to both the British Olympic rowing team and chess squad, and an all-round clever clogs), are excellent tools for summarizing complex relationships in a visual format. Experience shows that highly intelligent people like Mind Maps: if you have bought this book, we are sure you will like them. If you have just borrowed it, you won't. If you want, you can download a free demonstration copy of a superb Mind Mapping program from www.mindjet.com. If you want bigger and better versions of the Mind Maps you can get them from our site at www.cobasco.com; they are free of charge and you can adapt them as you want.[3]

There are also lots of diagrams, 'word bites' and illustrations. Again, some people will like them and others won't. But most people remember messages in diagrams better than they do plain text, simply because their brains are hardwired to do so. If you like diagrams and other stuff, great. If not, don't worry. It probably means that your primary channel of communication is other than visual and this is not really a problem, unless you plan to become a creative accountant or fashion designer.

## TABLES

There are many tables in this book, which summarize what would otherwise be massive amounts of text. The problem with tables is that people skip over them, blank out and glaze over and thus miss important messages. We strongly recommend that you take a few minutes to read each table carefully and use a highlighter pen to mark those bits you think could be important to you.

*You can learn a lot from tables, if you read them*

## ADAPTING THE TECHNIQUES

The techniques in Chapters 5 to 8 are directed at the most difficult interviews of all, where serious dishonesty is suspected. These are referred to as 'tough interviews'. However, the approaches suggested may be adapted for any meeting or interview in which it is important to get the truth from people opposed to telling it.

Being able to recognize lies and to deal effectively with them is a really valuable tool, which will:

---

[3]  Providing you don't remove our copyright symbols, in which case your computer will self-destruct

- ensure that your decisions are based on accurate information;
- avoid unpleasant surprises in your business and commercial life;
- make you more capable and confident in your job, whatever it is;
- enable you to conduct audits and special investigations more effectively;
- enable you to find the truth when dishonesty is suspected.

By understanding the nature of deception, obtaining the tools and honing your interview skills you can quickly get to the truth in 97.24 per cent of all cases and you can do so politely, in your own way and without causing controversy.

*Who knows wins*

We also hope you will find this book interesting and fun. Not everyone has a sense of humour and the idea of having fun at work may be abhorrent. This is a serious book, but humour has its place and helps you remember important points because it registers in the brain in a different way from most other memories.

## INTERNALIZING TECHNIQUES

You can internalize – or make second nature – most of the techniques recommended in this book by:

- highlighting the points you believe are most relevant and putting Post-it® notes on pages you regard as important to you;
- thoroughly examining the tables and diagrams, again using a highlighter;
- consciously watching and listening to what people do and say in every meeting from today onwards: if you take a real interest in people you will find discovering the truth is easy;
- watching television programmes very carefully, especially interviews with politicians and football managers and, of course, *Blind Date* (where contestants say one thing and their bodies say another);
- trying out the techniques in day-to-day conversations.

Within a short time, the techniques will become second nature. Please believe this!

For any liar reading this, remember: if we or any of our readers (who have this book on their desk and in their golf bags) ever have to interview you, you will be a very soft touch simply because you will know – without being able to remember all of the detail – that you have two uncontrollable monkeys on your back. These are your subconscious and memory and they eat into liars' brains.

## INTERVIEWING SKILLS

### General

This book covers 'interviewing skills', which can be defined as:

- the capability to find the truth;
- in all situations;

- in compliance with the law and ethical standards, through specified *processes*;
- in a way which leaves everyone involved with the most *positive feelings* possible under all of the circumstances.

Interviewing skills consist of two main elements: *capability* and *understanding*.

*Capability* is based on a deep *understanding* of the nature and mechanics of deception, and the ability to be able to deal with the conflict between the liar's:

- subconscious (which will usually try to tell the truth) and controlled consciousness (which may wish to misrepresent it);
- memory (which will know the facts) and imagination (which will distort them to suit the liar's conscious objectives).

*The memory and subconscious are referred to as the 'two monkeys' that sit on the liar's back, constantly reminding him of the truth*

*Understanding* is the second vital element of interviewing skills, and includes:

- An *appreciation* of the questions we can ask and statements we can make to get to the truth, and especially:
  - The capability to *influence* and *persuade* the liar to the point where he loses all confidence in his ability to cope with the anxiety created by his deception.
  - The capability to *recognize* when the suspect is confronting himself with the dilemma (the 'pivotal point') of whether or not to release his anxiety by telling some or all of the truth.
  - The capability to create *rapport* and *empathy* with the suspect to enable him to resolve this dilemma by telling the truth and to clear up other matters with which he may have been concerned while retaining his *self-respect*.
- An *acceptance* of the ethical, moral and social values concerned, including:
  - human rights,
  - privacy,
  - the policies and procedures in your organization,
  - the applicable laws, rules, procedures and codes of practice against which our actions will be judged by others and, more importantly, by ourselves as professional interviewers.

The definition includes three very important words, and these are 'respect', 'rapport' and 'empathy'. Let's look at these words in more detail.

## Respect

We should always show respect for the person who tells lies, no matter how bad a person he really is, and must never become emotionally involved, through anger, sarcasm or discourtesy. Respect means honouring the suspect's legal rights and treating him fairly. It also means that you can sleep soundly at night, knowing you have done your best and have acted professionally.

## Rapport

Rapport is defined as *'the process of establishing and maintaining a relationship of mutual trust and understanding between two or more people'*. It means 'seeing eye-to eye' or 'getting on the same wavelength' as someone else. It does not mean being condescending or obsequious. We should always try to establish rapport with the subject of an interview, while remaining firmly in control.

There is overwhelming evidence that people tell more of the truth, more often, to people they believe really understand and empathize with them. As a rule, if you show someone you don't like him by what you say, how you say it, or through your body language, he will not like you, and rapport goes out the window.

Within the first few seconds of meeting someone, you will subconsciously decide – based on their 'emblems' (see Chapter 4, Table 4.9, p. 128) – how your relationship will develop (see Figure 1.2). We all form immediate impressions of people based on their 'emblems' and the circumstances in which we meet them. Once an impression has been formed, we are reluctant to change it and, as a result, can be badly misled, simple because our minds are closed to conflicting input. In investigative interviews, we must always keep an open mind. However, if your mind is left too open, your brains will spill out.

To establish rapport we must take conscious control of our prejudices and first impressions. The ways in which we can consciously establish rapport are described in Chapter 6, page 219, but please remember the word: it is very important.

**Figure 1.2**   Who will you get on with?

## Empathy

This is another weighty word and goes a step beyond 'rapport', bordering on a low-level telepathy. It means that we are able to put ourselves in the other person's shoes, appreciate how he feels and, among other things, use this understanding to bring him face to face with reality, so that he tells the truth.

Where a liar is fighting with the two monkeys of subconscious and memory and deciding whether to tell the truth or not (the 'pivotal point'), an empathetic approach is critical. Chapter 7, page 277–8 says more about empathy, but remember that, like rapport, it is a really influential word. And you must have lots of it.

*Empathy is sympathy without sadness*

## THE DEEP TRUTH

Really skilful interviewers don't just find the truth about the topic in which they are interested. They find the deep truth and get a brain dump from the subject of all matters that could be of interest. Once issues of immediate concern have been dealt with, they move on to explore other areas in which the subject may have been involved or may possess knowledge of naughtiness by others.

From now on you should focus on finding the deep truth and trying to get the subject to tell you *everything* that could be important, rather than just a confession to the limited matters at hand.

*The person who confesses is a most valuable source of information on other matters*

# Disclaimers

## LEGALITY

Every reasonable effort has been made to ensure that everything in this book is legal in civilized jurisdictions (i.e. excluding Cheam and Islington) and complies with legal, human rights, privacy and other legislation. However, neither the authors, publishers or Spot the Dog can be held responsible for the outcome of any particular interview and, in really difficult cases, especially involving criminal prosecution, you should seek specific legal advice.

It is also possible that some of the techniques for finding the truth – especially if they are quoted out of context – could be offensive to liars and people who believe in tooth fairies and that the rights of crooks, cheats and ne'er-do-wells should always prevail over those of their victims. We do not apologize for this but later on we include a specific health warning because it is totally contrary to human nature to ask questions that elicit the truth. Everything we suggest is fair, ethical and directed towards finding the truth, which means clearing the innocent as well as exposing the guilty. If readers of the *Independent* and residents of Cheam and Islington don't agree, so be it.

## SEXISM AND OTHER STUFF

Women make superb interviewers, mainly because their brains have evolved more efficiently than men's (see page 46). However, given that the population is divided almost equally between males and females,[4] it is amazing that proportionately less women are *detected* in dishonesty. This could be that they are innately more honest than men, more clever, or, more likely, both.

To simplify sentence construction, the masculine gender is used throughout and we hope this does not offend anyone.

## GIVING THE GAME AWAY

Some people might believe that writing books like this helps liars plan their defences and therefore should be suppressed. This is wrong and, on the contrary, the more the liar knows and becomes anxious about the clues he is emanating into the ether, the more likely he is to fail.

### THE TURN IN THE BARREL

Where a person is being questioned about dishonesty, the world ceases to exist outside the room in which the interview is taking place. Family, friends and other problems disappear into the background while the subject focuses on surviving the interview. At this time, it is a closed world in which the more he understands, the more difficult it becomes to repress the truth.

*Liars know too much; if you think telling the truth is difficult, try lying.*
*When it is your turn in the barrel, things look different*

## Misconceptions and myths about deception

### WHAT INTEREST IN SOLUTIONS?

There are few subjects which are as fraught with misconception, danger and emotion as the art of deception and the quest to identify and isolate its symptoms. Paradoxically, once symptoms have been recognized, there appears to be little interest in actually resolving them. This unwillingness to expose deception is clearly demonstrated in a recent book by a respected academic which devotes 220 pages to reviewing abstruse publications by his colleagues on the nature of lies and four and a half pages on how to resolve them!

*It is easier to identify a problem than to suggest a solution*

It is easy to discover when people are lying: in fact we are flooded with clues. What you do once you are put on notice is an entirely different matter, and it is in this area that the void of knowledge and lack of applied techniques are at their most extreme. No one, except for a few American investigators and lawyers, seems prepared to offer advice on how lies should be tackled and the deep truth exposed, except in the case of exculpatory lies. This is another paradox because, for the reasons explained later, it is much better to catch lies in the achievement stage, before the damage has been done.

*People want to know how to detect lies but not how to tackle them*

---

[4]    Except in Cheam and Islington

Getting to the deep truth can be simplified as a three-stage process:

1   Recognizing that a lie has been told.
2   Using interviewing skills to get to the deep truth.
3   Using a legal and morally defensible process.

Stages 1 and 3 are easy and, for this reason, everyone seems to have concentrated on them, including academics, lawyers etc., etc. Police training throughout the world is focused on process rather than on deep-truth interviewing skills. If you don't believe this, just read the transcript of the interview with OJ Simpson (http://simpson.walraven.org) which from a procedural point of view was uncontentious but which had no chance of ever getting off the ground and into the deep truth.

*Process suppresses skills*

This is not to say that processes are not important, but they must be set against the skills and techniques necessary to get to the deep truth. Figure 1.3 shows the relationship between skills and processes and the fact that the two must work together. It shows that methods currently forced on law enforcement agencies and the courts are dominated by the requirement to comply with set processes, thereby reducing the likelihood that the deep truth will emerge.

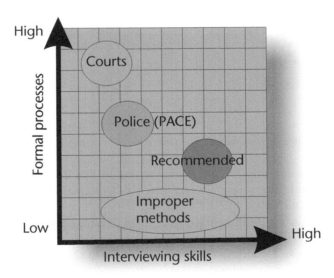

**Figure 1.3**   Interviewing skills and processes

Without process controls, 'skills' may go over the line into extreme areas such as violence, torture, deprivation and truth serums. However, the methods currently used by law enforcement agencies are too process-orientated and do not encourage the use of interviewing skills. The result is that the deep truth never surfaces.

Putting down in writing the skills, tools and techniques needed to get to the deep truth in all situations – involving achievement and exculpatory lies – is difficult and if there has been any applied research on the subject, it is not visible.

Many groups are involved in the detection and resolution of deception, including academics – ranging from anthropologists, psychologists, psychiatrists to zoologists – politicians, lawyers and do-gooders down to the great unwashed such as police, customs, the intelligence services, auditors and business managers. Their work is fragmented and often conflicting.

For example the interests of results can be summarized as in Table 1.1, which shows the lack of interest in dealing with both achievement and exculpatory lies.

**Table 1.1**   Interested parties in deception

| Interested group RESEARCH Application Both | Achievement lies | | | Exculpatory lies | | |
|---|---|---|---|---|---|---|
| | Detection | Resolution | | Detection | Resolution | |
| | | Skills | Process | | Skills | Process |
| ACADEMIC | RESEARCH | | | PRIORITY | | PRIORITY |
| Lawyers | | | | Priority | | Priority |
| US training agencies John E. Reid Inc. LSI Others | | | | Priority | | |
| UK law enforcement | | | | Interest | | Priority |
| Businessmen | Interest | | | Interest | | |

*This is the first table. Please don't just gloss over it, but read it carefully. It is important.*

The table indicates, for example, that academics have a limited interest in deception and that few people or organizations have produced anything of great value on resolving either achievement or exculpatory lies.

It is worth spending a few minutes examining these disparate interests so that this book can be seen in context. *Deception at Work* will not be everyone's cup of tea, because, in Chapters 5 to 8, it suggests applied solutions which, in the cold light of day, may appear too harsh, pedestrian or irrelevant. But the fact is that they work.

## ACADEMICS KNOW THE TRUTH

Currently academics dominate the play in the field of exculpatory lies and rarely a month goes by without some new pronouncement or suggestion, ranging from vaguely sensible to utterly nutty.

## THE SILENT STALKER

In late January 2003, Dr Zuhair Bandar, Dr Janet Rothwell and her colleagues at Manchester Metropolitan University announced a new lie detection machine, called the 'Silent Stalker' which was 'fast, cheap, non-invasive and works virtually in real time'. The system consists of a television camera focused on the subject's eyes, linked to a computer. It detects tiny movements of muscles around the eyes and mouth, cheeks and forehead, which are continuous when a person is being deceitful (i.e. micro tremors see pages 7 and 125). 'The current results are good enough to aid in many situations, to change a line of questioning, to reinterview someone and such things. For example, the Yorkshire Ripper was interviewed at least five times. I'd like to think that it wouldn't happen with the Silent Stalker around.' The system has a claimed accuracy of 80 per cent.

Supposedly banks and insurance companies have already expressed an interest in the Silent Stalker, which could be used in everything from job interviews to police investigations.

It's a nice story that again raises the reluctance to provide applied solutions and the partitioning of some academics from reality.

## THE REAL WORLD

It is true that Peter Sutcliffe, the Yorkshire Ripper, was interviewed a number of times, in the dead of night, in the street by uniformed officers. Is the suggestion that every police office should be given a Sainsbury's trolley to wheel the Silent Stalker equipment around? Does anyone really believe that such equipment would get past human rights and the other smelly-socked legislation; and so what if the machine does say – with 80 per cent accuracy – that someone is lying? What does the interviewer do with this knowledge? Perhaps he says, 'Eh by gum, Peter lad, it is obvious from this gizmo that you are telling porkies' to face the riposte: 'No comment except stick the machine where the sun don't shine'.

*In deception there is an absence of applied solutions*

Most academics hold firm in their belief that unless something can be measured, dissected and scientifically proven down to the last microdot it is of no value. This is why they dismiss the polygraph, VSA SCAN and some good suggestions in relation to exculpatory lies made primarily by American training agencies such as John E. Reid.[5] People who use the polygraph or the Reid method know they work but applied knowledge seems to count for nothing with academia. This is a great shame.

---

[5]  See www.reid.com

## TRANSACTIONAL ROLES

As a probably irrelevant aside, it is interesting to note the way that academics are taken seriously and robotically adopt the role of Critical Parents when dealing with the great unwashed. In one encounter, a brilliant police detective with years of success interrogating criminals and terrorists of all shapes and sizes was counselled by a young, spotty academic who told him his methods were 'outdated and ineffective' but suggested no alternative other than a few mealy-mouthed words such as 'paradigm shifts' and 'sonomic responses'. The detective appeared to shrink and take on the role of an Adaptive Child.

Possibly he was so exhausted and dispirited that he did not have the energy to object or maybe he was genuinely impressed by the spotty youngster's qualifications and emblems. Either way what was being suggested was impractical rubbish.

Precision and proof is supposedly in the blood of academics, yet their own conclusions on deception are almost entirely based on artificial tests under laboratory conditions using innocent, compliant subjects: they are not for real.

## DEAFNESS IN FROGS

The research is much like the experiment concerning deafness in frogs. Scientists found that when they said 'jump', frogs did so with great enthusiasm but when they cut off their legs they did not respond. This proved that frogs detected sound through their legs

*In research all findings have to be proven, except your own*

A possible exception in the case for alleging academic irrelevance is the recent study by Dr D.D. Langleben and his colleagues at the University of Pennsylvania, which used functional magnetic resonance imaging (fMRI) to monitor brain activity during simulated deception. If the results can be validated in real-life situations with real liars, we might be getting somewhere, although any practical benefits in improving interviewing skills are likely to be decades away.

Sometimes academics can go too far and get too carried away. Robert Matthews, a British statistician, published a truly amazing article in the *Daily Telegraph*:

## FALSE LOGIC

In an article headed: 'Logic says that a confession often spells innocence', Robert Matthews proposed an 'Interrogator's Fallacy'. In the case of IRA bombers called 'the Birmingham Six', he wrote: 'Who is more likely to confess when subjected to extreme (interrogation) methods? A committed terrorist trained to resist interrogation or some innocent person dragged off the street and accused of murder and questioned for days on end? Indeed the only logical conclusion one can draw is that the existence of a confession increases the probability that the person is innocent.' This is much like the experiment involving deafness in frogs and overlooks the facts of the particular case.

The distinguished statistician – like some other boffins who make pronouncements on lying – has probably never interviewed a crook, terrorist or ne'er- do-well in his life and apparently misunderstands the nature of a 'confession'.

In most of the cases Mr Matthews seems to have reviewed, the defendants did not confess along such lines as: 'It's all down to me Guv. Only you are clever enough to have caught me and you should get a promotion out of this.' What they did do, is prevaricate, lie, refuse to answer questions, make contradictory statements and small admissions, thus leading a jury to convict them. Subsequently, the interviews were judged unreliable, mainly because of procedural mistakes by the officers or lawyers concerned. Convictions were not overturned because the defendants were innocent or because confessions had been forced from them and it is misleading for the statistician to suggest this.

*Academic research on deception, like that on multiple orgasms, must be treated with suspicion*

## LAWYERS KNOW THE TRUTH

Most people would presume that if anyone can expose deception, courts, lawyers and the legal system can. Unfortunately, this is seldom the case and what takes place in court is usually a sanitized version of pseudo-truths. But, these days, before a serious case even gets to court in the UK it has been dissected by the Crown Prosecution Service (CPS), which applies a dual test. The first is whether or not prosecution is in the public interest and the second is whether or not there is a good chance of obtaining a conviction. Determination of what is and what is not in the public interest appears to be an imprecise science. If you are a high-profile television presenter or politician who, ten years ago, is suspected of having put it about in places where it should not go, the chances are you will face a high-profile arrest and prosecution with the media in tow. You are relatively less likely to face prosecution if you are a nobody and all you have done is ripped off your employer for a few million. To a large extent the CPS has usurped the role of the courts, but its decision-making process is opaque.

To the cynical observer the term 'public interest' might mean 'publicity value' in promoting the impression that the criminal justice system is a deterrent and that our political leaders are interested in crime. These days the criminal justice system is mainly driven by funding, budgets and out-turns and, to that extent, falls into the same hole as the UK National Health Service.

## THE GREAT UNWASHED DON'T KNOW THE TRUTH

At the end of the line are the poor so-and-sos who day in, day out have to face and deal with deception, sometimes in difficult or violent circumstances. The most exposed of all are police and other law enforcement officers who are hog-tied by deftly crafted processes inflicted by academics, promoted as 'initiatives' by politicians, enforced by lawyers and supported by the smelly socks. Today, to effect an arrest a police officer may have to complete up to 38 separate forms and if he says one word out of place or makes a procedural mistake his career may be at an end. It is no wonder that experienced detectives are finding nice comfortable posts in quiet backwaters to wait out their retirement.

The irony is, that of all the parties involved, front-line police and other investigators have probably the best insight in how to get to the deep truth, using legitimate persuasive skills, but are prevented from doing so by artificial or ineffective processes that give priority to form over substance (see page 17). The result is that villains are never brought to face reality, cases are thrown out by the CPS or argued endlessly in court, incurring massive costs and burdens on the criminal justice system. The use of effective interviewing skills in the early stages of an investigation would encourage guilty pleas from the guilty, resulting in both justice and savings in time and costs.

## A POTENT HEALTH WARNING

The point of the above is not just to take a gratuitous smack[6] at academics, lawyers and others who have the luxury of second guessing, but to issue a potent health warning. This book is based on over 40 years of applied experience of both achievement and exculpatory liars, including successes, failures and many hard-learned lessons. Not every technique can be proven scientifically or measured, and in the abstract some – especially those at the pivotal point – may appear clichéd or pedestrian.[7] Some ideas may not be suitable for the golf club or the Women's Institute. It is up to you to decide how you will deal with deception, but it is evil and ruins the lives of honest people. We hope this book will help you until such time as something better comes along. It should also lead you to conclude that prevention is far better than cure because once you are forced to deal with exculpatory lies it could be too late.

*Prevention is better than cure*

# Conclusions

The bottom line is that people will always answer questions and admit the truth providing you have a cunning plan and use your powers of persuasion.

## UNDER-AGE DRINKER

In an American case a man with a shotgun appeared before the cashier in a small grocery store and filled up a paper bag with the contents of the cash register. Nothing unusual in that, you say, but not satisfied with just the cash the robber saw a bottle of whisky on the shelf behind the trembling cashier and ordered him to hand it over. The cashier said he would not do so as the robber was under age. The robber claimed he was over 21, but the cashier argued. The argument went on for a few minutes but was resolved when the robber produced his driving licence showing his name, address and photograph, proving that he was over 21. The cashier examined the licence, remembered the details, and handed over the whisky. Two hours later the robber was caught sitting in his apartment counting the cash, with the bottle unopened.

This case demonstrates that anxiety can cause people to do things they would otherwise not do. You can always get to the deep truth by using a cunning plan: someone will always give the game away.

---

[6]   However satisfying this might be
[7]   But they usually work

## BUZZ LIGHTYEAR

In November 2002, the *Daily Telegraph* reported an interesting case involving the *Toy Story* character Buzz Lightyear. For those of you not involved in academia, Buzz is a small spaceman whose main catchphrase is 'To infinity and beyond'. A thief hiding in the bushes after stealing a Buzz Lightyear toy from a shop was caught after Buzz blurted out one of his catchphrases. Police with sniffer dogs were about to give up the chase for the thief who had set off the store's alarm, when the intergalactic law enforcer blurted out, 'Buzz Lightyear, permission to engage'. The thief realized the game was up when a police dog ran to his hiding place and began growling at him.

The first rule of interviewing is never give up and the second is if one person won't tell you the truth, somebody else will. If you want to really find out what is going on in an organization, go to the area where smokers congregate, speak to the tea ladies or the chauffeurs or play golf with the senior managers. The world is full of Buzz Lightyears who blurt out the truth and all you have to do is to recognize it at a conscious level and then deal with it.

'THINGS HAVE NEVER BEEN THE SAME SINCE HE BOUGHT THAT BLOODY BOOK'

# **2** *Taxonomy*

*If at first you don't succeed, try lying*

## The basics

### WHAT IS A LIE?

A lie is a communication which the person conveying it:

- does not believe to be true; *or*
- has good reason to suspect is incorrect *(that is, wilful blindness)*.

A lie is communicated with the conscious objective of misleading the victim to achieve an advantage for the liar or for someone else.[1] Thus, to tell a lie the liar must first know the truth. Truth is the baseline cognitive state and a lie a distortion of it.

> *The liar always makes a conscious decision to lie.*
> *A person lies because the truth is not to his greatest advantage*

A liar has conscious control over most of the words he utters, or the content of his story, but in all cases unconscious clues – including incongruencies in the syntax, paralinguistics, non-verbal communications and attitude – will always give the game away.

## CLUES FROM EVERY PORE

Sigmund Freud said, 'He that has eyes to see and ears to hear may convince himself that no mortal can keep a secret. If his lips are silent, he chatters with his fingertips. Betrayal oozes out of every pore.'

*A liar will always fail against an effective interviewer*

As we shall see in Chapter 3, the human brain is hard-wired in a way that makes repression[2] and concealment of the symptoms of deception impossible, simply because emotions and autonomic actions driven by the lower – reptilian and mammalian – brain cannot be hidden. In simple terms we can consider a liar's memory and subconscious as two monkeys sitting on his back, chattering away, creating anxiety, and liable at any moment to blurt out the truth.

---

[1]   St Augustine defined a lie as 'an intentional negation of a subjective truth'
[2]   Unconscious concealment

## CHANNELS OF COMMUNICATION

Untruths – which will have one or more critical issues – can relate to future intentions, and are thus usually classed as 'achievement lies', or past events, usually 'exculpatory lies' that can be communicated in what we will refer to as a 'story' (Table 2.1).

**Table 2.1**   Methods of communicating lies

| Channel of communication | Delivery of the lie | | |
|---|---|---|---|
| | How expressed | | Examples |
| Verbal Consisting of content, lexicon and syntax | Speech Auditory | | In face to face conversations In meetings During negotiations Over the telephone |
| | V I S U A L | In writing | In correspondence In forms In statements and affidavits In accounting and financial records In spreadsheets In business proposals In agreements and contracts In academic research and surveys |
| Non-verbal | | Other than in writing | In pictures, photographs and diagrams In physical objects |
| | | | Sign language, flags, smoke signals and symbols |
| | | Emblems | In appearance, such as clothing, hair or jewellery In appearance of an object, such as an office or a car |
| | | Body language Kinaesthetic | Through gestures Facial expressions Proximity or personal space |
| | Paralinguistics Phonetics | | Non-verbal sounds such as grunts and sighs Speed, tone and pitch of delivery |
| | Sensory | | Smell (olfactory) Touch (tactile) Taste (gustatory) |
| | Extrasensory | | Demeanour Attitude Telepathy |

Channels of communication can also be summarized in the following way (see Mind Map 2).

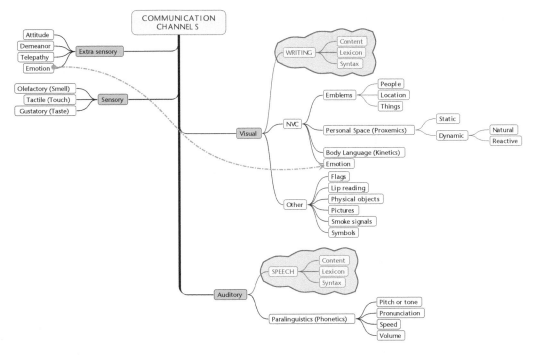

**Mind Map® 2**   Lies and channels of communication

Mind Map 2 shows that there are four channels through which we can communicate with others, the two most important are:

- auditory (hearing);
- visual (seeing).

We will discuss these channels of communication and their significance when we talk about finding the truth in Chapter 3. However, it is important to recognize from the outset that people always communicate:

- what they intend to communicate (conscious communication);
- other things they do not intend to disclose (unconscious communication).

Unintended or unconscious disclosures – which include body language, paralinguistics, proximetics, kinetics, attitude and emotions – are very important in guiding us to distinguish truth from lies. We will return to this point later.

Often lies will be communicated through more than one channel. For example:

## THE TASTY DISH

A menu might give a written description which is nothing short of mouth-watering; the chef might tell us that the meat is delicious and arranges it so that it looks appetizing and covers it with a sweet- smelling sauce. The waiter may provide us with a knife so sharp it would cut through concrete. Only when we start eating the meat do we realize that it tastes like an old sock and is as tough as an army boot.

Lies usually come in clusters, with signals through the different channels of communication being incongruent. The liar has no conscious control over such incongruencies.

## COMPONENTS OF A LIE

A lie consists of a number of components:

- The *content*, which is the words the liar consciously selects (or fails to select) in giving his story.
- The *syntax*[3] or the technical construction of the sentences in the story, which is mainly driven at an unconscious level.
- The tone, volume and speed with which the explanation is given: called *paralinguistics*, again usually directed at an unconscious level.
- The *non-verbal communications* (or body language), some of which may be consciously controlled, although most come straight from the autonomic system and are instinctive.

In a truthful story all of these components are more or less compatible, but in lies there is usually a conflict between them or incongruencies which reveal the underlying untruth.

## THE ALIENS

In the mid-1970s mysterious circles and patterns appeared in fields of wheat and corn throughout the UK and the tabloids spread doom and gloom, as they do, to the effect that aliens had landed. In one case the words 'We are not alone' appeared in the patterns, thus confirming that aliens spoke English. Granny Smith immediately placed a curfew on her cat and Tommy Jones would not eat meat for weeks. There was great panic and the tabloids had a field day.

However, within the statement the lie is glaring, because aliens would have said 'You are not alone' or 'Earthlings are not alone'. The fact that the syntax included the personal pronoun 'we' showed that the supposed aliens included themselves in the same category as humans. Eventually, two jokers from Southampton admitted their responsibility.

---

[3]   Including the person's lexicon (or dictionary of words he uses), semantics and pragmatics (the meaning he attaches to words)

The problem with stories like the above is that humans tend to make deductions from apparent facts and thus come to the wrong conclusions. For example, the fact that the Southampton cornfields incident was a sham does not mean that all such cases fall into the same category and it is quite possible that there are aliens out there.

As we will see later the pronoun 'we' – and syntax, generally – is very important in detecting deceit. In many cases syntax conflicts with the content of the story.

## THE PRIZE WINNER

Soon after the hoax was exposed, the same Granny Smith received a very posh letter announcing, 'I am pleased to inform you that you are to receive a cash amount. We are currently holding a corporate cheque for £50 000 and await the filing of your Winnings Claim Form.'

Read the sentence carefully and you will see that no one was saying that Granny Smith would get anything more than a 'cash amount' and certainly not the fifty thousand smackeroos she expected. Incongruencies also appear between other channels of communication and particularly between content and non-verbal communication.

The truth lies in detecting small deviations and incongruencies, but the problem is that we do not think deeply enough about what we hear, see, feel or read and ignore our unconscious concerns. This is a bad mistake.

*The truth is always in the detail*

## THE COMPONENTS OF A STORY

A 'story' is the total proposal, explanation, statement or answers a person gives about a particular matter and it may contain both truth and lies. They may be 'freestyle' when the person has total control over what he communicates or 'guided' when a template is provided by questions asked by an interviewer or in a form left blank for completion. As we will see later, it is often easier to find the truth in freestyle stories. Stories may be oral or written.

Written freestyle, and some template, stories usually consist of a background introduction (or scene setting), factual and emotional clarification and one or more topics, scenes or events in:

- *a prologue*: the introduction to the matter concerned;
- *critical issues*: the key aspects of the proposal or explanation;
- *an epilogue*: the closing of the matter concerned.

A story, whether initially in writing or transcribed later, takes on an identity of its own, distinct from the reality it purports to represent. For example, an event that took two hours in real life may be represented in the story by one line of text or a very short oral explanation, whereas something else that was over and done with in two or three minutes may, in the mind of the subject, justify pages or hours of explanation (see Figure 2.1).

The fact that the person allocates a disproportionate number of words to a topic indicates it is very important to him: it should therefore be important to you. The same is true of the sequence in which topics are dealt with.

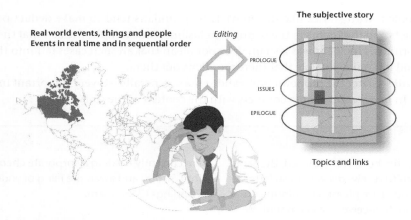

**Figure 2.1**  Real and story or subjective time

In most truthful freestyle stories, whether written or oral, the divisions between the pro-logue, critical issues and epilogue are more or less equal and comments in the background consistent with emotions and the sequence of scenes or topics. In deceptive stories the pro-logue and epilogue may be extended, usually because the liar unconsciously prevaricates before bringing himself to address the critical issues and, when he does, he may extend the epilogue to soften its impact. Such prevarication is true of a deceptive story as a whole, for sentences within it and within answers to specific questions. For example, the pseudo-denial by Bill Clinton:

> *I would like to tell the American people, and I will say it again, I did not have sex with that woman, Monica Lewinsky.*

This is an instance of an extended prologue, within an answer, and, as we will see later, it is also a subjective truth. Both are strong indicators of deception.

## Types of lies

### GOOD AND BAD LIES

Not all lies are intended to cause the victim harm.

---

*Example*: A doctor may understate the seriousness of an illness to reassure his patient that he will recover. A smarmy employee might compliment the boss on his new tie when it looks like a dog's blanket. A golfer may boast about the length of his drive or the fisherman the size of his catch. Such lies are unimportant and, in fact, if we always challenged them we would soon become very unpopular.

---

Altruistic, boastful, joking, social or *good lies* involve no serious penalties if exposed, and may even be authorized by the victim, or justified by the circumstances in which they are communicated. If good lies don't exactly make the world go round, they do little harm either.

*Bad lies* have a negative or evil intent. They are not authorized by the victim, justified by the circumstances or expected. They are normally intended to cause damage to the victim or to someone else. Their discovery would normally result in adverse consequences for the liar. In some cases bad lies become so ingrained that they are accepted, including: 'The cheque is in the post', 'Mr Smith is in a meeting and cannot take your call, but will call you back straight away', or 'Billy is sick this morning and will not be able to come to work'. They are still damaging and should be dealt with.

*This book concentrates on bad lies*

## ACHIEVEMENT AND EXCULPATORY LIES

Lies can be told to provide the liar with a *benefit not already obtained* and these are called 'achievement lies'.

> *Example:* The job candidate may claim to have a degree in zoology when he can't tell a camel from a goat, a car salesman might lie about the age of a car or the number of previous owners to get a better price, the social security claimant might feign illness when he is as fit as a butcher's dog, and the businessman might try to convince a banker that an investment is sound when it is built on sand.

*Achievement lies* are usually based on a *falsification* (rather than concealment) of what we can regard as a *central issue* in one or more of three aspects:

1  *Personal* misrepresentation

> *Example:*
> - The liar claims to be someone he is not. This is essentially identity theft, which is an increasingly nasty problem (see www.identitytheft.com).
> - He claims a relationship he does not have (for example, a woman claims she is the widow of President Abacha of Nigeria and has $25 million ready to send to you).

2  *Physical* misrepresentation

> *Example:*
> - The liar misrepresents the quality or quantity of goods being delivered.
> - He deceives an insurance company over the extent of damage to his car.
> - He falsifies an injury to claim compensation.

3   *Commercial* or *financial* misrepresentation

---

*Example*:
- The liar produces false accounts to obtain a loan from a bank.
- A manager overstates the results of his department.
- A potential borrower pretends to own assets he does not own.
- He exaggerates the gains to be made from an investment.
- He claims false professional or other qualifications to obtain employment.
- He inflates his performance.
- He anticipates results not yet achieved.

---

In such cases, liars must *create* explanations, forge or falsify documentation or *make up* falsehoods to achieve their objectives and cannot claim the right of silence. For example:

## THE ESTATE AGENT

The house was described in the glossy brochure as 'boasting a wonderful outlook over the rolling hills with planning consent to build an observatory over the adjacent wildlife park.' When you go to look at it, and find that it is in the middle of an abattoir, not unreasonably you ask the estate agent to explain. He cannot respond: 'I am saying nothing until I have first spoken to my lawyer.'

In *achievement lies*, the liar cannot refuse to answer: he has to falsify. Also, achievement lies are very dangerous for the liar, because they leave him little opportunity to provide a plausible excuse if they are detected.

*Exculpatory lies* usually occur after the liar has obtained an advantage and are necessary to justify or substantiate an earlier deception. There is a close relationship between achievement and exculpatory lies (see Figure 2.2).

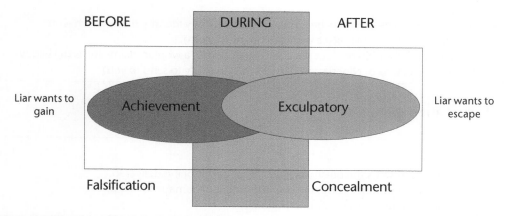

**Figure 2.2**   Achievement and exculpatory lies – showing that an achievement lie today may have to be explained away by an exculpatory lie tomorrow

The relationship between achievement and exculpatory lies is important, especially from a fraud prevention point of view, because the more false detail the liar can be committed to at the achievement stage, the more likely it is he will be deterred or detected. Moreover, barefaced achievement lies may be impossible for the liar to explain later on. Ways of dealing with achievement lies are discussed – see p. 341.

*For every exculpatory lie there has already been an achievement lie that succeeded*

## CONCEALMENT LIES AND FALSIFICATIONS

Lies can be used to *conceal* information adverse to the liar, such as responsibility for a criminal act, a bad credit record or previous deception. Concealment is used in both achievement and exculpatory lies.

*Concealment lies* are used to deceive the victim by:

- failing or refusing to answer questions;
- feigned cooperation;
- suppressing or evading the truth;
- attacking the victim, physically or verbally, as a means of deflecting his questions.

Concealment lies are the most common and the most beneficial when viewed from the position of the liar. If they are challenged, the liar is usually able to say that he misunderstood the question or forgot to mention an important detail. In 95 per cent of cases, lies occur because a person does not tell the *whole* truth. If he succeeds, the interviewer is to blame because he did not ask the right questions and press for detailed answers.

*Every concealment is a step away from the truth, while every falsification is a step towards finding it*

### AN EXAMPLE OF CONCEALMENT

'I understood Michael Heseltine wanted to know whether I had a "financial relationship" with Ian Greer by which Fayed money could have found its way into my pocket … the term "relationship" implied some element of continuity. The receipt of two single commission payments … carrying no implication of further obligation does not constitute a "relationship". This has been described as a semantic distinction, but I was answering the question I was asked. If I had been asked whether I had ever received a payment of any kind from Ian Greer I would have said that I had. But that was not the question.'

*Neil Hamilton MP before the Select Committee on Standards and Privileges*

In *falsifications*, the liar has to make up a story or invent details that are not true. Falsification calls for good imagination, excellent short-term memory, anticipation, composure, assertiveness and confidence. What starts out as a concealment can quickly turn when the victim challenges it, forcing the liar to falsify.

There is no excuse for a barefaced lie and a skilful liar will try to make sure that, if he is compelled to give an answer, the words he actually utters are as near to the truth as possible.

These, as we will see later, are referred to as 'subjective truths' and their recognition is very important in exposing deception.

## REHEARSED AND SPONTANEOUS LIES

Most achievement lies are rehearsed and some salesmen are trained in delivering them.

---

**PENSION SWITCHES**

Thousands of British workers were persuaded to remove their pension funds from 'earnings related' to individual 'money pool schemes'. Investigations revealed that salesmen, working for apparently reputable companies, had systematically lied about the benefits of making the switch, primarily to increase their own commissions.

---

A liar may also rehearse for exculpatory interviews but will still be unable to suppress all clues and incongruencies in the various channels of response. On the contrary, the fact that a liar has rehearsed his responses may make him more vulnerable to surprise questions.

## DIRECT AND INDIRECT LIES

Lies may be communicated directly to the intended victim or they may be relayed through a third party who has himself been deceived.

---

*Example:* A parent who believes incorrectly in his child's innocence will be a fierce defender.

---

## LIES IN WRITING

Even when the liar has extensive time to plan and write down his untruths, he still leaves clues. This includes achievement lies, such as false business proposals, application forms, or Nigerian 4-1-9 scam letters (see the excellent site www.ed-u.com/nigerian-scam-letters.htm), and exculpatory lies, such as false statements and affidavits in legal proceedings or in correspondence.

## PASSIVE AND ACTIVE COLLUSION

Experience suggests that over 90 per cent of all deception involves collusion between two or more people, which can be viewed in two categories:

- *Active collusion*, in which all the people involved participate and share in the benefits and are personally liable if the dishonesty is detected.
- *Passive collusion*, in which people know of dishonesty by others but do not benefit or participate or report their suspicions and are not at risk of criminal prosecution. The Buzz Lightyear example in Chapter 1 is an example of how the liar can be exposed by others, possibly inadvertently.

In most cases of fraud there will be a number of passive colluders or bystanders, most of whom do not wish to become involved or to voluntarily report their suspicions. However, they often retain detailed records, copies of correspondence, tape recordings and diaries for their own protection if they ever fall under suspicion. Establishing that such unofficial and personal records exist and obtaining them is critically important in interviews with witnesses.

## INDIVIDUAL AND TEAM LIES

Lies can be told by one person to another or they may involve groups of people who actively collude together to deceive others.

Members of collusive groups usually rationalize their behaviour as acceptable and take strength from each other. They will sometimes dress, look and act alike to reinforce the bond

---

*Example*: Many employees of the failed Bank of Credit and Commerce International (BCCI) maintained false achievement lies of the bank's finances for many years. In fact, BCCI is alleged to have had a special office whose only job was to create fraudulent documentation.

---

between them. When they involve collusion, lies are usually easier to prove, simply because the people involved are scared that their associates will capitulate to save their own skins. Their fear is usually justified and someone will always inform on the others. Collusion is always a fertile ground for developing witnesses and informants.

## Lies in the animal kingdom

The fact is that the ability to deceive is, to a large extent, ingrained in both humans and animals and, according to Prince Charles, in plants, because it is useful. In his excellent book *The Human Mind*, Professor Robert Winston[4] explains how the brain develops, making and reinforcing connections that are used and useful and disregarding those that are not. Thus if deception had not been worthwhile it would have been atrophied and forgotten long ago.

In addition some forms of deception are hardwired or appear in a physical form. Robert Mitchell and Nicholas Thompson[5] set out four levels of deception in animals:

1   Because it is designed or hardwired to deceive.

---

### THE BUTTERFLY

The Viceroy butterfly mimics the markings of a Monarch butterfly, which is noxious to predator blue jays. Some orchids mimic the appearance of female insects, to deceive males of a rogering disposition, into pollinating them. The Blenny has evolved with the markings of Cleaner fish that bond with and remove parasites from larger members of the species. The crafty Blenny hides in the reeds, by its appearance assuring the larger fish of his good cleaning intentions and then pops out and rips chunks of flesh out of him.

---

4   Bantam Press ISBN 0593 052102
5   *Deception*, State University of New York Press, ISBN 0887 061087

## DAY OLD CHICKS

If you hold a cardboard cut out of its mother in front of a day old chick, it will open its mouth to be fed. Do the same with a cut out of a hawk and it will tremble.

2    Deception is instinctive but occurs only when there is some other creature in the vicinity to be duped.

## CUCKOOS AND STICKLEBACKS

Cuckoos lay eggs in the nests of other birds. Female fireflies flash to attract mates and each species has its own codes. Most complex is *Photuris* whose females imitate the flashes of other species and when the rogering male appears, eats him. The most interesting case was reported by Jeremy Campbell as follows:

'Consider the case of the ten spiked stickleback *Pysgostoeus Pungitious* recorded by Robert Trivers of the University of California. Males of this species build nests shaped like small pipes into which females swim to lay their eggs. Sometimes when one female is spawning in a male's nest, another female appears a short distance away. The male swims to her and invites her in, hoping to double his reproductive prowess. The female is supposed to lay her own clutch of eggs whereupon the male moves in and fertilizes, as he fondly supposes, both clutches. Fooled you! On some occasions, the second female is actually a male, who sneaks in and fertilizes the first and only clutch of eggs. The trick is worked by the impostor altering its bright breeding colouration, which advertises its masculine gender, to the dingy cryptic, nonbreeding colouration of the female. The intruder is so thorough in his chicanery that even while fertilizing the eggs, effectively cuckolding the other, unsuspecting male, he affects the posture of a female laying eggs.'[6]

3    Deception is non-automatic but can be learned by trial and error and is repeated if it is successful.

## CRAFTY DOGS

Dogs may fake a limp or a fox play dead to deceive an opponent. All the deceiver knows for sure is that the trick works (i.e. that he has no scientific proof) and routines are learned by experience and practice.

4    A deliberate intention to deceive is modified according to what the deceptive clues mean to those being misled. This is mainly a human trait, although some animals can operate at this higher level of deception.

The fact is that the more practiced a liar becomes, the greater is his or her ability to succeed simply because the deceptive neural connections are reinforced and become more automatic. However, the interviewer can minimize this advantage by ambushing the liar with aspects for which he and his brain are not prepared. We will see how to do this later.

---

[6] *The Liar's Tale*, Jeremy Campbell, W.W. Norton, ISBN 0 39302 5594

# Why people tell lies

People tell lies because they believe at the time it is to their advantage to do so or to help someone else. Men tend to tell more self-serving lies – even good ones, such as boasting about their golfing prowess – than women, and this seems to be in their nature. Women are much more likely to lie to help someone else to prevent their feelings being hurt.

In most frauds the liar has no alternative but to lie if he wishes to achieve an advantage and a confidence trickster cannot elect to remain silent or claim the 'Fifth Amendment'. When a story is challenged, the liar has three options:

- fight
- flight
- appease.

Reactions to any threat are triggered by the limbic system (see pages 40, 42 and 43), are often based on fear and are, initially at least, unconscious. Neurotransmitters bursting out of the lower brain may, or may not, be refined by the upper brain before the liar says or does something, but even when he consciously tries to control his reaction, he will radiate with clues to deception.

Exculpatory lies are normally in response to a challenge and are communicated for a number of reasons. The most important is that the liar wants to give the impression of innocence and thus appease his opponent. He knows refusal to answer will be treated with suspicion and is tantamount to a fight.

The liar answers questions because he believes he can bamboozle the interviewer by deception, evasion, concealment and all the other tools available to him. The decision to answer questions is usually taken consciously.

In some cases the liar will refuse to answer questions but will present a plausible justification for non-cooperation, the most usual being based on legal advice which he may, or may not, have taken. He may claim mental or physical incapacity or make promises to answer in the future, which he has no intention of keeping.

# The lack of an endgame

In both achievement and exculpatory lies, the liar seldom plans his endgame with precision and his thinking is essentially short term.

## THE ROUNDABOUT

A fraudster working for a bank created fictitious loans for non-existent borrowers and converted the funds to his own use. As they became due for repayment he created new and larger loans, siphoning off further funds. When he was caught he was asked how he planned to bring the fraud to a close. He looked puzzled and said, 'I never thought about it. I was just living from day to day.'

This lack of planning for the endgame is a serious problem for the liar which can be exploited by asking the right questions at the appropriate time (see pages 269). It is, as they would say in Latin, his Achilles heel.

'WE ALWAYS GET MRS BIRT THE CLEANER TO CHECK OUT JOB CANDI-DATES AS HER CORPUS CALLOSUM IS MORE DEVELOPED THAN OURS'

# 3 *The Human Mind*

*Never believe in superstition as it makes you unlucky*

## Introduction

This chapter examines some of the important psychological, physiological and other theories that have proven themselves important in practice, and sets the background for getting to the deep truth. Its bottom line is that the symptoms of deception can never be hidden, mainly because contention between different elements of the brain when lying always surfaces in recognizable profiles. We usually know when we are being deceived; we just don't want to deal with it.

*Darwin said that repressed emotion always surfaces*

## Freud's model of the mind

Sigmund Freud theorized that there were divisions in the human psyche (Figure 3.1).

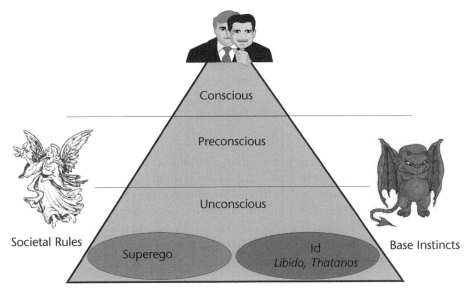

**Figure 3.1**   Freud's model of the mind

Freud believed that the very idealistic superego is challenged by basic drives from the unconscious, resulting in conflict and stress. Practical experience suggests that this is especially true when people are being deceptive

The id contains the primitive biological urges like needing to be loved, cuddled or rogered. It also drives aggression and destructiveness and hostility towards anyone or anything that interferes with the pleasures we seek. The id is not rational or realistic: it has no morals and seeks immediate satisfaction, on the basis of 'if it feels good – do it'.

Although Freud believed that his model was representative of physical structures in the brain, he was never able to prove it. However, recent research using magnetic resonance imaging (MRI) seems to confirm that at a subconscious level only reality and deep truth exists, and that the subconscious cannot lie. Jung believed the subconscious to be the reservoir of 'transcendent truth' and that it dominated human behaviour.

Freud also identified what he regarded as the main drivers of human behaviour: *eros* or libido, which centre on life's pleasures and erotic thought, and *thatanos* or death instincts. Unsurprisingly, the erotic bits have been given the most attention, especially in such academic journals as the *Sun* and *Mirror,* but the death-wish instincts are also important. They explain why smokers are not deterred by death warnings on tobacco or why some people are sadists or masochists.

Experts in subliminal advertising – especially those employed by Silk Cut cigarettes – have replied upon the instinct of self-destructive behaviour to the extent that the urge for a drag is excited by advertisements that non-smokers would regard as bizarre. In short, the 'smoke this and die a painful death' warnings are a great way of increasing sales. Similarly, if you believe that banishing smokers to a freezing spot alongside the dustbins deters them, dream in technicolour: they love it and are encouraged by the pain.

Freud also suggested that unconscious emotional responses always occur ahead of conscious reactions to the same input, but may be repressed before intruding into awareness, concealed by mental constructions (such as self-deception) or through obsessive behaviour, such as repeated washing of the hands or cleaning of the carpet. Even then, the repressed thoughts continue to affect conscious behaviour.

Freudian theories thus suggest that to succeed with deception, a liar has to block out damaging information from his subconscious, especially his real memory, feelings and attitudes. He then has to consciously present the filtered results. This is very difficult for even the most accomplished liar to do. The subconscious and memory are monkeys on the liar's back that make him anxious and may cause him to blurt out the truth.

*The subconscious is the first monkey on the liar's back.*
*The second is his memory*

It is obviously impossible for us to remain in conscious control of everything we do. For example, it is estimated that the human brain receives two million bits of information every second. If we had to deal consciously with our breathing or the carbon dioxide levels in our blood, we would never cope. The subconscious represented mainly in the limbic system (cerebellum or mammalian brain) and brain stem (or the reptilian brain) are the autopilots, controlling our vital bodily or autonomic functions, most of which are hard-wired and, to a large extent, non-variable.

*Question: Why are you breathing so heavily?*

Until you thought about this question, you were not consciously aware of your breathing, but now you are.[1] It is a simple example of how stimulation can bring thoughts from our unconscious into awareness.

*Question: When people dress, why does a woman put her left arm in first and men their right? And why do they cross their legs in different ways?*

Most people react to deception at an unconscious level and may have an intuitive feeling that they are being misled without quite knowing why. For example, we notice other people's body language and emblems and, once we have made an unconscious determination, our minds may become closed to further input. To get to the deep truth it is imperative that we remain alert to everything around us and elevate our suspicions to conscious level.

*If it does not look or feel right, ask yourself, 'Why?'*
*Never consult a psychiatrist whose office plants have died*

# The brain and mind

## EVOLUTION (IN VERY BASIC TERMS!)

Some 3.5 billion years ago (can you even imagine how long ago that was?) single cells floated around the planet, with no brains, spines, eyes, ears, legs or even golf clubs. The best they could do was to drift towards a light source and if they bumped into something, chomp away at it. You can still see this behaviour today as kids chomp away in McDonald's. Bumping into things and then chomping at them is an inherited instinct.

Darwinism, which has held to be accurate except in the case of investigators, proposes that the human gene pool was refined as a result of natural selection, sexual selection and inherited instincts.[2] Faculties that were useful were incorporated and subsequently hard-wired by the development of new cells in both the body and brain. Patterns that were beneficial to survival were replicated and those that weren't were thrown in the bin through a process known as atrophy. If lying had been bad for survival of the species – any species – it would have atrophied during earlier evolutionary periods. The fact is that deceptive instincts and abilities are ingrained in humans, animals and – according to Prince Charles – in plants, because they are useful.

Some researchers believe that deception is instinctive and is the baseline cognitive state, overridden in humans by conscious intervention. We are not clever enough to know the answer, but nature suggests that both hard-wired and learned deception evolves depending on the ability of opponents to detect it.

*The rule in life is 'If you don't use it, you will lose it'*

---

[1]    You thought to yourself 'Bullshit', but now you are thinking about your breathing: go on admit it
[2]    Lamarkianism

## BRAIN HARDWARE

### The basics

The human brain, at its present state of evolution, is a complex, modular system (rather than a homogeneous lump of stodge), around three pounds in weight and consisting of the useful parts not atrophied from reptilian and mammalian eras, plus a newly added (i.e. 60 million years ago) cerebrum, or outer brain (Figure 3.2).

We can summarize the components of the human brain, as in Table 3.1.

The amygdala plays an important role in lots of things, including deception. It is one of the basal ganglia, small islands of grey matter in the limbic system, and consists of two almond-shaped, fingernail structures that are reciprocally connected to most brain areas. Its main task is to filter and interpret incoming sensory information in the context of survival and emotional needs and to trigger appropriate responses. It also encodes or lays down emotional memories.[3]

Sensory receptors (such as eyes, ears, nose, mouth, hands) detect something and then direct signals to the appropriate part of the brain, which fires up neurons and sends them on. Senses and movements on the right side of the body are processed by the left hemisphere and vice versa (except for smell which is handled simultaneously by both hemispheres). Funny that!

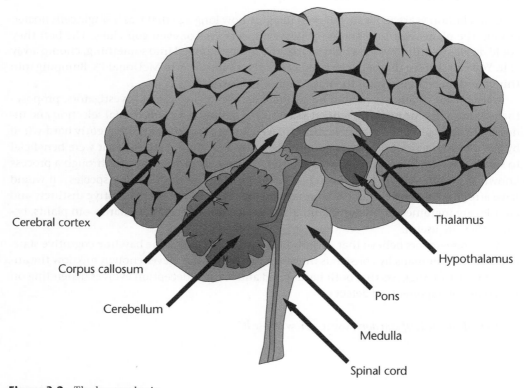

Cerebral cortex

Corpus callosum

Cerebellum

Thalamus

Hypothalamus

Pons

Medulla

Spinal cord

**Figure 3.2**   The human brain

---

[3]   Definition based on www.ascd.org/pdi/brain/amygdala/html

**Table 3.1**   Important elements of the human brain

| Area of the brain | Sub area | Evolutionary stage | What it does |
|---|---|---|---|
| Forebrain or upper brain | | | |
| Cerebral cortex *A thin sheath and other layers of the cerebrum and cerebellum* | | | Super fast transmission system between most areas of the brain |
| Cerebrum *The major part of the brain – gives humans 'self-awareness' – or consciousness Divided into two hemispheres which appear identical but in fact operate differently It controls impulses* | Occipital Lobe | Human | Visual processing and some memories |
| | Temporal lobe | | Sound and speech, spiritualism and some memories |
| | Parietal lobe | | Movement, calculation, recognition and some memories |
| | Frontal | | Integrated functions, thinking, conceptualizing, also consciously processes emotion and stores some memories |
| | Motor cortex | | Handles bodily movement |
| Midbrain | | | |
| Corpus callosum *Transmission system* | Connects the left and right hemispheres | Human | A sheath-like membrane connecting the two hemispheres of the brain |
| Hindbrain or lower brain | | | |
| Limbic system or cerebellum *Totally unconscious Creates impulses* | Known as 'the little brain' | Mammalian | Directly connected to the cortex |
| | Thalamus | | The brain's central switch between the cortex and sensory organs. Also influences mood |
| | Hypothalamus Pituitary gland | | Adapts the body to the environment and its internal state |
| | Hippocampus | | Lays down and controls long-term memory |
| | Amygdala in the medial temporal lobe | | Deals with emotion and especially fear. Acts as memory store for emotions |
| Brainstem | Connects the two cerebral hemispheres to the spinal cord | Reptilian | Handles transmissions to the body, determines the brain's level of awareness, regulates breathing, heart beat and blood pressure etc. Also directs most eye movements |

Engineers (bless them) see the brain in a slightly different way and represent its processes as shown in Figure 3.3.

The engineering representation is important because it shows the connection between a sensory input and the resulting action, passing through a number of conscious filters. As we will discover later, when a person is being deceptive, some of these filters break down.

The different areas of the brain are related through a web of more than a 100 trillion (again just think how many this is) neural connections, which receive and send a complex array of neurotransmitters for even simple tasks.

*Darwin made a Freudian slip: what he meant to say was 'survival of the fattest'*

The way the brain processes information is truly incredible.

## HOW MANY FS?

Look at the following sentence and count how many occurrences of the letter 'F' there are:

FINISHED FILES ARE THE RESULT OF YEARS OF SCIENTIFIC STUDY COMBINED WITH THE EXPERIENCE OF YEARS

Most people will say there are three, but in fact there are six. The reason for overlooking three of the little critters is the way we process information. All written language is handled by the brain's auditory processing systems and not the visual centres. We learn the alphabet by looking at the letters but listening to the associated sounds. When a fluent reader is reading alphabetic characters he is, in fact, internally listening to the sounds in the left hemisphere of his brain. In English the word 'of' is usually pronounced 'Uh-v' and not as 'Uh-f' and you thus ignore the 'f' sound. This is why the three 'fs' in the word 'of' are missed.

## Hemispheres of the brain

### Divisions

The human brain is divided into two hemispheres each with the same component parts (except for the old pineal gland):

The left hemisphere is concerned with:

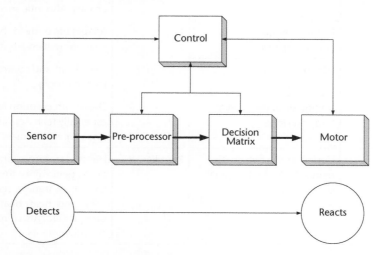

**Figure 3.3**   An engineering representation of the brain

- *logic* and analysis and is conscious of time;
- verbal communication and *words*;
- *control*, linear, serial and sequential thinking;
- movements and sensory input on the right side of the body;
- dissection and separation of thoughts;
- autonomic control of the right side of the body.

It processes information in a logical way and is closely associated with a person's conscious state. When different parts of the brain are in contention for control, it is usually the left hemisphere cortex that acts as the final arbiter and failure in this control region can be disastrous for the liar.

The right hemisphere is concerned with:

- creativity and perception;
- *visual* communication, pictures and even Mind Maps;
- *imagination*, mood and emotion, *including humour;*
- movements and sensory input on the left side of the body and the autonomic management of most non-verbal communications;
- whole or holistic relationships;
- synthesis and connecting things together;
- autonomic control of the left side of the body.

The right hemisphere of the brain processes information in a non-sequential, spatial, holistic and relational way and is closely associated with a person's subconscious.

*Twice as many twins are left handed (20%) as single births (10%)*

The pineal gland (which is not duplicated in both hemispheres) is a pea-sized module, which Descartes described as: 'The seat of the human soul'. In fact, it is a biological master clock, setting body rhythms for night and day. In reptiles and birds the pineal gland is just under the skin and needs no input from the eyes to distinguish between night and day. It also seems to be sensitive to magnetic waves and helps birds with navigation.

The limbic system (and especially the amygdala) is a very emotional little organ and has direct access to the motor cortex. In people under the age of 20, the controlling frontal lobes in the *cerebrum* are not fully developed and thus emotional reactions from the amygdala are likely to burst out, sometimes with devastating results.

## KEVIN THE OBNOXIOUS TEENAGER

You were wrong when you criticized your eighteen-year-old son, Kevin, for being a bolshy so-and-so: his problem is a hard-wired, over-active, amygdala over which he has no conscious control.

### Job gravitation, hobbies and personal interests

People tend to behave and take up interests and jobs that match their dominant hemisphere. This is admittedly a sweeping statement but most accountants, actuaries, lawyers and even some investigators are left hemisphere dominant whereas HR specialists and artistes tend to be driven, more often, by the right hemisphere. There are exceptions and a few accountants, such as some of those employed by Enron and WorldCom, are dominated by their right hemi-spheres and thus may be exceedingly creative.

### Getting on the same wavelength

You can predict, more or less, how a person will react once you determine which hemisphere is dominant and if you wish to create rapport with a left hemisphere driven, dreary and humourless accountant,[4] you should try a logical, step-by-step unemotional approach. With an arty, creative, right hemisphere inclined advertising executive, you should normally work on a more visual, intuitive and emotional basis. If you try things the other way around, you are unlikely to succeed. As we will see later, establishing rapport, or 'getting on the same wavelength', is important.

*You can establish rapport with anyone, if you try*

### Men and women

It may not be politically correct to repeat what scientists have said about the evolution of male and female brains, but it is relevant. Men, traditionally, have been the hunters, gather-ers and stalkers, and are very preoccupied with sex; while females have evolved as nurturers and homemakers. Thus male and female brains have advanced in slightly different ways. It is a physical reality that the corpus callosum (which acts as the conduit between the right and left hemispheres of the brain) has a greater bandwidth in women than men.

## A PROVEN FACT

MRI scans reveal that between 14 and 16 areas in both hemispheres of a female brain are active when she is communicating face to face. These areas decode words, note non-verbal communications and result in what is known as 'woman's intuition'. A male brain uses only four to seven areas for identical tasks because it has evolved for spatial tasks rather than for communication.[5]

Women are thus hard-wired to multitask faster and more efficiently than men, process seamlessly in both hemispheres of the brain and are more prepared to take emotional stimuli on board. Men tend to be more pedantic and logical although, as in all walks of life, there are exceptions to every rule.

*The term 'opposite sex' was not coined by accident*

## DECISION CONFLICT

The brain is the ultimate in multitasking and multi-programming. It is like a giant committee of the Women's Institute when discussing whether to serve cream teas or muffins at the vil-lage fete. All relevant sectors of the brain – logical, emotional, visual, sensory and so on – are canvassed, in milliseconds, on what to make of a stimulus. Each involved area has an input with the frontal lobes of the cerebrum normally trying to resolve disputes, before sending signals to the motor cortex for action to be taken.

It is generally believed that stuttering is caused through interference by the right hemi-sphere in verbal construction and linguistics delivery handled primarily by the left. Similarly,

---

[4]    And believe it or not there are some like this!
[5]    See *Why Men Lie and Women Cry,* Allan and Barbara Pease, ISBN 0 75284 727 9

there is an illness called the 'alien hand' in which (usually) the left hand opposes actions both contemplated and completed by the right. It is very common in investigators, whose right hands often don't know what the lefts are doing.

## ALIEN HANDS

In one sad case a lady would pick her dresses from the wardrobe with her right hand and the left would put them straight back.[6] She could not pack suitcases. One man used to put his cufflinks on with his right hand and immediately take them off with his left.

## KNEE-JERK REACTION

A tap on the knee of a person sitting down with his legs crossed produces a message to the spinal cord, which sends a pre-processed message to the leg to respond with an upward jerk. The brain is not involved in this movement and hence the phrase a 'knee-jerk reaction'. The body uses such reflex arcs when a rapid reaction is needed.

When a person is anxious, under pressure, fearful, angry or lying, the cerebrum (upper brain) has difficulty controlling other parts that are inputting, contending or thrashing about to be heard. One reason for this is that the neurotransmitters going up from the limbic system are more powerful than those coming back down from the upper brain. However, as adults we regard it as 'immature' to react to emotional stimuli and try to suppress them.

One of the most important results of brain thrashing is when the limbic system causes uncensored bodily movements and especially facial expressions. Such 'micro-expressions' occur for milliseconds usually before the upper brain can control them and produce a more reasoned reaction.

## THE NANNY

You may remember the case of the young British nanny who was accused of killing a baby in the USA. At her trial, when she was asked whether she killed the baby, she said, 'No', but a micro-smile seemed to influence the jury, who found her guilty. This was a great shame if, as she claimed, she was innocent.

*Micro-expressions are very important*

## BRAIN FINGERPRINTING

Brain fingerprinting works by flashing words or pictures relevant to a crime or other incident, together with irrelevant words or images. When the subject recognizes information brain pulses, called MERMERS (or P300 waves), are involuntarily emitted around 300 milliseconds after stimulation. Thus when details of a crime, for example the scene of a murder, are shown to the guilty subject he MERMERS, where innocent people do not. This activity can be detected on a headband equipped with sensors and MRI scanning.

---

6   This might explain why it takes your wife so long to get ready to go out

To find the truth, we have to overload the liar's brain (see the difference between creating fear – a definite no-no – and increasing anxiety, pages 71–72) so that he loses confidence in his ability to succeed. This is referred to as the pivotal point and it is critical in finding the truth.

*Most liars succeed because they are not taken to the pivotal point*

## NEUROLINGUISTIC PROGRAMMING (NLP)

You either like NLP or you don't and even its greatest supporters have difficulty in explaining what it is. The simplest definition is that 'NLP concerns itself with modelling existing cognitive processes, and designing interventions, based on redirecting resources that the person already has.' The word 'neuro' refers to an understanding of brain functions; 'linguistics' to communication; and 'programming' is the behavioural and thinking patterns that people follow. The pseudo-science was founded by John Grinder and Richard Bandler in 1975 and has come into and fallen out of favour ever since.[7]

The bottom line from a practical viewpoint is that there is a two-way feedback between a person's inner thought processes and his actions. In simple terms, the subconscious will normally drive most non-verbal communications, paralinguistics and so on, but if an external stimulus can be introduced there will be a corresponding impact on the person's thinking, feelings, attitudes, anxiety, verbal responses and so on.

### NEUROLINGUISTIC PROGRAMMING

NLP is the art, science or pseudo-science concerned with programming the brain (see www.NLP.org) to act in a certain way. For example, if you consciously feel the emotion of happiness, neurotransmitters will be sent to the amygdala and you will genuinely feel happy. Moreover, the more you repeat the process (called 'feedback'), the more the emotion becomes a reality.

If a child is feeling unhappy, with his head down and perhaps in tears, the mother's normal reaction is to place her fingers gently under his chin and raise it: the child cheers up. This is another example of NLP. It is very difficult to remain depressed when your eyes are open and looking upwards. If you don't believe this, try it.

### LOOK UP NOW

Look towards the ceiling for a minute or two. Are you feeling any different? You may even feel happy that you bought this book.

Recent research, including MRI scanning, confirms this feedback relationship between the brain and bodily movements. Neurotransmitters, coming from the amygdala, result in facial expressions, such as smiles and other activity. But consciously driven activity can affect the brain, including emotions. Thus the old saying 'smile and the world smiles with you' is true.

---

[7]    The website www.skeptic.com sets out to debunk NLP and it is well worth visiting

In all interviews we should consider using NLP and feedback techniques to our advantage. The way of doing this is described later but you should always programme yourself when dealing with suspected liars by imagining two monkeys on their backs.

# More on channels of communication

## PRINCIPLES

Primary channels of communication are normally aligned with the dominant hemisphere of the brain. For example, right hemisphere-inclined people react better to visual input and are less linear in their thought processes; they also react strongly (both positively and negatively) to emotional and sensory stimuli. The language a person uses and his eye movements (see Table 3.2, column 3) when processing and retrieving information will *usually* reveal his primary channel of communication.

There is a very important point to note in relation to Table 3.2. It is that there is an exception to every rule. To test how a person reacts you should ask a few control questions, which are

**Table 3.2**   Primary methods of communication for right-handed people

| *For right-handed people* | | |
|---|---|---|
| Dominant method of communication | Examples of language used | Eye movement when retrieving from memory for a right-handed person <br> *Eye movement when calculating or imagining something* |
| Auditory <br> Usually left <br> hemisphere dominant | 'I haven't *heard* any reason why I should help' <br> 'It *sounds* to me that you have already made up your mind' <br> 'You are barking up the wrong tree' | Horizontal and left <br> Then straight ahead <br> *Horizontal and right* <br> *Then straight ahead* |
| Visual <br> Usually right <br> hemisphere dominant | 'I don't *see* why you have asked to see me ...' <br> 'It *looks* to me that you have already made up your mind ...' <br> 'In my *view* ...' <br> 'You cannot *read* too much into this' <br> 'You're *looking* at the wrong person' <br> 'We don't see eye to eye' | Upwards and left <br> Then straight ahead <br> *Upwards and right* <br> *Then straight ahead* |
| Sensory and emotional <br> Usually right <br> hemisphere dominant | 'I *feel* you are looking in the wrong direction' <br> 'You are not *handling* this very well' <br> 'Just get off my *back* ...' <br> 'I do not *believe* ...' <br> 'That is really *heavy* man' <br> 'It *strikes* me you are on the wrong track' | Downward <br> Eyes closing or fluttering <br> Expression before verbal statement <br> *To the right* <br> *Verbal statement before expression* |

non-threatening, and monitor his eye movement. This will set the baseline standard against which you can monitor his response to relevant questions.

*When you are watching people in live interviews on television, determine their primary method of communication and observe their eye movements – it will soon become a habit*

## HOW INFORMATION IS CONSCIOUSLY ABSORBED

People become consciously aware of information through their sensory receptors (eyes, ears etc.) and process it through their primary channel of communication: some people learn best by listening, others by reading or watching and others by touching, feeling or through emotional stimuli. Experience shows that visual inputs have a very powerful effect on all people and for this reason, your appearance, the way you present documentary and other evidence and the layout of the room in which the interview is held are all very important.

| VISUAL INPUT |
|---|
| Images sensed by the right visual field of both eyes are processed by the left hemisphere of the brain and vice versa. Thus, documents and other visual prompts will have the greatest emotional impact when they are presented into the subject's | left field of vision because they hit his emotional right hemisphere and create a direct link to his memory. We will come back to this important point later on (see pages 207–8 and 221). |

*Impact is enhanced when all channels are used together*

## UNIQUE COMMUNICATION CODES

Everyone uses reasonably consistent protocols for communication, both linguistic and non-linguistic. For example, some people use hand movements a lot and others don't; others use big words[8] and complex syntax, some speak slowly and others quickly. Deviations to a person's baseline communications code – in response to a specific question or stimulus – are normally a strong sign of deception.

Generally highly educated or intelligent people use non-verbal communication less than dummies.[9] But please remember everyone has his own baseline communications code.

*Communication codes are disturbed by anxiety caused by being deceptive*

Our communication codes are mainly determined at an unconscious level, except when we try to impress others by using big words or by 'dumbing down', for example in the mistaken belief that we can establish rapport with a rapper by talking rap[10] or by trying to get on the same wavelength as teenage kids by doing moonies. Artificial changes to your communication codes can make you look a plonker and destroy, rather than create, rapport.

---

[8]   Their lexicon or dictionary
[9]   Possibly because dummies are further down the evolutionary chain
[10]   Never try doing this: it will make you appear a condescending nerd and will destroy rapport (no pun intended)

Linguistic codes (which are part of the wider communication codes) are also reasonably consistent but may change over time with the adoption of vogue words: these days everything seems to be an 'issue' or a 'fury' or, in government circles, 'an initiative'. Sometimes organizations and divisions within them create their own vocabularies and linguistic codes. There is nothing sinister in this and it simply goes towards building group identity and rapport. However, the use of common codes tells you that people are part of a group and may stick together.

Sometimes the extended use of esoteric linguistic codes can cause problems.

## THE INTERNATIONAL COMPANY

Supposedly to simplify communications, a leading international company used acronyms in place of virtually all proper nouns. It did not refer to the Marketing Department but to 'EMCS' (Marketing Central Services) and it referred to the Human Resources Department as 'GER' (Global Employee Relations). In its reports it did not refer to John Smith, but to 'JS', or to Bill Jones, but to 'WEJ'. It had printed a glossary of over 500 acronyms, which employees (and external consultants) were expected to learn. There was no consistent structure to the acronyms. For example, common sense would suggest that the first letter should always be the geographical area ('E' for Europe, 'G' for global and so on) but this was not the case. An enormous amount of time was thus wasted in trying to decipher what was meant. There were also serious misunderstandings, which were put to rest when a senior manager sent out an instruction that in future 'all UOAANST[11] would cease'. This caused an uproar, but it made the point.

We should consciously tune in to a subject's communication codes – think what he is really saying and why. We should also remain on the lookout for changes in his codes, or incongruencies between his various channels of communication, because these are always good clues to deception.

## INVESTIGATOR'S LINGUISTIC CODES

Some investigators, in their more enlightened moments, grunt in staccato bursts accompanied by a great waving of hands and serious readjustments of their genitalia with both hands. This is their baseline communications code and is often accompanied by a verbal expression such as 'what a load of twaddle'.

## EMBEDDED COMMANDS

Obviously people do not *always* stick to their primary channel of communication or codes, nor do they think exclusively with one hemisphere of the brain. To complicate matters further, the subconscious registers communications totally missed at a conscious level. Subliminal advertising[12] or muzak to encourage sales in retail shops are examples of communications aimed directly at a person's subconscious. These are sometimes referred to as 'voice to skull' communications because they bypass conscious filters.

---

[11]  Use of acronyms, abbreviations and non-specific terms, i.e. UOAANST
[12]  There is still a big debate over whether this works: the balance of professional opinion is that it does in certain circumstances

We often pay too little regard to the importance of smell and its impact on the subconscious. The Greek Orthodox Church incorporates all five senses into its services, including the burning of incense. Aromatherapy was first practised by the ancient Egyptians and there is a strong connection between the impact of smell and memory.[13]

## DEBT COLLECTION AGENCY

A London debt collection agency sprays demanding letters with a clear non-smelling solution of the pheromone andosterone. This odourless stuff is normally emitted from men's armpits[14] to warn away others, but it improved debt recovery by over 17 per cent. The trouble is, pigs like pheromones and eat the letters and women find them a turn-on.

## DEJA VU

Some scientists believe that déjà vu is a phenomenon where a smell too faint to be consciously recognized registers in the subconscious, triggering memory and an inexplicable sense of familiarity.

## KEYBOARD ERRORS

When the odour of jasmine or lemon was diffused into a room, keyboard errors fell by 30 per cent. According to research by Neil Martin of Middlesex University, smell has a significant effect on the way people behave. Subjects were asked to smell a number of odours including chocolate, spearmint, coffee, almond, strawberry, baked beans, rotting pork and garlic. They sat in special smell-proof rooms and wore clouded goggles and earplugs so that they were forced to concentrate on the smells provided to them. While they sniffed away, their brain activity was monitored. Chocolate consistently suppressed theta waves, making it more difficult for the subject to concentrate or carry out complex tasks.

The human brain is truly amazing: some people are able to speak in reverse and to decipher a tape recording played backwards. The subconscious also reacts to what are called 'embedded commands', and these are very important. They can be considered an adjunct to neuro-linguistic programming (see p. 51).

## DON'T SPILL THAT!

When Johnny walked across your new carpet carrying an overfull bowl of mulligatawny soup and you told him, 'Don't *spill* that', that is exactly what he did. Until now, you probably thought he was a careless little critter and deserved a smack round the ear. You could be right, but chances are his subconscious recognized the embedded command *'spill that'*, which is precisely what he did.

If you are not convinced about embedded commands, let's look at another example:

---

[13]  Aroma processing is wired directly into the limbic system, where much memory is stored and emotion resides
[14]  Don't ask how the chemical is collected

## DON'T LIE

If you want to challenge a lie, you should emphasize the word TRUTH. This seems, in practice, to be recognized as an embedded command.

## NON-VERBAL COMMUNICATION

### The reptilian-mammalian heritage

Our reptilian and mammalian ancestors communicated primarily through body signals. Rita Carter in *Mapping of the Mind* (ISBN 0520 219376) states:

## MAPPING OF THE MIND

Once, no doubt, all living things communicated only to the extent that they reacted to changes in others' behaviour or appearance in much the same way as they reacted to environmental signs. Those that were good at reading these changes must have had a major advantage. If you react to a neighbour's reaction to a rustle in the bushes rather than hear the rustle itself, you speed up the process of fleeing from a potential predator. Similarly, those that gave big noticeable reactions must have given a survival benefit to those around them, so their genes were passed on preferentially.

In this way Darwinian selection must constantly have improved communications between individuals until some species became adept at reading the slightest facial expression, body movement or visible physiological change in others of their kind.

Hominids, blessed with their free moving, flexible hands developed gestures, which were supplemented by proper language some two million years ago. This gave humans the tool needed to elevate themselves to a higher level of consciousness ... while still retaining many of the other forms of communication.

Try describing a spiral without using your hands. It is also much easier to point to an object rather than describe it. Thus body language is still an integral part of human communication and a lot of it is instinctive and unconscious. As we shall see later, body language is very important in building rapport.

As finders of the truth we should be primarily concerned with four main aspects of non-verbal communication:

- personal space;
- emblems;
- body language;
- facial expressions.

What we do about this form of communication is explained at page 242 but first we should have a basic understanding of its significance. Body language can be driven unconsciously by the lower brain when it is really significant or consciously controlled, when it is less important. We will describe later how conscious and unconscious non-verbal communications can be profiled and how you should react.

## Personal space

All people have an elliptical zone around their bodies, which their reptilian brain unconsciously defines as their personal space and in which they feel comfortable (see Figure 3.4). It is an embodiment of the inherited instinct to establish territorial possession.

*The phrase 'Too close for comfort' has a deep meaning as does 'Looking over my shoulder', 'Keep at arm's length' or 'Get out of my face'*

*Remember the saying 'Keep at arm's length'*

People raised in large cities and in large families tend to be comfortable with smaller personal zones, but whatever their history the way a person stands or sits in relation to others is part of his communications code. Research indicates that psychopaths and hardened criminals are very sensitive to violations of their personal space.

Liars usually change their baseline communications code by trying to increase their personal space by:

- moving their body away from the interviewer;
- leaning backwards and especially towards the nearest door;
- moving their chair away from the interviewer;
- walking around.

They may also sit with their legs in a position to make a run for the door.

## THE START OF THE MEETING

Bill Jones walks into your office and you guide him to a chair, which he immediately pulls away from you. This deliberate move to increase his personal space should alert you to the possibility that he intends to mislead you or, at least, sees you as an opponent.

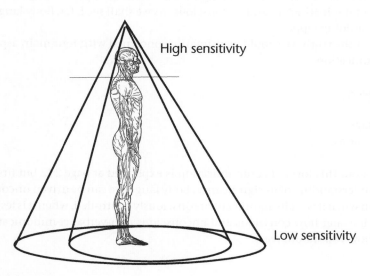

High sensitivity

Low sensitivity

**Figure 3.4**   Personal space

Liars may also try to protect their personal space by erecting large barriers, such as crossing their arms high on their body or over their genital regions, protecting themselves with a file or standing behind a piece of furniture. They may also build protective barriers around their desks, such as laying out files, fruit, drinks etc. in a set defensive pattern.

People also find comfort in occupying territory they believe belongs to them. For example, board members usually take the same seat at every meeting, and if someone changes the routine everyone becomes uncomfortable. The same applies to animals. Try entering a dog's kennel and see what happens.

There are also personal space rituals in many aspects of life. Watch how people behave in lifts, toilets, on public transport or in queues. An obvious example is holidaymakers who mark out their territory by throwing towels on sun beds. This is the human equivalent of dogs establishing territorial rights over trees, lampposts and the neighbour's car.

## THE LITTLE BLACK DRESS

You are feeling really good because at your next door neighbour's party his niece (who was wearing a revealing black mini-dress and had legs to die for) told you she found elderly, tubby, grey haired men, who are good at golf, a 'real aphrodisiac'. What a great night it was and to make matters even better you planned to play golf at 8.30 the following morning at Wentworth.

You return home and as you start taking off your purple flares and yellow Hush Puppies you notice your wife has a face like a 'robber's dog'. 'What's up dear?' you innocently ask, 'another migraine?'

Then you get it full blast: 'You know what's up, you lecherous bastard. Who was that girl you were talking to?' Of course, you know perfectly well who she means

but decide to play for time and admit nothing: 'What girl, I spoke to lots of girls. I always speak to girls, they are much more interesting than that gawky accountant you were talking to.' Not deterred your wife says: 'You know who I am talking about, the one with that silly black dress and the fat, hairy legs.' You are sure your wife could not have heard the talk about aphrodisiacs and all the other stuff, so where did you go wrong?

The answer is your body language and use of personal space. You stood too close, were too frontally aligned and when you were talking to her, you were looking at her mouth and neck. In short you were giving her all of the clues that you were in an amorous mood and it serves you right.

If you think this is all psychobabble, why not try a little experiment.

## A LITTLE EXPERIMENT

If you have someone you don't trust and think he may lie to you, walk up to him and stand slightly to his left. This will force his eyes to move left. In this position, if the NLP theories are correct, he is programmed to access his memory and is more likely to tell the truth. Then ask him some really nasty questions. Moving his eyes right (to contrive access to his imagination and lie) will be even more obvious than usual. It is likely that

he will try and change his position so that he looks naturally to the right. Please try it.

In one such experiment a local rogue builder danced around the room to get himself into a position where he was to the left of the interviewer. As the interviewer resumed his position there was further dramatic movement to get back into a natural deceptive position.

Maybe you have not noticed, before, just how sensitive people are to their personal space but from now on handle it consciously. Make sure your towel is on the right sun bed and that you keep well away from the neighbour's niece with the little black dress and legs to die for.

Anxiety usually increases when there is an unauthorized intrusion into a subject's personal space, especially when he is approached from behind or when you upset his ritual (like moving the towel on another holidaymaker's sunbed). But if you consciously invade someone's personal space to increase his anxiety, you must be careful, as you can never tell whether the anxious result is because the suspect feels 'pinned down' or whether your socks smell.

We have unconscious protocols for setting our positions with other people. Maybe you haven't noticed this, but it is true. When you happen to meet Joe Jones in the corridor you will both unconsciously negotiate a position with which you are comfortable. There will be a certain distance between you and you will align at an angle which will be to the left or right. If one of you changes position the other will normally move. Just try it.

Personal space also has some interesting sub-plots. In most cases the guilty suspect will try to distance himself from incriminating evidence and especially documentation. Thus if you hand a damaging exhibit to the subject and he quickly drops it on the desk, hands it back or shoves it away (usually in small increments while it is in his space), you know it is causing him anxiety (see Figure 3.5).

You can increase this anxiety by pushing the offending document back into the suspect's personal space and in his left field of vision. This, again, is a useful NLP technique that appears to work in practice because it impacts on the liar's more emotional right hemisphere.

Indicative of innocence                    Indicative of guilty knowledge

**Figure 3.5**   Handling incriminating evidence

## Emblems

An 'emblem' consists of all those visual, verbal and sensory images through which a person, consciously and unconsciously, presents himself to the world, including clothing, hairstyle, glasses, shoes, tattoos, jewellery, the tone and strength of his voice and the accessories and accoutrements he uses and the people who accompany him.

*You can tell a lot about a person by the company he keeps*

It also includes other sensory images such as smell (nice perfume or bad breath) or touch, such as the strength of a handshake. Emblems are an inherited instinct intended to show, or impose, the social status of the animal.

In the olden days, great store was put in physiognomy and the supposed relationship between a person's looks and his character. To an extent, we all still react to a person's physical appearance and form conclusions based upon it.

Emblems are selected both consciously and unconsciously to represent the way the person feels about himself and how he would like others to perceive him.

The trouble with emblems is that we tend to accept them without thinking. This is a big mistake because the impression we form may permanently influence our transactional relationships.

## THE TRAMP

An actor dressed as a tramp stopped people in Victoria Street in London and asked them for directions to the Houses of Parliament. Some people avoided him; most were curt and did not want to be bothered. The next day, in exactly the same spot, the actor was dressed as a top businessman and asked the same question. The responses were fast and friendly.

We are also subliminally influenced by a person's accent and we all tend to work on stereotypes.

## BRUMMIES ARE NOT TO BE BELIEVED?

A report from Doctor Mahoney and colleagues from the Worcester College of Further Education was presented to the British Psychological Society in the autumn of 1997 and concluded that people speaking with a Birmingham (or 'Brummie') accent are twice as likely to be convicted or, if not convicted, disbelieved in court. The doctor and his team hired male actors to reproduce interviews with suspected armed robbers and cheque fraudsters. The actors used Brummie, 'standard' and other regional accents before a panel of 119 students from the college. The results showed a dreadful bias against Brummies, who were seen as 'less intelligent', 'working class' and 'socially incompetent'. This is extremely interesting, as many of the students on the panel were from the Birmingham area and the city produces many highly intelligent people including, even, some lawyers and investigators.

Thus the rule is to be very careful with emblems, both your own and your interpretation of others. Look, listen and smell carefully and consciously determine what the person is telling you about himself. Pay particular attention to incongruencies between a person's emblems and his communications through other channels.

## JOB CANDIDATE

If the job candidate turns up for interview in a pink suit, flowery shirt, yellow Hush Puppy shoes and long, frizzy hair dyed pink, he is more likely to be a right hemisphere type, with a visual channel of primary communication. He may, of course, be simply an investigator, but only if he keeps rearranging his genitalia.

## BAD TASTE OF THE WEEK

Two lawyers at a court in New Orleans have been reprimanded for wearing ties decorated with a hangman's noose and the grim reaper at a murder trial.

So who dares say that emblems are not recognized?

## Body language

Chapter 4, pages 126 to 133 goes into interpreting body language signals in depth, so it is not necessary to repeat them here, except to say that the liar's body is like a monster BBC transmitter, driven by unconscious commands from the limbic system and reptilian brain, often resulting in contention and conflict with the cerebrum.

For example, some hand movements (called *manipulators*, see Chapter 4, pages 130 and 242) are used unconsciously to relieve stress. Actions like rubbing the back of the neck, putting hand to mouth, crossing arms and legs or brushing non-existent dust off clothing are examples of manipulators. If the person is deprived of the comfort of these, anxiety is increased. For example, if a person is getting comfort from crossing his arms high up his body, we can increase his anxiety by handing him a piece of paper to examine, thereby compelling him to change his position. Also, if we unobtrusively mimic manipulators or comment on them he will stop using them and will be denied their soothing effect.

Other non-verbal communications are called *demonstrators* and these again are hand movements (like describing a spiral) used to reinforce a verbal explanation. When being deceptive a liar's demonstrators usually stop or deviate from his baseline patterns.

## Facial expressions

In 1862, Guillaume Duchenne carried out experiments on facial expressions and especially smiles. He discovered, by applying small electrical currents to his patients' faces, that genuine smiles (thereafter known as 'Duchenne smiles') were quite different from those that were artificial, mainly because in the latter the *pars lateralis* (bloody Latin again) did not move and some muscles in the cheeks remained passive (see Figure 3.6).

In our world there are seven primary facial expressions:

- anger;
- anxiety;
- disgust;
- fear;
- happiness;
- sadness;
- surprise.

In most cases, an expression representing a genuine emotion is spontaneous and takes place before any associated verbal response. Spontaneous reactions are driven by the lower brain. With feigned expressions of emotions the reverse is true and they are often preceded by micro-tremors around the eyes and mouth that give the game away.

**Figure 3.6**  Duchenne's experiments. (Poor fellow: he only intended going out to buy some milk for his cat. But note the striped trousers, suggesting that the patient is an English solicitor, and Duchenne's knotted eyebrows, suggesting that he should not become a used car salesman.)

Eckman and Friesen (see www.2cs.cmu.edu) have proposed a Facial Action Coding System, based on the relationship between expression and emotion. They identified 46 different Action Units (AU), which are mainly unconscious, and 14 miscellaneous mainly conscious expressions. For example AU 20 is called the 'lip stretcher', which involves the *risorius w/ platysma* muscle (Figure 3.7); the 'lip corner depressor' involving the *depressor anguli oris* (or *triangularis*) muscle (Figure 3.8).

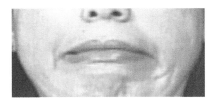

**Figure 3.7**  Does this remind you of anyone? Her name is Doris.

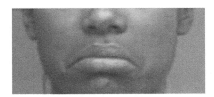

**Figure 3.8**  Looks like Tiger Woods after missing a 40-foot 'tap in' putt

This is all very interesting stuff, but the expressions were all posed mainly in response to stimulation by smell: in the case of Doris (Figure 3.7) by showing her a Big Mac. To that extent the results have to be regarded as artificial and in any case do not take you very far. You could hardly say to her: 'Look here, Doris, I know you are unhappy because your *risorius w/ platysma* muscle has pulled your expression into AU 20.' Try this and you are likely to get a smack with her handbag.

*The problem is not in recognizing when a person is lying, but what you do about it*

However, the Eckman–Freisen research is important in confirming the relationship between apparently genuine emotion and facial expressions. We will return to this point in Table 3.8, page 73.

A person's eye movements, including their direction (left, right, up or down), the size (or dilation) of their pupils, gaze intensity and blinking rates are mainly driven unconsciously and, when a person is lying, are different from his normal communications code. The normal reaction when a person is recalling from memory (probably true) or constructing a story (probably false) can be summarized as in Table 3.3.

**Table 3.3**   Eye accessing clues

| Channel of communication or type of memory being accessed | Construction of a lie | | Remembering the truth | |
|---|---|---|---|---|
| | Eye movement from the subject's position | | | |
| | Vertical | Horizontal | Vertical | Horizontal |
| Visual | UP | RIGHT | UP | LEFT |
| Auditory | AHEAD | RIGHT | AHEAD | LEFT |
| Emotional | DOWN | RIGHT | DOWN | LEFT |

## A LITTLE TEST

Try this little test: concentrate on which way your eyes are drawn in answering the following questions.

- What is the date of your mother's birthday?
- What is the result of multiplying 72 by 6?

It probably won't work because you are thinking consciously about eye movements, but unconsciously to the first question your eyes would drift to the left (and up if you are trying to picture her) and to the second question your eyes will be pulled to the right.

There are obviously exceptions to the rule,[15] but it is very easy (with a little practice on your granny or by watching politicians on television) to work out what the subject's baseline patterns of eye movements are and to determine which way they move when they are truthfully retrieving facts from memory or untruthfully contriving them in the imagination. You then have to remain consciously alert to changes in the response to relevant questions.

---

15   Especially with left-handed people

*Eyes left usually means the truth is being told*

The direction of a person's gaze, his rate of blinking and the size, or dilation, of his pupils tells you a lot about what he is thinking. If you are sexually interested in someone, the chances are that you will unconsciously focus on their mouth: if you are not, the direction of the gaze is towards the forehead, unless you are severely anxious, when you may try to avoid all eye contact or just stare (see Figure 3.9).

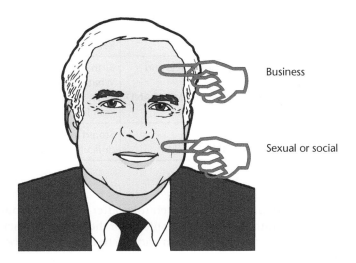

Business

Sexual or social

**Figure 3.9**   Direction of gaze

*Never say to someone, 'You can't look into my eyes and say that'*

Normal eye contact is for around 40 per cent of the time a person is speaking and 75 per cent when he is listening. The baseline human blink rate is six a minute and the average gaze for between one to ten seconds. Remain consciously aware of a subject's baseline behaviour and deviations from it: these are often signs of deception.

People's pupils become enlarged (dilated) when they are emotionally aroused and blinking rates noticeably increase or decrease. These can all be considered as deviations from the person's baseline communications code and you should consciously register them.

# Memory and imagination

## TYPES OF MEMORY

Input to memory is encoded in a number of ways, both consciously and unconsciously, and can be considered under four main headings (Table 3.4).

Each type of memory has short-term and long-term stores hard-wired into the brain in the areas shown in column 2 of Table 3.4. What moves between them and when is usually directed at an unconscious level.

Experiments suggest that information is held in memory in chunks and that it has many handles through which it can be retrieved. The short-term memory in the cerebrum can nor-

**Table 3.4**  Types of memory

| Type of memory | Function<br>AREA OF THE BRAIN IN WHICH STORED | Examples |
|---|---|---|
| Procedural | How to perform tasks<br>CEREBELLUM AND PUTAMEN | How to ride a bicycle or drive a car<br>How to get home from work |
| Semantic | Relating to ideas and concepts<br>CORTICAL AREAS AND TEMPORAL<br>LOBE | Recognizing different colours<br>Feelings and emotions<br>Shapes and colours<br>Relationships |
| Episodic | Relating to events, people, facts and<br>learning<br>ENCODED BY THE HIPPOCAMPUS AND<br>STORED IN CORTICAL AREAS | Birth dates of your children<br>What you did last week<br>What someone told you yesterday<br>Your last annual appraisal |
| Emotional | Emotional experiences<br>Amygdala in the LIMBIC SYSTEM | Stored in the amygdala and very<br>difficult to forget |

mally hold between five and nine topic-related chunks, after which it becomes overloaded and either throws the excess into the waste bin or files it for the long term. Each experience is encoded in chunks in different parts of the brain and can be considered to be a highly complicated relational database.

We can, of course, override the unconscious processing of memory and make a conscious decision to remember something such as an important telephone number, name or date. We may make a note to remind us, but the irony is that when we do this, our subconscious reminds us at the appropriate time and we never have to refer to the note. Similarly, if we set our alarm clock to wake us for work particularly early, our subconscious will wake us up every 90 minutes throughout the night.

*You can never forget something you really want to remember*

Episodic memory (relating to people, places events etc.) is the most short-term and transient. Some input is consciously or subconsciously flagged as important and is retained in long-term memory: unimportant matters are not flagged and recollection quickly degrades.

Other inputs may not be consciously flagged on being laid into memory but still can be quickly retrieved when prompted by a cue. *For example, the cue of 'What were you doing on 11 September 2001?'* will undoubtedly remind you where you were and what you were doing, mainly because of the emotion involved and the scale of the visual impact. The cue of 18 February 2002, may not have the same effect unless, of course, it was your wife's birthday and you forgot it and found your supper in the dog rather than in the oven.

*The more handles, or cues, there are, the easier it is to remember*

## THINGS WHICH ARE NOT FORGOTTEN

Whether they like it or not, criminals and liars unconsciously commit emotional details of their dishonesty to memory; 'handles' guiding them to stores in the lower brain will trigger other parts of memory into action, such as the date their dishonesty started, what their feelings were at the time, what they did and thought about doing with the money and who else was involved. Once one handle gets pulled, neurotransmitters fire away and activate other memories.

When someone responds to a question with 'I don't remember', this may or may not be true. Everything depends on what the person is being asked to remember, the type of memory involved and the number of handles potentially available.

In all cases, a spontaneous statement that a person does not remember, when he has made no attempt to access his memory, is a very powerful sign of deception.

*If you genuinely don't remember, how do you know there is anything to forget?*

## REHEARSING FALSE EXPLANATIONS

In some cases, a liar will carefully rehearse how he plans to deal with questions and will try to commit the answers to memory, but they will go into a different area of the brain to a real experience.

### MEMORY CORRUPTION

Extracted from *Mapping of the Mind*:[16]
[Most] memories are not pure recordings of what happened but are heavily edited before being laid down. The process of falsification gets another boost each time memory is recalled. As we go over things that happened we add a bit, tweak a bit, lose a bit, tweak a fact here, tinker with a quote there and fill in any little bits that may have faded. We may consciously embellish the recollection with a bit of fantasy – the biting comment that we wished we had said but that was only thought of later. Then this new, re-edited version is tucked back in storage. Next time it gets an airing it may pop up with the fantasy comment still attached, and this time it will be difficult to distinguish it from the genuine memory. So by gradual mutation our memories change.

However, MRI studies suggest that the brain activity used in recalling pure memory differs from that which produces a false recollection.

When interviewed, the liar may deliver his answers too quickly or have varying response times that do not correspond with the complexity of the question or matter concerned. He may spontaneously list out alternatives, but they will normally be concerned with the content of the story. Unless he is an exceptional liar, his answers will lack commitment and his non-verbal responses will not be synchronized.

*Evidence that answers have been rehearsed is often a strong sign of deception*

---

[16]  By Rita Carter, ISBN 0520 219376

## THE BENEFITS OF RECOVERING MISPLACED MEMORY

A great deal of information which appears to have been genuinely forgotten can still be re-trieved, providing the right stimulus is provided and handles pulled. In Chapter 9, page 377, cognitive and other methods of helping witnesses dig deep into their memories are explained. Most are based on presenting the subject with as many handles as possible to help him retrieve memory chunks. Similarly, by asking the right questions, we can cause a suspect to bring disa-greeable information to a conscious level, which obliges him to either tell the truth or repress it, significantly increasing his anxiety. Either way, he is faced with a problem.

*The memory is the second monkey on the liar's back.*
*Liars have more memory failures than truthful people*

## PRACTICAL DIFFERENCES

The truth comes from memory and is consistent with the person's unconscious deep knowl-edge. When a person lies, he has to overrule his subconscious, wipe the truth from his memory and draw the detail from his imagination.

*Truth comes from the subconscious and memory.*
*Memory is recalled in the past tense*

The difference between memory and imagination is true whether the lie is a falsification or a concealment and whether the response is rehearsed or not. In concealments the liar has to select from memory only those portions of the truth he wishes to reveal, and has to imagine that the remaining negative detail does not exist. In falsifications he has to invent something that did not happen. Lying successfully is very difficult, since the liar has to try to juggle a number of connected elements (see Table 3.5).

Making sure that all of these elements are consistent, especially with the liar's normal or baseline behaviour and communications codes when not lying, is virtually impossible.

*If there is one single indicator of deception, it is the incongruence of a person's responses when compared to his normal baseline behaviour*

The difference between memory and imagination has a computer equivalent. The first is similar to a computer chip that can be accessed rapidly at any point. Memory has separate brain areas for storing visual, auditory and sensory information. Data drawn from memory can be repeated consistently and confidently, and the visual, auditory and sensory responses are congruent.

Imagination is like a tape that starts as a blank and records lies as they are told. The tape has to be replayed carefully to check earlier answers each time a new question is asked. Moreover, the tape may have no track – or a corrupted track – for visual and sensory information, and thus responses are likely to be incongruent.

**Table 3.5**  Difference between memory and imagination

| CHANNEL OF COMMUNICATION Elements of a lie | True and from memory and subconscious | False and consciously drawn from the imagination |
|---|---|---|
| | Examples | Examples |
| VERBAL The content of what the person says; the story | Natural and spontaneous, consistent in detail Demands the right to explain Commitment to the explanation | Censored and lacking detail Claims the privilege of silence Uncommitted |
| VERBAL The words used. The syntax or construction of the story | Consistent with the content | Inconsistent with the content |
| VERBAL AND VISUAL How the answer is delivered: sometimes known as 'para-linguistics' | Relaxed and confident Possibly angry at accusations of responsibility | Cautious Will not make an enemy of the questioner |
| VERBAL, VISUAL AND SENSORY The person's attitude to honesty and the offence in question | Consistent and likely to condemn the act in question | Inconsistent and insincere; unlikely to condemn the act in question |
| VERBAL, VISUAL AND SENSORY Emotional reactions | Superficial Non-verbal expression appears before a verbal response | Repressed The verbal response appears before the non-verbal reaction |
| VISUAL AND SENSORY Non-verbal, body language clues | Consistent with the words used. Hand movements will be mainly demonstrators, which emphasize points being made | Defensive, inconsistent with the words used. Hand movements are restricted to manipulators, which are soothing movements |

# Transactional analysis

## THE THEORY

Professor Eric Berne, a distinguished American psychologist, developed a theory called 'transactional analysis' (TA), which suggests that in our relationships with other people (called 'transactions') we adopt one of three ego states, referred to as 'parent', 'adult' or 'child'. Parents are further sub-divided into 'critical' or 'nurturing', and children into 'rebellious' or 'adaptive'.[17]

---

[17]  Eric Berne subsequently revised his theory slightly to introduce two categories of rebellious child: the 'natural' child and the 'little professor'. They do not affect the basic principles

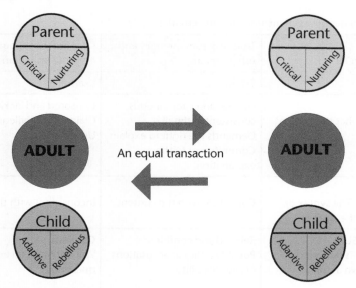

**Figure 3.10**    Transactional analysis

These roles – shown in Figure 3.10 – are further illustrated in Table 3.6.

TA is relevant in all meetings and interviews and we must elevate our subconscious behaviour to a conscious level.

*TA is a very powerful tool in establishing or destroying rapport*

**Table 3.6**    Roles in transactional analysis

| Ego state | Primary channel of communication | Role model example *Attitude* |
|---|---|---|
| Parent: critical | Whatever is normal for the person concerned plus emotional | Father or mother who disciplines a child *Assertive, disciplinary, punishing, censuring* |
| Parent: nurturing | | Father or mother who nurtures and comforts a child *Consoling, teaches, guides, mentors, encourages, empathizes, helps sort out problems* |
| Adult | Normal for the person concerned | The usual ego state in business *Controlled – logical – responsible – political – unemotional* |
| Child: adaptive | Whatever is normal for the person concerned plus emotional | Emotional and willing to comply *Willing, cooperative, loving* |
| Child: rebellious<br>• Natural<br>• Little professor | | Awkward and looking for trouble, either as the natural child or the little professor, who is manipulative *Truculent, angry, emotional etc.* |

## BORINGLY OBNOXIOUS

Chances are that there is someone in your life that you do not like: maybe you find him boring, rude or otherwise obnoxious: he might even be an investigator. Rapport will be totally absent and chances are he does not like you. Why not try a little experiment.

Elevate to a conscious level all of those things that you don't like about him, the symptoms and prejudices. Next time you meet, carefully observe him, ask him nice questions and show an interest. You may find you begin to like him and he will you[18.]

On the other hand, if you want to create disharmony you simply take an approach that you know will not align with the subject's dominant hemisphere, impose a crossed transactional relationship (see pages 65 and 216) and create negative rapport. We will return to the important art of deliberately winding people up later.

## EQUAL TRANSACTIONS

Transactions are regarded as 'equal' when the parties to them accept their roles. Equal transactions build rapport. In business, most transactions take place on an adult-to-adult level and can be regarded as more or less 'equal' (Table 3.7).

**Table 3.7**    Equal transactions

| Person 1 | Person 2 | Examples |
| --- | --- | --- |
| Adult | Adult | Normal business relationship |
| Child | Child | Normal relationship between children |
| Critical parent | Adaptive child | Parent instructing a compliant child |
| | Rebellious child | Parent instructing a naughty child |
| Nurturing parent | Adaptive child | Parent comforting a distressed child |
| | Rebellious child | Parent counselling a naughty child |

Equal transactions are normally harmonious and rapport building and they can be consciously controlled.

---

[18] If at the end of the experiment he asks to borrow £100, you know it has failed

## DRIVING OFFENCES

If you are pulled over by a traffic cop on the way back from a boozy night at the golf club annual dinner and dance, the worst thing you can do is to get off on the wrong transactional footing, if you want to avoid a night in the slammer. Get out of your car, nice and quietly, walk slowly towards the officer in an appeasing way, perhaps gesturing by clasping your hands to your forehead, and make a conciliatory remark such as, 'I am so sorry, officer, I just did not see that pink elephant. How could I be so stupid?' You might get your ass verbally kicked but you should escape, simply because few animals attack if they already know they have won.

If you sit in your car, with a defiant expression, or your wife comes out with a load of verbals such as 'Tell the pig who you are, Stan, and that you play golf with the Chief Constable', you have had it. Getting to the right transactional relationship is the key.

## UNEQUAL OR 'CROSSED' TRANSACTIONS

Negative emotion – usually fear, anger or anxiety – is generated when one person tries to impose a transactional role on another that he is not willing to accept. For example, you will become angry if you treat a colleague on an adult-to-adult basis but he treats you as he would a child. Such misalignments are referred to as 'crossed' transactions, and they always generate strong emotions. You can totally unbalance people by deliberately crossing a transaction.

## THE DOMINEERING BOSS

Many years ago a young investigator had a boss who was an ex-major in the Colonial Army, rigid, domineering, plain nasty and with a pencil thin moustache. Everyone was afraid of him. He was the ultimate 'critical parent' and they the 'adaptive children'.

Every day the major would bring to work a box, packed by his devoted wife, containing nicely cut brown bread and two hard-boiled eggs. He would sit at his desk, reading *The Times*, tuck a beautifully clean napkin under his chin, crack the first egg, peel it and eat it. He would then eat some brown bread and crack the next egg.

One day, the young investigator went to a local grocery store, bought two raw eggs and substituted them in the major's lunch box. When he began to peel the first egg, it exploded and dropped in his lap. Foolishly, though, he opened the next egg and the same happened. The major's investigation quickly identified the person responsible and rather than being outraged, laughed and thereafter treated the investigator as a 'rebellious child' (an equal transaction) and from that time onwards got on well with him.

## NEGOTIATION OF TRANSACTIONAL ROLES

Transactional roles are usually negotiated (much like personal space) between the parties at an unconscious level and are dynamic over the course of a meeting or interview. Most people are not aware of ego states or how they affect them and thus lose the opportunity to get into the transactional relationships that lead to the deep truth. Moreover, the opening phases of a conversation with someone you have never met before usually set the transactional relationship for everything that follows.

First impressions will be influenced by various factors, including:

- The person's position, reputation, wealth etc.
- The location at which the meeting takes place, including visual, auditory and sensory inputs.
- The person's intended or unintended emblems, such as clothes, hair, office, car or speech.

The lesson is always to try to consciously register transactional roles, emblems and communications codes and to get to the deep truth by arriving at the position where you are a nurturing parent and the subject an adaptive child.

*The deep truth comes in the relationship between a nurturing parent and an adaptive child*

## CONSCIOUSLY CONTROLLING ROLES

If you want to raise the temperature of an interview or meeting and, for example, challenge the honesty of the other party, you must be prepared to cross the transaction and become a critical parent. If you want to establish rapport, you must recognize the other person's ego state and act accordingly. If you want to put someone off, adopt the role of a rebellious child.

Police officers and lawyers in court are perceived to be, and often act as, critical parents. In fact, the environments in which they operate and their personal and associated emblems, including uniforms, helmets or wigs, are deliberately used to reinforce a critical parent role and to increase anxiety in the minds of people around them. The fact that people in positions of authority rarely consciously move to become nurturing parents is one reason why there are so few deep confessions in court, and why those made to police are sometimes alleged to have been obtained through oppression.

*If you can't understand people, don't interview them.*
*If you can't become a nurturing parent, you will never get to the deep truth*

---

**BIG TIPS**

Research in the USA shows that waiters and waitresses who touch their customers get 20 per cent greater tips than those that don't.

The light physical contact shows they are interested and nurturing.

---

# Emotions: from anxiety and panic to relief

## WHAT ARE EMOTIONS?

Emotions may be defined as 'strong, positive or negative feelings' and they are usually an important factor in deception. They affect both the subject and the interviewer and are mainly triggered in the lower brain at an unconscious level.

## THE EMOTIONAL PATH

Emotion always surfaces either obviously or by displacement into other verbal, non-verbal or sensory disclosures. The stronger the emotion, the more obvious are its symptoms and the more difficult to repress.

The normal sequence of emotions involved in deception is illustrated in Figure 3.11.

A person's ability to reason decreases as his emotions move up the scale. When anxiety turns to panic, the liar finally loses confidence in his ability to succeed with lies and at the 'pivotal point' (see pages 48, 70 and Table 6.1, page 199) may try to negotiate to minimize the consequences of his acts before accepting the truth.

We are primarily concerned with seven emotions:

- anger;
- anxiety;
- disgust or contempt;
- fear;
- happiness or deception delight;
- sadness;
- surprise.

These all originate mainly in the lower brain and are neurotransmitted to the cerebrum (to be precise the ventromedial or subgenual cortex), which consciously examines them before sending signals to the motor cortex for action. There are two potential problems for the liar. The first is that the emotional neurotransmitters going from the amygdala to the cortex are more powerful than the ameliorating signals going the other way. The second is that, to achieve the fastest survival reaction when facing a severe threat, the amygdala can go straight to the motor cortex. Thus, in genuinely emotional reactions, body movements and facial expressions occur before any conscious verbal reaction driven by the upper brain. We will see the significance of this hard-wiring when we try to distinguish genuine from feigned anger.

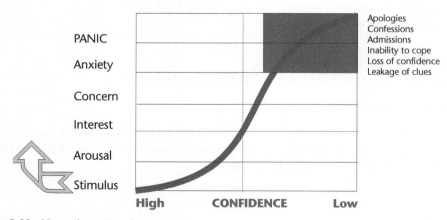

**Figure 3.11**  Normal emotional sequences

## SCRATCHING

| If you have a genuine itch, the chances are you will scratch it five times. If you | consciously move to make a scratch it will be more or less than five times |
|---|---|

## HAPPINESS AND DECEPTION DELIGHT

Some people enjoy lying and this is especially true of achievement lies when the victim is being misled and taken like a lamb to the slaughter. The liar feels that he is in a dominant position and his approach is akin to an attack. Ways of dealing with achievement lies are discussed in Chapter 9, page 341 and they are, unfortunately, very common in business. Delight or happiness are the starting emotions for achievement lies because the liar is in the driving seat. This can quickly turn to anxiety when the lie is challenged.

## FEAR

Fear is a very strong emotion, initially based on an unconscious perception of a specific external threat, like being chased by a sabre-toothed tiger; or your wife after the neighbour's party. In the modern day truth-and-lies world, fear may result from, amongst other things:

- torture and physical pain (i.e. working for an investigations consultancy);
- an improper threat to lock him up or beat him (as above);
- loss of livelihood, family or friends;
- not being believed;
- becoming involved in something he would rather avoid;
- some other reason unknown to the interviewer.

You should never assume that the reason for a person being afraid is because he is guilty of the matter in which you are interested. Innocent people can be afraid, for genuine reasons. Thus, fear is not an emotion you should stimulate, although anxiety is.

*Usually genuinely frightened people don't have the time to be anxious*

## ANXIETY AND PANIC

### Principles

Although fear and anxiety are closely related, the latter is internally generated through a combination of factors resulting in an elaborate and continuing neurotransmitted dialogue between the lower and upper brains. Anxiety is mainly a conscious emotion and it can result in near panic when the person internalizes that he is unable to cope. Whereas fear is a response to a specific threat, anxiety is usually caused by a combination of small factors, which accumulate to become overwhelming.

Anxiety in a guilty suspect varies directly with:

- His analysis of the situation, including:
  - the strength of the evidence currently against him and the potential penalties (this is the balance at the pivotal point);

  – other evidence he believes might be *discovered and not just that which the interviewer has currently available*;
  – his perception of the skills of the interviewer;
  – his ability to explain and evade questions;
  – his ability to succeed with an attack.
- The penalty if earlier lies are revealed.
- Other unrelated problems such as:
  – poor mental and physical health;
  – tiredness.

The more the liar has to falsify an explanation, the more his anxiety increases. And it is not always one large problem that causes anxiety, but rather a combination of small issues which cumulatively lead the suspect to conclude that he cannot cope. This is an important point to remember. Although we would always like to have overwhelming evidence, the fact that we have many small items of incriminating intelligence, or use NLP techniques, can be just as effective in increasing the suspect's anxiety and getting him to the pivotal point and then to the deep truth.

## Raising the pavement

If most people were asked to walk on a narrow kerbstone at the edge of a pavement, the probability is that they could do so successfully and without anxiety because they have the balancing skills to succeed.

However, if the pavement were raised, so that there was a sheer drop of 30 feet over the edge, the balancing skills needed would be just as before. But anxiety, caused by the consequences of failure, would increase, in turn leading to a possible loss of balance. A few people might try to walk along the edge and succeed. Others would try and fail, but the majority would take the safe course and either refuse the invitation, or accept but leave a wide safety margin so that they would not fall off the edge. The same principles apply to deception and are manifested, primarily, in a lack of commitment that results in panic when the penny drops that the person simply cannot cope. In finding the truth, this is referred to as the pivotal point.

*Always raise the pavement to get to the pivotal point*

## ANGER

Anger is a negative, initially unconscious, emotion directed externally and is consistent with a person's decision to fight rather than flee. It may also be a battle against reality. Anger may spring from frustration, anxiety or fear, or from some totally unrelated reason; in the animal kingdom, it is used to establish dominance or protect territory. The basis may be genuine, or contrived, but in most cases anger is intended to cause the adversary to withdraw and run off.

Some people will take a conscious decision to simulate anger, again to frighten off an opponent, but the difference is obvious (see Table 3.8).

You should remember that an angry person is directly connected to, and thrashing with, his subconscious and is vulnerable to making mistakes, Freudian slips and blurting out the truth. If you can talk him out of his anger, you are likely to get to the deep truth (see the methods of dealing with anger in Chapter 7, page 238).

**Table 3.8**   Genuine and contrived anger

| Genuine anger (driven unconsciously by the sympathetic system) | Contrived anger (conscious action by the para-sympathetic system) |
|---|---|
| Bodily signs | |
| Adrenalin flush, fast heartbeat and heavy breathing | Normal heartbeat |
| Apparently enlarged body | Normal, ambivalent or 'image-managed' posture |
| Pallid complexion (often extreme) | Flushed or reddened complexion |
| Face inclined forward | Face pulled back |
| Tightly drawn lips | Exposed teeth |
| Profuse sweating | No discernible activity |
| Hair standing on end | |
| Dry mouth caused by reduced salivation | |
| Clenched hands or pointing finger gestures | |
| Fixed stare with dilated pupils | Variable gaze |
| | Displacement movements to relieve tension, such as false scratching, rubbing hands, winding his watch or cleaning glasses: gasps and sighs |
| Voice | |
| Raised with a fast delivery | |
| Attitude and demeanour | |
| Not quickly forgotten | Transient |
| Will not defer to interruptions by the interviewer and will be assertive | Will usually defer to interruptions |
| May terminate the interview and storm out | Very unlikely to terminate the interview |
| Focused on a specific issue or event | Unspecific, often unjustified and at the start of the interview |
| Throwing or breaking things | Threatening but not doing |
| Timing | |
| At any time in an interview and usually in response to a specific statement | Usually at the start of an interview, without any obvious reason |
| Non-verbal expression appears before a verbal outburst and is symmetrical | Verbal outburst precedes the non-verbal expression. The facial expression may be asymmetrical |
| Justification | |
| Often a good basis for complaint | Spurious grounds for complaint |
| Anxiety decreases | Anxiety remains |

## SADNESS AND DEPRESSION

Depression can be regarded as anger directed inwards and is often an isolation from reality. It usually has the same roots as anger and leads to increased, rather than reduced, anxiety and can result in a mental block. However, depression is often an unconscious excuse in anticipation of failure. Signs of depression include:

- complaints about poor health and particularly mental problems;
- self-pity;
- paranoia;
- comments such as *'I wish I had never been born'*;
- self-deprecation, e.g. *'No one will ever believe me'*, *'I am not clever enough to lie'*.

It is also not uncommon for suspects to feign depression to get the interviewer to pull back, using phrases such as *'If this doesn't stop, I will kill myself'*. Depressed people do not usually confess and the ways in which a subject can, and should, be talked out of this negative emotion are explained in Chapter 7, page 240.

# Other characteristics of deception

## A COMPLEX ARRAY

There is also a range of other emotional and emotionally based reactions that can surface during an interview.

## SELF-DENIAL

The human body has a powerful ability to anaesthetize itself against pain, and the mind has an equivalent capacity to block out unpleasant facts from consciousness. This self-denial may take a number of forms, both conscious and unconscious (see Table 3.9).

**Table 3.9**   Examples of self-deception

| Category | Effect | Examples and comments |
|----------|--------|------------------------|
| Repression | Keeping bad news from the consciousness | *Like the ostrich: burying his head in the sand* |
| Denial | Deliberate refusal to accept things as they are | *Pure self-deception and a most common feature in lies* |
| Projection | Refusal to see himself as being personally involved | *Seeing the problem in an impersonal way. For example, Richard Nixon often referred to himself in the third person as 'The President'* |
| Obsession | Displacing anxiety to a manual task | *Compulsive washing of hands etc.* |
| Isolation | Acceptance of the facts while not accepting blame, guilt or emotion | *Admitting the transgression but without intention or guilty knowledge* |
| Rationalization | Consciously defending, justifying or downplaying the bad news | *Minimizing the seriousness of the problem* |

*Inattention to painful truths shelters us from anxiety*

Before the truth can emerge, we may have to bring the liar to face the truth at a conscious level and to overcome his self-denial. There are two main ways of doing this and both are founded on the relentless pursuit of detail, what you believe to be the truth and arousal of the two monkeys: the memory and the subconscious.

This action will either lead the subject to lose confidence in his ability to cope with the continuing anxiety created by deception, or to be forced into telling more and more extreme lies.

*When in doubt, press for detail*

## NEGOTIATION

The subject may seek clarification, usually at the pivotal point, to help him decide whether or not he should confess. The object is usually to help him decide whether the consequences of confession are tolerable and whether he has more to gain by telling the truth than not. Symptoms of negotiation include:

- Asking for clarification about the possible outcome: 'What usually happens in cases like this? Do they get reported to the police?'
- Posing hypothetical questions about the possible consequences: 'I didn't do it, but if I said I did, what would happen?'
- Accepting a justification for their action, without specifically acknowledging guilt: 'You are right in suggesting this started by mistake.'
- Seeking sympathy: 'How would you feel in my position?'
- Asking to speak off the record.
- Body posture opens or leans forward: arms and legs may unfold.
- Eyes look upward, with slow blinking or head drops.
- Rubs chin: his chin may appear to quiver.

You must recognize negotiating symptoms and take your time. It is likely that the suspect will be communicating on an emotional and sensory level and you must mirror this. It is not the time to say too much and under no circumstances should you discuss the potential penalties or make any promises that cannot be kept (see pages 13, 215, 272, 282 and 284).

## ACCEPTANCE AND ADMISSION

If the suspect believes he has more to gain by confessing than from continued denial, he will begin to make admissions. Signs of acceptance include:

- tears and deep sighs;
- eyes looking downward, often accompanied by slow blinking and with virtually no eye contact with the interviewer;
- head and shoulders drop;
- body posture opens further and the suspect may appear to look smaller;
- appears that he is about to faint.

Again, such communication will be at an emotional level and you must remain patient, adopt the role of a nurturing parent and help him get the monkeys off his back. We will return to this point in Chapter 7, page 277.

## CONFESSION: THE DEEP TRUTH

It is one of the great ironies of life that most religious orders see confession as a positive, natural and healing process, whereas lawyers and smelly socks[19] seem to assume that they can only be obtained through improper means. In a tough interview, the suspect definitely finds confession cathartic.

Over the years we have tried to find what caused suspects to confess. We did this after the deep truth had been revealed, empathetic relationships established and a bond of mutual trust formed with the suspect, by simply asking them.[20] People said they confessed because at the time they were convinced that:

- The truth would emerge regardless.
- They could not cope with the anxiety created by their own deception.
- They had lost confidence in their ability to succeed with lies.
- They believed that telling the truth might be beneficial to:
  - gain an advantage,
  - minimize punishment,
  - start life again,
  - feel better,
  - clear the position for colleagues,
  - avoid disadvantages,
  - avoid the involvement of family,
  - terminate the investigation,
  - prevent matters becoming worse,
  - avoid their home being searched,
  - avoid the involvement of police,
  - avoid dismissal,
  - avoid publicity for the case.
- They were able to internally excuse their own behaviour and save face with their family and colleagues, both in defending the transgression and their admission of it.

They also said they believed that the immediate consequences of confession were tolerable and that they could rebuild their lives. It should be noted that very few showed any genuine signs of remorse.

## PROJECTION AND REVENGE

The relationship between a suspect, who has confessed, and the interviewer is usually very close, often based on a child-to-child transactional relationship. Most suspects are relieved

---

[19] 'Smelly socks' is a generic term relating to people who live in a dream world, believe in Father Christmas and the tooth fairy, and think that the Data Protection Act achieves any useful purpose for honest humans
[20] 40 years later we still get Christmas cards and emails from people who have confessed

that they have told the truth. However, in the days immediately after the interview, when the suspect has discussed his confession with his colleagues and lawyers, it is not unusual for him to turn and make allegations of improper treatment and to go on the attack. There is little you can do about this except to know in your heart that you have acted properly, fairly and reported the facts accurately.

## Monkeys on the liar's back

Always remember that the liar has two monkeys on his back (see Figure 3.12). The subconscious monkey always wants to blurt out the truth and give away what the person is really thinking, his emotions and attitudes. It is the ultimate 'supergrass'. It is a very dangerous monkey, and the liar has to try to keep it carefully and consciously under control. The memory monkey also knows the deep truth: it is a database of unbridled accuracy. When set free, it will always state the facts.

From now on, when you are confronted by someone you suspect is not telling you the truth, put on some new spectacles and look at him in a different way.

So from today onwards become a keen observer of human behaviour and remember the monkeys on the liar's back. It will make you a much more effective truth finder!

**Figure 3.12**    The two monkeys – the subconscious and memory

'I HAVE TO TELL YOU, MR PARKER, YOUR CONVICTIONS FOR MURDER ARE A POTENTIAL RED FLAG'

# 4 *Signs of Deception*

*The total amount of evil in a person remains constant*

## Introduction

Finding the truth is a seven-stage process (see Mind Map 3).

This chapter examines how a liar leaves clues as a direct result of his conscious objectives and, much more importantly, scattered unconsciously in ways he never intended.

| MILLER'S LAW[1] | |
|---|---|
| In order to understand what a person is telling you, you must first accept that what | he has said is the complete truth and then ask yourself what it is true of. |

The bottom line is that there are so many clues that we cannot consciously remember them all and have to rely on our subconscious to warn us. Once we get the warning – which may be as weak as an intuition – we have to decide if the matter is important and, if it is, to elevate our suspicions to a conscious level and deal with them.

Thus dealing with deception is a three-stage process:

- Let our feelings and intuition run free (that is, don't immediately suppress them and test the story against the clues you can consciously remember).
- Decide whether the suspected deception is important: if it is not, just enjoy it. But if it is important, take a conscious decision to deal with it.
- Adapt the cunning plan to suit the circumstances.

The Mind Maps in this chapter summarize everything and Chapters 6 and 7 set out the methodology for handling tough interviews where fraud or other gross deception is suspected. Working copies of the Mind Maps can be downloaded from www.cobasco.com.

*Deciding that a person is not telling the truth is the easy part.*
*Dealing with it is more difficult*

---

[1] George Miller, US psychologist

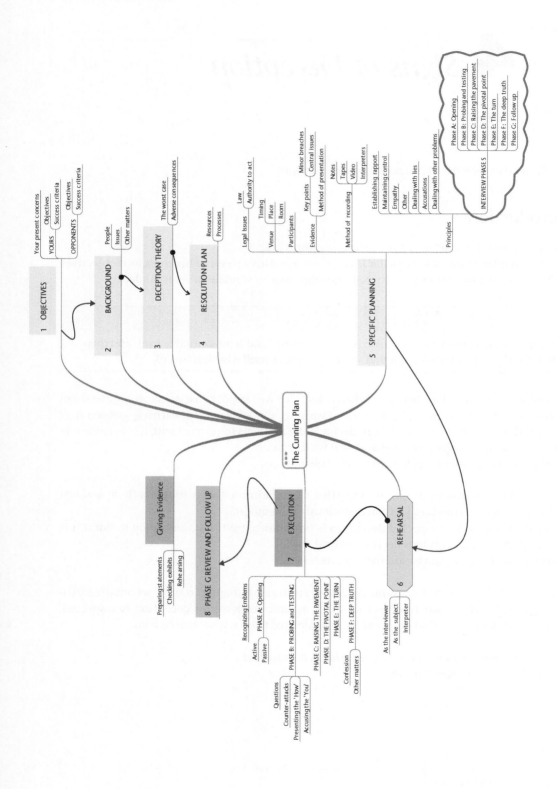

**Mind Map® 3**   Stages and phases in finding the truth

# The liar's *conscious* objectives

## BACKGROUND

In most cases, a liar has conscious objectives, which are to distort what he knows to be the truth and to communicate the modified story to another person with the intention of misleading him. Achievement lies are told before the event, to provide the liar with a financial or other benefit and are usually based on falsification.

*Everything is said for a reason*

Exculpatory lies are usually told after the event with the conscious objective of:

- *Permanently removing suspicion* or stopping the enquiry:
  - by attacking,
  - by convincing you of his innocence.
- *Escaping*, taking a line of appeasement, without incriminating himself:
  - by *avoiding making admissions* and ensuring he does not increase the evidence against himself in any other way,
  - by diverting, distracting, *evading* or attacking so that the matter is not effectively pursued.
- *Finding out what you know* and planning so that he can take appropriate action.
- *Minimizing the penalties*, if there is no escape.
- *Frustrating follow-up action by further attacks.*
- *Possibly returning to the deception* as soon as he believes it is safe to do so.

These conscious objectives are mainly achieved by concealment and falsification of the content of a story. Few liars appreciate the importance of syntax, paralinguistics, non-verbal communication and attitude. Even if they did, they could not consciously control them. Also, lying is easier when the liar knows he has left no repudiatory evidence.

*Liars usually concentrate on the content, but know too much.*
*They fail to say things an honest person would*

If the liar cannot succeed with an achievement lie, possibly because he is effectively challenged, his fall-back position is to try to escape by removing suspicion: if this is not possible he will fall back to minimizing the penalties or making sure action cannot be taken against him, so that he can walk away to fight another day, with another victim. In fraud cases, achievement liars usually revert to their dishonesty once they believe it is safe for them to do so. Thus, this makes it imperative that suspicions of dishonesty are resolved. However, in most cases, liars and fraudsters have not planned their endgame and this is their weakest link.

*If you currently have suspicions, you should make every effort to resolve them*

## ACHIEVEMENT LIES

These lies, which are an integral part of most frauds, hit you when you least expect them. The liar chooses the time, the circumstances and the weapons: everything is in his favour but he will usually assess his chances of success and decide whether or not to engage in what is effectively a fight with the victim. If the fraudster believes the balance is not in his favour, he will deflect to another victim, to another time, place or another method. Thus, a deep awareness of your risks and the circumstances in which you may be deceived is a great defence. That is why this book should be carried with you at all times. Also the personal manifesto should ensure that you do not become the victim of achievement lies. They are always preventable if you ask the right questions at the right time.

> *For every credibility gap, there is a gullibility fill.*
> *If it looks too good to be true, it is*

## EXCULPATORY LIES: PERMANENTLY REMOVING SUSPICION

### Objective

Totally stopping an investigation and removing himself from suspicion is an ideal outcome for the liar and he has two options, based on the 'fight, flight or appeasement' decision discussed in Chapter 2, page 37.

### Attack

The option to attack will be used if the liar believes it will achieve his objectives.

---

### AN ATTACK: THE SWORD OF TRUTH

'If it has fallen to my destiny to start the fight to cut out the cancer of bent and twisted journalism in our country with the simple sword of truth and the trusty shield of British fair play, so be it. I am ready for the fight.'
Jonathan Aitken, former Defence Minister, author of the book *Nixon: A Life*, and later jailed for perjury

'A few weeks later, there was a moment of absolute stillness in the court as Jonathan Aitken, once dubbed the tallest, handsomest man in British politics, bent over to study the documents that had just been placed in his hands. They revealed that the testimony he had recently given on oath had been a lie.'
*The Guardian*

---

The attack may include:

- *Challenging*:
  - the motives, authority, skill or independence of the victim or the interviewer,
  - the evidence.
- *Threatening or using*:
  - violence,
  - legal action,
  - any other action that could damage the victim, including blackmail.
- *Interfering with the evidence*:
  - destroying records,

- threatening witnesses,
- creating false evidence and alibis.
• *Complaining*:
- about alleged unfair treatment,
- about infringement of his human or other rights.

Attacks – especially at the start of an interview, or during it, when they are unjustified in the circumstances – are usually contrived to deflect you off course.

---

## NOW WHAT DO YOU HAVE TO SAY ABOUT THAT?

In a very high-profile British murder case, an experienced detective began to interview a 15-year-old suspect in the presence of his lawyer. The detective opened the interview politely and explained to the suspect how it would be conducted. Without warning, the suspect leapt from his chair head-butted the detective (breaking his nose) and said, 'Now what do you have to say about that?'

---

An attack may also come at any point when the suspect believes the balance falls in his favour and can be encouraged by your lack of confidence or determination. Thus, it is critical that you remain in control of every important interview, because if you fail to do so you increase the chances of an attack. The good news is that the subject who launches an attack and fails is extremely vulnerable, and thus you should look upon anger as a step towards reaching deep truth.

*Strong objects cannot be shaped without the application of heat*

### Convincing of the truth
The liar will try to convince you of his innocence, but if the right questions are asked, this is a dangerous course, requiring him to falsify information and to tell barefaced lies. More often the liar will give the impression of truthfully answering questions but, in doing so, he leaves abundant clues. These are analysed later.

## EXCULPATORY LIES: TO ESCAPE

### Objectives
If the liar believes he cannot stop the investigation – through an attack or convincing you of his innocence or appeasement – he must either make sure that he does not make the case against himself any worse, or try to cloud the issues sufficiently to prevent any action being taken against him. Again, he is unlikely to have planned his endgame.

### Avoid making admissions
The liar may avoid making admissions in a number of ways, including not appearing for the interview at all, refusing to answer questions, evasion, feigned anger or sickness, alleged memory failures plus a host of other tactics described later in this chapter. By deciding to answer questions the suspect consciously enters into a battle of wits that he believes he can win and, unless you can take him by surprise through your own cunning plan, his prepared responses may prevail.

*Liars are more evasive than honest people*

## Finding out what you know

The liar may also ask questions ('fishing questions') to find out how much you know and what action you plan to take. This, again, is much like a game of poker and you must control any disclosure. If you say too much (perhaps through the questions you ask) the liar is able to plan future answers and actions, interfere with witnesses or destroy evidence. For this reason, the fact that you have suspicions should be treated in confidence, especially when fraud is suspected. It is critical that the suspect is ambushed.

## Minimizing the penalties

Where a suspect's guilt is overwhelming, he may try to minimize his punishment by providing a plausible excuse, the most common being that he is suffering from a terminal illness or has a personal crisis of some sort, the common theme being that people should take pity on him.

Excuses are the manifestation of the 'flight' or 'belly up' decision by animals who know they have lost the fight. Experience shows that many excuses are totally false but even so, people seem to accept them. Even the highest courts in the land fall for sob stories without verifying them and thus allow villains to walk away laughing.

Thus the rule is that if at any time an excuse is presented, consider it to be no more than an achievement lie and deal with it accordingly.

---

## GOD'S LITTLE MIRACLE

Tommy Taylor stole £100000 from ABC Ltd and admitted his sins to his manager. If anyone was facing a term of imprisonment, Tommy was; until God intervened. The day after making his admissions, Tommy and his crying wife saw the head of personnel and explained that he had a terminal illness and was unlikely to live for more than a few months. A letter from his doctor – backed up by very bleak test results – confirmed the tragic news.

Human resources recommended that Tommy be allowed to resign and die in peace, and any idea of prosecuting him was abandoned. In fact he was given time (something of an irony under the circumstances) to repay.

A few months later, Tommy appeared on a national television quiz show and was a picture of health. God had intervened with a miraculous cure and, six years later, Tommy is still alive and well and probably still cherishing the letter, supposedly from his doctor, and test results which his wife had dutifully forged on her laptop computer.

---

*Never accept an excuse without verifying it*

## Frustrating follow-up action by further attacks

It is not unusual for people who have confessed to change their minds and make complaints of unfair treatment or to threaten blackmail. Such allegations, which can be days or even months later, can be successfully defended if the interview has been properly conducted and recorded.

*Always expect a counter-attack and never give in to blackmail*

## TACTICS

To achieve his objectives a liar may consciously use a number of tactics in the following ways.

### Silence or explanation

Innocent people who believe they are being wrongly accused usually demand the right to explain. Their emotions run deep and are consistent. They are committed to their positions and little will deflect them. On the other hand, liars frequently claim the privilege of silence – either directly or, more usually, through their legal advisers.

> *Innocence demands the right of explanation.*
> *Guilt claims the privilege of silence*

In 99.24 per cent of cases, refusal to answer a question has to be viewed as an admission that there is no believable explanation. Of course, there are exceptions, such as where a person has been treated unfairly by the organization concerned or has no confidence that his explanation will be reported accurately. Genuine cases of this nature are very rare. It is also very unusual for a suspect to commit himself so that he accepts personal responsibility for refusing to answer questions. Usually his failure to answer is blamed on his legal advisers, some feigned illness, deafness, inability to speak the language, muteness, unavoidable absence on a prolonged trip to Mongolia, family catastrophe, religion, curvature of the earth – or legitimized in some other way.

---

### TERMINAL CANCER

Two senior businessmen based in Singapore were suspected of stealing $35 million from their employers and failed to turn up for interviews with auditors on the grounds that the first had checked himself into hospital with terminal stomach cancer and the other had seen the error of his ways and joined a monastery. A few weeks later investigators were retained, and true enough both men were indisposed although they were known to be talking regularly with each other on the telephone. Investigators established that the cancer victim's daughter was about to get married and they kept observation on the wedding service and checked into the hotel where the reception was to be held. Sure enough the manager did look ill and walked into and out of the church with great difficulty.

But later on, at the reception, he was the life and soul of the party and was seen drinking vast amounts of brandy and eating anchovy and tuna sandwiches by the score. He was intercepted while in the throes of doing a vigorous dance to the Chubby Checker record 'Let's do the twist' and taken to a private room for an interview. Although he initially claimed he was too ill to cooperate, he eventually relented, and called his colleague out of the monastery to join him; together they ate more anchovy and tuna sandwiches while they confessed to fraud and told investigators where the proceeds had been stashed. It all seemed to be going so well until defence lawyers argued that they had been under the influence of alcohol at the time and thus their confessions would not be admissible in the criminal courts. The case was settled by negotiation and to no-one's amazement the cancer was cured and the religious zeal dissipated. Both men went back to their usual ways, although they were $20 million less rich.

It is very rare for a liar to make a commitment and carry the personal responsibility for not answering questions.

*Silence is an admission that there is no believable answer*

## Concealment and falsification

Both consciously and subconsciously, liars do not want to get caught in a barefaced lie for which they have no plausible excuse. Thus, where you permit him to do so, the liar will conceal the truth rather than falsify it (Table 4.1).

**Table 4.1**   Concealment and falsification

| Concealment | Falsification |
|---|---|
| He omits to mention important and usually incriminating information | *He makes up facts, events and other things that did not take place* |
| He does not have to remember what he has already said and is therefore less likely to give a conflicting answer | *He has to be careful to make sure untrue details provided are not contradictory and to avoid 'Freudian slips'* |
| If it is discovered that he did not volunteer the truth when asked, he can always say he had forgotten the detail or misunderstood the question. There is usually a plausible excuse for concealment | *If the suspect is caught in a falsification, he may be unable to provide a plausible excuse. There is no excuse for a barefaced lie* |
| Low anxiety | *High anxiety resulting in the surfacing of repressed emotions through non-verbal and other communication* |
| This is the safe course, chosen by 99 per cent of all liars in 90 per cent of all cases | *Inexperienced liars and suspects under professional questioning falsify rather than conceal* |

When you are in doubt over whether a person is telling the truth or not, press for more detail and make him falsify. Pin down his explanation, listen carefully and get more and more detail. In this way the liar's confidence decreases, anxiety increases and his non-verbal and verbal clues spiral out of control. You then confront him with these as part of the cunning plan.

*The devil is always in the detail*

# The clues

It does not matter how skilled the liar is, his conscious and unconscious objectives will always leave clues to deception (Table 4.2).

**Table 4.2**   Objectives and clues

| Objectives CONSCIOUS *Unconscious* | Where the lie is revealed | | | | |
|---|---|---|---|---|---|
| | Content *What he says* | Syntax *Words used* | Paralinguistics *Ancillary verbal communication* | Non-verbal *Body language* | Attitude |
| LACK OF COMMITMENT | Page 88 | | | | |
| SUBJECTIVE TRUTHS | Page 89 | | | | |
| FAILURE TO ANSWER | Page 90 | | | | |
| GENERALIZATIONS | Page 91 | | | | |
| SUPPRESSING GUILT | Page 92 | | | | |
| Inconsistent detail | Page 93 | | | | |
| Reducing anxiety | Page 94 and 100 | | | | |
| Failure to deny | Page 95 to 99 | | | | |
| Irrelevant support | Page 100 | | | | |
| Contextual clarification | Page 100 | | | | |
| ATTACK | Page 102 to 104 | | | | |
| AVOIDING BAREFACED LIES | Page 104 | | | | |
| ALLEGED MEMORY FAILURES | Page 104 | | | | |
| **CONTENT** | Page 104 to 111 | | | | |
| **Syntax** | | Page 114 to 123 | | | |
| **Paralinguistics** | | | Page 123 to 126 | | |
| **Nonverbal clues** | | | | Page 126 to 133 | |
| **Attitude** | | | | | Page 133 to 135 |

*Also, the liar's attitude will be revealed mainly in the content*

There are also peripheral clues, in content, syntax and so on, arising from the way a liar seeks to minimize punishment and frustrate follow-up action. In fact, we are flooded with signs of deception but often fail to consciously register and deal with them.

*We may unconsciously recognize a lie, but consciously fail to challenge it*

# Unconscious symptoms of deception in the content
## GENERAL

We can easily recognize a liar's conscious objectives by relying on our deception theory and resolution plan but unconscious clues are less easy to spot although they are equally important. But please remember, there is seldom one perfect clue to deception, short of a full confession. We must always look at clusters of responses and gauge them against the subject's baseline responses to non-threatening, or 'control' questions. We must also look for incongruencies in the different channels of communication (oral, visual, paralinguistics and body language).

*Incongruency is the best single indicator of deception*

However, the four most important clues that a liar unconsciously leaves are:

• lack of commitment;
• reducing anxiety within his response;
• from his attitude and especially *not doing and saying the things an honest person would*;
• not reacting as an innocent person would.

These are discussed below.

## LACK OF COMMITMENT AND SPONTANEITY
### Generally

Most liars (but there are always exceptions) will make every effort to avoid being caught in a barefaced lie for which they have no plausible excuse. They will dance like a dervish around difficult topics, squirming and using every option to avoid commitment. The liar will try to keep his options open, so that he is not pinned down to a barefaced lie or any other position from which he cannot escape and will consciously use a number of techniques, such as evasion, appeasement, deflection, ambiguity etc. to do so.

*Liars rarely answer a relevant question with a binary 'yes' or 'no'*

Another critical factor is the liar's lack of spontaneity and 'naturalness' in his answers to questions and his failure to volunteer information, especially if it might show him in a bad light.

*What a liar does not say can be more important than what he says*

Even when a person seems to be committed to an explanation, the syntax used can still give the game away.

## THE BODY[2]

| | |
|---|---|
| 'Around 5:00 am/5:30 am I, John A. Woods Jr, was in the process of giving my son, John A. Woods III, his scheduled feeding. During this feeding he bucked and fell approx. 2 ft to the floor, hitting his head on the floor. | His body landed head first; I attempted to catch him but was unsuccessful. When I picked him up he cried for about 90 sec. then started to gag. His eyes were glazed. I immediately called 911.' |

Can you spot the hidden clue? It is that he referred to the 'body' (a dead one) before it supposedly hit the floor.

Lack of commitment is often concealed by alleged memory failures such as:

---

[2]  From the excellent site www.theirwords.com

- 'I am not sure about this …'
- 'Don't hold me to this …'
- 'To the best of my recollection …'

Such phrases are always an indication of deception, especially when the subject has made no effort to access his memory. You should never let them succeed with this ruse.

*It is a proven fact that liars claim to have more alleged memory failures than truthful people.*
*If someone genuinely does not remember, how does he know there was anything to forget?*

## Subjective truths

A liar will unconsciously try to reduce his anxiety when giving a false explanation and this may be achieved by omission, deflection or other contrivances. Perhaps more importantly, he will try to make sure that the precise words he utters are technically true or justifiable and these are referred to as 'subjective truths' or 'internalized definitions'.

### TONY BLAIR AND THE SECRET UNDERSTANDING

Tony Blair was asked about a secret agreement between him and Gordon Brown to the effect that he would resign and let the Tartan Terror take over as Prime Minister before the next election. Blair said, 'What Gordon and I say when we are asked this question is "no".'

Think about it. What Mr Blair said is subjectively true in his own mind, even if there is an agreement in blood, more so if it is not a 'secret'. The wording is typical of a subjective truth and, therefore, of deception. Time will tell whether Mr Blair and the Tartan Terror have such an agreement, 'secret' or otherwise.

### THE AFFIDAVIT

John Smith was accused of taking bribes from a customer and in his statement to the Employment Tribunal he said:
'I have been accused of taking money from a customer. *I would like to state* categorically that I have never taken money. I know the company's policies *and I would be stupid* *to risk my job by doing anything underhand.* I do know the customer concerned and from time to time have played golf with its Managing Director, but I would like to repeat that I have never taken money, except for small winnings on our games.'

There is no doubt that he 'would like to state' but he is not actually stating it. Equally, the voluntary admission over golf winnings was a pre-emptive defence or a denial of an allegation not made. The statements are typical of deception.

Bill Clinton also relied on subjective truths.

### NOT A SHRED OF EVIDENCE

During an interview with Jim Lehrer of PBS, Bill Clinton said: 'There is not a single solitary shred of evidence of anything dishonest in my public life'. Most people hearing this would understand it to be a total denial of wrong-doing and Mr Clinton clearly intended this to be the case.

However, more careful reading shows that Mr Clinton did not deny acting dishonestly: merely that there was no evidence of it. His further qualification concerning dishonesty in his 'public life' suggests that the denial did not apply to his private life.

## BILL CLINTON

No one could forget President Clinton's emphatic, but rehearsed, finger jabbing denial that: ' I would like to tell the American people, and I will say it again, I did not have sexual relations with that woman: Monica Lewinsky'.

This apparent denial was based on his internal rationalization that what he was saying was true, and resulted from his very mealy-mouthed definition of 'sexual relations'. At another point in his testimony we find another classic statement: 'It all depends what the definition of "it" is'.

A classic example of a subjective truth is the statement made by a person who stole £100000 through a wire transfer fraud. He said: 'As I told Mr Smith last week, I did not take the money'. The statement that he 'told Mr Smith' is subjectively true (and thus minimizes the liar's anxiety in saying it) even if he did make the transfer as, in fact, he did. It is also true because he did not take 'money' but merely rearranged a few electronic impulses.

Subjective truths often appear in pseudo denials (see page 95). For example, when the subject is told, 'I think you are involved in this, Bill', he responds, 'I would have been crazy to do that', which is subjectively true and not a denial.

Job candidates are great at subjective truths and the phrase 'I pursued a degree course in mathematics' does not mean that he caught up with it and actually qualified.

Subjective truths can arise because the liar has rearranged his memory (see page 63) and given himself the benefit of the doubt. His anxiety in delivering the lie is thus reduced because he has rewritten history. This is a very common form of deception in business, which makes it imperative that you have an accurate record of conversations in which achievement lies may have been told.

## THE TRUSTY BUSINESSMAN

A businessman and an apparent pillar of society routinely makes promises which, possibly, he may intend to keep at the time. However, on reflection, he believes they were too generous and convinces himself he did not say he would do something, merely that he would 'do his best' or would 'consider'

doing what in fact he had promised.

The routine is made even more abhorrent because he systematically delegates execution to his deputy, who denies all knowledge of any promises made by his boss. The only way to deal with such people is to tape-record their every word.

Truth is always in the detail and subjective truths must always be challenged.

## Not answering the question

Although it is rare for a person to accept personal responsibility for saying, 'I am not going to answer that question', there are many other ways in which the liar can achieve the same result including:

- waffle and ambiguity;
- answering a question with a question such as *'What do you expect me to say?'*;
- attacking or praising the question such as *'That is a good question'* or *'I don't know how you can ask me that'*;
- avoiding detail, often claiming loss of memory;
- answering a totally different question *(this is a common ploy by politicians)*;
- limiting phrases such as *'That's about all I can tell you'*, *'I can't think of anything further'*, *'That's about it.'*

## DISCONTINUITY PHRASE

The subject said: 'We went to the billiard hall, then to the pub and began to drive towards Central London. Later on, we called in at the club'. The phrase 'later on' is a discontinuity statement indicating that something has been omitted (and probably important) between 'starting to drive towards Central London' and calling at the club.

It is truly amazing how often politicians are allowed to escape in television and radio interviews without answering the question.

## THE HEAD IN THE SAND AND THE TARTAN TERROR

Or as George Carman QC said of The Right Honourable David Mellor MP: 'He buried his head in the sand, thus exposing his thinking parts'. On Sunday 26 January 2003, Tony Blair was interviewed by Sir David Frost. Quentin Letts reporting in the *Express* said:

'Later stages of the interview were devoted to domestic problems: college fees and immigration. Mr Blair's tone deepened. Maybe he thinks these are more of a threat to his electoral chances. And then, just as the distinguished guest was at last relaxing, old Frostie produced a kidney punch. He asked about Mr Blair's relationship with Gordon Brown. Could both men still be in their jobs in a year's time? Would Gordon soon be looking for a new place to live? Mr Blair stared in astonishment. Motionless. When he recovered himself he said lamely: "Gordon does a fantastic job." "Marvellous," said Frostie, with a clap of the palms.'

What Sir David should have done was to press home the question, maybe by crossing his transactional relationship with the Prime Minister and to continue doing so until he got an answer. Why he did not do this raises more questions than answers, but it is typical of all humans in that they would rather be deceived than confront a lie.

*The golden rule is to make sure that every relevant question is fully answered.*
*Relevant questions have to be repeated before a liar gives a meaningful answer*

## Generalizations

Generalizations may be used to craft a false explanation by drawing in general practice to avoid answering a specific question.

## OJ SIMPSON AND THE BRONCO

| | |
|---|---|
| Tom Lang: | And where did you park it when you brought it home? |
| OJ Simpson: | Ah, the first time probably by the mailbox. I'm trying to think, or did I bring it in the driveway? *Normally, I will* park it by the mailbox, sometimes … |
| Tom Lang: | On Ashford, or Ashland? |
| OJ Simpson: | On *Ashford*, yeah. |
| Tom Lang: | Where did you park yesterday for the last time, do you remember? |
| OJ Simpson: | Right where it is. |
| Tom Lang: | Where it is now? |
| OJ Simpson: | Yeah. |
| Tom Lang: | Where, on …? |
| OJ Simpson: | Right on the street there. |
| Tom Lang: | *On Ashford?* |
| OJ Simpson: | *No, on Rockingham.* |
| Tom Lang: | You parked it there? |
| OJ Simpson: | Yes. |

In this case, Mr Simpson's generalization that the car was 'normally' parked on 'Ashford' was flushed out by specific questions, revealing that it had been parked 'on Rockingham' where it was found in a blood-drenched state. The interviewer should have pressed home this deception by asking, 'Then why did you try to mislead us by implying that you had parked it on Ashford?' In a very poor interview, he did not do this and in fact had no plan to bring OJ to the pivotal point. Had he done so, the result of his criminal trial might have been totally different.

*Responding to a specific allegation with a generalization is a sign of deception*

## Suppressing guilty knowledge

The fact is that in most cases the liar knows too much, has to suppress the truth and has to be careful he does not inadvertently leak clues.

## KNOWING TOO MUCH

Some sensitive files were stolen on a Saturday from a storeroom in company Y's offices. Employees were told only that 'information' had been stolen over the 'weekend' and asked to write down in free style all they knew about the thefts. One statement said:

'I had nothing whatsoever to do with the removal of the *files* and I can account for every second of my time last *Saturday* 14th.'

He knew and said too much and he later admitted his guilt. It is a great shame that not all cases are this simple.

*Liars always know too much*

The way a subject reacts to documentary and other exhibits (which have a powerful visual impact on the right hemisphere of the brain) can also tell you a great deal about his guilt or innocence, as in the following example.

## THE ARSON CASE

Two very serious fires had been started on board a British seagoing oil tanker (a very large crude carrier). They could have killed the 54 crewmen. The police in the country concerned had investigated the cases and advised that the fires had been accidental. We were called in to investigate and immediately searched the ship from top to bottom and found a third fire, in a storeroom, which had not flared. We took photographs of the piles of wood, newspaper and about 50 empty matchboxes and hundreds of matches. We also tried to raise fingerprints from the matchboxes, but without success. We did find some fingerprints on a light switch, but they were far from illuminating!

The photographs were enlarged and stuck all over the walls of the cabin in which it was planned that the crewmembers would be interviewed. The matchboxes were laid out on a table and the fingerprint slides cut to the same size as the matchboxes and set out in front of them. The impression was that fingerprints had been raised from the matchboxes.

Other evidence suggested that one or more of five crewmembers could have been responsible for all three fires. The first suspect was asked into the interview cabin. He appeared fairly relaxed.

The first question was: 'Is there any reason why your fingerprints should be on all of those matchboxes?'

He asked where the matchboxes had been found, what the photographs were all about and tried quickly to put the question in context. He had no objection to providing his fingerprints. Subsequent questions established his innocence.

The second suspect came into the cabin and immediately his eyes focused on the photographs, matchboxes and fingerprint slides. When we asked the question: 'Is there any reason why your fingerprints should be on all of those matchboxes?' he did not ask any questions about them, but sat silent for a full two minutes and then said 'Yes'.

He gave an unconvincing explanation that he may have handled all of them while working in the ship's bar. Five minutes later he confessed to starting the fires and gave details that only the arsonist would know. He also explained his motive and made a voluntary written statement.

This is a classic example of the suspect knowing too much and of not asking the questions an innocent person would ask.

*Liars don't ask the questions an innocent person would.*
*Guilty people make assumptions of facts known only to the perpetrator*

## Disclosing inconsistent detail

An absence or excess of detail is vital in assessing the truthfulness of a story. Some people have good memories while others cannot even remember their wife's birthday or wedding anniversaries (bless them!). Absence of detail should always be treated with suspicion, especially when the person's memory – on other events at around the same time or regarding topics of equal importance – is good.

Inconsistencies indicating deception include:

- lack of detail relating to significant, and especially emotionally charged, events;
- jumbled sequences of important topics within a story;
- significant changes in an explanation to fit newly revealed facts;

- failure to explain an admitted inconsistency;
- Freudian slips;
- admissions of having failed to volunteer information, possibly in response to a 'blocking question' (see pages 118, 202 and 247);
- rigid recollection of some facts (such as times) but not others of equal significance.

Other inconsistencies, such as variations in estimates of time, distance, size etc. are not necessarily indicators of deception, but they should still be carefully examined.

Unnecessary or apparently irrelevant detail may unconsciously expose a chain of events or subject matter which the subject has tried to conceal.

## WHAT IS OJ CONCEALING?

| | |
|---|---|
| Vannatter: | You haven't had any problems with her lately, have you? (This is a bad, negative, leading question.) |
| OJ Simpson: | *I* always have problems with *her*, you know? *Our* relationship has been a problem relationship. Probably lately for *me*, and *I* say this only because *I* said it to Ron yesterday *at the* – Ron Fishman, whose wife is Cora – at the dance recital, when he came up to me and went, 'Oooh, boy, what's going on?' and everybody was beefing with everybody. And I said, 'Well, I'm just glad I'm out of the mix.' You know, because I was like dealing with him and his problems with his wife and Nicole and evidently some new problems that a guy named Christian was having with his girl, and he was staying at Nicole's house, and something was going on, but I don't think it's pertinent to this. |

There was a reason why OJ did not simply reply to the awfully bad question with the word 'yes' rather than go into the unnecessary detail about Ron, Cora etc. The likely answer is that he unconsciously associated these people with a real problem that he did not want to reveal. Unfortunately, he was never asked to explain so we will never know the answer.

Consistent detail – in response to both control and relevant questions – indicates that the subject is being truthful.

> *There is no such thing as irrelevant detail.*
> *The subject says everything for a reason*

## REDUCING ANXIETY WITHIN THE RESPONSE

### Generally
The liar will try to reduce his own anxiety by consciously avoiding a barefaced lie, avoiding detail, by evasion, deflection and so on. But he will be also driven by his subconscious monkey to make sure that anxiety is reduced and this may be manifested in the content, syntax, paralinguistics and non-verbal communications of his responses. Obviously, the lack of com-

mitment discussed above minimizes anxiety but there are subtler and more telling clues, and failure to deny an accusation is the most telling.

*Falsely denying an allegation requires commitment and raises anxiety.*
*For this reason, liars don't react in the way an honest person would*

## Failure to deny

It is critical that you confront a liar with what you believe really happened and with the symptoms of his deception (see pages 95–6 and 258). The way he reacts to accusations such as:

- 'Bill, I have to say that I believe you took the money.'
- 'The evidence shows clearly that you did this.'
- 'I can see no other explanation than you did this.'

is critical.

A truthful denial of an accusation is normally a positive and committed assertion, such as 'I did not do it', and when the syntax used is in the first person singular, past tense, the denial is usually true. Most guilty people cannot commit themselves to utter this barefaced lie but will use pseudo denials, objections, partial denials and subjective truths.

*Any deviation from a first person singular, past tense denial must be regarded with suspicion*

Frequently, as in the case of Bill Clinton (see pages 30 and 89), they will prevaricate and use superfluous words before and after what appears to be a denial. A person making a false denial is at great risk from a statement along the following lines.

### THE ULTIMATE IN COMMITMENT

'So, Bill, there can be absolutely no doubt about this, can there? If I prove that what you have said is not true, the only explanation is that you have told a barefaced lie and deserve all the punishment possible: isn't it?'

In over 40 years of practical experience a proven liar has never once answered this question with a simple 'yes', although many people wrongly suspected have.

### THE GREAT ANSWER

In one case, where a dishonest but legally qualified senior manager was confronted with this question, he responded: 'This is not fair. If you have this evidence, you should tell me before I answer that question'. As always, it is a different matter when it is your turn in the barrel.

If the response to the statement is in the affirmative, the liar is denied a plausible excuse.

## F LEE BAILEY AND MARK FUHRMAN

F Lee Bailey:    Do you use the word 'nigger' in describing people?
Mark Fuhrman:    No, sir. (A subjective truth because he does not use the word currently.)
F Lee Bailey:    Have you ever used that word in the past ten years?
Mark Fuhrman:    Not that I recall, no. (Lack of commitment.)
F Lee Bailey:    So anyone who comes to court and quotes you as using that word in dealing with Afro-Americans would be a liar ...
Mark Fuhrman:    Yes, they would. (Again, a subjective truth, depending on Mr Fuhrman's definition of an 'Afro-American'.)

Tape recordings made between 1985 and 1994 by Laura Hart McKinny, who was carrying out research for a film script, of conversations with Mr Fuhrman revealed that he had used what became referred to as the 'N-word' on no less than 40 occasions to denigrate black citizens of Los Angeles (i.e. but not necessarily 'Afro-Americans'). This evidence, which the jury believed, confirmed OJ Simpson's defence claim that he had been framed by racially motivated cops and was the turning point in the trial.

Liars are also much more passive in the way they respond to accusations and, when these are repeated throughout the interview, their pseudo denials become weaker (Figure 4.1).

Feigned anger over being accused is transient and quickly dissipates. On the other hand, innocent people, wrongly accused, react strongly and their protests increase if the accusation is repeated. Their anger is deeply felt and, usually, not quickly dissipated.

An objection sounds like a denial but it is far from it. A statement along the lines of 'I could not have taken [Note: not 'I did not take'] the money *because* I did not know the combination of the safe' is almost certainly untrue. An objection usually contains a justification within the sentence concerned, which probably results from the liar's unconscious acceptance that

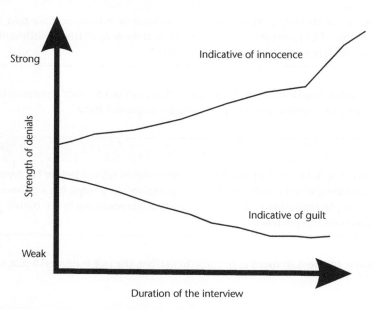

**Figure 4.1**   Declining and increasing strength of denials

he knows his denial is unconvincing and which he internalizes for reinforcement. Objections often include the word 'because' and are a strong clue to deception.

A pseudo denial will often contain superfluous words which are an indication of the subject's prevarication in bringing himself to address a critical issue.

---

*For example*: 'You have accused me of a very serious offence that strikes at the heart of my relationship with the company and I would like to tell you I did not do it.'

---

It should be noted that this statement also contains a subjective truth, as there is little doubt the liar 'would like to tell you'. He is not saying that this is what he is actually telling you!

No one in the UK will ever be able to forget the recent case of Neil and Christine Hamilton who were arrested on suspicion of rape, based on a story which was brokered by the publicist Max Clifford.

## NEIL AND CHRISTINE HAMILTON

Neil Hamilton said: 'Given that the name of Max Clifford has been mentioned in this context, a man that brought you "Freddy Starr ate my hamster", and can be believed to that extent, there is no truth whatsoever in the allegations.'

Taken by itself, the prevarication before the pseudo-denial is very suspect, but in the same interview the Hamiltons made many FPSPT (first person singular, past tense) denials which were totally committed. The lesson is that clues come in clusters and seldom is a single statement conclusive of deception.

Superfluous words at the end of a pseudo-denial indicate a lack of commitment. For example, the statement 'I did not do it, *as such*' tells you all you need to know, that the denial was too committed for the liar's comfort.

The various forms of denials and pseudo denials can be summarized as in Table 4.3.

*Any deviation from an FPSPT denial through a single word or short phrase should be treated with suspicion*

Finally, the English upper classes (including royalty, politicians and those investigators who wear 'Hush Puppies' and red suspenders) have what appears to mere mortals to be a pretentious habit of referring to themselves with the reflexive pronoun 'one', such as *'One would not do such a thing'*. This subtle way of avoiding the dreadfully committed pronoun 'I' should be treated with suspicion unless the person concerned is a Raving Rupert or an estate agent.

Because so much emphasis is placed on the strength of denials, you may believe that a liar could prepare himself to respond in the right way and thus deceive you. This is not the case.

## YOU WILL NEVER GET ME

At a celebratory dinner following a very successful investigation when ten employees confessed to fraud, a senior manager told the investigators, 'I am bloody amazed that these guys confessed. If ever you came after me, I would say nothing'. One investigator – who did not like or trust the senior manager – replied, 'It's a different matter when you are in the barrel, Bill. If ever we had to interview you, you would be a soft touch, so remember that.' Everyone went quiet but the matter dropped.

A couple of years later investigators discovered that the senior manager had incurred thousands of pounds in costs by entertaining his mistress at a local hotel but had them misdescribed as dinners or meetings with clients, trade union representatives etc. and paid for by his employer. The hotel reported the investigation to the senior manager, explaining that it had no alternative but to supply the correct documentation. When the manager appeared at the first interview with the investigators he said, 'I remember what you told me at that dinner. I am dead in the water and I will tell you everything. I do not want to go through the pressure of trying to lie to you. I have not slept for days thinking about this moment.'

*Deception seems easy until it is your turn in the barrel.*
*If you think telling the truth is difficult, try lying.*
*Making first person singular, past tense denials is hard if you are lying: they are too committed*

**Table 4.3**  Summary of denials and pseudo-denials

| Wording of the apparent denial | Interpretation |
|---|---|
| 'I did not take the money'<br>'I did not do it' | FPSPT, bold, brief and totally committed<br>*Probably true* |
| 'I don't steal' (in response to a specific question: 'Did you take the cash from the safe?') | This is not a denial to a specific accusation but a generalization and is *probably false* |
| 'I *would not* steal from the company'<br>'I should like to think I would never be suspected of that' | Conditional-passive<br>*Probably not true* |
| 'I could not have taken the money, *because* I did not have the keys to the office' | This is an objection<br>*Probably untrue* |
| 'I know in my own *mind* I am innocent' | Any reference to his internal thoughts, 'heart' or 'mind' should be treated with great care<br>*Probably untrue* |
| 'There is not a shred of *evidence* and no *proof* that I took the money' | This may be a subjective truth, but is not a denial<br>*Probably untrue* |
| 'I have been with the company for 40 years and have *worked hard and loyally*. I am upset that anyone should think I was responsible for this. I did not do it' | Extended introduction to what appears to be a bold denial<br>*Probably untrue* |

| | |
|---|---|
| 'I had a great time in Florida and the hotel was great. The hire car was excellent, *but I did not meet any nice-looking blondes with long legs*' | Denial of an allegation not made and *probably false* |
| 'I did not take the money, as such' | End softening and extraneous words after the denial<br>*Probably untrue* |
| '*I know you may accuse me of taking the money, as well as all of the other things, but I would like to make it clear* that I do not need to do this' | Self-deprecation and a denial of an allegation not made: a pre-emptive denial<br>*Probably untrue* |
| 'Oh, and I suppose you believe I stole the crown jewels as well?' | Joking or dismissive reply<br>*Probably untrue* |
| 'If I had, do you think I would admit it?'<br>'No one would admit to that, would they?' | Not a denial and *probably untrue* |
| 'You have accused me of taking the money and of falsifying the accounts. I have never taken any money from this company' | Limited denial: does not deny falsifying the accounts<br>*Thus the allegation not denied (i.e. he falsified the accounts) is true* |
| 'There will be no whitewash in the White House. The "President" would not do such a thing.' President Richard Nixon in referring to Watergate | Projection to the third person<br>*Probably untrue* |
| 'I know you will not believe me, but I am telling you I did not do anything wrong' or 'I am not clever enough to lie' | Self-deprecation and a subjective truth<br>*Probably untrue* |
| 'I did not take the money simply because I did not know the combination to the safe' | An objection and *most likely false* |
| In response to the question 'Did you take the money?' the subject replies 'no' and has words before or after this binary answer such as 'No. I was not there' or 'The reply to that question is "no"' | *Probably untrue* |
| In response to the question 'Did you take the money?' the subject replies 'I would be crazy to do that' | Subjective truth and *probably untrue* |
| When asked a non-threatening question the subject responds 'Are you accusing me?' | *Probably guilty* |
| In response to the question 'Did you take the money?' the subject replies 'No' | *Probably true* |

## Irrelevant support

A truthful person will usually be confident in his own position and will convey his explanation. He will also answer closed (binary) questions with a committed 'yes' or 'no' with no prevarication before or softening words afterwards. Liars, knowing the weakness of their position, will often go too far in trying to convince you by providing inappropriate support for a false explanation.

> *For example*: 'I did not steal the money and if you don't believe me, you can ask my mummy; she will tell you I don't steal and that I always eat up my cabbage.'

They may also suggest corroboration for their lies from a source that is impossible to verify. For example: 'Bill Smith would confirm my explanation, but it is a great pity he died last week'. Dishonest job candidates often use the same ploy by claiming to have worked for companies they know have gone out of business.

## Contextual clarification

Liars are hindered by the fact that they do not understand how an innocent person would react and may seek clarification through phrases such as: *'I am not sure what I should say about that', 'I am not sure what I am expected to say',* or *'How should I know that …?'* Such phrases should be treated with suspicion.

## Other anxiety reducing responses

The liar will unconsciously use a range of techniques to reduce his anxiety when delivering an untruthful response. Possibly the most important are his use of manipulators, defensive body language and from his attitude, but other clues are summarized in Table 4.9, page 128.

## Clues from an attitude

Liars, like alcoholics, are inclined to minimize the seriousness of their problems by using soft, non-emotive words or unwanted words at the end of an apparently strong sentence. The words 'really', 'actually' or 'as such' are good examples. They may minimize important topics with words such as: *'as an aside,' 'perhaps I should mention in passing,' 'incidentally,' or ' by the way'.*

The liar may use self-deprecating phrases such as *'I know it sounds incredible but …'* He may even be excessively submissive and use phrases such as: *'If you want me to say I did it, I will'.* He may introduce an excuse before one is justified or deny allegations that have not been made.

### SELF-DEPRECATION IN GOLF

Some golfers who stand on the first tee of an important competition use self-deprecation such as 'I had a really late night last night and still feel a bit pickled' to unconsciously reduce anxiety by providing an advance excuse for what they fear will be a poor shot. By doing so they use NLP to prepare themselves for a duck hook into Granny Smith's garden.

You should not allow suspects to find comfort in self-deprecation but they should be told something along the lines: 'Forget that, just tell me ...' If your golfing partner self-deprecates say the same sort of thing and try to make him focus. If your opponent self-deprecates you might say: 'Yes, you do look a bit pickled and you are aiming miles to the left. Watch out for Granny Smith's garden.'

A suspect may refer to his own state of mind such as *'I know in my own mind I am innocent of this'* and give away other clues that he has internalized the problem. Experience shows that when a person refers to his own mental state, he is struggling with the truth. When he refers to his 'mind' or 'heart' he is usually drawing information from his imagination.

A profile in family murder cases is that the attacker will not refer to his victim by his given name or by his exact relationship. For example, he will refer to the victim as 'the child' or 'my child' rather than 'my daughter'.

Most crooks (whether white collar or otherwise) tend to be non-judgemental, do not have clearly ingrained beliefs and tend to assume everyone is as crooked as they are. In management fraud cases, the guilty person will often fail to clear himself or blame someone else. For example, if he is asked the question, *'There were four of you on duty at the time and someone took the money. Who can you absolutely clear of this?'* the person responsible will seldom give the answer 'me'. If he does, the chances are he is innocent. But if he says 'me, *because* I just love pussies', by now you should know what this means. Through such attention to fine detail the truth is exposed.

Perhaps the greatest example of attitude giving the game away is the story of King Solomon.

## KING SOLOMON

Two women were in dispute over a baby: both said they were its mother. King Solomon said the baby should be cut in two and half given to each. He knew that the woman who accepted this decision was not the real mother.

*Attitude is critically important in revealing the deep truth*

The real bottom line is that liars do not do or say the things an innocent person would and do not show congruent emotions.

## OTHER UNCONSCIOUS CLUES

Virtually all of a liar's syntax, non-verbal communication, paralinguistics, and clues to his attitude are driven at an unconscious level and are summarized in pages 114 to 136. But the most important thing, in all of the ways lies are communicated, is that liars do not do or say what an innocent person would do or say.

*Liars focus on what they do and say but omit innocent reactions.*
*It is not only what liars say, but what they don't say that is important*

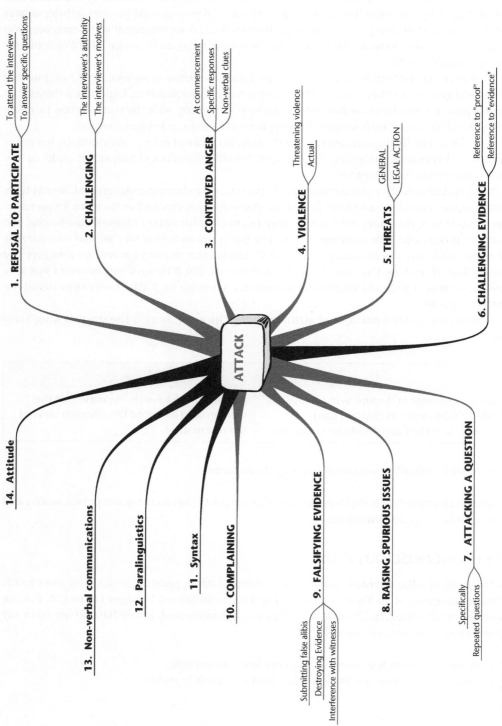

**Mind Map® 4**  Attack

# Detailed symptoms of truth and lies

## FROM OBJECTIVES TO DETAILED LEAKAGE

The truth is that we are flooded with symptoms of deceit, so much so that there are far too many to consciously remember. The good news is that all of the clues are already embedded in your subconscious and you should always try to elevate – to a conscious level –*why you have the feelings you do. Detecting deception is not difficult but resolving your suspicions is less easy unless you have a cunning plan. Chapter 1 contains such plans.

Deception is communicated through one or more of four channels (see Chapter 2, page 26), the most important being auditory, in speech and paralinguistics, or visual, in writing and non-verbal communications. This section summarizes the most important conscious (IN BLOCK CAPITALS) and unconscious clues under the headings of:

- Attacks.
- What the liar says:
  - content,
  - syntax,
  - paralinguistics.
- Non-verbal communication.
- Attitude.

You will not be able to remember them all, so don't worry. The important thing is that once you believe a subject is lying, you must use a cunning plan to clear him from suspicion or nail him.

It is also important to emphasize that where a person consistently responds with answers that do not fit the profile of deception, the chances are he is innocent. So always keep an open mind.

## ATTACKS

Attacks are communicated through verbal, visual and sensory channels but are of such importance that they warrant being treated as a separate division. The main clues, which mainly result from the liar's conscious decisions are listed in Table 4.4, and further illustrated in Mind Map 4.

**Table 4.4**    Attack

| Symptoms of deception CONSCIOUS and unconscious | *Examples and comments* | Significance 10 = High 0 = Low |
|---|---|---|
| ATTACK REFUSAL TO PARTICIPATE ON THE GROUNDS OF ALLEGED INJUSTICE | *'You have not been fair in the past and I do not trust you'* <br> *'You cannot be trusted to report the truth'* <br> *'The Audit Department is total crap'* | 10 |
| CHALLENGING THE INTERVIEWER'S AUTHORITY, MOTIVES, INDEPENDENCE ETC. | *'You have already made up your mind'* <br> *'You are not interested in hearing the truth'* <br> *'You have been trying to catch me out for years'* <br> *'You have never liked me'* <br> *'You have no right to treat me like this'* | 10 |

| Symptoms of deception CONSCIOUS and unconscious | Examples and comments | Significance 10 = High 0 = Low |
|---|---|---|
| CONTRIVED ANGER AT THE START OF THE INTERVIEW OR NOT IN RESPONSE TO A RELEVANT QUESTION | Note that the verbal outburst of feigned anger usually occurs before the facial expression and is transient. Genuine anger usually results from a specific stimulation, such as a question | 10 |
| THREATENING VIOLENCE | 'I know where you live and you will be getting a visit from my brothers' 'You and I better step outside, right now and sort this out' | 5 |
| ACTUAL VIOLENCE | If the suspect attacks you, he has lost the fight | 10 |
| THREATENING OTHER PROBLEMS AND DIRE CONSEQUENCES | 'If you try and carry on with this investigation I will have a few things to say to the Inland Revenue' 'I will report the company to the Fraud Squad' 'I will expose the MD for his shenanigans' | 8 |
| THREATENING LEGAL ACTION | 'That is slander and I am going to my lawyer' 'I will prosecute you personally' 'You are discriminating against me' | 5 |
| CHALLENGING THE EVIDENCE | 'You have no evidence of that ...' 'There is no proof' 'There is not a shred of evidence in my public life of any wrongdoing' (Bill Clinton) 'You will have to prove that' 'I hope you have some evidence of that' | 10 |
| ATTACKING A QUESTION | 'That is a stupid question' 'I do not have to answer that sort of crap' 'I am not going to justify that with an answer' 'I can't believe you asked me that' | 8 |
| RAISING SPURIOUS ISSUES | 'Before I answer that, you better tell me about the company's problems with tax evasion' | 8 |
| FALSIFYING EVIDENCE SUBMITTING FALSE ALIBIS, DESTROYING EVIDENCE AND INTERFERING WITH WITNESSES | Producing false documents Producing deceitful witnesses Threatening witnesses | 10 |
| COMPLAINING ABOUT UNFAIR TREATMENT | 'I have never been treated fairly here' 'You have always wanted to fire me' | 5 |
| SYNTAX | Using obscenities | 8 |
| PARALINGUISTICS | Shouting, fast speed of delivery | 10 |
| NON-VERBAL CLUES | Aggressive body language Using pointing gestures or a closed fist Aggressive facial expressions | 10 |
| ATTITUDE | Feigned anger Irrational justification of his position | 10 |

The vast majority of attacks are intended to deter the victim from pursuing his rights. Ways for dealing with them are explained in Chapter 7, page 240, but the rule is don't panic and treat them for what they are.

## THE CONTENT OF THE STORY

The content, or what the person says *and does not say,* contains many clues to deception. You should always consciously consider why the liar:

- chose to say what he did and, sometimes more importantly, what he did not say;
- chose how to say it and in the order he did.

Clues in the content of a story are summarized in Table 4.5 and Mind Map 5.

*What the suspect does not say is almost as important as what he does say*

You will note that the subject has conscious control over most of the content. The same is not true on other areas where unconscious clues are scattered into the ether.

**Table 4.5**   Clues in the content

| Symptoms of deception CONSCIOUS, unconscious or *both* | Examples | Significance[3] 10 = High 0 = Low |
|---|---|---|
| AVOIDING BAREFACED LIES | | |
| LACK OF COMMITMENT CONCEALMENT, OMISSION, EVASION, DEFLECTION ETC. DELIBERATE AMBIGUITY SUBJECTIVE TRUTHS OBJECTIONS RATHER THAN DENIALS GENERALIZATIONS FAILURE TO DENY | *'I did not have sexual relations with that woman: Monica Lewinsky'* *'There is not a shred of evidence of any wrongdoing in my public life'* | 10 |
| LACK OF COMMITMENT | | |
| AVOIDING THE BAREFACED LIE ALLEGED MEMORY FAILURES | *'I am not sure about this, but …'* *'To the best of my recollection …'* *'Don't hold me to this … but I believe …'* *'I am not sure about this …'* *'As far as I recall'* *'I believe'* *'I would have thought'* *'I can't really remember'* | 8 |

| Symptoms of deception CONSCIOUS, unconscious or *both* | Examples | Significance 10 = High 0 = Low |
|---|---|---|
| DELIBERATE AMBIGUITY | Long rambling sentences | 10 |
| REDUCING THE SIGNIFICANCE OF A TOPIC | *'As an aside ...'* *'Incidentally ...'* *'By the way ...'* *'I would just like to tell you ...'* | 8 |
| SUBJECTIVE TRUTHS | *'When Gordon and I are asked that question, we say there is no secret agreement'* *'I would have been crazy to do that'* *'How can you think I did that?'* | 10 |
| SELF-DEPRECATION AND OVER-APOLOGETIC | *'I know you won't believe this ...'* *'I know this sounds incredible but ...'* *'I am not clever enough to lie'* *'I know you think I am a crook but ...'* *'I know I look foolish'* *'I know I will fail to convince you'* | 5 |
| *Projection* | *'The President of the United States would not do such a thing'* | 5 |
| *Referral* | *'As I told Mr Smith, I was not in the room at the time'* | 10 |
| *Prevarication, especially before a pseudo-denial* | *'I would like to tell the American people, and I will say it again, I did not have sexual relations with ...'* | 10 |
| *Evasion and omission* | *Various techniques* | 10 |
| *Contextual clarification* | *'I don't know what you expect me to say'* *'How can I answer that?'* | 8 |
| *Suppression of detail* | *Unwillingness to falsify a statement* | 10 |
| CONCEALMENT | | |
| FAILING TO APPEAR *In effect saying 'I don't want to answer questions, because I have no answer, but I do not want to take the responsibility for this decision on my own shoulders'* | *' I would like to see you, but my wife is ill'* *'My lawyer has told me not to see you'* *'I have had a heart attack and cannot see you, as much as I would like to help'* | 8 |
| FAILURE TO ANSWER *Usually by blaming someone else or through a legitimization* | *'I cannot answer that because of the Data Protection Act'* *'It is not company policy to discuss such matters'* | 10 |

| Symptoms of deception CONSCIOUS, unconscious or *both* | Examples | Significance 10 = High 0 = Low |
|---|---|---|
| *Inconsistent coverage of topics* Sequence violations in an explanation or story | In freestyle stories or responses to open questions, the liar prevaricates and delays in reaching the critical issue and thus extends the prologue. In various topics in a story, the subject allocates a disproportionate amount of his explanation to one over another. Often the most important topic is dealt with superficially (indicating omission) or a less important topic given excessive coverage (indicating that there is some hidden reason why the subject believes this is important). In some cases, topics are dealt with out of sequence (indicating omission) | 7 |
| *Omission* *Limited answers* *Containment* | DELIBERATE OMISSION OF INCRIMINATING INFORMATION *'I am not going to answer unless my lawyer is present …'* *'I don't have to answer that …'* *'I can't answer that …'* *'I can tell you this …' [probably meaning there are other things he cannot or does not wish to tell you]* *'There's not much I can say …'* *'Oh yes, and then I murdered the chairman …'* *'I am not going to dignify that question with a reply'* *'That's a stupid question'* *'Company policy prohibits me from answering that question'* *'I cannot answer that question until I have spoken to my manager'* *'That's about all I know …'* *'That's all I can tell you …'* Such phrases usually mean that there is other information the liar is not prepared to reveal | 10 |
| RELUCTANCE TO PROVIDE DETAIL | Inconsistent recollection of detail. Typically the liar will have a good and detailed recollection of non-controversial matters within the time frame concerned. Only when questions focus on critical areas will his recollection become vague. The liar is drawing the content of this explanation from imagination. He knows the more detail he provides, the greater the chance he will give contradictory answers. Thus avoiding detail seems the safe course | 10 |
| FAILURE TO VOLUNTEER | Failing to volunteer information to open or blocking questions or to admit facts which are known | 7 |
| COMPRESSION | Instead of giving detail such as *'I went to Sainsbury's and bought an egg, then to Tesco and got some bacon, then to Homebase and bought a ladder,'* the subject says *'I went shopping'* | 5 |

| Symptoms of deception CONSCIOUS, unconscious or *both* | Examples | Significance 10 = High 0 = Low |
|---|---|---|
| *Discontinuity words and phrases* | *'Later on', 'The next thing we did', 'Subsequently', 'We began to discuss'* Indicates that important information has been omitted before the discontinuity word | 8 |
| *Unopened or unclosed actions* | *'I then left the office'* (without explaining when he entered it) | 8 |
| *Inconsistent and missing detail* | Different levels of detail between control and relevant questions | 8 |
| EVASION AND DEFLECTION DIVERSIONARY ADMISSIONS RAMBLING ANSWERS | *'I have made small mistakes … I will admit that'* Long rambling answers which are off the point *'Before I answer that, I want to tell you about …'* | 10 |
| LIMITED ANSWERS | *'Basically …'* *'As a rule …'* | 8 |
| ADMITTING ONLY WHAT CAN BE PROVEN | And changing his explanation in response to enticement questions (see pages 256, 265 and 268) | 10 |
| FOCUSING ON NON-ISSUES | Using ambiguous words and phrases (see also 'subjective truths') Admitting only what is provable Focusing on non-issues and elevating their importance | 7 |
| GENERALIZATIONS | In answer to the question *'What did you do last Friday?'* the suspect responds, *'I usually go to the club on Fridays'* | 8 |
| REHEARSED ANSWERS AND FOCUSING ON NON-ISSUES | *'I could not have done it (1) because I did not have keys to the office (2) because my car had broken down (3) because I am not that sort of person (4) etc …'* Listing of this nature indicates the answer has been rehearsed | 10 |
| CONTRIVED ANGER | An honest person may become genuinely angry at suggestions that he has done something wrong. A guilty person's anger is usually contrived and short term *'Are you accusing me?'* *'That is a stupid question …'* *'I will not dignify that question with an answer …'* | 8 |
| LEGITIMIZATION | *'I would like to answer that, but it is a state secret'* *'It is not company policy to disclose this stuff'* *'I cannot answer because of the Data Protection Act'* | 10 |
| FALSE PROMISES | *'I will get the papers for you next week'* *'I have to see my accountant first'* | 7 |

| Symptoms of deception CONSCIOUS, unconscious or *both* | Examples | Significance 10 = High 0 = Low |
|---|---|---|
| **FEIGNED COOPERATION** | | |
| *Feigned submissiveness and cooperation. Flattery and misplaced humour* | Using permission phrases such as: *'Can I please explain ...'* *'Will you give me time to think about this?'* *'You are obviously a very, very clever interviewer ...'* *'I would never do anything to upset you ...'* | 7 |
| Offers to confess | *'If you want me to say I did it, I will'* *'If it will help, I will take the blame for this'* | 10 |
| Responding with a question | *'Why should I do that?'* *'What do you expect me to say?'* | 8 |
| Repeating words from the question | Using some or all of the interviewer's words | 7 |
| Contextual clarification | Saying something like *'Who, me?'* when he is the only person in the room or when the question is obviously addressed to him *'How should I know that?'* *'What do you expect me to say?'* *'Why do you think I can answer that?'* *'I don't get the question'* *'I don't see what you are driving at'* | 10 |
| REPEATING THE QUESTION | Using exactly the same words as the interviewer | 8 |
| PRAISING THE QUESTION | *'That is a great question'* *'I knew you were going to ask me that ...'* *'The answer to that question is ...'* | 8 |
| ASSESSMENT QUESTIONS | *'Have you spoken to Bill Smith?'* *'Will you be able to get the Swiss bank accounts?'* *'What do you plan to do?'* | 10 |
| **ASSERTIONS OF VIRTUE** | | |
| Religious assertions Ethical assertions Other assertions | *'I have done many good things in my life ...'* *'I have always worked hard for this company ...'* *'I swear on the Bible ...'* *'I am an honest, God-fearing man ...'* *'I would never do such a thing'* *'I swear on my mother's life.'* *'Let God strike me down if I am not telling the truth ...'* | 10 |
| **Abnormal assumptions** | | |
| Inside knowledge of critical issues known only to the perpetrator Failure to seek clarification | Failing to ask for clarification of facts that would not be known to an innocent person. For example, a guilty person will rarely ask about the significance of exhibits displayed in the interview room | 10 |

| Symptoms of deception CONSCIOUS, unconscious or *both* | Examples | Significance 10 = High 0 = Low |
|---|---|---|
| *Denials* | | |
| *Failure to deny* | See page 95 and Table 4.3, page 98 | 10 |
| *Passive reaction to accusations and lack of commitment* | Denials get weaker as the interview progresses | 8 |
| *Declining strength of denials* | Throughout the interview, an innocent person's denials usually become stronger. A guilty person's objections become weaker | 10 |
| *Pseudo denials Generalizations Limited denials* | In response to the question *'Did you take the money?'* the suspect responds *'I do not steal.'* This is also a generalization In response to the question *'I think you are a crook and a liar,'* the reply *'I am not a liar'* | 10 |
| Objections rather than denials | A denial is a solid, usually first person, past tense statement along the lines *'I did not do it'* and is usually a sign of innocence. An objection is used because the suspect knows his case is weak and looks for reinforcement. Typical objections are: *'I could not have done it because I did not have the key to the safe ...'* *'I would not do such a thing'* *'I am not that sort of person'* *'I have no reason to do that'* | 10 |
| *Conditional denials* | *'I would never do such a thing'* | 7 |
| *Unsolicited denials* | For example: *'I had a great time in Florida and the hotel was great. The hire car was excellent but I did not go out with any nice-looking blondes.'* This unsolicited denial suggests that blondes came into the picture | 7 |
| *Prevaricated denials* | Superfluous words before or after the apparent denial | 8 |
| Softened denials | *'I could not have done it, **really** ...'* *'I was not there, **as such** ...'* *'essentially'* Coughing or other non-verbal sounds at the start or end of sentences | 10 |
| *Motivational denials* | *'I have no reason to do that'* *'I would have been crazy to do that'* | |
| *Unjustified support* | Going too far in trying to convince Referring to an unverifiable or irrelevant source for corroboration. For example, *'I did not take the money and my mummy will confirm that'* or *'Bill would confirm he gave me permission but unfortunately he died last week'* | 8 |

| Symptoms of deception CONSCIOUS, unconscious or *both* | Examples | Significance 10 = High 0 = Low |
|---|---|---|
| MINIMIZING ANXIETY WITHIN THE RESPONSE | | |
| Subjective truths | | 10 |
| *Projection* | Stepping outside his own body and seeing the accused as a separate person. Referring to himself as a third party. For example, in the Watergate case, Richard Nixon did not deny erasing tapes, but used phrases such as: *'The President is innocent of this …'* *'One would never do such a thing'* | 7 |
| *Permission phrases* | See above | 5 |
| *Self-deception and challenging evidence or proof* | *'I would like to think I would not do such a thing'* *'I know in my own mind I did not do it'* *'There is no evidence of wrongdoing in my public life'* *'If you think you have the evidence, then go ahead'* | 7 |
| Diversion to safe ground | *'Can we just go back and deal with (some minor issue)'* *'I think we should first deal with …'* | |
| *Reducing the significance of a response* | *'By the way …'* *'Incidentally …'* | 8 |
| *Referral statements to a past (and successful) lie* | *'In my own mind I know I did not do this …'* *'As I said in my speech last month …'* *'As I told Mr Smith last week …'* *'As you know …'* | 9 |
| *Layering* | This partly conscious and unconscious ploy can be confused with excessive or omitted detail. The subject starts off on an important topic, then diverts to a subtopic, then from the subtopic to a sub-subtopic and so on. The result is that the original topic is lost and this may be deliberate. | 6 |
| *Avoiding binary answers* | Not using *'yes'* or *'no'* without some qualification or prologue | 10 |
| *Using soft words* | Using *'borrowed'* rather than *'stolen'* | 6 |
| *Prevarication* | Using surplus or esoteric words | 6 |
| *Inappropriate humour* | | 6 |
| AVOIDING COMMITMENT | See above | 10 |

| Symptoms of deception CONSCIOUS, unconscious or *both* | Examples | Significance 10 = High 0 = Low |
|---|---|---|
| FALSIFICATION | | 10 |
| ADMITTED LIES | Falsification is a dangerous game for a liar and calls for composure and good memory. In exculpatory interviews falsification is manifested in most of the symptoms explained above | 10 |
| *Obvious lies* | | |
| *Contradictions* | | |
| *Changing explanations to fit new facts* | | |
| *Unintended disclosures* | | |
| FALSE ALIBIS | | |
| FALSE EXCUSES | | |
| *False and inconsistent detail* | | |
| FALSE CONVINCING | | |
| ADMISSIONS AND CONFESSIONS | | 10 |
| | *'OK, It's all down to me and only you are clever enough to have caught me'* | |

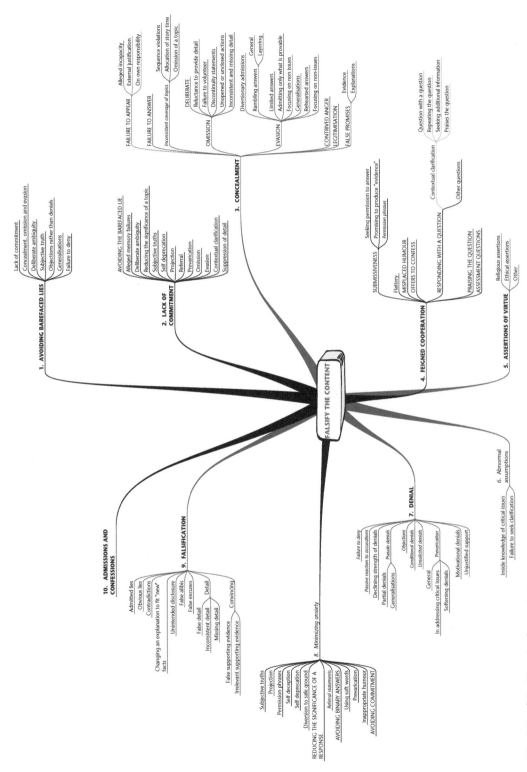

**Mind Map® 5** Clues in the content

## THE SYNTAX

### General

The construction of sentences is mainly unconscious and based on the person's unique communications code and may be incongruent with the content of a freestyle story or an answer to an open question.

### Sentence construction

The construction of sentences may be stilted, excessively short or rambling. They may also be deliberately ambiguous, riddled with subjective truths or incomplete.

---

### OJ SIMPSON AND HIS ALIBI

In explaining what he had done on the night his wife was murdered, OJ Simpson said: 'Eight-something, maybe. He hadn't done a jacuzzi, *we* had … [unfinished sentence but probably referring to a discussion about his wife] … went and got a burger, and *I'd come* home and kind of leisurely got ready to go. I mean, *we'd* done a few things.'

Note also the mixture of and missing personal pronouns.

---

Often an incomplete sentence, or changes in content or syntax midway through a sentence, result from severe editing and are indicative of deception.

With the brain in a thrashing mode a liar may use esoteric words such as *'I am positively asserting that I can exculpate myself from this abhorrent predicament'*. Such phrasing is a sign of severe editing – a deviation from his communication code – and deceptive unless, of course, the subject is an estate agent, when any language is possible.

In another part of OJ's interview he says the following:

---

### OJ SIMPSON

'I recall bleeding at my house. *The last thing* I did before I left, when I *was* rushing, was […] went and got my phone out of the Bronco.'

The phrase 'The last thing' suggests that something important was omitted between the time he 'recalled' the bleeding and left the house. Also the missing pronoun 'I' before 'went and got' and the change from past to present tense may also be significant. The statement is unlikely to be true.

---

Statements such as the above, and especially changes in tense, should be carefully analysed for their real meaning. But please remember the analysis proves nothing. It is only of any value if you consciously deal with it and it leads to other evidence, admissions and confessions.

In written stories, especially, punctuation can reveal important clues. Direct speech, reported within inverted commas, is normally a sign of commitment and is more likely to be true than not. However, if you are a follower of the comedian Billy Connolly, you will have seen him use hand signals to indicate inverted commas in parts of his speech. Liars do the same. So if someone says, ' I spoke to my wife' and signals inverted commas when saying 'wife' you know something is amiss.

## Use of verbs and adverbs

- *Verb* n. a word that applies to an action (doing).
- *First person singular* 'I' 'me' or 'my'.
- *Tense* n. (Gram.) form taken by a verb to indicate the time (also continuance or completeness) of the action etc. (present, future, past, conditional, imperfect, perfect).
- *Active or passive* 'I kicked Bill' or 'Bill was kicked'.

A person may unconsciously use different verbs in a way that exposes his inner thinking. *For example, a story may contain the verbs 'said', 'tell', 'conversing', 'conversed' and 'discussed'* which appear synonymous but may reveal important differences. Analysis might reveal that the subject used the verb 'told' and the past tense when he was describing a friendly conversation and consistently used 'conversing' in the present tense when he was on the receiving end of a tirade. Such minor differences may be important and they should be consciously examined.

*Liars consistently use less past tense verbs than honest people*

## LINGUISTIC CODES

A defendant's affidavit[4] was described by the complainant's lawyer as 'being convincing beyond peradventure'. The defendant stated that on various specific times and dates he 'went', 'saw', 'spoke to', 'bought', 'purchased' and each one was supported by detail. The critical point was precisely when and where he bought a specific item. The affidavit addressed this purchase as follows: 'During the week commencing Monday 8th April (i.e. not a specific date and time), I attended upon a retail store in Central Essex and acquired the said items.'

This sentence was a glaring breach of the defendant's linguistic code and is therefore highly suspect.

*Memory speaks in the past tense*

Great care also has to be taken over verbs that do not have any associated action. For example, *'I started to mend the computer'* does not mean he mended it, or even that he made a reasonable effort to do so. 'Tried', 'thought about', 'considered' etc. (which can be referred to as 'unverbs', or 'political verbs', because the only action associated with them is cerebral) should be carefully examined for their real meaning.

## CEREBRAL VERBS

You should always ask for an explanation of unfinished verbs. For example, 'I started to mend the computer.' Question: 'Did you actually mend it?'
Reply: 'No, Tom came into the office and interrupted me.'

First person singular, past tense (FPSPT) commits a writer to an explanation. Use of other than the FPSPT or a mixture of tenses within a topic dealing with past events are all signs of deception.

---

4   Most affidavits cannot be considered to be freestyle stories

## MORE OF OJ SIMPSON

In answering questions about the unusual way in which the Bronco had been parked Mr Simpson said, 'Well, it's parked because … I don't know if it's a funny angle or what. It's parked because when I *was hustling* and the end of the day to get all my stuff, and

*I was getting* my phone and everything *off* it, when I just *pulled* it out of the gate there … it's like a tight turn.' The change of tense suggests that the story is untrue, as does the preposition 'off' rather than 'from' (the Bronco).

## PAST TENSE FOR LIVING PEOPLE

In a recent high-profile case, three children had been abducted and the fear was that they had been murdered. The mother and father appeared on television appealing for their kids to be returned. He consistently referred to them in the present tense: *'are*

lovely kids' etc. The mother, however, referred to them in the past tense: 'they *were* home loving and caring', revealing that she knew they were dead. She was later convicted of their murder.

Passive sentences or statements normally reflect a lack of commitment. For example, *'He was seen by us'*, rather than *'We saw him'* suggests a problem. Similarly the difference between *'I went at around 10.00pm'* and *'It would have been around 10.00 that I would have gone out'* is significant: the conditional statement is suspect.

The possibilities of deception, especially in exculpatory stories can often be determined by verb usage (Table 4.6).

*Any contrived avoidance of FPSPT should be treated with great caution*

Adverbs are normally used to add detail to a verb by qualifying such things as who, why, how or how much etc. If the adverb or adverbial phrase is consistent with the story, and especially any emotion involved, it is normally true.

**Table 4.6** Verb usage

| Probably true<br>Committed | Probably deceptive<br>Uncommitted |
| --- | --- |
| PAST TENSE<br>*I saw* | Other than past tense, especially if the syntax is contrived<br>*'When I got to the door I could see'*<br>*'I would have seen'* |
| FIRST PERSON SINGULAR | Other than first person singular |
| ACTIVE<br>*'I hit Bill'* | PASSIVE<br>*'Bill was hit'* |
| ADVERBS AND ADVERBIAL PHRASES<br>*'I was very, very angry'* | Absence of adverbs and adverbial phrases, especially when recalling an emotion |
| SUBJECT – VERB – OBJECT<br>*'Tom took the money'* | OBJECT – VERB – SUBJECT (or no subject)<br>*'The money was taken by Tom'* |

## Use of nouns

---

- *Noun* n. (Gram.) word or phrase used as name of person, place or thing.
- *Synonym* n. (Gram.) word or phrase identical and coextensive in sense and usage with another of the same language.

Nouns may be *proper* when they refer to a specific entity (such as the King) or *common* when they refer to a general class such as 'investigators'.
   The *gender* of a noun may be masculine, feminine or neutral.

---

A writer may give away a great deal of information in the way in which he uses nouns and pronouns to 'label' people and things.
   Changes in the use of labels when they are not consistent with the writer's likely emotions are suspect.

## FROM GENTLEMAN TO YOB

'I saw this *gentleman* walking along. *He* and a *youth* appeared to be drunk. The *man* walked up to me and said, "Up yours." The *fat pig* then hit me in the face without any provocation and I fell to the ground, the youth just stood there. If I get my hands on this *yob* again I will kill him.'

   The change of labels for the same person from *'gentleman'* to *'man'* to *'fat pig'* to *'yob'* is interesting. On the one hand it could accurately reflect the changing emotional state of the writer when reliving the real-world events. On the other, at the time the story was written, the writer had already decided that the man was a 'yob', so why did he refer to him as a 'gentleman'? This is inconsistent and the phrase 'If I get my hands … again' reveals that the writer was far from a passive victim and had probably already given the 'gentleman' a smack or two. The syntax throws great doubt on the truth of the story. However, the consistent use of the noun 'youth' suggests he was a passive bystander and that he could be an important witness.

The label used, and changes in the noun or pronoun for the same thing or person can also be revealing. The excellent website – www.TheirWords.com – contains the statement quoted on page 88 made by a man following the death of his baby son. The interesting point is that he refers to his son as 'his body', suggesting he was already dead before he hit the floor
   Also significant is the use of a synonym (rather than a pronoun) when the person refers to himself.

## PROJECTION TO A THIRD PERSON

In the 'Praise the Lord' scandal, Tammy Bakker said, 'No one would believe that *Jim and Tammy* would do such a thing.' She could have said, 'We didn't do it', which would have been much more convincing. Similarly in Watergate, Richard Nixon frequently used the word '*President*' when referring to his part in the deletion of tapes. In both cases the writers appeared to be standing outside their own bodies, thus distancing 'I' from the unpleasant truth.

Such phrasing is referred to as a 'projection' because the subject seems to disassociate himself from personal accountability.

## THE FOOTBALL MANAGER

Kevin Keegan, the ex-England football manager, often referred to himself as 'Kevin', especially when he was trying to justify poor results.

## Use of pronouns

- *Pronoun* n. (Gram.) word used instead of (proper or other) noun (without naming) the person, place or thing already known from the context. There are different types of pronouns. Examples:
  - personal (first person) – I, me, mine, myself;
  - personal (second person) – we, us, you, he, she, it, they;
  - possessive – my, mine, ours, hers, his, its;
  - demonstrative – this, that;
  - distributive – each, either;
  - impersonal – any, some, anyone, something;
  - interrogative – who, what, which;
  - relative – who, what, which, that;
  - reflexive – myself, oneself, one, himself.

Everyone subconsciously selects pronouns. Generally 'I', 'me' and 'my' (first person singular) indicate a positive commitment and their use in the past tense is consistent with the truth. Clumsy construction of sentences to avoid FPSPT is a clear warning of deception. Also a mixture of possessive and demonstrative pronouns, especially with the definite article 'the', can be interesting.

## THE CAR

The subject said: '*My* Jaguar was parked on the drive. I had owned it for a few years. I jumped in *the* car and then it just exploded. I had nothing to do with it, honest. *That* car just went up in the air … woosh!'

Also, the stilted or exaggerated use of 'I' can be a sign of concealment or deception, possibly resulting from a discontinuity in the process of imagination.[5] For example:

## STILTED USE OF FPS

'I am the manager. I know about the system. I have no reason to take the money. I do not know Bill Smith.' This extract is a sign of extreme censorship.

---

5   Memory of events is usually in chronological order: imagination is jumbled

Normally, before the collective pronouns 'we' or 'us' or 'they' are used, the other people concerned should be introduced by name; failure to do so (i.e. the use of 'we' without explaining who is referred to) suggests that the relationship between the subject and the other party is not harmonious.

## Use of adjectives

> • *Adjectives* n. (Gram.) word or phrase naming an attribute, added to a noun to describe a thing more fully.

Adjectives, and adjectival clauses, add detail to a topic and when consistently used are more likely to be truthful than not.

## Use of prepositions

> • *Preposition* n. word governing and normally proceeding a noun or pronoun, expressing its relationship to another word (for example, 'at', 'in', 'off', 'to', 'with' etc.).

The liar may unconsciously use wrong or inconsistent prepositions. *In the OJ Simpson case he referred to taking his telephone 'off' his car rather than 'from' it.* Again this suggests that the explanation is unreliable and that his brain was struggling to find a suitable answer.

## Use of definite and indefinite articles

The use of 'the'[6] and 'a'[7] or 'an' can also be revealing. In our analysis of the dingo case (Chapter 5), the subject speaks of seeing 'a' dingo and later refers to 'the' dingo. This progression is natural: but immediately referring to an individual member of a general class as 'the' indicates deception or omission.

## Conjunctions

These words, such as 'and', 'but', 'because' etc. connect words and phrases and usually indicate a continuity of thought or of memory retrieval. An absence of conjunctions is indicative of deception.

## Interjections

A person may interject with an exclamation such as 'oh' or 'shit' which does not grammatically fit into a phrase or sentence. Interjections are normally true.

## Summary of clues in the syntax

Clues in the syntax of a false explanation are illustrated in Mind Map 6 and summarized in Table 4.7.

---

6   Definite article
7   Indefinite article

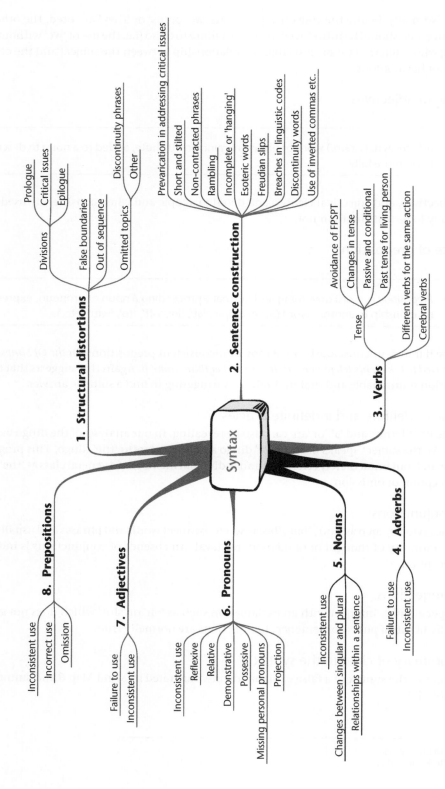

**Mind Map® 6**   Clues in the syntax

## Syntax

### 1. Structural distortions
- Divisions
  - Prologue
  - Critical issues
  - Epilogue
- False boundaries
- Out of sequence
- Omitted topics
  - Discontinuity phrases
  - Other

### 2. Sentence construction
- Prevarication in addressing critical issues
- Short and stilted
- Non-contracted phrases
- Rambling
- Incomplete or 'hanging'
- Esoteric words
- Freudian slips
- Breaches in linguistic codes
- Discontinuity words
- Use of inverted commas etc.

### 3. Verbs
- Tense
  - Avoidance of FPSPT
  - Changes in tense
  - Passive and conditional
  - Past tense for living person
- Different verbs for the same action
- Cerebral verbs

### 4. Adverbs
- Failure to use
- Inconsistent use

### 5. Nouns
- Inconsistent use
- Changes between singular and plural
- Relationships within a sentence

### 6. Pronouns
- Inconsistent use
- Reflexive
- Relative
- Demonstrative
- Possessive
- Missing personal pronouns
- Projection

### 7. Adjectives
- Failure to use
- Inconsistent use

### 8. Prepositions
- Inconsistent use
- Incorrect use
- Omission

**Table 4.7**  Syntax

| Category of response | Examples | Significance 10 = High 0 = Low |
|---|---|---|
| **Structural distortions** | | |
| Distortions between the time in real life and story time. Prevarication in addressing the critical issues Out of sequence and omitted topics | Most freestyle stories can be divided into a prologue (or introduction), a critical issue or issues and epilogue. An expanded prologue is a sign of prevarication and possible deception In real life an event that took one hour is explained in one sentence. Another that took two minutes is explained in ten pages | 8 |
| **Sentence construction** | | |
| Prevarication | In addressing the critical issues through an extended prologue | 10 |
| Use of short stilted sentences | *'I went out. We saw the car. It was a dark car'* | 5 |
| Non-contracted phrases | *'I did not go'* rather than *'I didn't go'* | 6 |
| Long rambling sentences | | 6 |
| Incomplete or hanging sentences | *'I went … er … no, we thought about …'* | 8 |
| Esoteric words | *'I can explicate myself from this abominable predicament'* | 6 |
| Freudian slips | *'Can I have a ticket to Titlochry please'* (see page 124) | 6 |
| Breaches in linguistic codes | See pages 51 and 115 | 10 |
| Discontinuity words and phrases suggesting a topic or detail has been omitted | *'The next thing I know …'* *'We then began …'* *'I continued …'* *'Later on …'* | 8 |
| Use of inverted commas in a written explanation | Usually means that the person does not accept the conventional interpretation of the words concerned. *'I knew the cheques were in the safe when I "left" that night'* | 8 |
| **Use of verbs** | | |
| Avoidance of first person, past tense For example *'I went …'* | In English, first person, past tense is a very precise and committed style of expression. Explanations in FPSPT are usually true | 10 |
| Passive rather than active phrasing Indicating lack of commitment | *'The tree was cut down'* as opposed to *'I cut down the tree'* | 10 |

| Category of response | Examples | Significance 10 = High 0 = Low |
|---|---|---|
| Changes, mid-story, between past and another tense | *'I went to the office and the next thing I know I am reading the computer files …'* | 10 |
| Passive and conditional tense, such as 'could', 'would' 'ought' etc. Both lack commitment | *'I would have …'* *'I could have …'* Are non-committal and more likely to be untrue than true | 10 |
| Past tense for a living person | *'They were happy kids'* | 10 |
| Different verbs for the same action | *'I talked to Bill then we discussed the game and chatted about golf'* | 6 |
| Use of cerebral verbs *These usually mean the act was not completed* | *'I then thought about going …'* *'I planned …'* *'I started to talk to …'* *'We talked about …'* | 6 |
| Use of adverbs | | |
| Failure to use and inconsistent use | These add detail to an explanation. When the detail is relevant, the chances are the explanation is true. Apparently irrelevant detail indicates an important topic has been concealed | 6 |
| Changes, mid-story, between singular and plural | *'I went towards the office and then we saw the door …'* | 7 |
| Use of nouns | | |
| Inconsistent use for the same thing or person | *'I got in my **car** then drove the **vehicle** to my home'* | 6 |
| Changes, mid-story, between singular and plural | *'We got into the car. Then as I was driving along we saw …'* | 7 |
| Relationships within a sentence | *'I went with Bill, John, Fred, Doris, Ethel and my wife.'* The distance in the sentence between *'I'* and *'wife'* suggests a poor relationship, as does the fact that she is referred to in her position, rather than by her name | 8 |
| Use of pronouns | | |
| Inconsistent use | *'I got in my car, then the bloody thing wouldn't start. Can you believe it, that car just blew up'* | 8 |
| Reflexive pronouns | *'One would never consider stealing from the company'* | 10 |
| Relative pronouns | *Inconsistent use of pronouns* | 6 |
| Demonstrative pronouns | | |
| Possessive pronouns | | |

| Category of response | Examples | Significance 10 = High 0 = Low |
|---|---|---|
| Missing personal pronouns | *'I went to the dance … then saw Bill … talked to him … drove my car to the cinema.'* The missing *'I'* before *'then'* etc. suggests a lack of commitment to that part of the explanation | 10 |
| Projection | *'The president would not do such a thing'* | 10 |
| Use of adjectives | | |
| Failure to use resulting in missing or inconsistent detail | Consistent use of adjectives is normally indicative of the truth | 6 |
| Use of prepositions | | |
| Inconsistent or incorrect use | See the OJ Simpson example of 'off the car' on page 116 | 6 |
| Use of definite and indefinite articles | | |
| Using 'the' to refer to an individual member of a general class without any introduction or the prior use of 'a' | Compare the difference between *'I went to the dance and saw a girl'* to *'I went to a dance and saw the girl'* | 7 |
| Use of conjunctions | | |
| Missing conjunctions | *'I spoke to the man. He said he was ill. I did not like the look of him.'* This shows a discontinuity that indicates deception | 8 |
| Use of interjections | | |
| | *'I said, "Holy shit".'* Probably he did say this | 8 |

Even with the most careful planning and rehearsal, it is virtually impossible for a liar to maintain consistency between false content and syntax; this applies whether the deception is oral or in writing. On the other hand, most people do not take syntax and semantics to a conscious level and thus miss important clues.

*Listen to and read every word; think what they really mean*

## PARALINGUISTIC CLUES

Paralinguistics is the study of auxiliary communications such as the tone, speed, volume and pitch of a person's voice. It is distinct from the content and syntax of the communication and body language and is mainly unconsciously driven. There are exceptions – such as when someone deliberately feigns a posh accent to convince the listener he is not from Birmingham.

The liar, who has to minimize the chance of saying something from his memory or subconscious that reveals his guilt, will usually edit his replies before delivering them. Pauses, long silences, deep sighing and clearing the throat are all signs of deception, as are changes in the tone of voice and the speed of response. This speed of response, known as 'response latency', varies from 0.5 seconds for truthful replies to 1.5 seconds for lies. Response latency is important and you should consciously monitor it and interject when the suspect's brain is thrashing for an answer (see pages 47, 72, 114 and 124).

*Remember: When a person is silent, thinking about how to lie, he is at his most vulnerable*

Even in writing, liars make Freudian slips which result from memory becoming confused with imagination and a fight between the conscious and subconscious monkeys. Things are blurted out that the liar never intended.

## WHAT IS A FREUDIAN SLIP?

Tom asked Bill what was meant by the phrase 'a Freudian slip'. Bill said: 'It is when the subconscious kicks in with something you did not wish to say. Let me give you an example. I went to buy a ticket to visit the famous Scottish town of Pitlochry. The girl at the ticket desk was really beautiful and wearing a low-cut dress. Instead of asking for *Pit*lochry I asked for a ticket to *Tit*lochry.

That is a Freudian slip.'

'In that case', said Tom, 'I have made a dreadful Freudian slip. Yesterday I was sat at breakfast with my wife and I meant to say, "Darling, would you please pass the toast". Instead I said, "I hate you – you dreadful old cow, you have wrecked my life." I told her it was a Freudian slip and she seems to have believed it.'

Freudian slips seem to result from thrashing between the person's conscious and subconscious and are therefore very important.

*Remain on the lookout for Freudian slips and challenge them.*
*Darwin meant to say 'Survival of the fattest'*

## ENRON

In the Enron case, a senior accountant meant to say, 'Ship the documents to the Feds,' but what he said was, 'Rip the documents to shreds,' and, as we know, this is what happened.

Freudian slips often appear as unfinished or 'hanging' sentences. For example, a suspect might say: 'We were just completing the annual accounts ... no, I am mistaken, we were talking about the weather.' At such points you should interject along the lines of 'Hold on a minute, Ralph, what were you going to say about the accounts?' so that you try to get him to complete the sentence.

'Insurance claims' below shows the effects of both open questions and Freudian slips.

## INSURANCE CLAIMS

- 'I knocked over my mother-in-law's bicycle but unfortunately she wasn't on it.'
- 'The pedestrian panicked and had no idea which way to run, so I ran over him.'
- 'The guy was all over the road. I had to swerve a number of times before I hit him.'

*Open questions get people thinking. This can be dangerous*

Paralinguistic clues can be summarized as illustrated in Table 4.8 and Mind Map 7.

*Paralinguistics are very important*

**Table 4.8**    How answers are expressed

| Category of response | Examples | Significance 10 = High 0 = Low |
|---|---|---|
| STALLING Delayed to give the suspect the chance to prepare the reply in his imagination | Long silences between a question and answer Disjointed replies Hesitant and cautious delivery Extended silences | 10 |
| DELIVERY (partly unconscious) | | |
| Changes in the tone pitch of the suspect's voice and speed of delivery (normally 120 to 150 words per minute) | Answers delivered slowly are more likely to be untruthful The pitch normally rises with deception and falls at the pivotal point Tone 8Hz to 12Hz micro-tremors Low volume: quieter replies may indicate deception | 7 |
| Stuttering and mumbling | | 8 |
| Delayed response Delayed to give the suspect the time to prepare a lie from his imagination | Micro-delays (from a normal response time of 0.5 seconds for truthful answers to 1.5 seconds for untruthful answers) Long silences between the question and answer Disjointed replies Hesitant and cautious delivery *'Please give me time to think'* *'I want to be certain, so give me time'* *'You are trying to trap me'* | 8 |
| Changes in volume | The volume of deceptive answers is usually lower than truthful replies (perhaps indicating a lack of commitment) | 5 |
| Extended silences | Response latency (see page 124) | 10 |
| Looking away when replying | See page 131 | 7 |
| Defers to interruptions | See Table 7.6, page 236 | 7 |

| Category of response | Examples | Significance 10 = High 0 = Low |
|---|---|---|
| **Non-verbal noises** | | |
| Extended sighs Clearing the throat Odd clicking sounds Tummy rumblings Extreme flatulence (stand back) Inappropriate laughter at the start or end of a response Grunts | | 8 |
| **Speech errors** | | |
| Missing words Freudian slips Spoonerisms Unfinished sentences Short, jerky sentences Corrections within a sentence Starting the sentence with 'Well ...' | Again this is usually caused by a conflict between memory and imagination, conscious and subconscious. Statements like *'I never let the wail tag the dog'* instead of *'tail wag the dog'* | 10 |
| **EMOTIONAL OUTBURSTS** | | |
| Anger Humour Tears | The main clue is that the emotion is inappropriate | 8 |

## NON-VERBAL CLUES

Non-verbal communication is normally managed unconsciously by the autonomic system and accounts for over 60 per cent of the messages conveyed between humans and 10 per cent between accountants. It dates back to over 500 million years ago before language evolved and was the only way that our ancestors could communicate. It is still highly relevant.

The body language of children is usually obvious, such as placing hands over their mouths, ears and eyes when they do, say, hear or see something naughty. As we get older, these childish movements are refined and substituted by disguised actions, such as false scratching, yawns etc. but they have the same objective of covering the mouth.

Non-verbal clues are especially important in assessing whether an emotion is genuine or not.

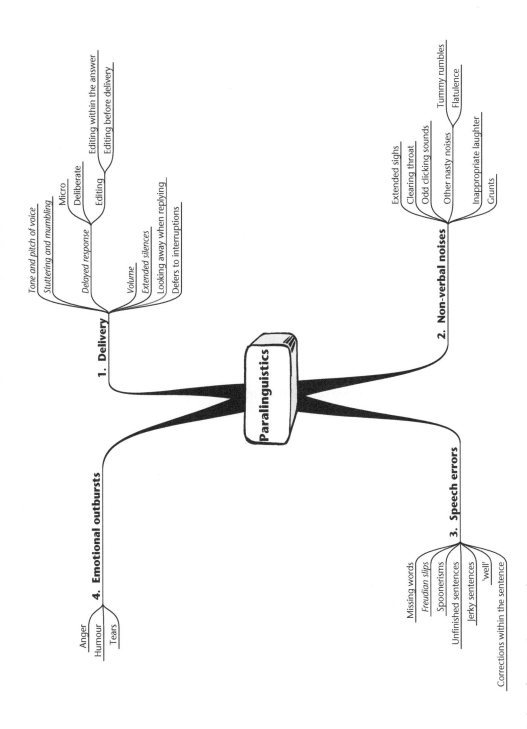

**Mind Map® 7**  Paralinguistic clues

## WHAT A LOVELY BABY: THE DUCHENNE SMILE IN REVERSE

All politicians love babies for three reasons. The first is that babies don't ask difficult questions. The second is they are camera ready and bring reflected glory. The third is that they show the politician has safe hands.

But next time you see a politician holding a baby look carefully and what you will see is him saying 'Coochy coo. What a beautiful little baby you are' and then put on a patently contrived smile. This is known in the trade as a 'reverse Duchenne smile' (see page 58). You know from the timing, lack of wrinkling around the eyes, the absence of dilation in the pupils and the uneven quick fade of the facial expression that the only thing the tub-thumper likes about babies is playing a part in their conception after an all-expenses-paid dinner at Langans (Table 1).

When emotion is genuine, the non-verbal clues are driven directly from the limbic system (see page 42) and appear before any oral expression. When false, they appear in reverse order and are usually transient. If you don't believe this, look closely at politicians on television: they usually get it wrong and smile milliseconds after they say how nice the baby looks.

*Watch for incongruencies between micro expressions and those which are consciously contrived*

Overall the body language of truthful subjects is more dynamic and relaxed with consistent use of demonstrators.

*Believe in body language*

Non-verbal clues to deception are summarized in Table 4.9 and Mind Map 8.

**Table 4.9**    Non-verbal clues

| Body element | Symptoms of deceit | Significance |
|---|---|---|
| Emblems (may also be unconscious) | | |
| SURROUNDINGS DRESS ASSOCIATES VEHICLES PREMISES Transactional role Incongruence | These are visual signals reflecting how the person sees himself and how he would like to be perceived by others. For example, police uniforms, barristers' wigs, punk hairstyles. Clothes, hair and especially *shoes and spectacles* inconsistent with the person's true standing or position and displayed with the intention of enhancing his ability to succeed with an attack or to deceive the interviewer | 10 |

| Body element | Symptoms of deceit | Significance |
|---|---|---|
| **Body posture (kinesics relates to body movement; proxemics to personal space)** | | |
| The body is the most reliable source of non-verbal communication. Posture is a reflection of the subject's confidence<br><br>OVERALL POSTURE<br>Large limbs and trunk into defensive positions<br>Leaning away<br>Body changes in response to a relevant question<br>Orientation of body<br>Defensive angles | Leaning or turning away from the interviewer. A person telling lies will rarely sit on the front of his chair, lean forward or sit or stand frontally aligned or 'face on' to the interviewer. He will usually stand or sit at an angle using his shoulders as a defensive barrier. Crossed legs and arms: the higher they are, the more defensive the barrier<br>Sits in a foetal position | 10 |
| | At the opening of the interview or in response to a relevant question, moves his body so that he creates a barrier with his shoulders and legs and is thus not frontally aligned<br>Changing posture before delivering a false answer<br>Generally the liar's main body movements are static (except when severely anxious) and are seldom inclined towards the interviewer | |
| Breathing | Shortage of breath<br>Increased heartbeat<br>Rapid pulsing of the carotid artery in the neck | 5 |
| **Personal space** | | |
| Initial position<br>Reactive movements<br>Responding to evidence | Liars will usually try to increase the space around them. They may lean away or pull their chair away from the interviewer at the start of the interview. Liars will usually push away incriminating reminders of their guilt such as documentary exhibits | 10 |
| Body element | Symptoms of deceit | Significance |
| **Legs** | | |
| Dynamic movements | While sitting down, moving legs towards or under the body or retracted<br>High crossing to create a defensive barrier<br>Crossing one on top of the other<br>Preparing to run | 10 |
| **Feet** | | |
| | Nervous tapping<br>Raised off the ground when seated or standing | 8 |
| **Arms** | | |
| | Crossed: the higher up the body the crossing of arms and the tighter they are together, the more defensive the intention<br>Moving towards the body | 10 |

| Body element | Symptoms of deceit | Significance |
|---|---|---|
| **Hands** | | |
| Manipulators are soothing, grooming movements near to or touching the body, the mouth, ears or back of the neck. They are usually an indication of deception and are a displacement activity<br><br>Demonstrators are used to emphasize a point and are usually movements away from the body. Consistent use of demonstrators – in relation to control and relevant questions – are usually an indication of truthfulness | **Manipulators**<br>Breaches of the normal communications code<br>Hand to mouth and head gestures<br>False scratching (a genuine scratch is usually five times, though be sympathetic to sufferers of eczema or those with fleas)<br>Grooming gestures, such as straightening the tie<br>Appearing to fall asleep<br>Brushing non-existent dust or hairs off clothing<br>Needlessly winding his watch or cleaning his glasses<br>Hands covering stomach or genitalia<br>Micro-expressions (see page 47)<br>**Demonstrators**<br>Breaches of the normal communications code<br>Hands moving inwards and close to the body<br>Use of hands to insert punctuation marks in conversation (such as inverted commas)<br>Failing to touch incriminating evidence<br>Frozen arms and hands<br>Jerky or nervous movements<br>Hand tremors or trembling<br>Pointing is a sign of anger or assertiveness. When people are telling lies, they do not usually point except when angry<br>Micro-expressions<br>**Other movements**<br>Excessive grip on an object<br>Clenched fists (a sign of anger)<br>Palms other than open; palms downwards; movements may be disguised and subtle<br>Displayed thumbs are a sign of defiance<br>Sits on hands or hides then in his pockets<br>Heavy sweating | 10 |
| Body element | Symptoms of deceit | Significance |
| **Face (may also be conscious)** | | |
| The face has over 100 separate muscle groups which produce around 20000 expressions. It is one of the most unreliable indicators of deception. However, the face makes micro-expressions which are straight from the subconscious and last for less than a second. You will notice these | Pallid or flushed complexion<br>Heavy sweating especially on the upper lip<br>Poker faced<br>'Stony faced'<br>**Micro-expressions**<br>False smiles (see page 58)<br>**Expression after an emotional outburst**<br>Transient expressions<br>Asymmetrical expressions: for example a 'crooked smile' | 8 |

| Body element | Symptoms of deceit | Significance |
|---|---|---|
| **Eyes (may also be conscious)** | | |
| Normally gaze is for between 1 and 10 seconds with around 6 blinks per minute. The speaker has eye contact for 40per cent of the time and the listener for 75 per cent of the time<br><br>People who are telling the truth look more and have better and more consistent eye contact<br><br>**Eye accessing clues**<br>Left to access memory<br>Right to access imagination | **Gaze and direction: gaze aversion**<br>**Variable or unnatural eye contact**<br>Generally a suspect will have poor eye contact when telling a lie. Thus the term 'shifty eyed'<br>Looking away and especially downwards and to the right<br>Eye contact is normally directed at the other person's forehead. When it is directed to the mouth or eyes, a sexual interest may be present<br>Dysfunctional gaze<br>Extended eye contact (staring)<br>**Size of pupils**<br>Pupils become enlarged (usually referred to as 'dilation')<br>Whites of the eyes become more visible<br>**Eye accessing clues**<br>Looking to right when accessing memory<br>**Blinking**<br>Eyes closed<br>Dramatic changes – increase or decrease – in the rate of blinking<br>**Other clues from the eyes**<br>Micro-tremors in the muscles around the eyes<br>Sweating below the eye lids<br>Hands over eyes usually as a disguised movement, but a reflection of 'see no evil' | 8 |
| **Mouth (may also be conscious)** | | |
| | Dry mouth: sometimes the person telling lies will drink vast amounts of water. Be particularly on guard when the subject brings his own bottles of water into the interview room<br>False yawning or any other movement that excuses the hands being put over or near the mouth<br>Biting, licking or chewing lips<br>Sighing and heavy swallowing<br>Narrowed, tight lips<br>Foam or spittle build up in the corners of the mouth | 10 |

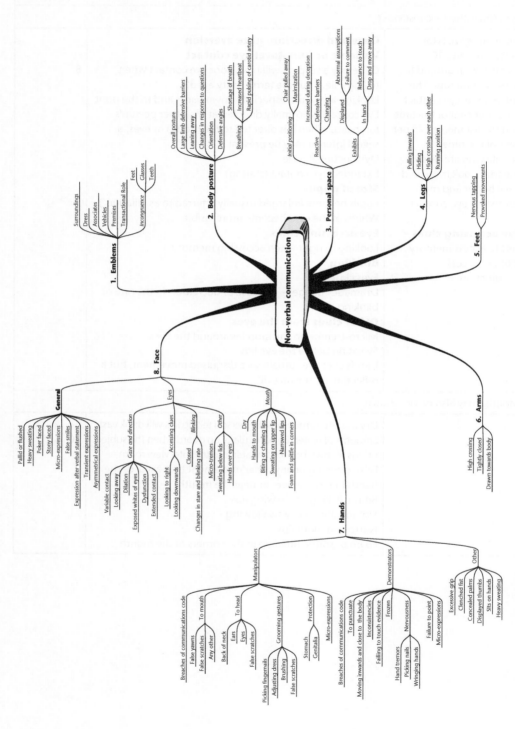

**Mind Map® 8**   Non-verbal communication clues

If you are not convinced about the merits of non-verbal communication, you are strongly advised to visit the website of Center for Nonverbal Studies (CNS) which is a private, non-profit research centre located in Spokane, Washington, and La Jolla, California. Underway since 1 October, 1997, the Center's mission is to advance the study of human communication in all its forms apart from language. The Center's goal is to promote the scientific study of non-verbal communication, which includes body movement, gesture, facial expression, adornment and fashion, architecture, mass media, and consumer-product design. On 12 January, 1999, CNS affiliated with the Center for Ethnographic Research (CER) at the University of Missouri in Kansas City.

The liar is well aware that subconsciously he is throwing away non-verbal clues and will try to disguise or consciously control them. This is virtually impossible and, if he knows you have noticed his struggle, it will increase his anxiety until it becomes a self-defeating spiral.

## ATTITUDE

The subject's attitude, which is communicated mainly in the content, also reveals important clues to deception (see Table 4.10 and Mind Map 9).

**Table 4.10**    Clues in the attitude

| Symptoms of deception CONSCIOUS, unconscious or *both* | Examples | Significance 10 = High 0 = Low |
|---|---|---|
| Absence of values | | |
| | The liar is usually focused on short-term goals and may find difficulty distinguishing right from wrong, having few values or principles to guide him He may consider himself 'above the law' Business liars seldom show remorse (until they are exposed) | 8 |
| Attitude to dishonesty and the matter in question | | |
| Non-judgemental of himself | President Nixon *'dissembled the truth'* President Clinton's relationship with Monica was *'inappropriate'* Clinton smoked pot, but *'did not inhale'* | 10 |
| Minimizes the seriousness of the matters in issue | Tends to minimize their seriousness, subconsciously reducing his anxiety Failure to deny Failure to become angry Contrived submission Contrived flattery | 8 |
| Unjustifiably passive Defers to interruptions Avoidance of hard words | Quietly accepts statements such as: *'I am not interested in that, Bill'* Like an alcoholic, the guilty person will usually minimize the seriousness of the problem, and will not use words like *'theft', 'fraud', 'steal'* etc. | 10 |

| Symptoms of deception CONSCIOUS, unconscious or *both* | Examples | Significance 10 = High 0 = Low |
|---|---|---|
| **Allocation of blame** | | |
| Blaming others | The white collar fraudster will not usually blame someone else for his dishonesty. For example, when asked the question, *'Who do you think is responsible?'* he will not name anyone | 7 |
| Anonymous blame | *'The company just wants to get rid of me'* *'I am always the scapegoat'* | |
| Clearing himself | When asked the question *'Who can you clear of this?'* he will not usually name himself *first*. An innocent person is more likely to do so | 8 |
| **Failure to deny (see content)** | | |
| | Failure to deny and pseudo denials (see Table 4.3, page 98) | 10 |
| **Rationalization (may also be conscious)** | | |
| Generally Specific issue Internalizes Admissions without guilt Honesty | *'Anyone would do the same'* *'I don't see what the problem is'* *Tends to believe everyone is dishonest* *'I may have done it, but it wasn't intentional'* *'OK just say I did it'* | 5 |
| **Self-deception** | | |
| Failure to accept the facts Failure to appreciate the consequences Self-deprecation Projection Unwillingness to touch incriminating evidence The false death wish (usually sarcastic or unemotional) | *'That document proves nothing'* *'He would say that, wouldn't he?'* *'I know I am stupid, but …'* *'The Sales Director [speaking about himself] is totally innocent, I can tell you that'* *'I wish I was dead'* *'Why don't I just kill myself right now'* | 8 |
| **Admits having considered the act in question** | | |
| | Will explain how he would have committed the act in question. An innocent person will rarely become involved in such a discussion. The explanation given may be obviously misleading or childish. However, sometimes the liar will give away facts known only to the perpetrator | 10 |
| REFERENCE TO HIS MENTAL STATE | *'I know in my own mind'* *'I would be bloody crazy to have done that'* | 8 |
| Reference to proof | Will tend to underestimate the significance *'You have no proof of that'* *'Show me the evidence and I will believe you'* | 10 |

| Symptoms of deception CONSCIOUS, unconscious or *both* | Examples | Significance 10 = High 0 = Low |
|---|---|---|
| Comments on the question | *'That is a good question'* *'How dare you suggest that'* Respond to a question with a question | 9 |
| EMOTIONS | Feigned anger etc. | 8 |
|  | Fluid emotions Failure to show the emotions an innocent person would Verbal expression before the non-verbal communication |  |
| Failure to act innocently | Failure to deny Failure to become angry or express the emotions of an honest person Goes too far to convince rather than simply convey Will usually deny having discussed the problem with his spouse or close family members as most innocent people do Admits to nothing in relation to the matter in issue, including small, irrelevant details | 10 |
| CONTENT | see page 104 |  |
| Syntax | see page 114 |  |
| Paralinguistics | see page 123 |  |
| Non-verbal communication | see page 126 |  |

*A liar's attitude is always different from a truthful person's attitude*

A great example of attitude shining through the mist and of people giving away their true feelings is contained in a press release put out by the Information Commissioner. The background was that a bunch of people had set themselves up as:

- Data Protection Registration Service;
- Data Registration Agency;
- etc.

They had been extracting money from mugs who thought they were dealing with the Information Commissioner: this was a pretty clever and lucrative scam. The press release opened:

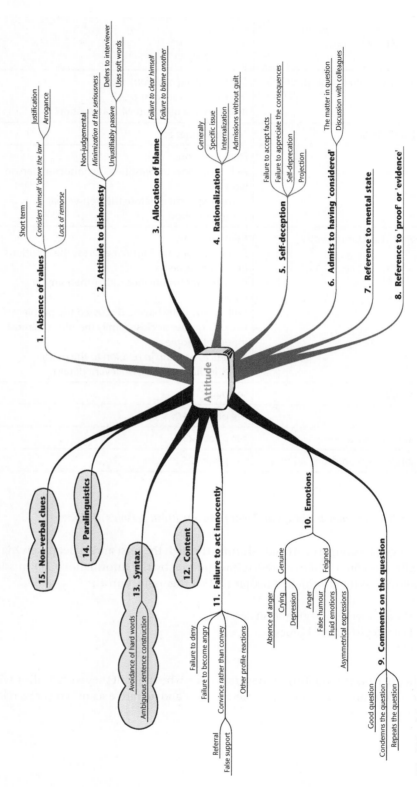

**Mind Map® 9**  Clues from the attitude

## THE INFORMATION COMMISSIONER

'The Information Commissioner, Elizabeth France, is concerned about the volume of telephone calls and correspondence received by her Office in relation to the above businesses.'

It later went on to say: 'She has been disturbed that a number of people have been confused and troubled by the wording and tone of some of the correspondence issued by these businesses.'

It would have been much more convincing if these sentences had been juxtaposed because they suggest that she is more irritated by having to respond to telephone calls and letters than she is about the poor so-and-sos who have been ripped off.

## Putting it all together

Academic research[8] indicates that for most people the chances of detecting lies are no better than 50:50 but since the research is always artificial – based on test conditions – it is not necessarily reliable in real life. In such experiments police officers and psychiatrists fared only a little better, although some individuals were accurate in almost every case, usually by following techniques of the type described in this book. Ironically, the most effective detectors of deceit *in the test cases provided to them* were a group of criminals serving life sentences! Estate agents were not scored.

## LIAR

The British television programme *Liar* asks the audience to decide which one of six candidates is telling the truth. Each candidate is asked questions, and in round one the audience dismisses the one it is most sure is a liar. Further rounds take place with a candidate being voted off each time until only two are left. They ask each other questions and the audience votes on which one is truthful. If the one and only genuinely truthful candidate of the original six is the winner, £10000 is given to the audience. If the person voted by the audience as the truthful candidate is a liar he keeps the £10000. As far as is known, the truthful candidate has never been voted the winner, but is often thrown off in the first round as being the biggest liar. The reason for this is that the truthful person is more likely to make mistakes and reveal small inconsistencies. For example, the only truthful candidate on one programme claimed to be a committed Christian yet, under the glare of the studio lights, she could not remember the Ten Commandments. She was immediately identified as a liar and thrown off in the first round.

The truth is that most people rely too heavily on the pure content of what is said and on facial expressions, which can be manipulated to some degree. The dark grey shading in Figure 4.2 represents their approach.

---

[8]   With all its limitations and under artificial conditions

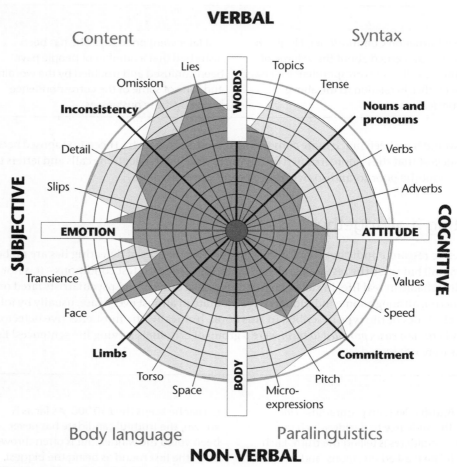

**Figure 4.2**    Methods of detecting deceit

Experienced interviewers take a holistic approach, *as shown in the light shaded area of Figure 4.2,* when assessing the truthfulness of an explanation and look for incongruencies rather than a single clue. This leads to far higher success rates in finding the truth. We suggest in future you take this approach.

You already know how and when you are being told lies. This is the easy part. You just have to consciously accept the reality. The following chapters explain the cunning plan necessary for dealing with them.

# PART 2

# *Countermeasures*

'I RECOMMEND BUYING THE SHARES ... THE FUNDAMENTALS ARE GOOD AND THE CASH FLOW POSITIVE AND WE DON'T EXPECT THE FINANCE DIRECTOR TO BE ARRESTED BEFORE THE FOURTH QUARTER OF 2005'

# 5 Planning Investigations and Legal Background for Tough Interviews

*Every falsification is a step towards the truth and every concealment a step away*

## Introduction

### THE BATTLEGROUND

Although the liar usually chooses the battleground, appears to have all of the advantages and believes he can win or escape, the balance is always in favour of the effective interviewer, providing he plans carefully. Successful interviewing is 95 per cent planning including:

- having clear objectives on the way the case should be resolved and the ideal outcome;
- knowing and complying with the law;
- fully understanding the case and every piece of evidence and intelligence that relates to it;
- having a clear theory on who and why the fraud happened and the key points that support it;
- having a sensible resolutions plan, showing who, where and by whom the investigation – and the interviews that form part of it – will be conducted including the place and timing of the 'first step', when the suspects will be confronted, preferably by a simultaneous ambush.

The balance of 5 per cent involves rehearsal of key interviews and their execution.

*Interviews are 95 per cent planning and 5 per cent execution*

### INVESTIGATION STAGES AND INTERVIEW PHASES

This chapter presents an overview of the legal background and planning steps that should be considered for difficult investigations of which tough interviews form a part.

Successful interviews do not require a harsh approach or raised voices – despite what many television detective programmes might suggest – but are founded on a relentless, professional dialogue that follows an established process as part of an overall investigations plan. The techniques are described in Chapter 7, but first it is necessary to review the legal environment in which investigations and interviews are conducted.

## RECOGNIZING THE REALITY

Although it is critical that investigations comply with the law and can be honestly reported without fear of *justified* criticism, criminals rarely intend to get caught and it is sometimes necessary to use techniques that could be regarded by anorak-wearers as controversial. But please remember that an ineffective investigation leaves a cloud of unresolved suspicion hanging over the heads of innocent people and allows crooks to escape and victimize others. *Thus the purpose of any investigation is to find the truth: to clear innocent people as well as to prove, beyond doubt, the guilt of those involved.*

Sweeping the symptoms of malpractice or dishonesty under the carpet, or going through faint-hearted investigations is not fair to the people suspected, to the victim organization or to honest employees; wilful blindness and apathy are not viable options.

### BRAND MANAGER

Allegations, in an anonymous letter, were made against a senior and very successful brand manager to the effect that he had taken bribes for passing business to an advertising agency. His managers decided not to probe the allegations, foolishly believing that an investigation would result in adverse publicity. However, they transferred the manager to low-level work, but refused to explain why. He became depressed and killed himself. At the inquest the truth emerged: the anonymous letter proved to be false, and the employer was heavily censured for its lack of action.

If the suspicions of dishonesty are ignored, chances are they will reappear, usually in a more damaging form.

*Fraud, malpractice and dishonesty is contagious.*
*If you have current suspicions you should resolve them*

### DECIDING ON ACTION IN THE ABSENCE OF THE FACTS

A director of human resources argued strongly that the police should not be called when clear signs of fraud were discovered in a computer department. He suggested that a witch-hunt would be bad for the morale of employees who were under extreme pressure to complete a large conversion project. Three employees were interviewed by personnel officers and issued with written warnings. Two years later over $3 million went missing. This time the police were called and two of the three men were prosecuted and imprisoned. However, the company's claim under its fidelity policies was, quite properly, denied on the grounds that the men's previous dishonesty disqualified them from cover.

There must be a clear distinction between finding the facts and the management decisions that have to be taken as a result. Deciding on the outcome of suspicions without knowing the facts is akin to signing a blank cheque.

# Important background on the law

## RIGHT TO ASK QUESTIONS

In most countries, any question can be asked of anyone, subject to their not being discriminatory on grounds of such things as sex, religion, ethnic origin, nationality, age or disability. There is also an inherent right against self-incrimination and limited rights of protection against intrusion *by agencies of the State* into the private lives of individuals under the human rights laws (see pages 148 and 151).

## RIGHT TO REMAIN SILENT

People suspected of a crime normally have the right to remain silent and to have access to legal advice once they have been arrested or are in custody. The exceptions include:

- certain regulatory, Serious Fraud Office and DTI investigations;
- health and safety enquiries;
- tax investigations (especially under the 'Hansard' procedure);[1]
- when required to answer under an employment or other contract.

In all other cases there is nothing to prevent you in a fair exchange from finding the truth by asking questions, challenging, persuading, leading or guiding someone else to tell the truth. It is a game of chess and a competition in which the liar engages because he believes he can win. Successful interviewers do not disabuse him of this misconception until it is too late.

# The Criminal Law in the UK

## SCOPE

Fraud victims have rights of recovery under both the Civil and Criminal Law, although many completely overlook the former and thus reduce their chances of success.

The hard truth is that most victims of fraud never get their money back, usually because of poor planning

The Criminal Law is defined by statute or common practice and breaches can result in punishment being imposed by the State, including imprisonment, restraining orders and financial penalties. Examples of crimes include theft, murder, treason, robbery and fraud. Also, attempts to commit crimes are usually punishable under the Criminal Law. An important objective of the criminal justice system is to punish offenders so that others are deterred and crime controlled but, judging by recent cases, this is not always obvious.

## HOW ACTIONS ARE STARTED AND PROCESSED

Most criminal prosecutions are undertaken by government organizations, such as the police, Customs and Excise or Inland Revenue but are usually based on a complaint by a victim. The accused or defendant may be arrested or summonsed to appear in court on a specified date.

---

[1] This procedure is used by the Inland Revenue where suspected tax evaders are invited to make a full frank disclosure. If they do so, a more sympathetic approach is taken on prosecution

The prosecution is managed by an official body such as the Crown Prosecution Service (CPS), the Serious Fraud Office (SFO) or a regulatory agency.

A victim may also start a private criminal prosecution by applying to a magistrates' court for a summons, requiring the accused to appear at a set date and time. Private prosecutions are both rare and hazardous but may be taken over and abandoned at any time by the Director of Public Prosecutions.

Even when criminal prosecutions are successful, any financial penalties are paid to the government and not to the victim. Equally, the costs of the prosecution are borne by the State. Thus, in criminal prosecutions, the State takes control and the victim assumes a secondary position.

There are some important differences between the objectives of fraud victims, the police and public prosecutors (see Table 5.1).

**Table 5.1**   Different objectives of police and civil investigations

| Police prosecution (or regulatory agency) | Victim company's objectives |
|---|---|
| Aims at a successful prosecution on a number of specimen charges | The victim needs to establish the full extent of the loss to maximize its recoveries |
| The police are not concerned with making financial recoveries | This may be a top priority for the victim |
| The police expect unrestricted access to evidence in the possession of the victim | The police have to release all evidence in their possession to the defence; this can seriously compromise the victim in civil actions |
| A lack of resources usually means the investigation will not be completed quickly | Delay always acts against the interests of the victim |
| Public prosecutors will not usually proceed with the case unless the chances of success are overwhelming and there can be no compromises | The victim may start a case to obtain injunctions or discovery of evidence with a view to a negotiated settlement |

In most cases, to get their money back, fraud victims have to take civil actions or negotiate. However, it should be noted that from 1 November 2000 the Criminal Proceedings Amendment Act (CPAA) 2000 permits fraud victims to apply to the police – through their lawyers – to inspect their case files. The extent to which any evidence obtained can be used in civil proceedings is, as yet, unclear.

## STANDARDS OF PROOF

To succeed with a criminal complaint, the prosecution has to prove – to the satisfaction of the magistrate, jury or judge – all of the elements of the offence and the responsibility of the accused 'beyond reasonable doubt'. This is an extremely high standard and any benefit is given to the accused. It is usually critical to show that the accused acted with 'guilty knowledge' or intent.

There are some criminal offences where proof of guilty knowledge is not required and these (such as failing to submit a tax return, not registering with the Information Commissioner or using a television without a licence) are referred to as 'absolute offences'. They have little relevancy to corporate fraud cases.

The trial judge will determine what evidence is, and is not, admissible, applying a rule of 'fairness' (Section 76 of the Police and Criminal Evidence Act 1984). If evidence has been illegally obtained, for example by making threats or promises to the accused or witnesses, the judge may still admit it but may make adverse comments that reduce its significance. This makes it imperative that victims understand and comply with the laws and evidential procedures and act fairly.

## DISCOVERY AND DISCLOSURE

In all criminal cases, the accused is not required to answer questions, produce evidence that could be against his interests or to give evidence in court, but there are exceptions. *For example, if the police execute a search warrant, any documents or other stuff recovered can be produced in evidence, although the accused is under no obligation to explain it.* However, under the Criminal Justice and Public Order Act 1994 if a person when questioned fails to mention any fact relied on in his defence, the court may draw such inferences as appear proper.

In England people accused of crimes are required to provide details of any alibi they intend to develop in their defence. For example, if a robber claims that he is innocent and at the time of the alleged offence was at ballet classes, he is required before trial, to produce details of the witnesses and other evidence he plans to call to support his alibi. The object of this is to prevent the prosecution being ambushed at trial by a spurious defence.

Criminal prosecutors are required (under the Criminal Procedure and Investigations Act 1996) to disclose, to the accused's representatives before trial, all of the 'prosecution material' they have, including that which is not part of their case.

This makes it imperative that all evidence (whether important or not) collected in a criminal investigation is catalogued and preserved so that at the appropriate time, the prosecuting authority can decide what has to be disclosed. It should be noted that many prosecutions fail because of technical problems with disclosure. It is a very important issue.

There are circumstances in which information that could be relevant to an opposing party does not have to be disclosed. In criminal cases this may include the name of a confidential informant or other material which should be protected in the public interest or by legal professional privilege (see below 'Information Privileged against Disclosure'). The procedures are complicated and will be handled by lawyers at the appropriate time, but the rule is total openness with the court.

## PENALTIES IN CRIMINAL CASES

If the defendant pleads or is found guilty, the magistrate or judge will impose what he believes is the appropriate financial, custodial or other sentence, supposedly having regard to the seriousness of the offence, previous convictions (which are not made available to the jury prior to its decision being reached) and any pleas in mitigation. The latter are often a work of art and victims of corporate fraud should try, through their counsel, to ensure that the most extravagant excuses are refuted. Victims should also press for financial compensation although in criminal cases this is always limited.

# The civil law in the UK

## SCOPE

The civil law deals with such things as breaches of contract and other wrongful acts or 'torts'. Most frauds result in breaches of the civil law and remedies can be sought in addition to criminal prosecution. It is important to recognize that the civil and criminal paths to recovery are not mutually exclusive but, in fact, complement each other. The primary focus of the civil law is to put the victim back into the position he would have been in but for the wrongful act. It is a bit like the *Match of the Day* action replay, but damages can be substantial.

Examples of civil law violations include:

* breach of employment or other contracts;
* negligence;
* breach of fiduciary duties;
* fraud.

Also attempts to commit a breach of contract, conspiracy or failure to act as agreed may be actionable under the civil law.

Civil actions may be brought to obtain compensation or injunctive relief preventing the continuation of an undesirable act (such as trespass), requiring a person or company to perform a specific act (such as complying with a contract) or to disclose evidence. Civil courts cannot impose custodial penalties except for perjury or contempt of court.

## HOW ACTIONS ARE STARTED

### Routine actions

Civil actions are normally commenced by private citizens, government agencies and organizations issuing a claim form (possibly supported by statements) through their lawyers setting out the nature of the complaint. The claim form obviously gives the defendant notice that trouble is brewing and allows him to take defensive steps, including interference with witnesses and hiding his assets.

### Pre-emptive actions

The law recognizes that people accused of wrongful acts, and especially fraud, are unlikely to make a full and frank disclosure in the normal course of events. It is therefore possible for claimants to carry out a pre-emptive strike by asking a High Court or other judge – *ex parte*, without the knowledge of the third parties involved – to issue orders of the type described in Table 5.2.

Pre-emptive orders are often the first indication a defendant has that civil action has been started and they are intended to take him by surprise.

To obtain such an order the claimant's lawyers have to convince a judge, sitting 'in camera', that there is 'good arguable case'. Most English judges are well-versed in fraud and realize that the evidence available to support an application is likely to be less than complete. *In fact, if the evidence were sufficient, there would be no need for a pre-emptive order.*

Until the human rights stuff came on the scene, judges would apply what was known as the *Cynamid* test and decide whether it was just and reasonable to grant an order. Now the

**Table 5.2**   Main types of civil orders

| Type of order | When used | Directed against |
|---|---|---|
| Freezing order<br>*Previously referred to as a Mareva Injunction* | To preserve assets<br>To locate (discover) assets and to prevent their dissipation<br>To require the defendant to account fully for his assets | Defendants |
| Search and seizure order<br>*Previously referred to as an Anton Pillar Order* | To enter and search premises for evidence where there are grounds for believing it might be destroyed or not produced under normal circumstances | Defendants |
| Production order (in various shapes and sizes) | To require the production of evidence | Defendants and witnesses |

judgment is more likely to be based on the notion of 'proportionality', which means that the relief requested should be commensurate with the seriousness of the case.

Courts usually require the claimant to enter into an undertaking on costs, so if their action is unfounded, the defendant is not damaged. Because of the checks and balances applied by good litigation lawyers and the judges themselves there are very few cases of pre-emptive actions going wrong. However, if they do the claimant can be heavily penalized for costs.

A *Search and seizure order* allows the claimant and his legal advisers to enter and search premises under the control of the defendant or third party and to recover evidence that would normally be available on discovery. If the defendant refuses to cooperate he can be held in contempt of court and imprisoned. Search and seizure orders are executed by the claimant's lawyers (accompanied by a specified number of assistants, investigators and representatives) by simply appearing on the defendant's doorstep. The order will also specify the name of a supervising solicitor. He will be from an independent firm and his job is to ensure that that order is executed fairly and that the defendant complies.

The defendant has a reasonable period to take legal advice, during which he can refuse to admit the claimant's representatives onto his premises. This is usually a critical period because it allows the defendant to conceal or destroy evidence. In practice, the supervising solicitor should seek immediate access, but again this can be a problem if there are a number of defendants in the premises and only one supervising solicitor, as he cannot watch them all. This aspect calls for very careful planning.

When a search and seizure order is executed, any material that the defendant argues is privileged should be retained by the supervising solicitor, who will refer the matter to the judge. In short, the self-incrimination argument should not be an issue. However, any case evidence recovered in civil proceedings is not normally admissible in criminal courts, but there are exceptions.

*Freezing orders*, which are often obtained in parallel with search and seizure orders, compel the defendant to disclose and preserve any assets which may, in due course, be recoverable by the claimant. They may also require the defendant to disclose under oath all of his income and assets. This is usually a very productive exercise and puts the crook in considerable difficulty.

*Production orders* can be issued on the defendant's bankers, financial advisers and others from whom the claimant believes useful evidence can be obtained. They are very powerful weapons in the fight against fraud.

## FURTHER PROCESSING

In the last couple of years the civil process has been streamlined (based on the Civil Procedure Rules) and involves statements of truth, discovery, interrogatories (written questions and answers) and submissions by both sides before trial. Such exchanges ensure that there should be few surprises at trial. There is often a mediation stage, when the judge will try and bring the sides together to reach a settlement before trial or during the trial itself.

Despite the improvements, proceedings can be very slow and costly as both sides take increasingly intransigent positions. Thus the main practical benefit of civil proceedings is to discover evidence and to bring the parties to negotiate. A full-blown trial should be avoided, almost at all costs. The better litigation lawyers are excellent negotiators.

*Before litigating, dig two graves*

## STANDARDS OF PROOF

To succeed with a civil case the claimant has to prove its case on a 'balance of probabilities' and may succeed where a parallel criminal prosecution fails. This is an important distinction

Trial judges are rightly concerned with the issue of fairness and this is critically important when injunctive relief or pre-emptive orders are being sought. The claimant must present all of the relevant information – whether it is good or adverse – and if it fails to do so the injunction will fail.

### ST MERRYN MEAT AND OTHERS V HAWKINS AND OTHERS QB2001

In this case injunctions were granted on the basis that evidence had been obtained by intercepting the defendant's office telephone. It subsequently transpired that this was untrue and that his home telephone had been tapped illegally, which the court viewed as a possible infringement of his rights to privacy under article 8(2) of the Human Rights Act.

The judge discharged the orders, not because of the human rights violation, but because he had been misled. It is possible that had he known the truth from the outset, he would have maintained the orders.

It is critical that courts are not misled for, if they are, the claimant can be very heavily penalized. Thus the judge should be advised at the earliest possible opportunity of anything that is unusual or could cause a problem.

## DISCOVERY AND DISCLOSURE

In routine cases the parties go through a process of 'discovery', which means that any evidence in their possession has to be disclosed to the other side. *For example the defendant might be compelled to disclose all of his assets or documentation which establishes his responsibility for wrongful acts.* The claimant also has to disclose any evidence which could conceivably assist the defendant and this aspect has to be carefully handled, usually by lawyers.

Again, a fundamental principle is that material that could be relevant to the case is disclosed to the opposing party – usually during the discovery process. For this reason investigators should catalogue all material collected during a case and make sure it is brought to the attention of lawyers.

Defendants in civil cases have no general right against self-incrimination, although some will argue to the contrary on the basis that disclosure could result in criminal prosecution or interfere with their human rights. The case of *Rank Film Distributors v Video Information Centre 1992* is an example of how the protection against self-incrimination is increasingly applying in civil cases. The point is particularly relevant when pre-emptive orders are being sought. Defendants may refuse to comply on the grounds that to do so could expose them to criminal liability. Thus the drafting of the pre-emptive order, in relation to future criminal proceedings, is vital.

## PENALTIES IN CIVIL CASES

Penalties in civil cases can include recovery of all losses, interest, costs and damages which are normally payable to the claimant. However, both parties are responsible for legal and other costs and the loser may have to compensate the winner. This can be a serious disincentive and, in fact, the party with the largest purse usually has the advantage.

# Information privileged against disclosure

In both criminal and civil proceedings certain material is classified[2] as 'privileged' and does not have to be disclosed to the opposing party including:

- all communications between a client (or his agent) and his solicitor (or his agent), in contemplation of proceedings, including requests for legal advice, reports and statements. This is usually known as 'Legal Professional Privilege' (or in the USA 'Client–Attorney' privilege) and it protects the client against adverse disclosure;
- 'without prejudice' correspondence;
- internal reports prepared by a Special Task Force specifically created to investigate an important matter;
- communications between employees and others who have a common business interest. For example, internal reports, staff appraisals and personal references are usually protected under the rule for common business interests. Also an accusation made about a suspected crime to the police with a view to detecting an offender is privileged (in the UK see *Kine v Sewell 1838).*

For all practical purposes, privileged information does not exist and protection is substantive rather than procedural, as was the case until a few years ago. Exceptions include cases where privilege is waived, privileged material is foolishly disclosed, where publication is excessive

---

[2] By legal advisers acting for one or more of the parties and ultimately by the trial judge

or malicious or when otherwise privileged information is obtained by illegal means *(see the cases of Dubai Aluminium and Memory Corporation v Sidhu (1999) where the courts ruled that the work product of investigators was not privileged because they had broken the law in obtaining it)*. But this does not necessarily mean that the evidence will be excluded although it may be regarded as 'tainted' and lacking credibility. Breaches may also be used to discredit the investigation generally or to undermine an otherwise solid case. The rule is that investigators must not break the law.

# Important developments in the UK law

## INTRODUCTION

There are a number of new and not-so-new laws that are relevant to investigations and interviews. The most important of these are described below.

## THE POLICE AND CRIMINAL EVIDENCE ACT

The Police and Criminal Evidence Act 1984 (PACE), sets out the framework for interviews by police officers and others 'charged with the investigation of crime' when – and only when – criminal prosecution in England, Wales and Northern Ireland is contemplated. Scotland has slightly different procedures, as it would.

The English rules are ambiguous and it is far from clear whether they apply only to full-time, professionally trained investigators or to anyone (such as a human resources manager) who happens to be 'charged' on one occasion to enquire into a small matter. Lawyers, especially when they are on fees, disagree over the applicability of the rules and stated cases go both ways.

However, your safe course is to assume the widest interpretation of the Act and thus, when you:

• have reasonable grounds to believe that the suspect has committed a criminal offence,
• *and* you intend to prosecute through the criminal courts,

you should caution him with the words:

---

*Example:* 'You do not have to say anything. But it may harm your defence if you do not mention when questioned something which you later rely on in court. Anything you do say may be given in evidence.'

---

You do not have to caution a subject just because your mother-in-law thinks he has shifty eyes or because he has a pencil-thin moustache or fancy shoes. But if you have good reasons for suspecting the person has committed a criminal offence and you do not administer a caution at the appropriate time, all of your interview evidence may be ruled inadmissible *in a criminal court*. This is true even if the subject is subsequently re-interviewed and cautioned.

Once the rules have been broken, it is very difficult to get back on track. For this reason, if you suspect a serious problem and intend to prosecute, you should make sure that all interviews are handled by an experienced investigator.

*If you don't plan to prosecute, forget all about the caution*

In practice, the caution is no big deal and is unlikely to stop an honest person from giving an explanation. If it is administered at the start of the interview, in a matter-of-fact way, possibly as part of the introductory statement (see page 244), it is unlikely to frighten even the most malodorous villain[3]. However, if the caution is administered immediately the suspect makes his first damaging admission, it may be a major deterrent if for no other reason than it destroys the empathetic relationship you have already established.

*When criminal prosecution is an objective, caution the suspect at the opening of the interview*

If criminal prosecution is not an objective, you can forget all about PACE and cautions. You can use all of your persuasive skills to encourage a suspect to confess, but remember everything you do may be examined under a microscope in court (see Chapter 10), so do nothing you cannot honestly defend.

## HUMAN RIGHTS

### Objectives
The objectives of human rights legislation is to protect citizens against improper intrusion into their private lives by instruments of the State. This is all to the good. However, the interpretation of the new laws and regulations by sandal-wearers goes well beyond their intent and it is therefore important to look at their genesis and evolution.

### The European Convention on Human Rights
*The role of the European Court*
All states that have contracted to the European Convention on Human Rights, with the exception of Ireland and Norway, have incorporated its principles into their laws, enabling their domestic courts to take full account of its provisions when considering any matter. If domestic remedies are not available (for example because the complained of action is not 'lawful' under local laws, as in the Halford case discussed below) or have been exhausted, an individual may seek redress in the European Court in Strasbourg. The Strasbourg process is not a substitute for national justice, but is in a sense an extension of it and a forum for final appeal. Maggie Thatcher was right: we should never have agreed to dig the Tunnel.

The Convention empowers the European Court of Human Rights to deal with individuals' petitions and inter-state disputes. The judges are independent and elected by the Parliamentary Assembly. When the Court finds that there has been a violation of a Convention right, and if the domestic law of the state concerned allows less than complete reparation to be made, it may award the victim of *unlawful action by the state* just satisfaction (Article 50). This generally involves the reimbursement of costs and expenses and, when appropriate, compensation.

---

[3]   Mainly because he has already figured out that he can beat you

In accordance with Article 53 of the Convention, the contracting states undertake to abide by the decisions of the Court. To date, states that have been ordered to make payments under Article 50 have consistently done so.

A finding by the Court of a violation of the Convention has often led the respondent state, and sometimes even other contracting states, to take general measures to comply. The Regulation of Investigatory Powers Act 2000 (see Appendix 4 and page 157) is an example of domestic laws being changed by European court decisions.

There are six points to note with decisions by the European Court of Human Rights:

- it takes years to get a case dealt with by the court: fast it is not;
- the judges assigned, usually mob handed, to any case have seldom agreed unanimously on anything: consistent it is not;
- the compensation imposed has been minimal;
- there are no criminal penalties for violations of human rights;
- it has avoided taking tricky decisions, like to what extent (under Article 8(2)) people are entitled to privacy at work.

Finally, lawyers and smelly socks engaged in the human rights area seem to have ignored all of the cases where the European Court has ruled in favour of law enforcement.

## A FORGOTTEN CASE

A classic example is the case of *LUDI v Switzerland* (17/1991/269/340: see http://hudoc.echr.coe.int/hudoc) where it was decided that people lost their rights to privacy when they engaged on a course of criminal conduct.

The European Court may be a dead sheep, but it is not an ass.

*Details on the Convention*

There are 59 Articles in the Convention, but those of interest in the corporate fraud and area are:

Article 6 – Right to a fair trial

1.  In the determination of his civil rights and obligations or of any criminal charge against him, everyone is entitled to a fair and public hearing within a reasonable time by an independent and impartial tribunal established by law. Judgement shall be pronounced publicly but the press and public may be excluded from all or part of the trial in the interests of morals, public order or national security in a democratic society, where the interests of juveniles or the protection of the private life of the parties so require, or to the extent strictly necessary in the opinion of the court in special circumstances where publicity would prejudice the interests of justice.

2.  Everyone charged with a criminal offence shall be presumed innocent until proved guilty according to law.

3.  Everyone charged with a criminal offence has the following minimum rights:
    (a)  to be informed promptly, in a language which he understands and in detail, of the nature and cause of the accusation against him;
    (b)  to have adequate time and facilities for the preparation of his defence;

(c) to defend himself in person or through legal assistance of his own choosing or, if he has not sufficient means to pay for legal assistance, to be given it free when the interests of justice so require;

(d) to examine or have examined witnesses against him and to obtain the attendance and examination of witnesses on his behalf under the same conditions as witnesses against him;

(e) to have the free assistance of an interpreter if he cannot understand or speak the language used in court.

Article 8 – Right to respect for private and family life

1. Everyone has the right to respect for his private and family life, his home and his correspondence.
2. There shall be no interference by a public authority with the exercise of this right except such as is in accordance with the law and is necessary in a democratic society in the interests of national security, public safety or the economic well-being of the country, for the prevention of disorder or crime, for the protection of health or morals, or for the protection of the rights and freedoms of others.

Article 10 – Freedom of expression

1. Everyone has the right to freedom of expression. This right shall include freedom to hold opinions and to receive and impart information and ideas without interference by public authority and regardless of frontiers. This article shall not prevent States from requiring the licensing of broadcasting, television or cinema enterprises.
2. The exercise of these freedoms, since it carries with it duties and responsibilities, may be subject to such formalities, conditions, restrictions or penalties as are prescribed by law and are necessary in a democratic society, in the interests of national security, territorial integrity or public safety, for the prevention of disorder or crime, for the protection of health or morals, for the protection of the reputation or rights of others, for preventing the disclosure of information received in confidence, or for maintaining the authority and impartiality of the judiciary.

Article 13 – Right to an effective remedy

Everyone whose rights and freedoms as set forth in this Convention are violated shall have an effective remedy before a national authority notwithstanding that the violation has been committed by persons acting in an official capacity.

These rights have all been incorporated in the Human Rights Act 1998.

### The importance of Article 8

This article is very important from a fraud investigation point of view. It consists of two sections. Article 8(1) deals with a right to respect a person's private and family life, his home and correspondence. The European Court has been consistent in its spinning – almost dervish-like – ability to avoid giving a precise interpretation of the four elements of:

- private life;
- family life;
- home;
- correspondence.

Most judgements have been concerned with the right to respect private life, although some have involved incidental claims relating to the home, family or correspondence. For example, in a 1997 decision (*Niemeitz v Germany*) the court seemed, under the particular facts of the case, to extend 'home' to include office premises. No general conclusions can be drawn from this, and if the Eurocrats intended that people were entitled to Article 8 rights in their business lives and offices, they would have said so.

They could never argue that they kept the Convention brief to preserve ink and paper.

Article 8(2) exposes three important principles:

1   There must be a specific legal rule which authorizes action by a public authority which makes intrusion into the private lives of citizens 'lawful'. If there is no such rule, the action is 'unlawful'. So, in Euro-speak, everything is 'unlawful' unless specifically approved.
2   The individual must have adequate access to the law in question.
3   The law must be formulated with sufficient precision to enable the individual to foresee the circumstances in which the law might be applied.

The way these principles apply can be seen clearly from the case of Allison Halford.

## THE HALFORD CASE

Alison Halford, was a senior police officer in the Merseyside Constabulary. During an employment dispute, her managers tapped her office telephone and, after exhausting her remedies under English law, she took her case to the European Court of Human Rights arguing a breach of her right to privacy in her private life under Article 8(2). The court found in her favour stating that the interception was 'unlawful'. This is a misleading term and what it meant is that there was no applicable law under which a public authority could intercept communications on its own internal networks. Since there was no law under which such interception could be regulated, the result had to be 'unlawful'.

The allegations and decisions, in relation to Article 8 and Ms Halford's office telephones, can be summarized as in Table 5.3.

It is obvious from Table 5.3 that the court's decision was based on the very unusual facts of an exceptional case:

• the employer was a 'public authority' or an agency of the State: this was a key factor;
• the matter being investigated was not a crime;
• the interception was not proportionate to the matters in issue;
• the intercepted telephone was specifically designated for her private calls;
• she had been assured that she could use the telephone to seek advice in relation to her case of sexual discrimination.

The court went to some lengths *not* to draw general rules on the application of section 8(2) and to what extent people were entitled to a private life at work. Rather than being an overwhelming victory for Ms Halford, the judgment was something of a damp squib.

**Table 5.3**  The decisions in relation to Article 8

| Alleged breach of | Provisions of the Article *Comments on the Halford judgement* | Finding of the court *comments* |
|---|---|---|
| Article 8(1) | 'Everyone has the right to respect for his private and family life, his home and his correspondence' *Note that in paragraph 1 the court uses the word 'may' when dealing with the general position. In paragraph 42, the court is dealing with the specifics of the Halford case in which:* <br>• *One telephone had been specifically designated for her private use (paragraph 44)* <br>• *She had been specifically assured she could use the telephones for the purposes of her sex discrimination case* <br>• *She was given no warning that her telephones might be intercepted* | **Paragraph 1** <br>Telephone calls from business premises *may* be covered by notions of 'private life' and 'correspondence' – the applicant had a reasonable expectation of privacy <br>Conclusion: Unanimously agreed <br>**Paragraph 42** <br>The applicant argued and the commission agreed that conversations made on the telephones in Ms Halford's office at Merseyside Police Headquarters fell within the scope of 'private life' and 'correspondence' since the court in its case law had adopted a broad construction of these expressions. <br>**Paragraph 44** <br>For all of the above reasons the court concludes that the telephone calls made by Ms Halford fell within the scope of 'private life' |
| Article 8(2) | 'There shall be no interference by a public authority with the exercise of this right, except such as in accordance with the law and is necessary in a democratic society in the interests of national security, public safety or the economic well being of the country, for the prevention of disorder or crime, for the protection of health or morals, or for the rights and freedoms of others' | **Paragraph 48** <br>(… The interception had) the primary aim of gathering material to assist in the defence of the sex-discrimination proceedings. This constituted an 'interference by a public authority' <br>**Paragraph 49** <br>Interference by a 'public authority' must be in accordance with the law. Such interference was not in accordance with the law since the domestic law did not provide any regulation of calls on telecommunications systems outside the public network |

Mainly as a result of the Halford case, panic set in. The UK Government had to pass laws so that interception of private networks by public authorities could be made 'lawful'. Members of the sandal-wearing class put forward the view that companies could no longer intercept internal communications systems for any purpose. OFTEL, the British telecoms regulator, put out 'guidelines' that were, by any measure, incredible. These stated that company telephone and communication lines could *never* be intercepted; that all employers had to provide separate communications facilities (for both voice and data) on which confidentiality was guaranteed, etc, etc. You can just imagine the smelly socks wetting their knickers with excitement at the idea that companies *must* provide secure lines so that their employees can download porn from the Internet in total confidence!

Fortunately the guidelines were ignored as being excessively Mandarinesque. Their appearance does, however, highlight the tendency of bureaucrats to apply their own liberal aspirations to interpretations of the law and there are plenty of example of this, especially involving the Data Protection Act (see page 162).

## Other interpretations

There have been a number of other decisions by the European Court of interest in the fraud area. They mostly centre on Article 6 and the right to a fair trial where the main stumbling block has been the failure by law enforcement agencies to produce undercover investigators and confidential informants as witnesses at criminal trials. Defendants have argued (sometimes successfully – but with minimal compensation) that by being unable to cross-examine confidential informants, their trials were not fair.

## Human Rights Act 1998
### Background and scope

This Act came into effect in England on 2 October 2000 and incorporates most of the provisions on the European Convention on Human Rights. English court decisions will be influenced by Strasbourg which is still the court of final appeal once all domestic remedies have been exhausted.

Again the Act is primarily directed at government agencies or 'public authorities' in their relationships with the private lives of citizens. The objective of the legislation is said to be 'to strike a fair balance between the demands of the community at large and the protection of individual Human Rights'. Any interference with these rights must be in accordance with the law (i.e. 'lawful'), necessary and 'proportionate'.

If 'public authorities' break the law, there is an extensive range of remedies available, including judicial review, injunctive relief and damages. For other than public authorities, the penalties for infringement are limited to reinstating the position had the claimant's rights not been violated. There is no criminal penalty and it should be remembered that there is a great deal of difference between someone making a complaint – often with the intention of frustrating an investigation – and succeeding with it.

> *Companies and private citizens have never been convicted of any human rights violations and arguably cannot be*

### Vertical and horizontal interpretations

The scope and extent of human rights legislation is endlessly arguable (especially if the time spent doing so is subject to fees) and some lawyers say that there are two possible interpretations. The first is known as 'vertical', which means that violations can only be committed by 'public authorities' and thus the bucket of mud only spills downwards.

The second interpretation is known as 'horizontal' and this – fully supported by the sandal-wearers – means that private citizens and companies *can* interfere with the rights of others (i.e. the laws do not just apply to public authorities). Under this interpretation, the bucket of mud flies in all directions and covers everyone who happens to be around. The 'horizontal' point has been raised in both criminal and civil cases and has generally had little impact except in the lower courts and industrial tribunals. Interestingly the Regulation of Investigatory Powers Act 2000 is based on a vertical interpretation of human rights.

There is no doubt that the Human Rights Act 1998 will be influential in supporting the dreaded horizontal interpretation in that it:

- imposes a duty on public authorities to act in a way which is compatible with convention rights;

- requires all UK legislation, whenever enacted, to be interpreted by both the civil and criminal courts in a way which is compatible with convention rights.

Thus it remains to be seen whether there will be any long-term, major impact on well-established laws and precedents in the fraud area. So far it has been containable and relatively sensible, except in employment tribunals where the smelly socks seem to have lost the plot.

### The bottom line of proportionality

The common theme in both the convention and the Human Rights Act 1998 is that the action taken to investigate crime must be *proportionate* to its seriousness. This is a sensible yardstick and one which should be addressed by all potential victims as a matter of policy and in investigatory procedures (see pages 161 and 166). Other than this, commercial victims of fraud need not be too worried about human rights legislation.

## REGULATION OF INVESTIGATORY POWERS ACT 2000(RIPA)

### Background and coverage

This Act was passed so that the UK would conform to the European Convention on Human Rights, primarily in the area of communications interception by public authorities on private networks and to make cases such as Allison Halford's 'lawful'. But like kids confronted with a cookie jar, English politicians and Mandarins could not resist the urge to take matters a few steps further and the Act was extended.

The introduction states 'The main purpose of the act is to ensure that the relevant investigatory powers are used in accordance with human rights' and 'to create a new regime for the interception of communications … it goes beyond what is strictly required for human rights purposes and provides also for the changed nature of the communications industry since 1985'. RIPA repealed the Interception of Communications Act 1985.

There are six things to be noted about RIPA:

- it is one of the worst drafted convoluted acts in the history of convoluted acts;
- it is primarily directed at 'public authorities' and intrusions into the private lives of citizens;
- it is based on a vertical interpretation of human rights legislation (see page 151);
- it creates masses of confusion and exceptions;
- there were no transitional arrangements;
- it adds unnecessary, and arguably insecure, bureaucracy to the investigatory process with the creation of quangos and jobs for the boys.

However, the act does not remove (at least yet) most of the investigatory powers needed by businesses to detect, investigate and recover from fraud. But victims do have to understand the fine print and have procedures in place to avoid violations of both the criminal and civil law. This is the key.

The coverage of the act can be summarized as in Table 5.4.

**Table 5.4**  Coverage of the Regulation of Investigatory Powers Act 2000 and Regulations

| Law | Applicability | | |
|---|---|---|---|
| | Public authorities acting as an agency of the State | Public authorities acting as a business See Section 4(7) of the Act | Companies and firms i.e. businesses |
| PART 1: Chapter 1: Communications: Interceptions of Communications Transmissions | | | |
| | Imposes criminal penalties and authorization methods | | |
| • Public networks | Home Office warrant | Not applicable | Not applicable |
| • Private networks | Permission of the person having control etc. (see below) | | |
| • Public postal service | Home Office warrant | Not applicable | Not applicable |
| • Private postal service | Permission of the person having control etc. (see below) | | |
| PART 1: Chapter 2: Acquisition and Disclosure of Communications Data (e.g. call logging) | | | |
| | Sets out authorization methods but no criminal penalties | | |
| • Public networks | Rights to obtain | Not applicable | |
| • Private networks | | | |
| PART 2: Surveillance and Covert Human Intelligence Sources | | | |
| | Sets out authorization methods but no criminal penalties | | |
| | Authorization methods | Not applicable | |
| PART 3: Electronic Data Protected by Encryption etc. | | | |
| | Sets out authorization methods but no criminal penalties | | |
| | Authorization methods Access rights | Not applicable | |

For each of these areas, the Act will *(but does not yet do so)* ensure that the law clearly covers:

- the purpose for which the powers may be used;
- which authorities can use the powers;
- who should authorize each use of the power;
- the use that can be made of the material gained;
- independent judicial oversight;
- a means of redress for the individual.

Various quangos have been established – such as the Surveillance Commission and the Interception of Communications Commission – to confirm 'lawful authority' monitoring and approval processes for public authorities. Also statutory instruments, rules, guidelines and codes of practice have been written, again primarily for *public authorities*.

# Communications interception
## Communications transmissions
Section 1 of Part 1, Chapter 1 makes it a criminal offence – punishable by an unlimited fine and up to two years imprisonment – for any person intentionally and without lawful authority to intercept a 'communications transmission' on a private or public network. Section 1(3) creates a separate civil liability for interception of communications transmissions without lawful authority.

## Definitions
A private communications system is defined as:

> any telecommunication system which, without itself being a public telecommunication system, is a system in relation to which the following conditions are satisfied:
>
> (a) it is attached, directly or indirectly and whether or not for the purposes of the communication in question, to a public telecommunication system; and
> (b) there is apparatus comprised in the system which is both located in the United Kingdom and used (with or without other apparatus) for making the attachment to the public telecommunication system;

Some lawyers have made the point that the word 'attached' is pivotal and thus argue that 'internal loops' or 'internal extensions' as well as 'radio extensions' are not part of the private system because they are not 'attached'. This is probably an unsustainable argument.

However, an 'entirely self-standing system' (such as an intranet) is not to be regarded as a 'private communications system'. The safe line for businesses is to work on the basis that any voice or data communications system is covered by the Act and regulations made thereunder.

The definitions of 'public telecommunications service', 'public telecommunications system', 'telecommunications service' and 'telecommunications system' are wonderfully owlish but mean what they say. They are communications systems provided to a substantial section of the public, such as that provided by British Telecom.

Section 2(2) states:

> a person intercepts a communication in the course of its transmission by means of a telecommunications system if, and only if, he:
>
> (a) so modifies or interferes with the system or its operation
> (b) so monitors transmissions made by means of the system
> (c) so monitors transmissions made by wireless telegraphy to or from an apparatus comprised in the system
>
> as to make some or all of the contents of the communication available, while being transmitted, to a person other than the sender or intended recipient of the communication.

## Interception of public networks

As far as the interception of communications transmissions on public networks is concerned, lawful authority comes from a specific warrant issued by the Home Secretary to a short list of eligible government agencies, such as the police, Customs and Excise or the security services. Companies and individuals cannot apply for a Home Office warrant to intercept communications transmissions on public networks.

## Interception on private networks

For a private communications system, removal of criminal liability under section 1(2) is achieved under four main provisions:

- Section 1(6) when the person with the right to control the system gives permission;
- Section 3(1) with the consent of both the sender and the recipient;
- Section 3(2) with the consent of either the sender or the recipient and, for public authorities only, subject to the surveillance conditions in section 48(2);
- Section 5 under the authority of a warrant signed by the Home Secretary.

Most businesses (and police when intercepting a private network) will rely on permission of the controller (section 1(6)) which removes criminal liability. However, there is a second condition of authorization for 'lawful authority'

Lawful authority to intercept communications on a private network will normally be derived from:

- a Section 5 warrant signed by the Home Secretary;
- the consent of one or more of the parties to the communication;
- compliance with the Telecommunications (Lawful Business Practice)(Interception of Communications) Regulations 2000 (the Regulations).

The Regulations came into effect on 24 October 2000 and are very important to businesses:

- Section 2(a) of the Regulations states 'references to a business include references to activities of a government department, or any public authority or of any person or office holder on whom functions are conferred by or under any enactment'. This implies that government departments are put on the same footing as businesses when investigating internal fraud relating to their statutory obligations.
- Section 3 sets out the conditions for 'lawful interception' including 3(1)(a)(iii) 'for the purpose of preventing crime' and then subject to section 3(2) which has three main conditions:
    - (a) the interception in question is effected solely for the purpose of monitoring or (where appropriate) keeping a record of communications relevant to the systems controller's business;
    - (b) the telecommunications system in question is provided for use wholly or partly in connection with that business;
    - (c) the system controller has made all reasonable efforts to inform every person who may use the telecommunications system in question that communications transmitted by means thereof may be intercepted.

Unsurprisingly, the Regulations do not state what constitutes 'all reasonable efforts', to advise users that communications transmissions might be intercepted, but common sense suggests that a statement in a staff handbook to the effect that employees are allowed to use communications systems on the express understanding that from time-to-time they might be monitored would be sufficient.

But what happens if a business discovers a serious fraud, where interception of communications would be proportionate, but has not already advised potential users of that possibility? Would it be 'reasonable' to publish a statement about communications interception and thus put the crooks on specific notice? Experts argue that it would be 'reasonable' to do nothing until the current suspicions have been resolved and then to issue a policy. The Home Office and police appear to have relied on this interpretation in a number of recent cases involving interception of private systems, although the issue has yet to be tested in court.

### Exceptions

It should be noted that the Regulations apply to interception of communications transmissions. They do not apply to cases where:

- a room is subject to audio or video monitoring using a linear microphone or other device that is licensed under the Wireless and Telegraphy Act, for example, by an adapted baby alarm, infrared or microwave transmitter;
- a linear microphone or other legal device is placed in a room or vehicle which incidentally picks up only one side of a communications transmission, even if the signal is transmitted to a receiver using telecommunications lines;
- emanations from a computer are collected on a passive receiver: neither would such a device contravene the Computer Misuse Act 1990;
- keystrokes entered into a computer terminal are captured by a buffering device and then transmitted by a legal transmitter to a receiver;
- a voicemail system is accessed after messages have been read by the intended recipient.

However, the techniques that a victim will use in any investigation should be approved as part of a fraud policy, which sets out authorization and other procedures. A model fraud policy can be downloaded from www.cobasco.com.

### Admissibility of intercept evidence

Section 17 of the Act repeats the principles of the Interception of Communications Act 1985 to the extent that transcripts of communications intercepted under the authority of a Home Office warrant – and any matters relating to them – cannot normally be introduced in evidence in legal proceedings, although there are some exceptions.

There is nothing to prevent intercept evidence being introduced in either civil or criminal courts when it was obtained by consent or under the authority of the system controller.

### Anomalies

If a private communications system is intercepted under the Regulations without employees and others potentially involved being informed, the behaviour is technically unlawful. If it is unlawful, it fails the second part of the test of Section 1(2) and should therefore be a criminal offence. This conundrum is resolved by Section 1(6) which is definitive. Thus it is not illegal to intercept communications transmissions on a private network without prior warning to the potential users. It might, however, still be unlawful under Section 1(3) and give rise to a civil claim for damages. What, if anything, these might be will be determined on a case-by-case basis but it should be emphasized that, in practice, neither the police nor the Home Office believe that a pre-warning is necessary. A decision chart summarizing the important aspects of communications transmission is at Appendix 4.

## Businesses and other sections of RIPA

No regulations have been issued for the business sector clarifying other sections of the Act covering the use of call-logging data, surveillance, or human and semi-human intelligence sources. Further regulations covering these areas is likely to coincide with the creation of the Security Industry Board (to be established under the Private Industry Security Act 2001: see www.hmso.gov.uk/acts/acts2001/20010012.htm) and goodness knows what will happen then.

Public authorities have been overwhelmed with paper on the rules covering directed, covert and intrusive surveillance, use of covert human intelligence sources, interference with property and officers working undercover (see www.homeoffice.gov.uk/ripa/). The point to note is that everything is directed at public authorities and based on the principles of lawful authority and proportionality.

Thus as matters now stand, business victims are able to access call-logging data, use covert, directed intrusive and other forms of surveillance and human intelligence sources without offending RIPA. The only restrictions are that the disclosure of call-logging data obtained from a public communications carrier must not contravene the Telecommunications Act 1984 (which it should not if the investigation of crime is concerned) and the Data Protection Act, of which more later. Surveillance must not contravene the laws on trespass or the Prevention from Harassment Act 1997. Also companies should consider their position on access to encrypted data and keys (Part 3 of the Act). All of these matters should be covered in a fraud policy (see pages 161 and 404).

## DATA PROTECTION ACT

This is another piece of legislation where liberal interpretation runs ahead of literal intent, and oiks up and down the country are using its provisions as a cover for their own incompetence or to build empires. The first thing to remember is that the Act only applies to personal data processed on a computer or through a relevant filing system. It is not a privacy act, nor a 'let's be nice to crooks' act, despite what the chattering classes might wish. Thus even the collection and use of even the most personal information does not fall within the data protection regime unless it is to be processed by a computer or retained in a 'relevant filing system', of which more later.

## THE SOHAM MURDERS

We should never forget the tragic murder of Holly Wells and Jessica Chapman in Soham and the outcry that followed the conviction of Ian Huntley. It emerged that this man had been recruited as the caretaker of the school, which the girls attended, without the management being told of his previous history of sex with under-aged girls and alleged rape.

The Chief Constable of Humberside suggested that to comply with the Data Protection Act his force had deleted intelligence records after a month, in the process removing those relating to Huntley. He was rightly pilloried and has since lost his job, but the Information Commissioner, whose statements and guidelines had run amok, ran for cover. He too should have been required to resign as most people involved in law enforcement had long complained that his interpretations of the act had been far too liberal and pervasive.

In December 2003, the Court of Appeal in the case of Michael John Durant and Financial Services Authority (see www.courtservice.gov.uk/judgementsfiles/j2136/durant v FSA) struck a blow to the heart of those that were building empires from data protection legislation by ruling on the definition of 'personal data' and the extent to which non-computerized manual filing systems fell within the provisions of the act. It was a landmark decision that totally exposes many of the Information Commissioner's guidelines on such things as CCTV monitoring, interception of communications and HR policies and procedures.

On the matter of what is and what isn't 'personal data', the Court of Appeal gave a very narrow definition (remember, in any event, it only applies to automatic processing) and excluded 'information which has as its focus something other than the individual (for example a transaction or document)' and continued that not all information retrieved from a computer search on an individual's name is necessarily personal data.

The court also ruled on what did and did not constitute a 'relevant filing system', resulting in the Information Commissioner conceding, '... Following the Durant judgement it is likely that very few manual files will be covered by the Data Protection Act'. For convenience, we refer to 'relevant filing systems' that might be covered by the data protection regime as 'structured'; there will be very few of them. For example, investigation case files (and thus data collected in respect of them) and most personnel files do not fall within the provisions of the data protection legislation. It is also likely that CCTV recordings will also be excluded, although this aspect has yet to be challenged in court. The bottom line of the Durant case is that it brought reality back to the data protection world: and not before time!

The Data Protection Act is based on the following important principles for the processing of personal data when it is being processed by means of equipment operating automatically. It must be:

- fairly and lawfully processed;
- processed for limited purposes;
- adequate, relevant and not excessive;
- accurate;
- kept no longer than is necessary;
- processed in accordance with the data subject's rights;
- not transferred outside Europe.

To comply with these very fair principles, controllers of computers and the *very rare* structured manual systems must register with, or notify, the Information Commissioner (the artiste formerly known as the 'Data Protection Registrar' or 'Data Protection Commissioner') and conform with various standards.

It is an offence under Section 17 to process personal data etc., without first making the appropriate registration. Under Section 22 the Commissioner is required to assess the notification and it may be declined if it appears that processing will cause substantial damage, distress or otherwise significantly prejudice the rights and freedoms of the data subject. Otherwise if the Commissioner is satisfied, the appropriate entry will be made in the register, which is accessible to the public.

Part IV of the Act makes substantial exemptions for specified purposes including (under section 29(1)) the prevention or detection of crime, the apprehension or prosecution of offenders and the assessment or collection of taxes. The Commissioner has extensive powers to issue enforcement notices and to require the production of information.

Section 55 makes it a criminal offence for any person, knowingly or recklessly, without the consent of the data controller to obtain or disclose personal data, except (under subsection (2)) when the person shows that:

- the obtaining, disclosing or procuring was necessary for the purpose of preventing or detecting crime or was otherwise authorized;
- that he acted in the reasonable belief that he had the right in law to procure, disclose etc.;
- that he acted in the reasonable belief that he would have had the consent of the data controller;
- that in the particular circumstances the obtaining, disclosing etc. was justified in the public interest.

Section 55(4) makes it a criminal offence for anyone to sell, or offer to sell, illegally obtained personal data. Interestingly, Section 56 states that it is a criminal offence for a person to require a data subject to supply a record which relates to his criminal convictions or cautions in connection with recruitment, continued employment or the provision of services, 'unless it is in the public interest'.

Section 56(4) clarifies the position and specifically states that requiring the production of certificates of criminal records (under Part V of the Police Act 1997) is 'not ... justified as being in the public interest on the ground that it would assist in the prevention or detection of crime'. This is a good example of political duplicity. On one hand businesses are held liable if they recruit bad people and on the other the law takes away a critical means of checking.

A few recent decisions also illustrate how the law is being applied and the scope of data protection legislation being extended far beyond its principles: the Soham case was just one of many.

## CLOSED CIRCUIT TELEVISION

In November 2001, the Information Commissioner put out guidelines for the use of closed circuit television (CCTV) in public places and the collection and processing of images. It is difficult to see how CCTV can be regarded as a computer or structured manual system. Fortunately, exceptions apply when a specific crime is being investigated, although for general crime prevention purposes, warnings that recordings might be made have to be displayed.

## NUMERICAL NONSENSE

Mandarins working for the Information Commission do not like British people being able to work out the identity and address of a telephone subscriber from his telephone number. Goodness knows why. In most other EU countries, whose laws are based on the same convention, the reverse telephone directory is part of the service. In France, not only can you reverse the number, the Website gives a street map showing adjacent subscribers, their telephone numbers and also the photographs of the buildings concerned.

Our requests to the Information Commissioner for clarification of its interpretation all went unanswered. The reason is obvious: they cannot justify it!

## CANCER RESEARCH

The Head of the Institute of Cancer Research has complained that the Department of Health would not supply information on doctors who have patients who could benefit from the treatment.

## DESTRUCTION OF EVIDENCE

In March 2001, the Divisional Court remitted a case for reconsideration in the Crown Court because, presumably under the Data Protection Act's retention provisions, police had destroyed video evidence that might have been potentially relevant. The defendant argued that absence of the evidence deprived him of the right to a fair trial. The court agreed.

The fact is that even the most sensitive data can be collected, processed and retained providing the proper registration has been made and other standards, subject to data access conditions are met and disclosure is made only to registered third parties. For example, data supplied by employees on their job application forms, pension plans, salary, transaction records and just about anything else can be processed for crime prevention and investigation purposes.

## OFFICIAL SECRETS AND POLICE RECORDS

Although the all-embracing Section 2 of the Official Secrets Act 1911 has been repealed, many of its provisions have been replaced by the Data Protection Act and the circumstances in which government bodies can disclose information are very limited.

Thus for any professional investigator, vehicle licensing, police and other governmental records are absolutely taboo and under no circumstances, short of a court order, should they be sought. Even the most mild attempt to obtain them can result in criminal prosecution under the Data Protection Act, and deservedly so.

However, at the appropriate time, suspects can be asked to obtain a certificate from the Criminal Records Bureau under Part IV of the Police Act 1997. The result is admissible in both civil and criminal proceedings.

## OTHER STUFF

In recent years, many of the large English Law firms put out papers, held lunches, breakfasts, teas, suppers, soirées, love-ins, workshops and clinics on the Human Rights Act 1998, RIPA and other worrisome legislation. It is flavour of the year. The result has been to spread panic and dismay among the great unwashed in investigative communities and to deter victims of fraud from retaining them, unless under the umbrella of the law firm concerned. This is clever marketing by the lawyers, and who can blame them?

The legislation, subject to forebodings of immediate doom has included those in Table 5.5:

**Table 5.5**   Effects of legislation on investigatory procedures

| Law or regulation<br>*What the chattering classes say you cannot do* | What you can do<br>How to do it |
| --- | --- |
| Computer Misuse Act 1990<br>*You cannot carry out a covert examination of an employee's computer*<br>*You cannot passively collect emanations from a computer* | There is no restriction on accessing the company's own equipment<br>A policy which would allow companies to examine personal computers owned by the employee and used for business purposes<br>There is no restriction |
| Copyright Act 1945<br>*You cannot photocopy trash without the owner's permission* | This may be a civil breach. The wronged party would have to show that he had been financially damaged |
| Criminal Justice and Public Order Act 1994 and Vagrancy Act 1861<br>*You cannot enter onto enclosed premises to pick up trash* | This act only applies where entry onto premises is related to a criminal act. Trash collection should never be a crime |
| Criminal Procedure and Investigations Act 1996<br>*You have to disclose intelligence to the opposing side. Therefore, it is best not to record it* | Disclosure will be determined by lawyers at the appropriate time. Confidential informants and privileged information can be protected |
| Customs and Excise Management Act 1979<br>*Impersonating an officer is a criminal offence* | CORRECT. This is illegal (under Section 13) and impersonating any official should not be contemplated |
| Data Protection Act 1998<br>*You cannot access call logging information*<br>*You cannot access personnel files*<br>*You cannot use personal data for automated fraud detection purposes*<br>*You cannot use pretext investigations*<br>*You cannot get out of bed in the morning* | All incorrect. It is wise to make sure that registration under the Data Protection Act is comprehensive. There are exceptions when crime is being prevented or detected |
| Freedom of Information Act 2000<br>*This will have a major impact on the access rights of people and companies to sensitive information* | The act has been delayed or abandoned until 2004 |
| Human Rights Act 1998<br>*May be used as a reason for doing nothing* | The act is not a charter for crooks and, properly interpreted is fair and sensible |

| Law or regulation<br>*What the chattering classes say you cannot do* | What you can do<br>How to do it |
|---|---|
| Official Secrets Act 1911 and 1989<br>*You cannot obtain details of a person's convictions or other evidence from an official database* | You can, providing the information is not required in connection with employment or continued employment. |
| Police Act 1998 and the Data Protection Act<br>*You cannot ask a person to produce a certificate of conviction during the recruitment process* | CORRECT. See above. You can ask under other circumstances. When the Criminal Records Bureau (see its website www crcb.gov.uk) is operational, employers will have access to information that can be used to eliminate unsuitable candidates |
| Police and Criminal Evidence Act 1984<br>*If managers and auditors do not administer a caution at the appropriate time, all interview evidence will be inadmissible*<br>*Auditors and others need to overtly tape record interviews and follow police procedures* | The need to caution is determined on a case by case basis and only applies to criminal proceedings. Each company should determine who is 'charged with the investigation of crime' and whether or not they should administer a caution and the procedure for tape recording |
| Prevention of Corruption Act 1906 and 1916<br>Public Bodies Corrupt Practices Act 1889<br>*You cannot pay for confidential information* | CORRECT. It is likely to amount to corruption |
| Privacy Act<br>*You cannot ask personal questions* | There is no Privacy Act in the UK, although smelly socks would argue that a combination of RIPA and the Data Protection Act achieves the same objectives |
| Private Security Industry Act 2001<br>*You must be an accredited investigator*<br>*You must hold the appropriate licence*<br>*You must be a member of a professional organization* | The Security Industry Board does not yet operate |
| Protection from Harassment Act 1997<br>*You cannot carry out surveillance* | The targets should never detect that they are under surveillance. Thus harassment should not be an issue |
| Public Interest Disclosure Act 1999<br>*You must have a whistle blowing procedure* | Optional. If you don't have a policy your rights of redress, if a malicious third party disclosure is made, are limited. So please get a fraud policy in place. A template can be downloaded, free of charge, from www.cobasco.com |
| Regulation of Investigatory Powers Act<br>*You cannot tap your own computer and communications systems*<br>*You cannot use intercepted material in evidence*<br>*You cannot obtain call logging data*<br>*You cannot search personal property on company premises*<br>*You cannot carry out surveillance (intrusive or otherwise)*<br>*You cannot use undercover investigators or informants*<br>*You cannot use vehicle tracking equipment* | You can, although public authorities must comply with codes of practice. Commercial organizations should have equivalent procedures, although this is not mandatory (see Appendix 4 and page 157) |

| Law or regulation<br>*What the chattering classes say you cannot do* | What you can do<br>How to do it |
|---|---|
| Rehabilitation of Offenders Act 1974<br>*You cannot ask about a person's criminal convictions* | You can. He is entitled, however, not to disclose 'spent' convictions |
| Telecommunications (Data Protection and Privacy) Regulations 1999<br>*You cannot intercept communications* | You can with appropriate authority. See page 157 and Appendix 4 |
| Telecommunications (Lawful Business Practice)(Interception of Communications) Regulations<br>*You cannot intercept communications* | |
| Telecommunications Act 1984<br>*You cannot obtain call logging data (Section 45)*<br>*Pretext calls are 'offensive' and contravene Section 43*<br>*Pretext calls are illegal because they are a 'nuisance'* | There is an exception for the investigation of any criminal offence |
| Theft Act 1978 et seq<br>*You cannot carry out pretext investigations*<br>*You cannot carry out trash searches* | You can under controlled conditions. See page 170<br>You can |
| Trespass (Civil)<br>*You cannot enter onto enclosed premises to pick up trash* | You can. If you are asked to leave, you must do so. There is an offence under Section 4 of the Vagrancy Act 1861 of being in enclosed premises for an unlawful purpose |
| Wireless and Telegraphy Act 1948<br>*You cannot use bugging devices* | You can, providing they are of an approved type and, when communications transmissions are being intercepted, comply with RIPA |
| Wireless and Telegraphy Regulations 2001<br>*You cannot use bugging devices*<br>*You cannot intercept communications*<br>*You cannot fit a tracking device to a vehicle personally owned by a suspect* | You can, especially when the prevention or detection of crime is concerned<br>There is no restriction providing only magnetic attachments are used and there is no damage to property. There is similarly no breach of RIPA or the Wireless and Telegraphy Acts |

A reason can always be found for doing nothing and it is true that great care has to be taken in all investigations. The best protection is always to work with experienced litigation lawyers and professional investigators.

## Intelligence and evidence

### INTELLIGENCE

A phrase often heard in investigations is: 'We know he did it, but we don't have any evidence.' This is rarely correct. In many investigations information (or intelligence, which is essentially the same thing and consists of knowledge, suspicions, deductions and extrapolations made therefrom) is uncovered suggesting that X did Y or something else happened. Often intelligence is dismissed but it is critical and turning it into 'evidence' calls for a combination of legal and investigative skills.

## EVIDENCE

*Evidence is simply facts, relating to a matter in issue, which are admissible in court*

Ultimately, the judge in the case concerned, will decide what is admissible and what it not. There is nothing magic or difficult about evidence. There are a number of categories of evidence as shown in Table 5.6.

**Table 5.6**   Types of evidence

| Type of evidence<br>*Examples* | How it is presented in court | How it is collated by the investigator |
|---|---|---|
| Oral evidence<br>*What the suspect said when he was interviewed* | Given on oath from the witness box by a person with first hand knowledge of the facts at issue | In statements (including his own), Proofs of Evidence, affidavits or transcripts of tape recordings |
| Documentary evidence<br>*False purchase invoices* | Produced by a witness as part of his oral evidence. Items which are produced to a court by a witness are normally called 'EXHIBITS' | Originals, copies and schedules prepared by the witnesses |
| Photocopies of original exhibits<br>*Photocopies of sales invoices* | Produced by a witness as part of his oral evidence, providing the court is satisfied that the originals are no longer available | Copies, extracts and schedules prepared by a witness |
| Copies of overseas bank accounts and other records | Produced by an employee from the bank concerned as part of his oral evidence or by another witness under the Criminal Evidence Acts | Certified copies and schedules prepared by the witness |
| Real evidence<br>*Stolen goods and weapons* | Produced by a witness as part of his oral evidence | Produced in court or illustrated by photographs |
| Tape and video recordings<br>*Of interviews with the suspect or telephone calls made by him* | Produced by a witness as part of his oral evidence | The original recording and a transcript may be produced in court |
| Expert evidence<br>*Opinion by a computer technician* | Expert evidence is one of the main exceptions to the hearsay rule. The Expert may give evidence under oath of his opinion concerning some or all of the facts in issue | Proof of Evidence or statement |
| Computerized evidence<br>*Disks, tapes, printouts etc.* | Produced by a witness as part of his oral evidence. The witness must be able to establish the exhibit was produced in the normal course of business on a computer of proven reliability | Proof of Evidence or statement. Original or copies of computer media |

Real evidence is a physical item that is relevant to the facts in issue, for example a gun in a murder case, a fraudulent invoice or a screwdriver used in a burglary. Real evidence is produced as an 'exhibit' by a witness who has first-hand knowledge of its relevance.

## THE NEED TO ESTABLISH CONTINUITY

Witnesses must be able to establish continuity or the 'chain' between the time an exhibit came into their possession and its production in court. *For example, an investigator will need to show how, when, where and by whom a document was recovered and how it was handled from that time to its production in court.* This makes it imperative that accurate records are maintained. Equally as important, the witness must satisfy the court over the integrity of the exhibit, confirming that it has not been altered in any way.

## HEARSAY EVIDENCE

Evidence in criminal cases must usually be given – under oath – by a witness who has first-hand knowledge of the facts in issue. *For example, if A who is accused of a crime, makes an admission to B who repeats it to C:*

- B can give evidence against A stating what A told him;
- C cannot give evidence against A because he was not present at the conversation between A and B. Thus his evidence is 'hearsay'.

In some civil cases, hearsay evidence will be admitted at the discretion of the judge.
Equivalent rules apply to documentary and other evidence.

> *Example.* A clerk who prepared a purchase order can go into the witness box, produce it as an exhibit and can be cross-examined by the opposing side about its contents. Any evidence from the clerk's manager (who has no first-hand knowledge of the document) may be excluded under the 'hearsay' rules.

There are some important exceptions to the hearsay rule. Some witnesses, who are recognized by the court as experts, are able to express an opinion.

> *Example.* A document examiner may express his opinion that a certain person's handwriting is on a document. Computer evidence may be exhibited by a witness who has no first-hand knowledge of the transactions concerned, but who is able to prove to the court that the records concerned were produced in the ordinary course of business by a system of proven reliability.

## ENTRAPMENT AND AGENT PROVOCATEUR

Lawyers will sometimes argue that their clients have been entrapped into committing a crime by an unscrupulous investigator or confidential informant. Again the allegation is easily made but far more difficult to sustain. Entrapment means cajoling someone into committing a crime they would not otherwise commit. If the crime – or a continuum of dishonest activity – is ongoing and an investigator or informant infiltrates it, this is not entrapment.

In some cases, and the brutal murder of Rachel Nickell on Wimbledon Common is a tragic example, investigators may approach the suspect on a pretext to gain his trust in the hope of discovering real evidence, such as the knife used or some feature of the crime known only to the perpetrator. The trial judge in Rachel's case was unjustly scathing over the approach used by the police and excluded damning evidence on grounds that were clear to him but less clear to anyone else. This case aside, investigators can infiltrate criminal groups with the resulting evidence being admissible.

However, whatever the circumstances, undercover investigations, infiltration and pretexts must be handled with care and under advice of experienced litigation lawyers. If the undercover investigator or confidential informant is not prepared to give evidence in a criminal trial, that fact should be made clear to the prosecuting authorities at the outset as the defendant's inability to cross-examine him may result in a breach of the fair trial principle under the European Convention of Human Rights.

## LIBEL AND SLANDER

People who are the subject of investigation sometimes threaten to take action because they claim that they have been libelled or slandered. In most cases, these threats should be viewed as being no more than a ploy to throw the investigation off course.

Libel is an untrue defamatory statement in a permanent form: usually in writing. Slander is oral libel and is governed by similar rules. It is obvious that anything which is true cannot be libel or slander.

An accusation made directly to a suspect that the interviewer believes him responsible for dishonesty is not slanderous. Similarly, an unproved, or even incorrect, allegation to a potential witness will not normally be actionable because it is privileged under the common business interest rule.[4] However, an unproved and untrue defamatory statement, for example, that someone is a thief, made in public or to a person who does not have a common business interest, may be actionable.

In proceedings for libel or slander, the claimant must establish that the words used about him were *untrue,* defamatory and lowered his estimation in the minds of right thinking people (i.e. not readers of the *Sun*). Interestingly, in the extremely nauseating fight between Neil Hamilton and Mohamed Fayed it was argued that neither could be defamed, as their reputations were already in tatters. This is an interesting concept, but not relevant to fraud.

In any case the claimant has to prove that the statement was made to at least one person, other than the defendant's wife, and that it caused him some quantifiable damage. There is a vast difference between threatening to take action for alleged defamation and succeeding. Besides that, during the discovery and legal processes, which result from the libel action, the claimant may be compelled to produce records that destroy his case and provide evidence of other transgressions. Threatening action for libel is easy: seeing it through to success can be a very unwise move for the crook.

There are a number of defences to actions for libel and slander:

- *Justification*: The burden of proof is on the defendant to show that the statement was substantially true. *For example, in the British case of the Observer v Redgrave the general article was substantiated although some words could not be justified. The court determined that libel had not*

---

[4]    See 'Information Privileged against Disclosure' earlier in this chapter

*been committed.* Thus if a defendant can prove that the allegations were substantially true, he will not be penalized.

- *Legal professional privilege*: Communication between a lawyer and his client is absolutely privileged (see pages 145 and 149).

Thus it is only in exceptional circumstances that the victim of fraud, or someone working on his behalf, could be successfully prosecuted for slander or libel. However, all Investigators must act fairly, and respect the rights of those with whom they deal.

## TAPE RECORDING

Laws vary from country to country on the legality of tape recording conversations without the consent of all of the parties concerned. In the USA, covert tape recording is legal in some states and illegal in others. In England recordings can be made secretly by any party to a conversation and the resulting tapes are admissible in civil and criminal proceedings.

## STATEMENTS AND PROOFS OF EVIDENCE

Statements made by suspects and witnesses are vital in fraud cases and are used by counsel to lead the witness through his evidence. If he fails to 'come up to proof' his statement can be used to cross-examine him as a hostile witness. In civil cases statements may be read by the lawyers concerned without the need to call the witness.

All formal statements (whether the witness is called or not) have to be disclosed to the opposing party but unsigned Proofs of Evidence *(obtained in contemplation of legal proceedings and possibly including the same material as in a statement)* are normally protected against disclosure by Legal Professional Privilege. Thus in the early stage of most investigations Proofs of Evidence are preferable to formal statements. Ultimately, lawyers will determine whether disclosure is necessary.

Under the Criminal Justice Act and the Magistrate's Court Act 1980, witnesses may make a statement on a special form which certifies that it is true and correct and on the understanding if it is untrue they could be exposed to criminal prosecution for perjury. Such statements are very useful, but should only be used by experienced investigators. An example of the form is at Appendix 3.

## DOCUMENTARY EVIDENCE

### General provisions

Documents, which are relevant to the facts in issue, may be produced in court (as 'exhibits') by a witness giving evidence under oath. In most countries, the originals are considered the best evidence but when these are not available, copies may be admitted.

In some developing and transitional countries, the original documents are vital and, if they cannot be produced, the evidence is lost forever. Unsurprisingly, there are a lot of document-eating dogs and spontaneous combustions in such jurisdictions.

There is no generally available authority given to a fraud victim to demand access to, or to search for, documents in the possession of third parties. This is the starting point, but there are some exceptions.

## Cooperation

Often third parties, such as customers and suppliers, will cooperate voluntarily in a fraud investigation and produce records in the hope that business relations with the corporate victim will not suffer. The victim's position is obviously enhanced if in its Standard Terms and Conditions of Business it has rights to audit the records of suppliers, distributors, agents and others with whom it has a commercial relationship.

## Civil Action for Discovery

Where the cooperation of third parties or defendants is unlikely to be forthcoming, lawyers should be consulted with a view to taking a civil action, to obtain pre-emptive orders for important evidence in the possession of innocent third parties as well as the suspects.

## Citizens' Arrest

In the UK under Section 24(4)–(7) of the Police and Criminal Evidence Act 1984, 'any person may arrest anyone without a warrant' providing:

- the person to be arrested is in the act of committing an arrestable offence (this includes all thefts and frauds);
- the person making the arrest has reasonable grounds for suspecting him to be committing such an offence;
- where an arrestable offence has been committed … a person may arrest anyone who is guilty of the offence or anyone whom he has reasonable grounds for suspecting to be guilty of it.

This is an important power, available to all citizens, especially if a person is caught while trying to remove or destroy evidence. All that is necessary is to tell the person he is being arrested and to take him to a police station or call for police assistance as soon as possible. Reasonable force can be used (see Section 3 of the Criminal Law Act 1967), but great care must be taken in all cases, especially when the villain is larger than the investigator and is with his mother or dog.

## Searches on the employer's premises

Employers are entitled to search anything, but not any person, on their premises. This means that desks, briefcases, cupboards or computers used by a suspect and owned by the victim may be searched. This has become a potentially controversial area (because of human rights legislation) but the dangers can be minimized by covering the employer's rights in a fraud policy.

## Searches of third party premises

The owner of any premises, or a manager in charge of them, may give permission to search. Permission may be revoked, in which case the documents or other evidence concerned must be returned without delay, although copies may be retained.

The consent of third parties must not be obtained by deceit or trickery, otherwise the Investigator could be accused of the serious criminal offence of obtaining property by deception under the Theft Act 1968 et seq.

## COMPUTER EVIDENCE

### Legality

Particular attention should be paid to the acquisition and preservation of computer evidence. Again, the investigator must comply with a raft of new legislation. Computers owned by the company can be accessed overtly or covertly without the user's permission when crime is being investigated. However, it would be illegal to access a laptop computer, Personal Desktop Assistant (PDA) or mobile telephone memory owned by an individual, even when it is on company premises, without his permission. If he has used diskettes paid for by the company, even on his personal computer, there is a strong argument that they can be copied and examined without his authority.

The Regulation of Investigatory Powers Act 2000 gives government investigators the right to demand the production of encryption keys. There is no equivalent in the business world. Thus businesses should address this issue in their fraud policy (see page 161).

### Evidence required

Wherever possible, original media, such as disks, diskettes, tapes etc. should be obtained. There are two main reasons for this:

- *Admissibility*: The courts in most countries have ruled that, to be held admissible, computer evidence must have been produced in the normal course of business and on a machine of proven reliability. Copies taken for other than normal processing requirements or special reports might be inadmissible.
- *Integrity*: It is possible original computer media contains data in image or digital form which will not be read by a copy program. For example, deleted files remain on the original disk until their space is overwritten by new data but are not read by normal copying and back-up utilities. Thus computers should only be examined by qualified experts so that full and accurate images are obtained.

## CONCLUSION

The laws are complex and evolving. It is essential that investigations comply with the highest legal and ethical standards, while standing a realistic chance of exposing crooks. Balance (or proportionality) is critical as is good advice from experienced litigation lawyers especially in difficult or complex cases.

However, the bottom line is – that despite the cravings of the Information Commissioner and other jobsworths – the law does not prohibit piercing investigations and interviews when crime is suspected.

# Steps in an investigation

## OVERALL PLAN

Most major investigations should be planned in the stages in Table 5.7.

Column 1 shows that time should be taken in planning the *first step*, which is the point at which those under suspicion first get to hear that this is the case. The first step must be an ambush.

**Table 5.7**   The eight stages of major investigations

| Stage | | Description | Principles |
|---|---|---|---|
| TAKE YOUR TIME | 1 | Deal with initial suspicions | Maintain total confidentiality<br>Assume the suspicions are true<br>Do not rush to report externally<br>Consider if and when the police should be advised |
| | 2 | Plan and prepare to strike | OBTAIN BACKGROUND INFORMATION<br>Prepare a dossier on the suspects<br>Prepare a dossier on suspect companies<br>REVIEW AND COLLATE EVIDENCE<br>Consider the evidence potentially available<br>Catalogue minor breaches<br>Consider blocking measures<br>Consider covert action<br>PREPARE A DIARY OF EVENTS<br>PREPARE NOMINAL SUMMARIES AND LINK CHARTS<br>EXTRACT THE KEY POINTS<br>DEVELOP A FRAUD THEORY<br>DEVISE A RESOLUTION PLAN AND FIRST STEP |
| | 3 | Set objectives | Normally these are to:<br>• Establish the facts<br>• Press for criminal prosecution<br>• Recover funds<br>• Prevent future losses<br>• Create a deterrent to others |
| | 4 | Obtain authority | Obtain authority from senior management<br>Align management's expectations |
| | 5 | Plan individual interviews | Determine the objectives<br>Plan the phases of the interview<br>Consider how the key points will be presented<br>Decide on the timing and venue<br>Arrange the interview room<br>Decide how the interview will be recorded<br>Consider using interpreters<br>Plan for interviews in the presence of the suspect's lawyer<br>CHECK THE LEGALITY |
| | 6 | Rehearse | Rehearse important interviews |
| | 7 | *The first step* | **Make the first step an ambush**<br>**Conduct important interviews simultaneously** |
| | 8 | Follow up | Complete this stage as quickly as possible |

## MAINTAIN TOTAL CONFIDENTIALITY

Do not discuss suspicions with anyone who does not have an immediate need to know. It may be repugnant, but you should assume collusion by at least one management level above the suspect's and that even honest managers may resist an investigation.

### TAKING THE SAFE COURSE

An undercover investigation in a multinational company revealed that unexplained losses were due to an entire country's sales force systematically defrauding its customers. Periodically, salesmen were the subjects of complaints by suspicious customers. The result would be promotion for the individuals concerned, so that they were kept away from hostilities in the field. Coincidentally, the complainants received the impression that the salesmen had been disciplined because they no longer saw them. Supervisors and intermediate managers demanded their share in a weekly division of the spoils, so the fraud had to be perpetuated to enable those involved to keep their jobs. If any new recruits showed signs of honest reluctance to participate, they failed their probation. There was no evidence that the subsidiary's top management were involved in the fraud, but they knew something was wrong.

Their reluctance to investigate was caused by fear of adverse publicity and its effect on their careers. They were replaced and the investigation was commenced. It did finish their careers, but only because they were too weak to initiate it.

*A little paranoia did no one any harm*

## ASSUME THE SUSPICIONS ARE TRUE

The safe course is to assume that your initial suspicions are true or even worse than they currently appear. You should not panic or rush to take action, but assemble your ideas and resources so that you can take the suspects by total surprise at the *first step*.

### A BAD CASE OF LEAKAGE

One auditor was worried that his findings seemed to implicate a sales manager in conflicting interests. To verify his suspicions, he checked whether the customer master file had been printed recently and contrary to normal practice. He found that it had been – by the sales manager. The following day, the entire sales force received an email from their manager explaining changes in the allocation of accounts which he had decided upon after studying the customer master file.

He had evidently miskeyed because the email was received by everyone, not just the sales department. However, the auditor was pleased that he had sought confirmation of his suspicions which he could see were unjustified. Six months later the sales manager had joined a competitor and was systematically targeting his former customers. Eventually it emerged that he had programmed the computer to warn him if the customer master file was interrogated. The email was untrue and its wide distribution was no accident.

The subsequent investigation proved that he had stolen proprietary information. Court injunctions were obtained to stop him and his new employer using it. However, much damage could have been prevented if the auditor had been less anxious to confirm his suspicions.

*The first step must be an ambush*

Also, unless there are exceptional circumstances, you should take no remedial – and especially disciplinary – action until you have established the facts.

## DO NOT RUSH TO REPORT EXTERNALLY

Do not rush to retain, or even advise, your external auditors or to inform insurers of your suspicions. Remember that evidence may subsequently justify legal action being taken against your external auditors for negligence or worse. Thus there may be a serious conflict of interest in retaining them to investigate because you may be asking them to build up a case of negligence against their audit practice.

Under most fidelity insurance policies, notice has to be given within a reasonable period (normally 'as soon as practicable') after discovery of a loss. Discovery means that evidence is available which would cause a reasonable person to charge another with dishonesty. This is a high standard. Mere suspicion, or the fact that a loss *might* have occurred, is not regarded as 'discovery'. There is no advantage in advising the insurer too early and many possible disadvantages.

---

**DODGY ACTION**

The victim reported its suspicions of a $10 million fraud to its insurance brokers and underwriters. In due course two very impressive lawyers turned up saying that they would adjust the claim and help the victim recover. What they actually did was to take the suspect employee on an all expenses Concorde trip to New York and take a statement from him that blew holes in the claim. The lawyers were not seen again until the Proof of Loss was filed and then they took a very negative position, waving the statement and saying that there was 'no causal link' because the employee never intended the victim to lose.

---

The greatest risks of giving notice too early are that:

- the insurer may start to make its own enquiries and thus confuse matters;
- it may dissipate your efforts by making unjustified and increasingly onerous demands for information;
- it may immediately deny coverage, thus cooling management's enthusiasm for pursuing the case.

However, dates for reporting the loss and filing a Proof of Loss must be carefully monitored so that they are not missed and notification given at the appropriate time and form.

*Never expect an easy ride with insurers*

The bottom line is that you should not report your suspicions to anyone outside your organization unless it is absolutely necessary to do so. For example, if you have to report to a regulatory agency, do so through the appropriate channels; hopefully as set out in your fraud policy (see page 161).

## WHEN TO ADVISE THE POLICE

If criminal prosecution is a definite objective (see pages 144 and 192), the police should be informed before any internal interviews with suspects take place. But please remember:

- Your objective is probably to establish the total amount lost, whereas the police will focus on proving a small selection of criminal charges.
- The results of internal company interviews can be made available to the police, whereas the results of police interviews will not normally be made available to you.
- Once a suspect has been interviewed by the police and cautioned, he is unlikely to cooperate in an internal investigation.

Do not be surprised if the police flatly refuse to take the case. Most police forces do not have the resources to investigate complex frauds and the worst thing you can do is to allow them to sit on the case for months, or sometimes years. If the police accept the case, a provisional timetable should be agreed and if it is not realistic, you should reconsider the advisability of criminal prosecution.

*Delay always acts to the victim's disadvantage*

It is impossible to set down rules that will apply in every case, but agreement can usually be reached with the police that will permit you to conduct your own investigation and subsequently make a formal complaint, consisting of your investigation report, statements and exhibits. This is usually the preferred route, where criminal prosecution is an objective.

# Obtain background information

## INTRODUCTION

You should never interview anyone without being fully prepared: who knows wins.

## GEORGE CARMAN QC

Mr Carman (see the excellent book *No Ordinary Man* (ISBN 0 340 82099 3)) was widely regarded as the best cross-examiner in the business and was known for his pithy comments and apparently throw-away lines like those in respect of David Mellor, MP when Mr Carman said, 'He buried his head in the sand, thus exposing his thinking parts'. What was not generally known is that Mr Carman prepared in the finest detail, and often took weeks to coin his memorable phrases. He also liked to ambush witnesses with evidence they did not know he had and to 'break the session overnight to give them the opportunity to fret'. He knew the value of detailed preparation in raising a subject's anxiety levels. This was described by one of Mr Carman's victims as 'being Carmanised'.

Gary Player, the great South African golfer said: 'Funny, the more I practice [and prepare] the luckier I become.'

*There is no substitute for hard work*

## PREPARE A DOSSIER ON THE SUSPECTS' BACKGROUNDS

Prepare a dossier on the background of each suspect person, reviewing and extracting information as set out in Table 5.8.

**Table 5.8**   Background on suspects

| Nature of information | Comments |
|---|---|
| **Personnel files** | |
| Annual performance appraisals<br>Applications for financial references<br>Bank and mortgage accounts<br>Car registration details<br>Conflicts of interest declarations<br>Credit card numbers<br>Date and place of birth<br>Details of loans and advances<br>Details of other family members, addresses and their employers<br>Details of previous employers, including the names of referees<br>Educational qualifications<br>Leave slips and holiday records<br>Name of next of kin<br>Name of spouse's employer<br>Passport and driving licence numbers<br>Pension and stock option plans<br>Photograph<br>Present and past addresses for the last 10 years<br>*Previous allegations made against the suspect*<br>Previous disciplinary warnings<br>Salary record<br>Sickness record<br>Surname of married daughters<br>Travelling expenses<br>Wife's maiden name<br>Handwriting samples | Look for discrepancies and catalogue them as 'Key Points' for the interview<br>Extract details for the diary of events |
| **Internal records and assets to which the suspect has access** | |
| Accounts payable and receivable<br>Asset registers<br>Cancelled cheques<br>Company telephone call logs<br>Email and correspondence files<br>Instruction and procedure manuals<br>Job descriptions, contracts of employment and authority tables<br>Mobile telephone records (if paid for by the company) | Consider a detailed covert audit of all relevant records before the *first step* or as part of it.<br>Catalogue any discrepancies<br>Add to the diary of events<br>Identify 'Key Points' |
| **Public records** | |
| Companies House<br>Credit and county court reports<br>Press reports (especially 'Reuters Business Briefing') | Directorships and shareholdings of the subject and his immediate family members |

| Nature of information | Comments |
|---|---|
| Previous statements on the subject | |
| Statements | Interview preparation |
| Interview notes | To detect conflicting evidence |
| Covert inspections | |
| Of the suspect's home(s) | Estimate of price<br>Building works<br>Cash spending |
| Of the suspect's office<br>Analyse an image copy of his computer (if company owned) | Analyse these carefully<br>Extract 'Key Points'<br>Add to the diary of events |

In important cases, examine the suspect's financial and domestic position, as these often establish his motive. It is also essential that you carefully analyse any explanations given by the subject. Important facts should be thoroughly checked and discrepancies should be scheduled as 'Key Points' so that they can be presented to him at the appropriate time.

## ON SMALL DETAILS

Background analysis of the type suggested in Table 5.8 has thrown up some critical clues and evidence. In a number of cases, suspects had authorized payments to fictitious vendors in the maiden names of their wives, to ex-employees who mysteriously appeared as vendors immediately after the suspect joined the victim employer or at addresses owned by a family member or at one of their own previous addresses. Inspection of a suspect's home revealed that he was living well beyond his means (and in one case a man on £25 000 a year had a £120 000 sports car parked on his drive). In other cases vacation addresses turned out to be a villa owned by a supplier. And in the most surprising case of all, involving manipulation of an electronic payments system, the suspect had noted the method of fraud used as well as incriminating memory dumps in copies of procedure manuals issued to him

An argument is sometimes put forward – based on a misinterpretation of the Data Protection Act – that information from personnel files cannot be accessed. This is incorrect and any data – even the most personal – can be used for the purpose of preventing and detecting crime.

## PREPARE A DOSSIER ON SUSPECT COMPANIES

Prepare a full dossier on the background of each suspect company, extracting details from:

- official files, showing names of directors, shareholdings, annual accounts etc.;
- credit agencies, such as Dunn and Bradstreet or Experian;
- bank references;
- trade directories;

- telephone books and Yellow Pages;
- indices of national and local newspapers and trade journals;
- press reports and especially 'Reuters Business Briefing'.

Again, make absolutely sure that checking does not alert the suspects

## THE IMPORTANCE OF PRESS REPORTS

A basic check showed that a suspect had been approved for a gold credit card issued in the name of one of his employer's suppliers. In another case, a routine check of the local press library revealed that the suspect had been provided with a £100 000 rally car and his expenses sponsored by a customer. In both cases, the suspects were given the opportunity to volunteer their benefits and failed to do so. Both were eventually prosecuted for corruption.

# Review and collate the evidence

## CONSIDER THE EVIDENCE POTENTIALLY AVAILABLE

Consider what evidence might be available to prove the worst case including that listed in Table 5.9.

**Table 5.9**   Potential sources of information

| Potential sources of intelligence and evidence | Purpose/significance | *How* and when obtained |
|---|---|---|
| Access logs to premises | For the diary of events<br>For comparison with expense statements | *Internal*<br>Planning stage |
| Accounts held at retail stores by the suspect | Signs of overspending<br>Check that private purchases have not been paid for by the company | *Seizure Orders*<br>First step |
| Accounts payable<br>All invoices approved by the suspect | Check against the suspect's expense statements<br>To identify personal purchases charged to the company | *Internal*<br>Planning stage |
| Address books (written and computerized) | Identify main/regular contacts<br>Trace bank accounts and other assets | *Covert search*<br>Planning stage |
| Aircraft log books (private jets) | Free travel provided to the suspect and others<br>Identify travelling companions | *Discovery*<br>Follow-up |
| Airline club mileage statements | Signs of overspending<br>Check against expenses<br>Check against travel agency invoices | *Covert search*<br>Planning stage |
| Application forms (any completed by the suspect for any purpose) | Log information<br>Note inconsistencies | *Internal*<br>Planning stage |

| Potential sources of intelligence and evidence | Purpose/significance | *How* and when obtained |
|---|---|---|
| Asset lists for the suspect's personal assets | Schedules to insurance policies<br>Identify expensive items and especially jewellery | *Seizure orders*<br>*Discovery*<br>Follow-up |
| Asset registers | Identify assets under the control of the suspect: especially computer equipment | *Internal*<br>Planning stage |
| Audio tapes | Recover and check all tapes<br>Recover deleted conversations | *Covert search*<br>Planning stage |
| Authority manuals | To prove the suspect's knowledge<br>Explain all highlighting and notes | *Internal*<br>Planning stage |
| Bank accounts used by the suspect | For evidence of over-spending and conversion | *Trash search*<br>*Covert search*<br>Planning stage |
| Boarding passes (aircraft) | Check against expense statements<br>Check class of travel | *Trash search*<br>*Covert search*<br>Planning stage |
| Boats and light aircraft registers | For assets owned by the suspect | *Public records*<br>Planning stage |
| Bookmakers' records and slips | For signs of over-spending<br>Track dates of large losses | *Trash search*<br>*Covert search*<br>Planning stage |
| Books on bookshelves | Establish the suspect's knowledge<br>Trace purchase of expensive books | *Covert search*<br>Planning stage |
| Brief cases | Check contents<br>Remove company property | *Covert search*<br>Planning stage |
| Call logs (internal) | See telephone call logs | *Internal*<br>Planning stage |
| Call logs (external and home) | | *Data Protection Act exchange*<br>*Crime investigation*<br>Planning stage |
| Cancelled cheques (on the accounts of the company) | For signs of false conversion<br>Track missing cheques | *Internal*<br>Planning stage |
| Car park receipts | For the diary of events<br>Check against expenses | *Trash search*<br>Planning stage |
| Casino records | As for bookmakers' records | |
| Certificates, academic and other | Check their authenticity<br>To identify associates | *Internal*<br>*Personnel files*<br>Planning stage |

| Potential sources of intelligence and evidence | Purpose/significance | *How* and when obtained |
|---|---|---|
| Cheque stubs | As cancelled cheques | *Internal* <br> Planning stage |
| Christmas card list | Identify close associates <br> Check names against accounts payable and receivable | *Covert search* <br> Planning stage |
| Club and other memberships | For the diary of events <br> For signs of overspending <br> Check how membership was paid <br> To identify associates | *Covert search* <br> *Trash search* <br> *Surveillance* <br> Planning stage |
| Company registration records | Directorships of the suspect and his family | *Public record* <br> *Planning stage* |
| Computers: mainframes and networked to which the suspect had access | Check all files and programs <br> Check logs against diary of events and expense claims <br> Check all email messages | *Internal* <br> Planning stage |
| Computers: personal | See 'personal computers' below | |
| Contract files | Check all contracts negotiated by the suspect | |
| Correspondence files (live and archived) | Proof of dishonesty <br> Diary of events | |
| Courier billing records | For the diary of events <br> For signs of conversion | |
| Credit agencies | Debt record <br> Financial position | *Public record* <br> Planning stage |
| Credit cards | For signs of overspending <br> To track assets and bank accounts <br> To confirm expense statements | *Trash search* <br> *Covert search* <br> Planning stage |
| Crime reports made privately by the suspect | To track assets | |
| Desk drawers | To recover diaries etc. | *Covert search* <br> Planning stage |
| Diaries and personal organizers | For the diary of events <br> To identify close associates <br> Compare against expense statements | *Covert search* <br> Planning stage |
| Dictation tapes | Check all tapes | |
| Disks and diskettes | For evidence of fraud <br> Unlicensed software | |
| Electronic mail | Reconstruct all mail | |
| Electoral roll | People sharing the suspect's address <br> Check all names for directorships | *Public record* <br> Planning stage |

| Potential sources of intelligence and evidence | Purpose/significance | How and when obtained |
|---|---|---|
| Expense statements | For the diary of events<br>Analyse for evidence of expenses fraud | *Internal*<br>Planning stage |
| Fax billing records | To identify associates<br>For the diary of events | *Internal*<br>Planning stage |
| Fax machines and memories | Print autodialler lists and memory | |
| Gift vouchers given and received | For signs of conversion and corruption | *Covert search*<br>Planning stage |
| Goods outwards passes | Identify goods removed from company premises by the suspect<br>Compare against the diary of events | *Internal*<br>Planning stage |
| Household bills | For signs of overspending<br>Identify expensive items (such as furniture and pictures) for which there are no purchase invoices | *Trash search*<br>Planning stage |
| Identification cards | Track club and other memberships<br>Identify associates | *Internal*<br>*Cover search*<br>Planning stage |
| Insurance policies held privately by the suspect | For compiling an asset list<br>Trace expensive items to source<br>Track discounted deals given by company insurers | *Trash search*<br>*Data Protection Act exchange*<br>Planning stage |
| Internet | Search for all references to the suspect | *Public record*<br>Planning stage |
| Keys | Withdraw company keys<br>Identify all other keys, especially for cars and safety deposit boxes | *Covert search*<br>Planning stage |
| Laptop computers | Examine forensically | *Covert search*<br>Planning stage |
| Leave slips | Showing vacation addresses<br>Possibly owned by a third party with whom the employee has dealings | *Internal*<br>Planning stage |
| Legal invoices | For intelligence purposes<br>To trace hidden assets and conflicts of interest<br>For identifying criminal convictions | *Internal*<br>*Accounts payable*<br>Planning stage |
| Manuals used by the suspect | Check all notes and highlighting<br>For proof of knowledge | *Internal*<br>Planning stage |
| Microfilms (and reproduction records) | For proving theft of confidential information | *Internal*<br>Planning stage |
| Mobile telephone | Address book<br>Last numbers dialled | *Office search*<br>Planning stage |

| Potential sources of intelligence and evidence | Purpose/significance | *How* and when obtained |
|---|---|---|
| Note pads | Explain everything<br>Consider an electrostatic document analysis (ESDA) examination | *Covert search*<br>*Trash search*<br>Planning stage |
| Overtime records | For the diary of events<br>Check against expenses | *Internal*<br>Planning stage |
| Pagers and billing records | For the diary of events<br>Identify close associates | *Internal*<br>Planning stage |
| Parking tickets | For the diary of events<br>To identify close associates<br>Check vehicle registration numbers | *Trash search*<br>*Covert search*<br>Planning stage |
| Passports | For the diary of events<br>Check against expenses<br>Check personal data | *Covert search*<br>*Discovery*<br>Any stage |
| Paying in books on the suspect's accounts | Identify cash deposits<br>Check against the diary of events | *Covert search*<br>Planning Stage |
| Personal computers (PCs) | Vital in all respects<br>Check everything | *Covert search*<br>Planning stage |
| Personnel files | Check against all application forms<br>Confirm personal details<br>Identify close associates<br>Identify and check out the employers of close family members<br>Note wife's maiden name and check out her directorships | *Internal*<br>Planning stage |
| Petty cash records | For the diary of events<br>Track personal purchases booked to the company<br>For signs of other fraud | *Internal*<br>Planning stage |
| Photocopy billing records | To identify theft of customer lists etc. | *Internal*<br>Planning stage |
| Photographs | To identify expensive assets (boats etc.)<br>To identify close associates<br>Compare with the diary of events | *Covert search*<br>Planning stage |
| Planning permissions | For spending on the employee's home<br>For signs of bribery | *Public records*<br>Planning stage |
| Press databases and other public records | Check the suspect's name against these<br>Especially Factiva Dow Jones (www.factiva.com) | *Public records*<br>Planning stage |
| Purchase invoices | See accounts payable for items approved by the suspect | *Internal*<br>Planning stage |

| Potential sources of intelligence and evidence | Purpose/significance | *How* and when obtained |
|---|---|---|
| References from past employers | Check authenticity<br>Consider the liability of the referee for providing inaccurate references | *Personnel files*<br>Planning stage |
| References for other people provided by the suspect | To identify close associates<br>Check the companies concerned against accounts payable and receivable lists | *Personnel files*<br>Planning stage |
| Safe deposit keys and receipts | To identify hidden assets<br>To track stolen funds | *Covert search*<br>Planning stage |
| Scrap disposal records | Check the legitimacy of approvals by the suspect for the disposal of company assets | *Internal*<br>Planning stage |
| Share dealing and stockbroker records | For signs of overspending<br>To trace assets | *Public records*<br>*Covert search*<br>Planning stage |
| Shorthand notebooks | Reconstruct all correspondence | *Covert search*<br>Planning stage |
| Shredder used by the suspect | Reconstruct contents | *Covert search*<br>*Trash search*<br>Planning stage |
| Tachometer records in company vehicles used by the suspect | For the diary of events<br>Identify and explain missing records | *Internal*<br>Planning stage |
| Tape recorders used by the suspect | Reconstruct all correspondence and conversations | *Covert search*<br>Planning stage |
| Tax returns submitted by the subject | For comparison against asset lists<br>For signs of fraud and illegal income | *Discovery*<br>Follow-up |
| Taxi billing records | For the diary of events<br>Check against expense statements | *Covert search*<br>*Expenses*<br>Planning stage |
| Telephone answering machines | Reconstruct all messages | *Covert search*<br>Planning stage |
| Telephone call logs | Schedule<br>Add to the diary of events<br>To identify regular contacts | *Internal*<br>Planning stage |
| Telephone directories | Confirm telephone numbers and address | *Public record*<br>Planning stage |
| Telephone memories | Print out autodial lists<br>To identify regular contacts | *Covert search*<br>Planning stage |
| Telephones: portable | Check as above | |

| Potential sources of intelligence and evidence | Purpose/significance | *How* and when obtained |
|---|---|---|
| Telex memories and billing records | See 'Fax billing records' above | *Internal* Planning Stage |
| Training manuals | See 'Manuals used by the suspect' above | *Internal* Planning Stage |
| Trash (search) | Everything! | *Search* Planning Stage |
| Travel agent's invoices | Check against expense statements For the diary of events | *Internal* Planning stage |
| Vehicle maintenance records | For signs of fraud For the diary of events | *Internal* Planning stage |
| Video archives | Public places | *Internal* Planning stage |
| Visitors' books | To identify close associates For the diary of events | *Internal* Planning stage |
| Voicemail | For the diary of events Associates | *Internal* Planning stage |
| Wall charts and display boards | For evidence of fraud | *Cover search* Planning stage |
| Waste bins | Recover all discarded documents | *Trash search* Planning stage |
| Wills and trust documents | To identify hidden assets | *Covert search* Planning stage |

Consider the way such information might be obtained before or when taking the *first step.*

*Remember, it is not the evidence you have which is important but the evidence the suspect believes you might be able to get*

## CATALOGUE MINOR BREACHES

Minor breaches of procedures, incorrect application forms, previous false explanations, abuse of discretion and errors or expense fiddles should be identified, catalogued and summarized on single sheets of paper as 'Key Points'. These may be used during the interview to demonstrate to the suspect that, whether he admits to the more serious matters or not, he is already exposed to censure and this may lead him to conclude that he has little to lose in leading you to the deep truth.

## CONSIDER FORENSIC EXAMINATIONS

You should consider having some or all of the evidence forensically examined:

* ESDA testing for latent impressions of other writings[5];
* handwriting analysis, to prove who wrote a document;
* fingerprinting, to prove who handled a document;
* enhancement of audio tapes from answering, voicemail and dictation machines;
* recovery of deleted computer files and emails.

However, it is essential that examinations are made without alerting the suspects that they are under investigation:

### THE BANK OFFICER

A senior bank officer, suspected of involvement in a major fraud, denied that he had seen a letter of authority, although he agreed he had seen and signed similar documents on the date in question. Forensic examination of the letters revealed an ESDA impression of the officer's signature on the unsigned document. It had obviously been included in the pack submitted to him for signature. This evidence was vital in obtaining his confession that he had seen the document and had *not* signed it because he knew it was fraudulent.

## CONSIDER BLOCKING MEASURES

Also, consider any actions that could be taken, at the appropriate time and probably before the *first step*, which might give wrongly suspected innocent people the chance to voluntarily disclose the facts.

### DECLARING A CONFLICT OF INTEREST

If an employee is suspected of running a competitive business, the employer might ask all employees – in a casual, low-key way – to submit a written declaration for 'insurance purposes' of their private interests. If the suspect fails to make a truthful disclosure, he is denied the opportunity of producing an innocent explanation later on. An honest response would normally be in the person's favour, but he can then be asked openly to produce the records of his private business interests for examination.

Whichever way the attempt goes, the results will be useful, and, at worst, bring forward the suspicions for discussion.

If the suspect does not volunteer the truth, when given the opportunity, it will make any subsequent explanations or denials less credible.

---

[5]   ESDA detects impressions made on paper from writing on other papers which at one time may have been made on papers resting above it. The leading company in the UK is Berkeley Security Bureau (Forensic) Ltd, 10 Grosvenor Avenue, London SW1W 0DH, www.bsbsecurity.com.

## CONSIDER COVERT ACTION PRIOR TO THE INTERVIEW

You should consider whether it would be beneficial to take covert action, before or after the *first step*, to detect the suspects in a dishonest act which cannot be excused, or to trace assets or accomplices

The possibilities include:

- *Interception and covert recording of company telephone, fax and data lines*: But first understand the legal position.
- *Intercepting company mail*: Including email and again subject to the legal issues explained in Appendix 4 and on pages 147 and 157.
- *Installing video or audio monitors*: In offices, warehouses or computer centres or on equipment which the suspects may use in carrying out the fraud.
- *Searching the suspect's work area or office*: Before doing this take a Polaroid photograph or video recording to help you make sure everything is put back in its original place.
- *Searching the suspect's PC*: Covertly copy his diskettes. Do not use standard software to take a secret copy of a hard disk as this may destroy the evidential value of what you find. It is much better to retain the services of a professional computer forensic technician. Consider carefully what rights you have to access the suspect's PC.

The possibilities should be considered and where appropriate included in the resolution plan. However, it is critical that the actions you take are proportionate to the seriousness of the suspected transgression

*Your action must be proportionate*

## PREPARE A DIARY OF EVENTS

From the first moment, you should start compiling a diary of events or chronology which shows, in date and time sequence, everything that happened from all of your sources, especially telephone call logs, expense statements and correspondence. It is a critical document and puts you in control. Table 5.10 gives an example.

**Table 5.10**   Diary of events

| Date | Day of week | GMT | Action or event | Comments | Source | Cross reference |
|------|-------------|-----|-----------------|----------|--------|-----------------|
| 2002 |  |  |  |  |  |  |
| Jan 1 | Wed | 14.00 | Bill Smith calls John Jones (14 mins) |  | Call Logs 1 |  |
| Jan1 | Wed | 14.15 | John Jones calls Zurich Bank (12 mins) |  | Call Logs 2 |  |
| Jan 1 | Wed | 20.30 | Bill Smith entertains Robinson at Hilton Hotel (Bill £145.76) |  | Expenses 1 |  |

Columns 2 and 3 can be particularly important in international frauds, involving different time zones and public holidays. The diary of events can be kept on Microsoft Excel, which has functions for calculating the day of the week (DOW) from any date, and superb sorting and analysis tools. It is also extremely important in interviews and enables you to quickly check and cross reference explanations given by the suspect.

## PREPARE NOMINAL SUMMARIES AND LINK ANALYSIS CHARTS

Again, from the earliest moments, you should prepare a schedule summarizing all of the detail on people and organizations potentially involved and keep it updated as the case moves forward (see Table 5.11).

**Table 5.11**    Nominal summaries

| Name<br>Date of birth | Address<br>*Telephone Nos[6]* | Role | Relationships | Comments |
|---|---|---|---|---|
| William J. Smith<br>Known as 'WJ'<br>Born 1.2.1969 | 53 Acacia Avenue<br>Slough SL34<br>*01444.577697 (H)*<br>*07723456 (Mobile)* | | Buyer<br>Husband of Jane<br>Robbins | Aged 45, heavy<br>build, dark hair,<br>glasses (see Photo 1) |
| Peter A. Mesat<br>Born 12.12.1964 | Not known | | Truck driver | |
| | | | | |
| | | | | |

In complex cases, you should consider representing this data on a link analysis chart (see www.i2.co.uk) or keeping all of the information on a customized program such as the excellent Case Map (see www.Casemap.com).

## EXTRACT THE KEY POINTS

Examine the evidence and the intelligence that has led to the suspicions and fully understand them. Pay particular attention to the *key points* that suggest the suspect's responsibility. Make sure your conclusions are correct; look for alternative explanations; pay close attention to detail.

Summarize each key point on a single sheet of paper that can be presented to the suspect during the interview (see pages 187 and 221). The more documented key points you have, the easier the interview will become.

# Develop a fraud theory

Before any interview takes place, you should have the clearest understanding of what you believe has happened and why, and why other things that might have happened didn't.

---

[6]   In practice telephone numbers would be shown in a separate column

- Who appears to be involved in the problem, based on the existing evidence? The safe course is to assume that other people are involved, possibly at more senior levels. Collusion is a factor in most fraud cases.
- Assuming the suspicions are correct, in what other and possibly much worse dishonesty might the suspect be involved: this is the worst case.
- What are the precise mechanics of the dishonesty suspected and the worst case (the '7HW mnemonic'):
  - How and how not,
  - What and what not,
  - When and when not,
  - Where and where not,
  - Which and which not,
  - Who and who not,
  - Why and why not.

In important cases, take a sheet of A4 paper and fold it vertically down the middle. In the left-hand column write down all those things that relate to the theory, where appropriate with dates and times.

In the right-hand column write down the evidence and the intelligence (i.e. the key points) that support the left-hand column and your theory. You may use a green highlighter to mark known facts and a blue maker for unconfirmed intelligence. When this has been checked, you can over-mark the blue with yellow, thereby turning it to green.

Compiling a fraud theory is like doing a jigsaw puzzle. If a piece does not fit, then your theory is wrong and you must revise it. Often pieces that didn't initially fit, result in the most important clues.

*The fraud theory is a jigsaw puzzle*

Consider other areas, possibly more serious, where the suspect might have tried to deceive you or others. Think carefully and develop a 'worst case theory'. Write this down, again on a sheet with two columns.

*Think like the liar*

Remember, there is no such thing as a coincidence. If a fact does not fit your theory, the theory is wrong. Have an explanation for every detail, document, coincidence or discrepancy. Summarize the key facts on which your theory is based and keep them updated.

# Devise a resolution plan and identify the first step

In parallel with the fraud theory, write down a resolution plan showing the steps that need to be taken, when and by whom leading to the first step (see Table 5.12).

**Table 5.12**  A simple resolution plan

| Ref No | Location | Aspect | Priority | Action by | Man days | Action required |
|--------|----------|--------|----------|-----------|----------|-----------------|
| 1 | Birmingham | Jones | 2 | JEF | 1 | Interview Smith and Co (Vendors). Obtain documents and statement |
| 2 | London SW1 | Jones | 1 | ABC KLM | 2 | Observation on XYZ and CO to check deliveries and goods inwards procedure |
| 3 | XXX | Smith | | | | |

Column 6 (Man days) enables budgets to be controlled. The table can be sorted by location, priorities etc.

The *first step* is critical. If the dishonesty is still continuing or is likely to be repeated, determine where and when the *first step* could be taken to catch the suspects in an act, with their pants down and backsides exposed, for which they cannot provide any plausible excuse. For example:

- while handling stolen goods or converting funds;
- while accessing premises or computer systems without authority;
- while involved in an obvious breach of procedures or deviation from honest practice;
- through pre-emptive legal actions, such as civil search and seizure orders.

It is much easier for the victim to seize the initiative if the fraud is continuing or might be repeated. If the problem is not continuing, plan how and when the first step can be taken with the maximum element of surprise:

- when the suspects can be kept apart and are unable to collaborate over their explanations: this is very important;
- when important records, computer and communication systems can be secured.

Review the resolution plan and decide upon the actions that should be taken simultaneously; remember international time differences. Simultaneous actions might include interviews with other suspects or witnesses, third-party audits or site visits.

Remember, make the *first step* a knockout blow.

## Determine your objectives

You should always decide what your objectives are before conducting any important investigation. In all cases, the initial goal is to find the truth and then to consider:

- *Disciplinary action*: You should make sure that any proposed action is permitted under local laws. But remember that taking a soft line against dishonesty is always counter-productive. It is also true that most cases of alleged unfair dismissal are no more than a ruse to weaken the victim organization's resolve, so do not take a soft line; where necessary select experienced litigation lawyers to assist you.

- *Criminal prosecution*: This is neither an easy nor necessarily a cost-effective option. It is true to say that most victims of fraud who prosecute are disappointed with the results. However, community responsibilities are important and it is morally indefensible to let fat cat fraudsters escape unpunished.
- *Civil litigation*: This again can be a costly and difficult process, but your chances of success are generally much higher through the civil, rather than the criminal, courts. You may also consider taking civil action to recover assets, to discover evidence in the possession of the suspects or third parties, to block funds or for some other reason. If civil action is an objective, you should instruct specialist litigation lawyers, as soon as possible, and follow their advice.
- *Recovery of the amounts lost*: This should be a primary objective and may be achieved, at the appropriate time, by negotiating with the criminals and their associates, through civil recovery or by claiming under fidelity or computer crime insurance. However, check your coverage now, before you need it and make sure it is appropriate.
- *Getting back to business*: Investigations take time and, unless properly controlled, they can be disruptive and costly. It is thus important to keep management of the investigation separate from ongoing business. Under no circumstances should the line manager responsible for the operation or area in which the problem is suspected be put in charge of the investigation. It is imperative that all serious investigations are professionally handled using specified procedures and skilled resources. The time to get these in place is now, before the worst happens.
- *Improving controls*: As soon as possible, controls should be reviewed and, where necessary, improved but do nothing before the first step that might alert the suspects and allow them to escape.

In most cases, the victims of fraud should take the toughest line necessary to get their money back and get rid of the crooks.

You should also consider the adverse consequences of pursuing your objectives. For example, the suspects may make allegations about, or threaten to expose other problems in, your organization, with the objective of stopping the investigation. The fact is that if you give in to blackmail you are headed on the path to failure and you should remember that the media is not interested in fraud unless it concerns Buckingham Palace or some sexual scandal.

*Publicity of fraud cases is very rare and transient*

# Authority to act

You must have the clearest understanding of your right to ask questions and the legal framework, bearing in mind your objectives, and consider:

- Is the subject required to answer questions under the terms of his employment or some other contract?
- Can the subject demand that a colleague, union representative or lawyer is present[7]?

---

[7]   In most investigatory interviews the answer is usually 'No'

- Do you have to administer a caution – but only in cases where criminal prosecution is contemplated – to comply with the Police and Criminal Evidence Act? Chances are, unless you are a full time investigator, you can forget about cautions.
- Can you tape record with or without the subject's knowledge?
- Are there disciplinary or other procedures that must be followed?

You should also think about the benefits of obtaining a letter from senior management authorizing you to investigate and conduct interviews[8].

## Align management's expectations

You should ensure that senior managers fully understand the case and the time and cost that may be involved in investigation. Many who watch television mistakenly believe that all investigations can be completed within 60 minutes including commercial breaks. This is far from the truth. The investigation should be independently conducted by internal audit, corporate security, the police or consultants and line managers should be prohibited from interfering. Ideally, this fact should be made clear, before the event, in a fraud policy.

*Managers are usually woefully misinformed about fraud*

## Conclusions

The level of planning recommended in this chapter will ensure that tough interviews that form part of an investigation are given the greatest chance of success, comply with the law and get to the deep truth. The next step is to plan each interview carefully. Most of the problems described in this chapter should be eliminated by the publication of a fraud policy, covering such matters as human rights, data protection, whistleblowing, rights to legal and other representation and investigatory processes. A model policy document can be downloaded, free of charge, from www.cobasco.com. It will remove the risk of bad decisions made in the heat of the moment.

---

[8]   Providing this does not alert the suspect to your interest in him

'I KNOW THEY LIKED THE BOOK ON RAPPORT BUT THIS IS RIDICULOUS'

# **6** *Planning Tough Interviews*

## Introduction

### OVERALL PLANNING

As a rule, tough interviews should be conducted as part of an overall investigations plan and in compliance with the legal background explained in Chapter 5.

*Never rush into any interview without careful planning*

### INTERVIEW OBJECTIVES

You should agree the objectives of each interview with your colleagues and legal advisers, and decide whether or not a confession is important (see Figure 6.1). The chart indicates that, in criminal cases where the evidence is already strong, interviews are less important. In fact, a badly conducted interview could compromise a winning case.

If the evidence is already overwhelming and the objective is criminal prosecution, there may be little to be gained from interviewing the suspect, other than being able to demonstrate that by going through a low-key, formal process, he had been given the opportunity of giving

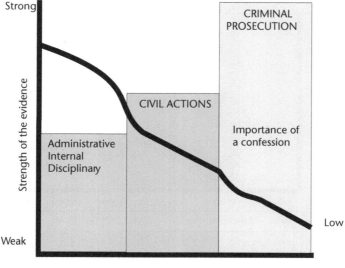

**Figure 6.1** Where confessions are not necessary

his explanation. This is the safe course because a badly conducted interview may actually reduce the strength of the case or, in the worst eventuality, get it thrown out of court.

*Don't go for a 'tough' interview unless you have to*

On the other hand, *properly obtained and admissible* admissions and confessions are important because they:
- add support to the existing evidence and intelligence;
- disclose previously unknown offences;
- identify accomplices;
- identify control weaknesses which can be corrected;
- speed up and simplify the legal process;
- enable the victim to recover more quickly and easily;
- reduce the chance of acquittals and successful appeals against conviction.

Also, the suspect with whom you have established a close relationship may become a valuable source of information on other matters.

*Good interviews are worthwhile.*
*Whenever you can, aim for a confession and the deep truth*

## PLANNING THE PHASES OF THE INTERVIEW

### Overview
Interviews should be planned in the five active phases as shown in Table 6.1 and Figure 6.2.

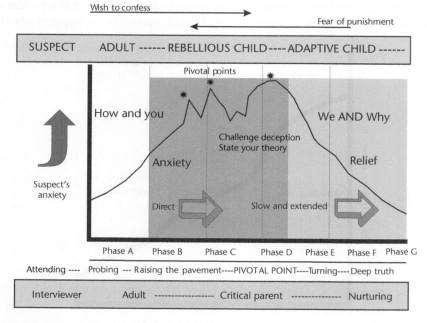

**Figure 6.2**   Phases of a tough interview

The specific coverage of each phase can be summarized as in Table 6.1.

**Table 6.1**   Phases of a tough interview

| Phase | Objectives and coverage | *Possible emotion* and APPROACH of the deceitful subject |
|---|---|---|
| PHASE A<br>Getting the subject to attend and the opening | Tempting the suspect to explain<br>Creating the right impression<br>Building empathy<br>Stating the purpose<br>Getting a detailed explanation | *Fear and anxiety*<br>*Anger*<br>FIGHT<br>FLEE<br>APPEASE |
| PHASE B<br>Probing and testing | Establishing whether the person is telling the truth or not with the interviewer acting as a human lie detector | |
| PHASE C<br>Raising the pavement<br>*PUTTING THE MONKEYS ON THE LIAR'S BACK*<br>Anxiety-inducing questions<br>Accusations | Pinning the subject down to detail<br>Increasing anxiety to the point where the subject loses confidence in his ability to cope and arrives at the pivotal point | *Increased anxiety*<br>*Depression*<br>QUESTIONS HIS ABILITY TO COPE<br>ESTABLISHES HIS INNOCENCE |
| PHASE D<br><div align="center">**The Pivotal Point**<br>*At which the suspect balances the relief given by confession and bringing the interview to an end with the potential consequences of a confession*</div> | | |
| PHASE E<br>Turning and empathy<br>*GETTING THE MONKEYS OFF THE LIAR'S BACK* | Helping the subject handle the critical decision whether or not to tell the truth<br>Taking an empathetic approach<br>Enabling the suspect to rationalize his behaviour | *Unbearable anxiety*<br>NEGOTIATION<br>ACCEPTANCE |
| PHASE F<br>Getting to the deep truth and arriving at a soft landing | Working with the subject as a nurturing parent to get to the deep truth<br>Leaving the door open for later contact | *Relief*<br>ACCEPTANCE<br>SUBMISSION |
| PHASE G<br>Review and follow-up | Transcribing notes and preparing an accurate record of the interview | *Relief*<br>ACCEPTANCE |
| | Reviewing your own performance, so that you can improve in the future<br>Identifying other actions<br>Keeping in regular contact with the suspect | *Anger*<br>ATTACK |

## More detail on the phases

In practice the phases run seamlessly together, but they provide the road map from the start to the end of a tough interview and enable you to backtrack to a safe point if an interview is blown off course.

*Phase A: Getting the subject to attend*

Wherever possible, the subject should be ambushed as part of the *first step* of the investigation and we recognize that this may not be the conventional approach. However, your objective is to find the truth and to clear the innocent as well as nail the guilty party. Experience shows that the *first step* must be a surprise. This makes it less likely that subjects can prepare excuses or interfere with the evidence.

> *The first step must be an ambush*

The invitation for a suspect to attend an interview, or meeting, should be carefully planned (see page 201) and should be made in a low key, unemotional way, ideally with the minimum of notice (see page 207) The objective is to entice the suspect into accepting the challenge of attending an interview. You can only do this if he believes he can win or has more to gain than lose by attending.

There are cases where people have no option but to attend an interview and answer questions, including investigations by the Serious Fraud Office, some health and safety enquiries, where employees are required to assist under the terms and conditions of their employment and when you are summonsed by your mother-in-law. But, in most cases, the willingness of the subject to attend depends on your persuasive skills.

A person invited to attend a tough interview will carefully assess his position. If he believes the evidence against him is damning and that he has no chance of escape, he is likely to flee, and refuse to attend. Thus the way you invite a subject to attend an interview is important.

## THE TELEPHONE CALL

You have been investigating for months and have reached the phase at which you would like to interview the suspect. You telephone him at home on a Sunday evening:

'Good evening, Mr Jones, this is Bill Smith from Audit. As you know I have been investigating you for six months and I have the strongest evidence that you are a malodorous scumbag who has ripped off millions from Sunshine Foods. My office is jam packed with evidence that incriminates you and you are in deep shit with no chance of escape. I would like to see you at 8.30 tomorrow.' Will he come? ... Would you?

You might think that conversations like this never take place, but unfortunately they do. In one recent multimillion pound case, auditors telephoned the suspect at home on a Sunday evening, telling him about their investigation and asking to see him in his office the following morning adding: 'Bring your laptop and backup files with you.' They were amazed that the suspect did not appear but had instead run off to Brazil. When he was eventually tracked down, he claimed his laptop had fallen into a river.

The lesson is not to make a big deal of the interview or meeting but to let the suspect form his own conclusion that, if he attends, he has a chance of winning or at least coming out no worse than he went in. Ideally you should give minimal advance warning or, better still, ambush him when his pants are down (see page 175 and Appendix 1).

## FALSE ARREST

A participant in a seminar on corporate fraud listened intently as the elderly speaker listed the ways in which false purchase invoices could be detected. A day or so later, he telephoned the speaker and said:

'I tried out the tests you suggested and picked up £70000 worth of false invoices. I interviewed the head of purchasing and he has confessed. I have locked him in the lavatory but I am not sure what to do next.'

The moral of this story is that although you should try and take the suspect by surprise you should not arrest him, unless it is vital to do so and permitted under the law. Arrest means detaining someone against their will, usually with the objective of bringing them before a court.

*You may invite a person to attend an interview, but you should not arrest him.*
*Let the liar think he can win*

If the interview can be arranged when the suspect is doing something he should not be doing, so much the better. For example, if an employee who is suspected of stealing can be caught loading company property into the boot of his car, the initiative swings quickly in your favour.

*It is very difficult for a liar to maintain his composure when caught with his pants down*

### Phase A: The opening statement

The way you open an interview is critically important. First impressions count and you must present an adult and professional image. In most cases you should explain, through some sort of introductory monologue (see page 244), selecting the best option:

**Table 6.2**    Opening statement options

| Title of opening statement | General nature and principles |
|---|---|
| OPTION 1<br>The Factual Testing Opening | Page 246 |
| OPTION 2<br>Blocking Questions | Page 247 |
| OPTION 3<br>The Introductory Monologue | Page 248 |
| OPTION 4<br>Direct Confrontation | Page 250 |
| OPTION 5<br>The Formality | Page 250 |
| OPTION 6<br>Elimination Interviews<br>Elimination Check List | Page 369 and Appendix 2 |
| OPTION 7<br>The Freestyle Story | Page 374 |
| OPTION 8<br>The Structured Check List | Page 375 |

Your choice of the best opening statement should be made based on the objectives of the interview and the strength of the existing evidence, as shown in Table 6.2.

Also depending on your objectives, you decide whether the suspect should be cautioned or not (see page 150). If your objectives are definitely not to press for criminal prosecution you do not have to administer a caution.

In all cases your opening statement and questions immediately after should:

- make it clear that you intend to find the truth and that you have limitless time and resources available to you;
- ask questions that commit the subject to detailed explanations;
- challenge untruths;
- state what you believe the facts to be, if necessary by making direct accusations.

If you are reasonably sure the subject is not telling the truth, you should proceed to Phase B

### Phase B: Probing and testing

In this phase you move from an adult to a critical parent role, continue to ask detailed questions and test the subject's reaction to the evidence and intelligence you have. You should focus on the key points and obtain detailed explanations on the mechanics (the 'how') of what you believe has happened. You will not remember all of the clues to deception described in Chapter 4, so rely on your intuition but elevate specific concerns into your conscious awareness.

**Table 6.3**  Interviewing objectives and options

| Objective of the interview | Strength of the evidence before interviewing | | | |
|---|---|---|---|---|
| | Conclusive on all aspects of the case (the worst case) | Strongly suggestive on some aspects | Uncertain with a single suspect | Uncertain with multiple suspects |
| Criminal prosecution | *Advise the police before interviewing*<br>*Agree objectives, timescale and action plan*<br>*Decide whether or not a caution should be administered* | | | |
| | Option 2: Blocking questions<br>Option 5: Formality | Option 3: Introductory monologue<br>Option 2: Blocking questions | Elimination Interview:<br>Method 1: Interview | |
| | *You may have more to lose by a poorly conducted interview than any potential gain* | *The interview may reveal evidence on the worst case* | Method 2: Freestyle statement<br>Method 3: Structured check list | |
| Civil action | Option 2: Blocking questions<br>Option 5: Formality<br>Option 4: Direct confrontation | Option 1: Factual testing<br>Option 2: Blocking questions<br>Option 3: Introductory monologue | | |
| Internal disciplinary | | | | |
| Internal decision making | | *The interview may reveal evidence on the worst case* | | |

If you believe the suspect is innocent or telling the truth or both, don't be afraid to admit it to yourself and move forward on that basis.

*One of the greatest failings of inexperienced interviewers*
*is that they will not admit that the subject is being truthful*

If you believe the suspect is guilty, telling lies or you are not sure one way or the other, you must move to Phase C.

## Phase C: Raising the pavement – putting monkeys on backs

It is crucial that the suspect's anxiety is taken to the pivotal point at which he loses all confidence in his ability to succeed and is willing to accept the consequences of confessing or sees an advantage in doing so.

You can lead the suspect to the pivotal point by taking a critical parent role and by provoking his subconscious and memory monkeys into states of intolerable anxiety by:

- preventing him from succeeding with concealment lies;
- provoking him into falsifying fine detail;
- challenging deceptive answers and non-verbal clues of deception;
- stating what you believe he did (based on the fraud and deception theories) through accusatory questions.

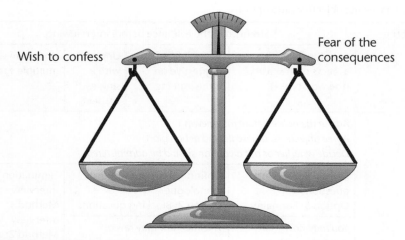

**Figure 6.3**   The pivotal point

You should emphasize the key points and keep the documentary summaries within his personal space; make sure all questions are answered fully, react coolly to counter-attacks and make clear what you believe has happened. You must state, repeatedly, what you believe the suspect has done.

The liar is at his most vulnerable at any phase of an interview when he is:

- emotional and especially angry;
- pausing for thought before answering a relevant question ('brain thrashing');
- caught out in a lie;
- forced to change an explanation or to admit he has been less than forthcoming in his answers.

However, he is totally exposed at the pivotal point. The way you handle this is critical in getting to the deep truth.

> *Put the monkeys on his back*

### Phases D and E: The pivotal point and turning
In this phase the suspect will consider confessing, usually for the reasons explained in page 76. If you miss your opportunity at one pivotal point, the chances are another will appear. The suspect may:

- Ask bargaining questions such as 'What might happen?'
- Show non-verbal and other signs of acceptance, such as dropping his head or rolling up into a foetal position; it may sound incredible, but at the pivotal point, many suspects appear to get smaller.

The suspect's primary channel of communication (both verbal and non-verbal) will almost certainly be emotional and you *must* tune to his wavelength by adopting the role of a nurturing parent. You must retain a low-key, sensitive and slow approach to the first and subsequent admissions: you should empathize with the suspect, make rationalization statements and slowly and carefully extend admissions into a confession. You should focus on the word 'we' and how the matter can be resolved.

If you handle this phase properly you should obtain admissions or confessions or conclude that the suspect is wholly or partly innocent. If you conclude he is innocent, truthful or both, you must be prepared to apologize for giving him a hard time:

---

*Example*: 'I am sorry, Bill, I had to put you through that, but it was very important to find the truth and I am satisfied that you did not … but I would like your help in moving this case forward.'

---

It is very rare, bordering on unique, for such an apology not to be accepted by an innocent subject. On the other hand, if the suspect has made admissions or confessions, this is where the hard work starts and you must take limitless time in getting to the deep truth.

*Turn from a critical to a nurturing parent*

### Phase F: Getting to the deep truth

This phase focuses on obtaining detailed admissions and confessions, using empathetic and emotionally challenging questions and getting to the deep truth. By this phase, the chances are you will have fallen naturally into the role of a nurturing parent and the suspect into that of an adaptive child. You should also explore any other cases of dishonesty that the suspect knows about and in which he may have been involved.

### Phase G: Follow-up

In this closing down phase, you will complete your notes or transcribe tapes. It is critical that records are accurate and securely retained. You should also prepare a list of further actions and review the results of the interview.

In the days following the interview, keep in contact with the suspect and try to obtain further details. Stay on cordial terms with him and speak to him as frequently as you reasonably can. Regular contact, after the interview, makes it less likely that the suspect will try and withdraw his confession, but don't be surprised if he turns against you once he has discussed his confession with accomplices, family and friends.

You should pay particular attention to the opening statement, how you will phrase accusations and present the key points. When you are planning and rehearsing the interview, consider the types of questions you will use by selecting the most appropriate from Chapter 7.

## CONSIDER HOW THE KEY POINTS WILL BE PRESENTED

You should identify, for each suspect, the most important evidence (the 'key points') you have and assemble them in such a way that their presentation will have the maximum visual and emotional impact:

- Enclosing documentary and other exhibits in clear plastic envelopes and marking them with exhibit labels and different coloured 'Post-It' notes. *(Usually an innocent person will ask about these and what they mean: the guilty party rarely will.)*
- Preparing weighty files of 'exhibits', which may be left out on desks in the interview room although never referred to. *(The anxiety of a guilty person will be increased by these, but he won't say anything!)*
- Preparing single page schedules summarizing important points: again these should be in colour, with important evidence highlighted or enlarged

The visual impact (as well as control of the interview) can be enhanced by using small coloured tabs, positioned to indicate the relevance of each document.

*The more evidence the suspect believes you have, the more likely he is to confess*

There are two ways in which the suspect can be confronted with key evidence. The first is to hold it in reserve until he has committed himself to a deceptive answer and then to ambush him with it.

## LOOK AT THIS

'Bill, you told me a moment ago that you have never been to Budapest. You said you were absolutely certain. I would like you to tell me about this receipt which shows that you stayed "with Mrs Jones" at the Hilton Hotel, Budapest from 1 to 12 April.' You should hand him the receipt and keep it in his personal space.

If you plan to do this, make sure you have backup copies of the evidence.

## EATING THE EVIDENCE

A young investigator found an airmail letter that totally proved a narcotics smuggling scheme. He interviewed the rather large Jamaican lady to whom it had been addressed handed her the letter and asked for her explanation. As quick as a flash she popped it in her mouth and ate it. 'What letter?' she asked. There was no backup copy.

Fumbling with papers in the interview reduces the chances of finding the truth, because it makes you appear incompetent and puts you in the transactional role of a child.

The second way is to display some or all of the evidence, by mounting it on walls around the interview room or laying it out on tables in the suspect's line of sight.

You will find that the guilty person seldom says anything about displayed exhibits, although you will notice his eyes drifting towards them, especially when he believes you are not watching him. Innocent people usually comment or ask questions about displayed exhibits.

## DECIDE ON THE VENUE AND TIMING

Ideally, interviews with suspects and important witnesses should be held simultaneously as part of the first step (see page 102) at a time and place when the suspects are most exposed or where they can be taken by surprise. If you cannot interview all suspects simultaneously, pay particular attention to the order in which they will be seen and, if possible, make sure they are not able to compare notes and coordinate their explanations.

If the suspect is a lark type – up early in the morning, all bright and cheerful – you may want to plan the interview for the late evening and vice versa if he is an owl. If you can catch him at a time when he is doing something he shouldn't be doing, so much the better. Always plan the venue and timing carefully: make sure they are to your advantage.

*The chance of finding the truth varies inversely*
*with the number of people present*

In complex cases, more than one interview may be required with some or all of the suspects but the first is usually the most productive because it should take the suspect by surprise. It is not uncommon for suspects to refuse to attend follow-up interviews simply because they have assessed their chances of success, decided the odds are against them and elected not to engage in battle.

*You may only have one bite of the apple*

## ARRANGING THE INTERVIEW ROOM

The layout of the interview room is very important in all serious cases. Always try to make the suspect play away from home or in an environment with which he is not familiar. Only in exceptional circumstances should the suspect be interviewed in his home (especially if he has a big dog) or office (especially if he has a fawning personal assistant). There are two reasons for this. The first is that the interview might be deliberately disrupted by family members or colleagues. Secondly, in his own environment, the suspect may feel in control.

Also think carefully before holding the interview in your own office, especially if it is small and untidy or displays your golfing memorabilia and photographs of you and your family on holiday in Benidorm. These can put you in the wrong transactional role.

Always remember that there are two interviews taking place, and if the suspect forms an opinion about you based on the appearance of your office, it may make it more difficult for you to adopt the transactional roles necessary to succeed.

Ideally the interview room should be small[1], private, reasonably soundproof and away from centres of earnest activity (the conference room in the Accounting Department may be ideal). People should not be able to look in from outside and the subject should be able to go in and out of the room without having to walk past 'rubber neckers'.

- Telephones should be disconnected and clocks and other distractions removed. (At the appropriate time, you must make sure all mobile telephones are turned off.)
- The room should be clean and tidy, bordering on clinical (a slight scent of antiseptic or of the confessional box does no harm).
- Furniture should be carefully arranged so that the suspect sits furthest from the door.
- At the start of the interview you should sit behind a desk with the suspect to your right.
- Seats for any corroborating witnesses should be placed out of the suspect's direct line of sight.

---

[1]  Around 10 feet by 10 feet

- If there are any pieces of particularly incriminating evidence, such as forged documents, you should consider enlarging them and having them pinned to the walls in the suspect's direct line of sight.
- If the suspect is known to smoke, the interview should be conducted in a smoking area.[2]
- If the interview is to be tape recorded, a test should be made to ensure that air conditioning and other ambient noise does not spoil the quality of the recording.

At the start of the interview you may plan to sit behind a desk to the suspect's left. As the interview progresses, through the pivotal point and the turn, you may move from behind the desk and sit alongside and close to him, thus reinforcing a nurturing parent role. But such movements have to appear spontaneous and natural. At the pivotal point you should be sitting close to the suspect and to his *left*.[3]

Under normal circumstances, a suspect should never be interviewed by more than two people at a time, and even then the second person should try and stay out of his direct line of sight and should remain silent unless the lead interviewer invites him to speak. The relationship between the interviewer and the suspect should be a one-to-one as far as possible and the room should be set up to establish the right transactional relationship.

After you have prepared the room and before the interview begins, ask a colleague who is not involved in the case to walk in and give you his first impressions. It must appear clinically professional.

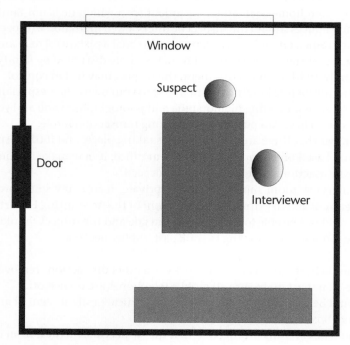

**Figure 6.4**   The interview room

---

[2]   Although denying the suspect the right to smoke may increase his anxiety it will be counter-productive in the later, empathy-building stages; also his smoking is likely to disturb his lawyer
[3]   By now you should know why but it is to connect to the right hemisphere and to the subject's memory (see page 60 and Table 3.3)

## NOTES AND RECORDS OF INTERVIEWS

## PRINCIPLES

It is important that a full and accurate record of each significant interview is prepared and re-tained[4]. The Codes of Practice issued under the Police and Criminal Evidence Act 1984, make it clear that lawyers would always prefer all interviewers to make contemporaneous notes as they do themselves[5]. The advice is detached from reality if the object is to establish rapport, create a free flow of information and get to the deep truth.

If you don't agree what a discouragement of the truth contemporaneous note taking is, try pulling out your notebook at the next cocktail party you attend but don't be surprised when no-one – except the odd accountant or lawyer – talks to you.

*Taking notes puts people off, including the note taker*

Worse still, while you are concentrating on joined up writing, you miss important clues. Contemporaneous note taking is at best a deterrent to finding the truth, and more often a displacement activity for anally retentive interviewers. It is the worst form of NLP and is tantamount to saying with each stroke of the pen 'Watch out what you say, old chum, you are really in trouble.'

Contemporaneous notes may, in exceptional circumstances, be made by a corroborating witness, but this practice is not recommended, again for the reason that it deters free flowing discussion.

### THE STENOGRAPHER

American lawyers insisted that investigators had a para-legal sit in on an interview with a fraud suspect. She was also a trained shorthand writer. She was told to remain silent, sit outside the suspect's direct line of sight and just take notes. When the interview got to the pivotal point and, in an emotional state, the suspect made his first serious admission, the para-legal could not contain herself and said 'Holy shit.' This threw the interview off track for at least an hour and could have been disastrous.

However, if a suspect is being totally unreasonable, you may decide to increase his anxiety by pulling out your note pad and committing him to false detail, which he will later find impossible to defend (see page 216).

In the UK you are allowed to tape record an interview without the subject's knowledge and for complex cases this is the safe course. However, if a long and important interview is not being tape recorded, trigger notes (such as names, addresses and other important information) may be made, but even then you must take great care. Never write anything down while the subject is speaking. Let him finish, make your note and then ask the next question.

*It is critical that you do not write down anything while the subject is speaking*

---

[4] You may use notes made at the time, or immediately after an interview, to refresh your memory when giving evidence in court.
[5] This is why lawyers seldom get to the deep truth

Notes of significant points, denials and admissions may be made at the end of the formal interview, jointly by you and any corroborating witnesses. These should then be shown to the suspect and his agreement sought. If he agrees they are correct, he should be asked to sign and date them.

A note should be made (again signed and dated) of any points with which the suspect does not agree. The notes should be annotated with the date and time they were completed and the names of the people involved. A photocopy of the notes may be handed to the subject for his retention.

## COVERT TAPE RECORDING

In most countries it is legally permissible to record any interview or conversation without the suspect's knowledge[6]. However, to ensure that recording is effective, the following procedure is recommended:

- An interview room with soft, sound absorbing furnishings should be selected, as air conditioning and other barely audible noises can completely obliterate a recording. A test should be made before the interview begins.
- Two high-quality stereo recorders should be used in parallel as Murphy's Law states that, 'the most important recording always self-destructs'.
- The recorder should have sufficient battery or mains power, memory or tape capacity to complete the interview without interruption.
- All end of tape buzzers and recording lights should be deactivated or covered with opaque tape.
- The tapes should be loaded and removed by an independent person (for example, the interviewer must not leave the room to change tapes!) who should keep a record of the time each tape was loaded and removed.
- Immediately after the interview has finished, the recording lugs on both sides of all original or master tapes should be broken to prevent over-recording.
- Two working copies of each tape should be taken as soon as possible and a note should be kept to establish the chain of evidence[7]. If necessary, the copies can be filtered to remove background noise, but under no circumstances should the original be modified.
- The original tapes should be delivered, as soon as possible after the interview has finished, to the company's legal representative against a signed receipt.
- Notes should be transcribed from the copy tapes and checked carefully.

The original tapes should be retained securely until all litigation connected with the interview has been completed.

When an interview is being covertly tape recorded, you should make a few trigger notes, if for no other reason than that by failing to do so, you may cause the suspect to ask the inevitable question: 'I see you are not making any notes. Is this being tape recorded?' If you are asked at any stage in the interview whether it is being tape recorded, you must tell the truth. You should not feel anxious or guilty but should respond:

---

[6]  However, check this with local lawyers. Some plonkers argue that covert recording contravenes the fair data collection rules of the Data Protection Act; this is nonsense, especially when crime is being prevented or investigated
[7]  In court you will have to prove the continuity of every exhibit from the moment it was obtained

> *Example:* 'Yes, we do this routinely on important interviews and you may have a copy at the appropriate time. If you would like to make your own recording now, we will provide you with a recorder. Let's carry on?'

You should then resume the interview as quickly and as quietly as possible. However, you must be prepared to present the tape – or copies of it – and transcripts to the suspect or his legal advisers and have them available for production in court.

Under no circumstances should covert tape recording be denied.

## MEMORY STICK

Investigators covertly recorded an interview using a Samsung recorder that uses a solid state memory rather than a tape. The suspect asked 'Is this being tape recorded?' and the investigators replied with the subjective truth 'No'. When the case came to court, the judge was very critical of the investigators' reaction and was not impressed with their statements that their reply was 'technically accurate' as the recording was not on tape. This foolishness caused the judge to lose all confidence in the investigation and the case was lost.

If you make a recording on a solid state recorder, you either have to maintain the device fully powered[8] until the recording is no longer required or copy the memory onto tape.

To transfer data from a solid state recorder to a CD, computer or tape:

- make a note of the length of the interview (e.g. 2 hours 42 minutes) from the display of the solid recorder;
- deliver the device to an independent laboratory (as soon as possible after the interview and against a dated and timed receipt) and get them to make at least three copies on tape or CD, noting the length of the interview (which should match the time recorded on the solid state recorder);
- obtain a witness statement from the laboratory;
- retain one copy of the tape or CD securely as the master version;
- use the copy to prepare a transcript and have the other delivered to the suspect at the appropriate time.

The danger is that if you make the copies yourself, you could be accused of tampering with the evidence. This is a bad scene.

## Overt tape recordings

Under PACE (see page 150), police are required to overtly tape record interviews with suspects, using approved double-reel tape recorders and to produce the recordings in court. Some police officers believe that overt tape recording increases the suspect's anxiety and makes it less likely to that he will lie, while others believe it is a big turn-off. There are no statistics to prove the point one way or the other but the reality is that anything that adversely affects the free flow of the interview at the pivotal point cannot be good (see page 199).

---

[8]   If you lose power the memory will be erased

If you decide that an overt recording should be made, tell the suspect – in a bland way – at the start of the interview: 'Bill, so that there is no misunderstanding, this interview is being tape recorded. We will give you a copy at the end of the investigation.' Then continue, without hesitation, with the opening statement. Do not make a big issue out of tape recording.

## CONSIDER USING INTERPRETERS

In some cases, interviews have to be conducted through interpreters, and this increases the difficulty. First, the presence of another human body may disturb the transactional relationship between you and the suspect: it slows down the pace of the interview and can lead to misunderstanding. If an interpreter has to be used (and bear in mind that some liars will deny their linguistic skills to give themselves more time to think):

- make sure the interpreter speaks and reads both languages fluently;
- choose an interpreter with experience of working with the local police or litigation lawyers;
- check the interpreter's background fully, especially his experience of giving evidence;
- make sure he has no relationship with the suspect, or anyone else involved in the case;
- translate the key documents, so that both versions can be shown to the suspect during the interview: pay particular attention to technical terms;
- obtain a letter of engagement and confidentiality agreement, signed by the interpreter, and check his references;
- explain the case fully and make sure he understands the evidence and the approach you intend to take;
- rehearse the interview (see page 222);
- tape record everything in the live interview if you can: experience shows this is a prudent step.

---

## WHEN IS A CONFESSION NOT A CONFESSION?

The interview was going badly and the interpreter did not seem interested. The interviewer suggested that they should take a break and he walked out of the room leaving the interpreter and the suspect together. Unbeknown to either of them, the interview had been, and was still being, taped.

The interviewer returned to the room and terminated the interview. A few days later when the tape was transcribed, part of the conversation between the interpreter and the suspect during the break read:

| | |
|---|---|
| *Suspect*: | I thought I was in trouble there for a moment. |
| *Interpreter*: | Trust me, the man's a fool. Keep calm. |
| *Suspect*: | How much longer will it be? |
| *Interpreter*: | Not long. He is giving up. He is a cretin: don't worry, my friend. |

It transpired that the suspect and the interpreter were first cousins who often went clubbing together. The real insult was that the off-record conversation was in English, a language the suspect said he could not understand.

During the interview:

- the interpreter should sit alongside you;
- you should address questions to the suspect and monitor his reaction – *especially noting if he appears to understand the question before it has been translated;*
- you should look at the suspect while the interpreter is speaking and while he is giving his response: *do not look at the interpreter.*

The interpreter can make or break an interview and it is vital that he is coached so that he can become actively involved.

## INTERVIEWS IN THE PRESENCE OF THE SUSPECT'S LAWYER

The UK Law Society published a paper in 1998[9] setting out the approach it recommends lawyers should take when their clients are being investigated and interviewed. It is not necessary to go into the gory detail, but sufficient to say that the recommended actions appear to be based on a Compulsive Interference Disorder (CID) and the assumption that their clients are always innocent.

The main problem is that the charisma of the suspect's lawyer will disturb transactional relationships and unless you take care, he will capture the role of the ultimate critical parent, forcing you into the role of an adaptive child. This is very bad news.

The recommended approach is to:

- Speak to the lawyer – in the absence of the suspect – immediately before the interview starts[10] and try to agree the ground rules to the effect that he is *not* a participant, nor a witness as to fact. His job is to advise the suspect on legal matters and not to argue the case on his behalf or to impede the course of justice. He is, after all, 'an Officer of the Court' and should act accordingly.
- If you regard his client as a peripheral player, or if there are mitigating factors, do not be afraid to say so. Clever lawyers will seize upon this and may change sides to support you.
- Try to establish an adult-to-adult transactional relationship with him. If this doesn't work, you should consider crossing roles in the interview (see page 67) but this is a high-risk strategy.
- Don't let the lawyer argue the case in the absence of the suspect but politely point out that 'your client should answer these questions and make these points, not you'.
- Outline the proposed interview structure, without necessarily revealing all of the 'key points' or your line of questioning. However, you must be fair.
- In the interview, direct all questions to the suspect and concentrate on him – not his lawyer, unless the latter is being unusually cooperative

Alternatively, you may decide to invite your legal representative to attend the interview and at least put the transactional roles in balance. However, you should recognize that the probability of getting to the deep truth varies inversely with the number of people present.

---

[9]  *Active Defence: Lawyer's Guide to Police and Defence Investigation and Prosecution and Defence Disclosure in Criminal Cases,* Eric Shepherd and Roger Ede, ISBN 18532 681 8
[10]  Try to make sure he is not able to brief his client on your conversation before the interview starts

## Your principles

### A LOW-KEY PROFESSIONAL APPROACH

As we have said it is not necessary to take on a macho, heavy-handed role, packed with testosterone and Tourette's syndrome. This is the opposite of what is needed and if such tactics are used, the result is likely to be a disaster. A quiet, confident, professional, empathetic but relentless approach is the most effective way of getting to the deep truth. Also never forget that everything you say and do may be examined in court, in the finest detail and under hostile cross examination (see Chapter 10 on giving evidence).

*Become quietly professional, but relentless.*
*Don't say or do anything you cannot honestly defend*

Some of the questions and responses discussed, especially in Chapter 7, may not suit your style.

### THE EMPATHETIC BANK INSPECTOR

An experienced interviewer was mentoring a team of bank inspectors. One inspector (who ironically became a very senior manager) could nor bring himself to turn at the pivotal point into a nurturing parent. 'I don't like people who defraud my bank', he said, 'and there is no way I can say all that crap, that I understand them or empathize with them'.

His supervisor pointed out that the empathic turn to nurturing parent had worked successfully for the department and that he should try it. His next interview was conducted brilliantly and the suspect brought quickly to the pivotal point. 'Why did all this start, Bill, you have always been such a good employee. Was it because you simply wanted money or was there some other reason?' The suspect thought for a few moments and then in a quiet and emotional voice said: 'I took the money because my wife was ill and she needed an operation, urgently.' The inspector's face became a mask of hate and he said: 'Bollocks, what was wrong with the National Health Service? It's good enough for my family and me. It should be good enough for you.' Unsurprisingly, all signs of empathy disappeared and it took another four hours to bring the suspect back to the point where he admitted the deep truth.

The decision on the approach you use is yours, but it is critical that you select tools and techniques appropriate to the situation concerned and with which you feel comfortable.

### ACTIVE LISTENING, OBSERVING AND VISUALIZATION

However, there is one critical point and that is to become an active listener and a conscious observer of human behaviour. Most people hear but don't listen, or see but don't observe, and thus miss important clues to innocence and deception.

Before every interview or meeting, make sure all of your senses are turned on and listen carefully to every word the subject says, how he says it and consciously monitor his body movements. Try to visualize what he is saying and picture if it makes sense and if you have any doubts press for more and more detail. Tune to the emotions involved and question whether they are genuine or false. Think how you would feel in his position and assess whether his reactions are consistent with his story. Remain consciously alert to the things the subject does not say that an innocent person would.

*You can learn a lot by listening and looking*

## TAKING A DEEP INTEREST IN THE SUBJECT

You always should try to remain emotionally detached and avoid being judgemental. Even in really tough interviews your job is to find the truth, within the law, while showing respect for the suspect's rights. If you take a genuine conscious interest in him (however bad his behaviour) and try to put yourself in his position, you will find interviews much easier and more effective. You will also get more easily to the truth.

*Take a deep, genuine interest in the subject*

## GET DOWN TO THE CRITICAL ISSUES

Wherever possible – and especially with people suspected of serious deception – you should try to get straight to the heart of the matter and be as direct as possible (see Figure 6.5).

If it becomes clear that the subject has no intention of telling the truth, you should switch your approach, take a few deep breaths and ask questions that force him into more and more detail – and lead to increasingly outrageous lies. Whatever the objective of the interview, lies to which the suspect has committed himself will come back to haunt him later on.

Ironically, if you take this indirect route, it is not uncommon to find that the suspect's anxiety is increased to the pivotal point, and he then decides to tell the truth.

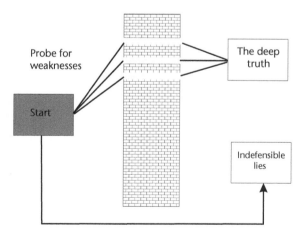

**Figure 6.5**   Direct and indirect approaches

## TRANSACTIONAL ROLES

You must consciously try to retain control of every interview or meeting. This may be easier said than done, especially if the suspect is an experienced crook, a senior businessman or represented by an overly aggressive lawyer. However, you should always aim to start every interview by consciously taking the role of an adult and be prepared to move into compatible transactions as the interview progresses (see Table 6.4).

You should remain consciously aware of the transactional dynamics in all meetings and be prepared to take action to change them.

## A GOOD EXAMPLE

If you want to see a good example of transactional analysis in operation, watch the television detective programme *Colombo*. This poor, untidy creature, who falls automatically into the role of a child, customarily seems to face murderers who are pillars of society and the ultimate critical parents. Colombo establishes an equal transaction with them and from time to time gains total control by picking up the suspect's most valuable possession – usually a vase or some other fragile gem – putting them in mortal fear that he might drop it. Certainly while it is in his hands, he has the suspect's full attention.

**Table 6.4**    Creating an adult role

| Aspect | What you should do |
|---|---|
| Dress and emblems | You must dress and appear professional. Do not wear your bow tie or Hush Puppies. Take great care over the first impression you will create with the subject |
| Interview room | The room should be clinically clean and tidy (see page 207) |
| Introduction | You should appear calm. Introduce yourself and your colleagues and offer to shake hands. Direct the subject to the chair in which you would like him to sit |
| Language | Your language should be professional and polite. Avoid childish chit-chat and humour. Try to get on the same wavelength as the subject |
| Body language | You should adopt an assertive, professional posture. Do not slouch in your chair |
| Documents to which you will refer which we call the 'key points' | You should make sure these are carefully arranged, so that their presentation is professional. Fumbling with documents will make you appear incompetent and childish |

To get to the deep truth it is usually essential that an equal transaction is created, with you in the role of a nurturing parent and the suspect accepting the role of an adaptive child. You will find that innocent and truthful subjects will be far more opposed to imposed changes in role than liars.

*Pay attention to transactional roles*

## CREATING RAPPORT

Your chances of getting to the deep truth are much greater if you consciously tune to the same wavelength and channels of communication as the subject. Thus before every important interview you should have thoroughly researched his background and know what makes him tick or tock.

For rapport building purposes, the population can be classed as introverts or extroverts and further categorized as in Table 6.5.

Table 6.5 shows how rapport can be established. However, in tough interviews you will still have to go through the roles of critical and nurturing parent to get to the deep truth.

**Table 6.5**   Character types

| Type and characteristics | Additional ways of creating rapport |
| --- | --- |
| EMOTION DOMINANT (arty types)<br>Wears his heart on his sleeve<br>Sometimes acts in a 'childlike' way<br>Takes things very personally and is inclined to worry<br>Extreme mood swings<br>Wants to please and be liked<br>May see himself as a victim of circumstances | Move slowly possibly on a child-to-child basis<br>Avoid aggression<br>Deal with problems on an emotional level (feelings etc.)<br>Build up case slowly and logically |
| SENSORY DOMINANT (SAS commando types)<br>High achiever<br>Appears fearless and a risk taker<br>Energetic and fast speech<br>Prepared to fight rather than flee | Avoid emotions<br>Move quickly and focus on concrete evidence (the mechanics)<br>Deal calmly with counter-attacks<br>Focus on the key points |
| LOGIC DOMINANT (accounting types)<br>Superior attitude<br>Exact, logical and precise, bordering on 'nit picking'<br>Cold and emotionally withdrawn<br>Logical<br>A Loner<br>Detached and indifferent to the problem | Take a logical approach and focus on detail<br>Make sure you are accurate<br>Show no emotion<br>Emphasize the key points |
| EGO DOMINANT (Managing Director types)<br>Assumes the role of a critical parent<br>Condescending, haughty and conceited<br>Pampers himself and is full of self-justification<br>Inconvenienced by the problem | Play to his ego (initially and to build rapport as an adaptive child)<br>Take a high-level view of the case and work on principles |

## SALES TRAINING

Some sales training courses encourage salesmen in rapport-building techniques. They are taught to show a deep interest in the prospects' hobbies, families etc., to mirror his dress, body language and verbal communications even to the point that if he swears a lot, they should do the same. The theory is that by getting on the same wavelength, rapport is established and sales improve. Also giving a small gift to the prospect or touching him has the same effect.

You can use some or all of the approaches listed in Table 6.6 – at appropriate stages of the interview – to establish rapport.

'We', 'us' and 'ours' are great rapport-building words, as are discussions about emotions, feelings and attitudes that hit directly on the subject's subconscious. Agreement on any point with the subject also increases rapport. However, never fall into the trap of believing that by self-deprecating you build rapport.

*Create a feeling of rapport*

**Table 6.6**   Methods of establishing rapport

| Aspect | What you should do |
| --- | --- |
| Transactional role | Adopt appropriate and equal transactional roles |
| Primary channel of communication | Tune to the subject's primary channel of communication |
| Careful listening | Listen carefully to the words used: use compatible language and don't talk up or down to him. If he is a rapper, do not pretend that you are some sort of jive bunny. Always act your age! |
| Words | Carefully repeat some words and phrases used by the subject |
| Method of addressing the subject | In the early stages of the interview you may refer to the subject as 'Mister' but use his first name, at the appropriate time, to support a nurturing parent role |
| Body language | Consciously use positive body language: mirror his eye contact and gestures |
| Mirroring | Adopt similar postures to the subject and use the same type of language, words and hand movements. When he picks up his cup of tea, you should do the same |
| Interests | Interests shared with the subject can be discussed to create rapport. However, make sure this does not become a displacement activity for asking relevant questions or used by the subject to ramble off the point |
| Shared professional qualifications, schooling etc. | |
| Emotions | Monitor the subject's emotions. Be prepared to communicate with him at an emotional level |

| Aspect | What you should do |
|---|---|
| Accusations and criticisms | Try to avoid being judgmental, but challenge all lies. Never attack the subject's character by calling him a 'liar' but you may destroy specific untrue statements by calling them 'lies'. It is, however, important to continually emphasize the embedded command 'truth' (see pages 51, 52 and 235) |
| Agreement | Confirm your agreement with the subject wherever you can. Try to find common ground. The more you are able to agree (even on small things), the more likely you are to get to the deep truth. The more the suspect says 'Yes' the less likely he is to say 'No' |
| Touch | Although touching the subject must be handled carefully[11], there is no doubt that with right hemisphere dominated (and tactile) people, touch builds rapport. However, never touch a member of the opposite sex, nor an accountant or lawyer |
| Appearance | Believe it or not, good-looking people are more easily accepted by others than those with faces like the back end of a bus. There is not much you can do about this if you are ugly, but it is a point worth noting |
| Compliments | Compliment the subject, without being patronizing |

## THE MODEST AUDITOR

An auditor for a very large conglomerate would – as a matter of course – try and get others to underestimate him by saying something along the lines: 'I know I am only a stupid auditor, but please tell me …' Rather than leading people into a trap, the words put him in the transactional role of a child and the embedded command 'stupid' stuck in the minds of auditees, who all seemed to agree with him. They also thought his approach was 'patronizing'.

*Don't self-deprecate: it will make your hair fall out*

As Forrest Gump would say: 'That's all we have to say about rapport' – at least for the moment – but it is a very important word.

## LOSING CONTROL

Remember there are always two interviews taking place and that the subject will evaluate you and recalibrate his approach accordingly. You may lose control of an interview if:

- you have not fully understood the issues or have misinterpreted the facts, so research carefully and check everything;
- you make wild allegations, so be careful how you phrase accusations;
- you bluff, bluster or show that you are angry or impatient, so remain emotionally detached;
- you let the subject succeed with lies, so always challenge them as politely as you can;

---

[11]  Excuse the pun

- you show your nervousness, so take a few deep breaths and focus hard on the suspect's nervousness as he has more to lose than you;
- you do not take on board facts which contradict your opinions: you must always keep an open mind.

You will definitely lose control if you have not fully prepared for the interview, lack commitment in the delivery of questions, succumb to an attack or do not adopt the appropriate transactional role. Good planning and rehearsal can eliminate all of these problems.

---

## THE BIG SHOT

A group of serious commercial villains employed a powerful ex-politician, who was also a brilliant lawyer, as a special adviser. He would be wheeled in to important meetings as the ultimate critical parent. Even experienced businessmen would tremble in his presence.

Lawyers had to try and negotiate a settlement with the villains and knew they risked being over-awed by the special adviser. For a few thousand pounds, they retained the special adviser's ex-political boss and presented him at the meeting. For a few moments, there was a transactional battle between the special adviser and the ex-boss, which the latter won and a fair settlement was reached.

---

*Keep control and remain emotionally detached.*

## DELIVERY OF QUESTIONS

Often questions have a much greater impact on the subject if they are delivered in conjunction with a visual and emotional stimulation, such as simultaneously handing him an incriminating piece of evidence or requiring him to look at a chart, physical object or picture. For this reason, it is a good idea to have every key point that supports the deception theory summarized on single pieces of paper which can be presented to the suspect at the appropriate time and kept within his personal space and in his left field of vision (see page 60, Table 3.3).

*Try and keep incriminating evidence within the suspect's personal space and field of vision*

Some interviewers like to use checklists which set the questions they plan to ask. Although in some circumstances this approach may be useful[12], it tends to make the interview too rigid and, for this reason, fails. A checklist may be referred to at the end of an interview, and before the subject leaves, to make sure you have covered everything you should. Lists may be used in formal interviews where you simply want to give the subject the chance to explain.

*Assemble key points in the order that you will deal with them*

For complex interviews, it is usually better to assemble all of the papers (summary single pages, exhibits, schedules etc.) in the order in which you plan to cover them and flag them

---

[12] Especially for elimination interviews

with highly coloured 'Post-it' notes summarizing the key points and other matters you want the subject to explain.

If the documents can be assembled in voluminous files, so much the better, as these will make it clear to the subject that he has a great deal to answer and thus increase his anxiety.

*Increase the visual impact of documents*

## NOTE TAKING

Taking detailed notes during an interview is a very bad practice and should be avoided at all costs. The detailed reasons for this, and alternative solutions are explained in pages 210 and 211. But please remember, from now on, that your chances of getting to the deep truth are significantly reduced if the suspect sees you, or anyone else, writing detailed notes. In any case, detailed note taking is usually no more than a displacement activity by inexperienced interviewers. It is really bad practice.

*Note taking disturbs the subject*

## BODY LANGUAGE AND PARALINGUISTICS

You must remain consciously aware of the way in which you ask questions and the effect your body language has on the subject. Try to deliver questions clearly, without prevarication and with real commitment. Try to make sure that your body language and channels of communication are consistent with the transactional role you are adopting (see page 66). This is especially important when you are in the role of a nurturing parent, when the tone and volume of your voice should drop and speed of delivery decrease. You should feel that you are talking to a child whom you are genuinely trying to help.

*Adapt your own body language*

## AWARENESS

You must always remain alert to the possibility that someone may try and deceive you: a little paranoia does no harm.

*Never take things at face value **but think what they mean***

This does not mean that you have always to express your concerns, but you should internalize and think to yourself 'What is the angle?' and 'Is this important?' If the lie is insignificant, such as a joke or a slight exaggeration, you are best advised to simply enjoy it, unless you dislike the person concerned and want to teach him a lesson. A lot of lies fall into this 'good' category and if you challenge them all, you will quickly become unpopular. Do this and your only option will be to become a lawyer, accountant or even an investigator.

*Decide which lies you wish to challenge*

## DEALING WITH NERVOUSNESS

Before the interview begins, you must plan the approach and techniques you will use. Never, ever go unprepared into an interview. In the opening phase you must adopt an adult and professional role.

Although it is usual for even experienced interviewers to feel a little nervous, you should remember that, deep down, the suspect is under much greater stress. Your nervousness can be reduced by good planning, knowing the facts inside out and through rehearsal.

# Check the legality

If the case is out of the ordinary or particularly difficult, you should check with qualified litigation lawyers in the country concerned that the planned approach will not contravene the law. It is especially important to confirm that privately conducted interviews are legal and admissible in court. Also, if you are not already certain, you should establish whether or not you are required to caution the subject to the effect that he is not obliged to answer questions and that, if he does so, the answers will be admissible against him in court. Finally, the position on covertly tape recording interviews should be confirmed.

# Rehearsal

If the interview is important, always rehearse it, if necessary with a colleague, your wife, kids, or in extreme circumstances, with your mother-in-law. The first rehearsal should be with you playing the role of the interviewer and the second in the shoes of the suspect. You will find this rehearsal is more than worthwhile.

*Practice makes perfect*

# The execution

If you have gone through the above process, the interview should be simple providing:

- you arrive early and get into the interview room first;
- you stick to your plan and remain in control.

As explained fully in Chapter 7, the process should take you to the pivotal point, with you in the role of a nurturing parent and the liar an adaptive child. From this point onwards, you must be driven by the circumstances of the case in question, but take your time and get to the worst case and deep truth.

## Conclusions

If you have planned properly and rehearsed thoroughly, conducting the interview should be the easy part, providing you remain emotionally detached with all of your antenna turned on.

THE INTERVIEW ROOM

# 7 *Conducting Tough Interviews*

## Introduction

This chapter sets out the potential strategies, tactics and questions for conducting tough interviews in the seven phases discussed in Chapter 6 and provides indicators of truthful and untruthful responses.

## Types of questions

### THE MENU

There are many ways in which we can deliver questions:

- some are general and set the scene;
- some will test whether the subject is being truthful or not;
- some will produce detail or fine-tune an answer;
- some will increase anxiety;
- others are empathetic and emotionally sensitive and can be used at the pivotal point to help the suspect conclude that it would be in his best interests to tell the truth.

The relevance of questions to the seven interview phases is usually as in Table 7.1.

Most questions will be directed and answered at a conscious level although, as we will see later, we can use embedded commands, NLP, non-verbal communications and other techniques to excite the monkeys on the liar's back.

### CONTROL AND RELEVANT QUESTIONS

Control questions are non-threatening and are used, among other things, to monitor a subject's baseline reactions when he is telling the truth. For example, under most circumstances, the question *'When did you start working here?'* could be regarded as a control question, as could *'Do you prefer rice pudding to treacle tart?'* The problem is that what you think may be a control, and unthreatening, question may hold a dreadful significance for the subject, especially if he has just stolen Granny Smith's rice pudding. Honest people take the same level of care with control as they do with relevant questions: liars relax but don't know how to deal with them.

**Table 7.1**   Question types and interview phases

| The types of questions that are most applicable to the following phases | Types of questions<br>*Transactional role* (see page 65) | | | | |
|---|---|---|---|---|---|
| | General | Testing | Accusatory | | Empathetic |
| | | | Probing | Increasing anxiety | |
| A: Opening | Introductory Statements<br>Yes<br>*Variable* | Possible<br>*Adult* | No | Possible<br>*Adult* | Possible<br>*Adult* |
| B: Probing | | Yes<br>*Critical parent* | Yes<br>*Critical parent* | Yes<br>*Critical parent* | No |
| C: Raising anxiety | | | | | |
| D: The pivotal point | | No | No | Yes<br>*Critical and nurturing parent* | Yes<br>*Nurturing parent* |
| E: Turning | | | | | |
| F: The deep truth | | Yes<br>*Nurturing parent* | Yes<br>*Nurturing parent or adult* | Possibly<br>*Adult or critical parent* | |
| G: Follow-up | | Possible<br>*Adult* | Yes<br>*Adult* | Possible<br>*Adult* | |

Relevant questions relate specifically to the matter in issue and will either require the suspect:

- to make an admission or confession; or
- to tell a lie.

Relevant questions thus stimulate an anxious response, usually within three to five milliseconds of being asked. Often the differences in responses to control and relevant questions – or 'response latency' – are glaringly obvious.

## THE OJ SIMPSON CASE

OJ Simpson was interviewed by two Los Angeles detectives the day after his wife was found butchered. The full transcript of this very poor interview can be downloaded from the Internet (simpson.walraven.com). Detailed analysis reveals some very interesting patterns (Table 7.2).

*Incongruence between the responses to control and relevant questions are vital clues*

Obviously, patterns such as those described in Table 7.2 are not proof positive of either guilt or innocence, but you should always consciously monitor the differences between the subject's response to control and relevant questions and incongruencies between content, syntax, paralinguistics, body language and attitude. This is the easy part, leaving you with the more difficult job of resolving your suspicions.

**Table 7.2**  Responses in the interview with OJ Simpson

| Type of question | Response to control questions | Response to relevant questions |
|---|---|---|
| Closed questions that could have been answered with a binary 'yes' or 'no' | 95 per cent of questions were answered only with a 'yes' or 'no' | None were answered with only a 'yes' or 'no' but were either prefaced by prevarication or closed with a softening phrase |
| Open questions | No requests for clarification were made and there was no stalling | 95 per cent of questions were clarified by a question from OJ |

## OPEN QUESTIONS

Open questions invite the subject to give an explanation in his own words, without prompting. They do not provide him with any sort of template for deception because they hide how much you know and don't know. Open questions such as:

*'Why?' 'What?' 'Where?' 'Who?' 'How?' 'Tell me everything you know about ...'*

allow the honest subject to respond with a detailed freestyle narrative, but they require a dishonest suspect to decide how much he will say and thus take a gamble: he does not want to volunteer too much detail (through which you may trap him later); nor does he want to be caught out in an obvious concealment (see Table 7.3).

**Table 7.3**  Reactions in the interview with OJ Simpson

| Reactions indicating innocence | Reactions indicating guilt |
|---|---|
| Gives a detailed, free-flowing account of the matters at issue, consistent with his baseline responses | Wants more information: 'Where do you want me to start?' 'I am not sure how far you want me to go' 'How much do you know?' 'You tell me what you want me to explain' |
| Retrieves the answer from memory: looks to the left while thinking | Creates answers in the imagination: looks to the right while thinking |
| Consistent detail | Lack of detail or inconsistent detail |
| Answers the question directly | Asks for clarification of the question such as 'Where do you want me to start?' |
| Immediately understands the context of the question | Does not know how much an innocent person would know. Thus asks clarification questions. 'How should I know that?' |
| Gives truthful responses to questions where you already know the answers | Gives evasive or untruthful responses to questions to which you already know the answers |

The most usual response from both honest and deceptive subjects to the question 'Tell me everything you know about x' is: 'Where do you want me to start?' Your response should be: 'Everything you think could be relevant'.

*Open questions provide no template for deception*

At this point the dishonest suspect will normally press for more clarification before responding, usually because he is concerned to find out how much you know. The innocent person is normally much more confident, not at risk and will just give his answers.

Always consider using open questions that focus on the subject's emotions, feelings and attitudes and which require him to consult with the subconscious monkey.

---

*Example*:
- 'What do you least like about yourself?'
- 'What is the worst thing you have ever done?'
- 'What were you *thinking* when you went to the post box?'
- 'What do you feel should happen to people who make false claims?'

---

If you ask a person, 'Please tell me everything you know about the missing money,' you give him no clues about how much you know and force him to define the boundaries of the story, prologue, critical issues and epilogue. If he asks, 'What do you want me to cover?', the answer should be, 'Tell me everything you think is relevant.'

## YOU KNOW WHY I AM HERE?

The head of accounting in the advertising division of a leading British retailer lived in a small apartment in an Essex estate. During the day he was a model of frugality and took the tube and corned beef sandwiches to work. At night and weekends and during holidays he was a raver. He owned a Porsche, fancy clothes, jewellery and generally lived the high life, drank champagne and ate caviar. His wealth was accumulated by setting up dummy companies that allegedly supplied his employer with signs, display boards and posters.

Over the course of a year his Porsche accumulated a bundle of parking and speeding tickets, mainly outside clubs in the West End of London, which the man ignored. The police became fed up and one weekend sent a young constable around to see him. When the man opened his front door the constable said, 'I am sure you know why I am here', and to his great amazement the man admitted to a £1 million fraud on his employer.

We should always be consciously aware of the assistance closed questions give a liar in framing his responses.

Questions about feelings and attitudes get directly into the subject's subconscious, making it more likely that the truth or Freudian slips will emerge, or that by bringing unpalatable facts into focus, his anxiety will increase.

## HOW DID YOU FEEL?

The Sales Manager of a company admitted to falsifying purchase invoices from an advertising agency and converting the benefits to his own account. Investigators believed that the Sales Director had intimidated the man into the fraud and that his confession was contrived to protect his boss. This appeared even more likely because the Sales Director was doing everything possible to impede the investigation and recommended that the Sales Manager should be allowed to resign and not even asked to pay back what he had stolen.

The investigators showed the Sales Manager a number of invoices and asked how he had falsified them. He replied 'I just did this on the copier.' This was clearly not the case, as the forgeries required careful alignment on a PC. This was pointed out and the Sales Manager asked to provide a demonstration of the process he had used to print them. He tried but failed to do so and became very agitated. He then made the incredible unsolicited denial 'I can promise you that the Sales Director was not involved in this. I only told him a couple of days ago what I had done.'

He was asked to relay the conversation he had supposedly had with his boss. He said 'I just told him I had forged some invoices.'

The Investigators asked: 'How did you feel when you told him this?'

| | |
|---|---|
| Response: | 'What do mean?' |
| Investigator: | 'How did you feel' |
| Reponse: | 'How should I feel? |
| Investigator: | 'You tell me' |
| Response: | 'He knew nothing before that' |
| Investigator: | 'What did he say when you told him' |
| Response: | 'I don't understand what you are driving at' |
| Investigator: | 'What did he say' |
| Response: | 'I don't remember' |
| Investigator: | 'Was he angry?' |
| Response; | 'Not that I recall … he didn't say anything' |
| Investigator: | 'Bill, we know what you are trying to do, but it's hopeless isn't it? You don't even know how to make the false invoices do you? Just tell us the truth' |
| Response: | 'His son did them on his computer and he told me to put them through. He kept most of the money' |

He then went on to make a detailed confession and produced overwhelming evidence against his manager.

## CLOSED AND LEADING QUESTIONS

Closed, or leading, questions can be answered by a simple binary: 'yes' or 'no'. The problem is that they often suggest the answer required and thus enable the subject to judge the extent of your knowledge.

*Example*:
- 'Did you go into the filing room?'
- 'Is this in your handwriting?'
- 'Did you speak to John Jones about this?'

Closed questions normally increase the pace of an interview and, if you change rapidly from one topic to another, the suspect may have great difficulty planning his responses and become anxious. You can tell a lot by how a subject answers binary questions (Table 7.4).

**Table 7.4**   Answers to binary questions

| Reactions indicating innocence | Reactions indicating guilt |
|---|---|
| Committed 'yes' and 'no' answers | Avoidance of a 'yes' or 'no' answer<br>Prevarication before saying 'yes' or 'no' or superfluous words following their use. For example, *'I would like to assure you the answer is yes'* or *'Yes, in truth it is'*<br>Lack of commitment to the answer usually by words such as *'to the best of my recollection'* |
| Denial of a specific point, often in first person singular, past tense | No denial, limited denial or objection |

Closed questions based on what is referred to as the '7WH mnemonic' of who, why, what, where, which, when and how are always useful. Closed questions do not usually result in a free-flowing dialogue, but should be used in Phases B and C to pin down detail on the mechanics of the suspected transgression. However, if the interview results in criminal proceedings, the suggestion may be made that responses to rapid-fire, closed questions were put into the mouth of the accused. Thus closed questions should be used carefully and corroborated by detail.

*Closed questions increase anxiety especially when you jump from topic to topic*

## COMPLEX QUESTIONS

Normally questions should be simply constructed, so that there can be no misunderstanding about the answer. Complex questions have more than one element and cannot usually be answered by a single response.

### THE ULTIMATE QUESTION

In the transcript of an interview, one question covered nearly eight pages of text and consisted of 1200 words. At the end of it, the subject said, 'Would you please repeat the question?'

You must try to ask simple questions so that misunderstanding is minimized and the subject is committed to his answers.

*Avoid complex questions*

But before you get on to this, think about the themes you plan to concentrate on in the interview and how you will lead the suspect to the pivotal point. Planning an interview is again like a jigsaw puzzle, so make sure all of the pieces fit. Also remember that to get to the deep truth, the suspect has to trust you, so do nothing that marks you out as untrustworthy: this does not mean that you should not be unswerving in your quest for the truth

# Important responses

## BACKGROUND

The normal sequence of interviews is question – answer – question and so on. But there are a number of possible responses that displace this sequence and which you should consciously plan to deal with.

## REFUSAL TO ANSWER QUESTIONS

### Background

Even if the suspect appears ready, willing and able to take part in an interview, there is still a possibility that he will not answer some or all questions. If he does this you know that the answers would not be in his favour and you should proceed on that basis and persuade him to answer by using some or all of the following approaches.

> *If someone refuses to answer a question, you know it would not be in his favour.*
> *That is all you need to know*

### Types of and reasons for refusal

Refusal to answer questions, which is a very strong indication of guilt and the epitome of the flee in the 'fight or flight' decision, comes in two guises – overt (conscious) and covert (unconscious), as illustrated in Table 7.5.

**Table 7.5**  Refusal to answer

| Category<br>Probable motivation | Examples |
|---|---|
| **Overt refusal** | |
| I cannot defend myself | *'I am not coming to see you'*<br>*'I am saying nothing'*<br>*'I am saying nothing unless my lawyer is there'* |
| I have had a bad experience before | *'I have already been interviewed by your colleagues and I am not going over it again'* |
| **Subtle refusal** | |
| I cannot defend myself but do not have the courage to refuse to answer your questions | Evasion<br>Pseudo-denials<br>Objections<br>Emotional outbursts<br>*'No comment'*<br>*'You have already made up your mind and there is no point in my explaining'* |

Refusal to answer may apply to the interview as a whole or to a specific topic or question. Either way it is usually an acknowledgement by the subject that he has no defence and that by answering questions he can only make matters worse.

## The soft approach

You may decide to take a soft, low-key approach to the suspect's refusal to answer:

• Concede his right to remain silent and point out your interpretation of his position.

> *Example*: 'I know you do not have to say anything and that is up to you. But this problem won't go away. I have been in this business for a long time and worked with lots of people in your position. In my experience, when people say what you have just said, they are afraid of something. Innocent people always demand the right to give their side of the story. Why don't you want to discuss this?'

• Try to build rapport and berate his decision to flee.

> *Example*: 'I understand how you feel and no one likes to feel they are under suspicion. I am very open-minded and we can call it a day now if you really feel that way. Do you want to give up now, or should we see how we get on, taking a step at a time? There are always two sides to every story and we should make sure that we get yours across. Shouldn't we?'

• If the suspect walks out of the interview you have lost nothing, but it is very unlikely that he will do so. If he stays, select the weakest piece of evidence you have or an unsubstantiated allegation and help him disprove it.

> *Example*: 'We know there are two sides to every story, so let's take an example. Someone said that you have just bought a villa in Spain for £100 000 in cash. This is not correct, is it? Shall we try to get this cleared up now?'

You should repeat this process, using the weakest evidence, until the suspect is talking freely: then turn quietly to the key points.

*Don't allow a liar to escape by not giving an answer*

## The direct approach

You may adopt the role of a critical parent and deliberately increase the suspect's anxiety by making statements summarizing the evidence and your belief in his guilt to the point where he concludes that it is in his interest to offer an explanation:

• Concede his right to remain silent and point out your interpretation of his position.

*Example*: 'Of course you do not have to say anything. If that is your firm decision you will have to live with the consequences. But in fairness to you I am going to tell you what evidence we have, how the investigation will move forward and what will happen. You know this will not go away just because you say nothing.'

- Pull out your notebook.

*Example*: 'I am going to tell you what evidence we have and I will ask for your feelings about it. If you choose to sit there and say nothing, that's up to you, but I will note down how you react, including 'no comment' and your non-verbal reactions. Do you understand?'

- Ask questions starting with a piece of weak evidence or an unsubstantiated allegation, which you know he can disprove.
- If he gives an explanation, compliment him, move on to another piece of weak evidence and keep him talking.

*Example*: 'You see how things can get cleared up when you are prepared to discuss them? Let's move on.'

*Once people start talking it is difficult for them to stop*

It is possible that the suspect will refuse to talk under either approach when incriminating issues are raised. Again, everything depends on your persuasive powers, but don't give up too easily.

## The dramatic approach
This approach should be considered only in extreme situations, but it sometimes works.

*Example*: 'Of course you do not have to say anything, but I am going to ask the questions anyway. And as you may know, 80% of human communication is though body language, the way you move, swallow, blink, move your eyes, legs, arms, body, breathe, react etc. I am going to tell you out loud how I interpret your reaction to each question and write down what I observe. Do you understand that?' Then you ask the first question and write down and say out loud: 'To that statement, Mr Smith swallowed hard, his eyes dilated and he began to sweat'. Then continue: 'Did you have access to the computer on the day in question?' Again write down and announce what you have seen: 'To that he moved his right leg, very defensively, blinked and sweat appeared on his upper lip. He had a very sheepish look about him.'

Suspects on which the above technique has been tested have begun to give oral answers after the fifth or sixth question, but you should use the technique only as the last resort and never in criminal cases, unless you want your ass severely kicked.

## The legalistic approach

This is a fairly high-risk strategy, but you may point out that the problem will not simply disappear and that by refusing to answer questions, the suspect is closing down the organization's options.

> *Example*: 'Bill, the company takes this very seriously and wants to give you the chance to explain. If you continue with the way you are going the company may be forced to take civil action against you. It could get an order to compel you to produce all of your bank accounts and other records and the truth will come out. Is this really necessary? Let's start with some simple issues that we can clear up quickly and see how we go.'

Alternatively, you may caution the subject.

> *Example:* 'Bill, I have to say I find your reaction incredible. I have never known an innocent person to refuse to answer questions. You give me no option but to tell you that you are not obliged to say anything and that anything you do say may be used in evidence.'

If all of these fail, the final option is to ask the suspect to produce a written narrative.

## The written narrative

You should again acknowledge the suspect's right to remain silent, but suggest to him that he might like to write down his explanation, without interruption. If he asks what he should cover, say: 'Everything you believe is important'.

> *Example*: 'I can understand that you don't like the idea of answering questions. But your explanation is very important and this is not going to go away. Please take this paper and pen and write down – in your own time and words – exactly what happened.'

This is a much more effective approach than submitting a list of written questions as these may reveal what you already know and provide the liar with a template for deception.

## DEALING WITH THE FACILE PHRASE 'NO COMMENT'

In a number of recent high-profile British cases (for example, the murders of Sarah Payne and Danielle Jones) the suspects, represented by lawyers, answered every question with the facile phrase 'no comment'. They were, nonetheless, convicted. Juries are not usually stupid and when they see videos of police interviews with suspects radiating non-verbal signs of guilt set against idiotic 'no comment' responses, they come to the right conclusion.

*Good lawyers encourage their clients to answer questions.*
*Bad lawyers get them to say 'no comment'*

The police approach in 'no comment' cases is usually absolutely correct in that they accumulate evidence through witnesses, forensic and other techniques, and go through the motion of asking questions, and video recording the responses. The rest is left to the wheels of justice.

In the business world the same approach is not usually possible and repeated 'no comment' responses must be dealt with as though they were pathetic refusals to reply. They are invariably an admission of guilt, based on very poor legal advice, low intelligence and a manifestation of the 'flee' response.

## DEALING WITH EVASION, PSEUDO-DENIALS AND OTHER STUFF

Subconsciously, most liars cannot bring themselves to be committed to a firm denial, in the first person singular, past tense, but will produce pseudo-denials (such as *'Why should I do that?'*) or limited denials or objections (such as *'I could not have done it because I did not have the access codes'*). Even more significant are those cases where a suspect *should* fail to make a denial.

*If a person does not make a spontaneous-committed denial, the chances are he is guilty*

Genuine denials are spontaneous, committed and can be in response to a vague allegation of responsibility or a direct accusation. *You should normally accept spontaneous-committed denials, especially when they are in the first person singular, past tense, as a sign of truthfulness.*

You can overcome psuedo-denials, evasions and other devices by emphasizing the strength of the evidence and pinning the suspect down to detail, thereby increasing his anxiety to levels at which he believes he can no longer succeed with deception. This usually calls for a professional and relentless approach, attention to the finest detail and focus on the suspect and the mechanics of what he has done.

## DEALING WITH FREUDIAN SLIPS AND SPOONERISMS

Most times, people let Freudian slips, incomplete sentences, changes in direction within a sentence and spoonerisms pass without comment; this is an opportunity lost. Such slips result from thrashing between conscious and subconscious states and between memory and imagination. Immediately after making them the suspect is vulnerable to further disclosures. You should stop the suspect at the first opportunity, point out the error and ask what he really intended to say.

*Freudian slips are direct from the subconscious and always have a meaning*

## DEALING WITH SUSPECTED LIES

### Principles
From now on, challenge every bad lie because if you fail to do so, problems will only get worse. As a minimum, press for more detail and make the liar falsify.

*Every falsification is a step towards finding the truth; every successful concealment lie is a step away*

## Making the right assumption

Although people tell lies for strange reasons, you should treat every provable lie, or failure to answer a relevant question, as though it were an admission of guilt. There will be occasions when this assumption is wrong, but it is the safe course to take.

There are two reasons why lies must be challenged. The first is that letting a subject succeed builds his confidence, reduces his anxiety and makes it less likely he will ever reach the pivotal point. The second is that it makes it more difficult for him to admit the truth later on, simply because he then has two problems to admit: the original transgression, and the fact that he lied to you.

*Lies must be challenged*

## Dealing with most lies

The main options for dealing with lies are detailed in Table 7.6.

**Table 7.6**   Dealing with lies

| Ways of dealing with a lie | Comments |
|---|---|
| **Low-key** | |
| Look away, up or down, pull your ear lobe, put your hand over your mouth, smile, or brush non-existent dust off your arm while the person is giving the false explanation | These are body language statements that tell the suspect that you do not believe him, without your uttering a word |
| Hold up your hand, like a traffic policeman | |
| Politely interrupt the lie by saying: *'I am having real difficulty understanding this. Help me understand and tell me why ...'* | This is a soft challenge |
| Point out that the suspect must have misunderstood the question and ask it again | This is a low-key approach, but achieves the objective of not allowing the person to escape with a lie |
| Interrupt the statement and say: *'Come on, Bill...'* | If he defers to this interruption, the chances are he is guilty and will confess |
| Say: *'That was not true, Mr Smith. I am going to ask the question again and please be very careful how you answer it ...'* | This raises the stakes. It will cause a liar to think carefully. An innocent person may object |
| Joke about the answer: *'Oh yes, and pigs fly ... now come on, Bill, what about...'* | This approach depends on the status of the subject, and his relationship with the interviewer. Don't try it on the chairman! |
| Say: *'Please stop right now. You are making things much worse'* | A statement along these lines should be delivered from the transactional role of a critical parent |
| Pull out your notebook and say something along the lines: *'That is absolutely incredible, Mr Smith ... I just cannot believe it is true. Please go over what you said again ...'* | This raises the stakes. It will cause a liar to think carefully. An innocent person may object |
| **Direct challenges** | |

You should use the suspect's vulnerability immediately after being detected in a lie to ask an important question to which you do not know the answer or where evidence is weak.

> *Example*: 'Bill, I am going to ask you another important question, and in view of what has just happened I want you to be very careful how you answer. Now what ... ?'

You should never, ever, whatever the circumstances call someone a 'liar' as it is a deep attack on his character and implies he never tells the truth. It is much better to attack the false or misleading statement (which is not a deep attack on his character) or specific action by saying something along the lines: 'Come on, Bill, you know that is not true.'

*Attack the false statement and not the person making it*

## Dealing with the obdurate liar

There will be some occasions when the liar will take an unshakeable position and has no intention of telling the truth. If this happens, don't give up but take your time and pull out your notepad and ask and repeat minutely detailed questions which lead the suspect into *barefaced, foolish, unbelievable* explanations, which even he may realize cannot be justified.

Depending on the nature of the case, you can also raise the pavement by saying something along the following lines.

> *Example*: 'As you know, we will be relying totally on the truthfulness of your answers for [e.g. paying this claim]. You know it is a criminal offence to try to obtain money by deception, and if you are not sure about [the lie], now is the time to clear it up. It is not too late now, but next week it will be. Shall we clear this up now?'

In extreme cases you may say something along the lines: *'This is totally unbelievable, Bill. I would like you to make a written statement about this'* (or agree a note on this). You should take down a statement or note, with as much detail *(most of which will be false)* as possible. When the statement has been completed, you should ask: *'Are you sure you really want to sign this? Do you want us to start again?'* If the liar refuses, at worst, you have a damning deceitful statement, which he will find difficult to defend later on. If he changes his mind, chances are you *will* get to the deep truth.

*Let the liar know his lies prove his guilt*

## DEALING WITH ADMITTED LIES

The suspect is brought nearer to the pivotal point every time he has to admit trying to mislead you, when he has to change a previous explanation or admit he has been less than frank. You should always press home your advantage by:

- Asking an important question where the answer is not already known or provable.

> *Example*: 'Tom, I am very disappointed that you tried to mislead me over this. I am going to ask you another very important question and I want you to think carefully before you answer it.'

- You should be prepared to compliment the suspect on an honest answer or admission along the lines:

> *Example*: 'Tom, it took courage to tell me that. Now let's deal with x.' (Another important topic.)

*Reward truthful statements*

## DEALING WITH ANGER

### Background

Genuine anger is the embodiment of 'fight' in the 'fight or flight' decision and may be directed at you, something you have done, or at a third party, and usually peaks and takes time to subside. Anger is an equal transaction between critical parents and rebellious children, but it is a very dangerous emotion for the subject for the following reasons:

- It opens a direct circuit to his subconscious (actually his limbic system), thus making it likely that he will make unplanned admissions or Freudian slips.
- A person who has gone overboard with an expression of anger usually becomes contrite and, thereafter, is vulnerable.

Thus you should always regard a suspect's anger – whether genuine or contrived – as a positive step forward in finding the truth. However, angry people do not make deep confessions, and so you must move the suspect to a less emotional position.

*Angry people are exposed to making mistakes*

### Method of approach with genuine anger

Remember you have all of the advantages: you are not emotionally involved or at risk, while the subject is. You must tune the subject off his negative, emotional wavelength:

- Try to understand the cause of his anger and whether it is genuine or contrived. Ask yourself what the subject is hoping to achieve by his outburst.
- Stay emotionally detached, take nothing the subject says personally and let him know his anger will not deflect you.

*Example*: 'Bill, I understand. It is a shame you are angry, but it is not going to make a scrap of difference to the way we resolve this. We can all get angry and that will get us nowhere. Now let's move on …'

- Turn to a nurturing parent role and state that you understand the subject's feelings, but do not concede the grounds for his anger. You may say you will review them later.
- Stress that you need to move beyond the present problem and try to resolve the larger issues.

*Example*: 'I can understand how you feel, but I cannot comment on [the reasons for his anger], but I promise I will look into that later. All I know is that we should move forward and try to sort out this problem. Now, what about [ask about a key point]'

- Go back to a previous point in the interview when the subject was not angry, and move forward from there.

*Example*: 'Bill, a few moments ago we were getting along fine and there is absolutely no reason why you and I should fall out. Now let's go back and start again …'

The key is for you to keep talking, to try to establish rapport with the subject and try to concede nothing. If this fails and genuine anger fails to dissipate, ask open questions.

*Example*:
- 'Let us go over what happened. Take me through the problem, step by step.'
- 'Tell me, what can we do to resolve this?'
- 'How can we make sure it does not happen again?'

Continue to ask open questions and, as soon as you can, return to the main focus of the interview.

*Never test the water with both feet*

## Method of approach with falsified anger

False anger is usually employed as a device to distract you. If you believe anger is being fabricated, adopt the role of a critical parent and say something along the lines:

*Example*: 'Come on. Let's move onwards. This is getting you nowhere.'

Your aim is to shock the subject on to a sensible course. If the anger proves genuine, this approach may raise the temperature for a few moments, but will enable you to regain control. You may also consider taking notes of the subject's complaints.

*Genuine and manufactured anger are totally different*

## DEALING WITH COUNTER-ATTACKS

This is one of the most difficult areas for the inexperienced interviewer, whose reaction is to panic when the suspect counter-attacks with statements such as:

---

*Example*:
- 'I am going to sue you.'
- 'My lawyer will be in touch.'
- 'Are you calling me a liar?'

---

If possible, you may pretend you have not heard the statement and carry on with the next question, regardless. If this does not work, you must stay cool and say something along the lines:

---

*Example*: 'I am not interested in that, Mr Jones, now what about …'

---

If this approach fails, you should say:

---

*Example*: 'Let's leave that until later; I am trying to find the truth. Please tell me why …'

---

It is vital that you do not get into an argument but ask the next question without hesitating. To the very common attack:

*'Are you calling me a liar?'*

you should respond:

*'No, but it is obvious that you have not told me the truth: now what about …'*

Only in exceptional circumstances should you back down or apologize. You must stay in control and move on to the next question without delay, as though it were the natural thing to do.

*Stay cool in the face of counter-attacks*

## DEALING WITH DEPRESSION

People in a depressive state seldom confess, simply because they are so immersed in their internal conflicts that they are unprepared to face reality. You must try to find out why the person is depressed and to focus on the future and how the problem can be resolved. Also try to get the person to look upwards by holding an exhibit (not one that is too incriminating) above eye level or pinning it to the wall. Also, if you can get him to laugh or smile, you may jump-start him into a more positive frame of mind.

## THE FAMOUS CASE OF ARTHUR

Arthur lived in South London and was a career conman. He gained employment, using false qualifications, as marketing director for a leading financial institution, which he then defrauded to the tune of £19 million. He initially refused to be interviewed by either the police or investigators employed by the victim company, but one morning investigators called at his house, without warning. Arthur, being a little short-sighted, mistook them for estate agents and let them in.

After more than a little prevarication he began to answer questions but when they turned to critical issues, Arthur threw himself on the floor and beat his hands, feet and head against it with considerable violence, saying: 'My life is in ruins: it has been destroyed. I am an unworthy father. I am going to kill myself.'

Investigators were not perturbed and gently placed exhibits under his prostrate figure and said, 'Come on, Arthur, what about this?' One eye furtively opened, then another and then further outbursts of sorrow and woe. 'I am going to jump out of the window, right now, and kill myself.' The investigators coolly pointed out that he was in his lounge which was on the ground floor and that he should stop 'fooling about'. Arthur burst into fits of uncontrolled laughter, cooled down and confessed. As the investigators were leaving he said: 'Do you know, I feel much better. Can you and your wives join my wife and me at a jazz dinner tomorrow? It should be a great night.' The offer was politely refused.

*Try to get him to smile*

## DEALING WITH WAFFLE AND RAMBLING

These diversionary tactics are very popular, especially among politicians. You should remain consciously on the lookout and stop the rambler in his tracks by interjections such as 'That is extremely interesting, Bill, but can we get back to x', or 'Can we stop there. I have only ten minutes left so can you please summarize your position in that time.'

*Stop waffle in its tracks*

## DEALING WITH SPONTANEOUS LOSSES OF MEMORY

Phrases such as 'I don't remember', when the person has made no attempt to access his memory, are signs of deception. Where you suspect deliberate deception, you should respond:

*Example*: 'How can you say that? You haven't given the question a single moment's thought. I am going to ask the question again, so please take a few moments and think carefully …'

If this approach does not succeed, you should ask detailed questions about emotions and attitudes, or reverse questions (see pages 64 and 377) and try to bring the suspect's memory to a conscious level. The liar will usually make no effort to latch on to the memory retrieval cues but will continue with an obdurate 'can't remember'. However, he *will* remember, and repression of memories will increase anxiety.

*Don't accept the answer 'I don't remember'.*
*Try everything to make the suspect remember*

## DEALING WITH BODY LANGUAGE

### Background
You must remain consciously aware of your own and the subject's non-verbal communications.

### The subject's body language
Let the suspect know you have noticed his negative body language signals and deny him the comfort of manipulators. You can do this by looking closely at the offending movement or moving slowly and deliberately to mirror it. If you are in any doubt, or don't know what a particular non-verbal communication means, mime it and let the subject see you doing it.

> *Example*: Any golfing reader who does not believe in the power of mimicry should, at a critical stage of a match, make an exaggerated copy of his opponent's putting stroke! Watch the very disturbing result. 'Do I really putt like that?' the gullible golfer says. 'Of course not,' you sincerely reply, smiling, but you know the seeds of doubt have been sown.

You may also get the subject to move from a negative posture (such as high, defensive crossing of his arms) by regularly handing him documents to read or by asking him to move to examine a chart on the wall.

*Deny the suspect the comfort of manipulators*

Similarly remain consciously alert to the way the subject uses his personal space. If he moves his chair away from you or leans back (both signs of withdrawal and possible deception), move your chair closer or get up and stand behind him. The object, again, is to deprive him of anxiety reduction positions.

### Your own non-verbal communication
Your own body language should be driven by your subconscious and therefore consistent with your verbal statements, emotions and attitudes. However, in the following circumstances you may decide to take conscious control (Table 7.7).

If you don't believe in the power of non-verbal communications, next time you speak to your boss, pull your ear lobe or slowly place your hand up over your mouth while he is speaking. See what happens; but be prepared for a change of job.

**Table 7.7**   The interviewer's body language

| Circumstances | Your body language |
|---|---|
| When the suspect does not tell the truth | • Pointing with the fingers<br>• Looking away<br>• Head moving slowly left to right<br>• Leaning forward<br>• Intruding on the suspect's personal space<br>• Hand over mouth<br>• Pull ear lobe<br>• Brush lint off your clothing |
| When the suspect tells the truth | • Palms upward gestures with the hands<br>• Looking at the suspect and smiling<br>• Head moving slowly up and down<br>• Leaning backward<br>• Increasing the suspect's personal space |
| When the suspect uses a manipulator such as brushing dust off his clothes | • Look carefully at the movement<br>• Mimic the movement (mirroring)<br>• Ask if the question is worrying him |
| Critical balancing point | • Mimic the suspect's body language |

## DEALING WITH FISHING QUESTIONS

Sometimes a suspect will say something along the lines:

*Example*:
• 'You tell me what you know and I will give an answer.'
Or
• 'I am not prepared to answer general questions: let me see the evidence you have and I will answer it.'

In such cases, the suspect is simply trying to find out how much you know so that he can deal with it without giving anything else away.

Your response should be along the following lines:

*Example*: 'I am trying to find out whether you are telling me the whole truth or not. It is a bit like being asked by Customs whether you have anything to declare. If you don't tell me the whole truth now, I have to draw my own conclusions that you are not being honest. Now please tell me everything, and I mean everything, about…'

A common fishing question is along the following lines at the pivotal point:

*Example*: 'I did not do it, but as a matter of interest, what could happen? Would the person be fired or what?'

Great care has to be taken at this stage. Obviously you would not say:

> *Example*: 'The bastard would go to prison and they would throw the key away.'

On the other hand, you must not mislead anyone. The safe course is to say something along the lines:

> *Example*: 'I don't know, Bill, but I don't think telling the truth can make it any worse. Now why did all this start?'

*Fishing questions are a step away from admissions*

## Introductory statements – Phase A

### THE OPTIONS

Your choice of opening depends on the strength of the existing evidence and the level of certainty in the suspect's guilt.

You may merge or adapt the alternatives but there are a number of common factors which are important (Figure 7.1).

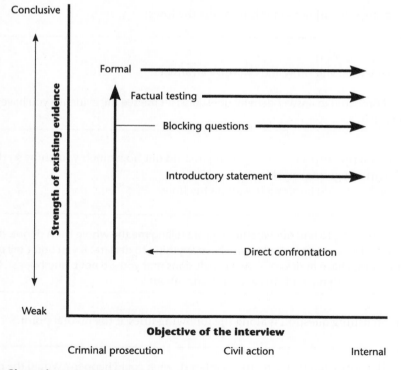

**Figure 7.1**   Chart of opening statements

## FORMALITIES

You must get into an adult-to-adult or critical parent role as quickly as you can and take command. You must be totally committed in everything you say, how you say it and in your body language.

If you are not already known to the suspect, you should either introduce yourself and any colleague, or be introduced by a very senior manager who will emphasize the importance of the interview.

> *Example*: 'Bill, this is Mr Jones, who is an HR adviser. We have asked him to investigate x and he has my full authority. He has worked on hundreds of cases around the world and has (list any impressive accomplishments). I am sure you will cooperate with him.' The manager should then leave the room.

You should always offer to shake hands and in the unlikely event that the offer is refused, look the suspect firmly in the eyes and say something along the lines of: *'That tells me all I need to know'*. Then continue, without pausing, to the opening. If he accepts the offer, make sure your handshake is not like a wet kipper: you must appear positive and committed.

## USING NAMES

If you do not already know the suspect, the safe course is to address him as 'Mister' followed by his surname. However, with senior people, and to establish an equal adult-to-adult transactional role, you should use his first name. If you want to unbalance a pompous suspect you might call him by his first name but refer to his and your colleagues – many of whom will be junior to him – as 'Mister'.

> *Example*: 'Bill, this is Mr Jones [the most junior member of HR]. I have spoken to Mr Smith [Bill's junior] and he will handle your calls for the next few hours, so would you please turn off your mobile telephone.'

You can further unbalance an overly important suspect if you start off calling him by his first name and later in the interview, when he is being deceptive, revert to 'Mister Smith' or start addressing him as 'Mister' and at the pivotal point use his first name. Small changes in the way you address the suspect will help you change roles from adult to critical parent and from critical to nurturing parent.

## AVOIDING PADDING

The natural instinct of most interviewers is to prevaricate (in much the same way that suspects do in bringing themselves to address critical issues), ask irrelevant questions with which they feel comfortable or talk about the weather, a current event or even golf. This is always counter-productive, because it gives the suspect time to settle down.

Avoid any social chit-chat and only ask questions on how a process operates or what work the suspect does, if:

- the information is vital and the suspect is the only person who can give an explanation;
- it is essential to prove the suspect's knowledge of the process and to block off an untrue excuse later in the interview;
- the suspect can be enticed into giving an explanation which will later trap him.

In other cases, questions about responsibilities and processes tend to reduce the suspect's fear of detection and his opinion of you. So get straight to the point. If you need to prove a suspect's knowledge of a process, you can summarize it in your own words and ask for his agreement that it is correct. This approach may avoid endless questions and puts you in control.

*Remember there are two interviews taking place and the suspect is trying to assess you*

## PREPARE FOR AN IMMEDIATE ATTACK

Even the best planning can be thrown off track if the suspect, or his lawyer, immediately takes a confrontational approach. Remember that attacks, especially at the start of an interview, are part of the liar's conscious fight or flight decision, and are most likely to be a deliberate attempt to gain control. Plan to deal with this as you would with any counter-attack (see page 240) and don't panic.

## PLAN SAFE HAVENS

From time to time, the interview may go off course and it is wise to plan the safe points to which you will return in times of trouble. This may be a single-page schedule of a key point indicating the suspect's guilt.

### THE SAFE HAVEN

At any point you can say: 'Forget about that, Bill, now let's come back to this.'

You should then move forward from that point.

## OPTION 1: THE FACTUAL-TESTING OPENING

This is probably the safest option when the existing evidence is uncertain or where you are unsure of the suspect's guilt. You will use the first part of the interview to test his reaction to questions and to decide whether he is being truthful or not. Even when criminal prosecution is an objective, you technically do not have to administer a caution with this opening because you will use it only when the suspect's guilt is in doubt. If you are less than 50 per cent certain that the suspect is responsible for the problems concerned, consider using the elimination approach suggested in Chapter 9. Where responsibility is over 50 per cent and less than 80 per cent certain[1] the opening statement should include:

---

[1]   As best you can approximate

- who you are and what you do;
- what the suspicions are;
- how the investigation has been and will be conducted;
- confirmation that the organization has limitless time and resources and intends to find the truth;
- your wish to give the suspect the chance to explain.

For example, the opening – with a purchasing agent who may have taken bribes – may be along the following lines:

## UNCERTAIN GUILT AND EVIDENCE

'I am Roger Jones from HR and I am investigating very serious allegations of corruption involving a number of vendors. The company takes this very seriously and will make every effort to find the truth. Investigations like this take time but I am sure you agree that bribery is a very big problem ...' [pause and note reaction] '... and it is usually the purchasing agent that takes all of the blame as vendors run for cover and to protect their other businesses say that they were forced into paying and had no alternative. In my experience, this is seldom the case, but that's the way it always seems to go.

'Vendors know that we can take civil action to force them to produce their records or get the police involved. They also know that someone will always talk to save their own skin.' [Pause] 'The facts always come out.

'We have got a lot of evidence already which we need to discuss. [To be fair with everyone involved and allow you to give your side of events, I have to tell you that you do not have to say anything unless *you* wish to do so and that anything you do say may be used in evidence.] I am particularly interested in AB Jones and Company Limited, what can you tell me about them?'

From this opening you can move into Phase B and ask more probing questions, if necessary increasing anxiety through Phase C until the suspect reaches the pivotal point. Alternatively, you may decide that the suspect is truthful and can be removed from suspicion. If this happens, don't end the interview too quickly, but try to encourage the subject as a witness or informant.

## OPTION 2: BLOCKING QUESTIONS

You may choose this opening when you have good reason to believe the suspect is responsible, but that he may be able to produce a plausible excuse. The object is to give him the chance to volunteer potentially incriminating information and, if he fails to do so, to block a plausible but deceptive excuse later on. For example, in a price-fixing case the opening might be as follows:

'We have received a complaint that some of our salesmen have been fixing prices with retailers and this could cause very serious problems. The company is determined to find the truth and will leave no stone unturned to do so. I know that these things happen and that sales people, to make a sale, sometimes bend the rules. But now is the time for everyone to clear the air. It's not the end of the world, but we need to know.

- Do you understand the rules on price-fixing?
- Have you ever fixed prices with retailers?
- Have you ever had discussions with retailers or anyone else on fixing prices?
- Has anyone ever discussed price-fixing with you?
- What would you do if anyone ever asked you to fix prices?
- What would you do if you knew about anyone else fixing prices?
- Is there anything you know which could be relevant to our investigation?'

From this opening you should move on to a factual analysis of the evidence and Phase B.

## OPTION 3: THE INTRODUCTORY MONOLOGUE

The introductory monologue is very important and should be used where there are reasonable grounds for believing that the suspect is responsible and may be deceptive. You should write down the words you intend to use and rehearse them so that you do not have to refer to your notes. If criminal prosecution is an objective, you should include the caution in an introductory statement consisting of five main elements:

- who you are and what you do (if you have not already explained this);
- how the investigation has been and will be conducted, and administer a caution;
- indirect or soft accusation;
- bridging statement;
- rationalization.

For example, the introductory statement in an interview with an insurance company employee who is believed to have colluded with a gang making false claims might be along the following lines:

'I manage a team of four investigators who investigate frauds against the company and we travel the world. We handle around 200 cases a year and most are successful. In some we press for criminal prosecution and in others – where the people concerned have helped us – we can take a more sympathetic approach. [Caution] I want us to work together on this. It is in everyone's interest that we establish the truth. [Pause]

'Some people seem to think that making bad claims is a bit like saving on income tax, but this is not so. Ultimately, other policyholders pay, and making false claims is a very serious matter, which results in the loss of jobs and damage to our reputation. [Pause]

'We have been investigating a case in which false claims have been made to us for medical insurance. The people concerned have been claiming serious injuries, but we know that many are untrue. Thousands of pounds are involved and the company is taking the matter very seriously and will leave no stone unturned to find the truth. We believe that at least one employee has been dragged into this [Pause] and this is what we are currently investigating.

'Before we conduct interviews, we do a great deal of background research. We keep surveillance on policyholders who claim they have been injured, take videos of them running around, playing tennis and doing all sorts of things they say their injuries prevent them from doing. We interview neighbours, family members and so on and we build up the evidence until we are really sure of our facts.

'As far as employees are concerned, we audit the claims they have handled very carefully and look for patterns. We sometimes keep surveillance on them and see them meeting claimants. Sometimes we see money being handed over. In other cases we have observed them going to nightclubs together and doing other things that would make it clear to the employee that the claimed injuries are fraudulent. Sometimes, with the permission of top management, we will monitor the employee's office telephone, inspect his computer and check his files. We take great care to establish the facts. [Pause]

'Sometimes employees get pressurized into cooperating with false claims and, when this is the case, we will try to support them if they are honest with us. [Pause]

'In other cases, we find employees drift into these cases. Not because they are really bad people, but they just drift, often without realizing the seriousness of what is going on. But at the end of the day, the claimants blame the employees to save their own skins. They do this because they think they can embarrass us into not taking action. This is never the case. But I see lots of really good employees in serious trouble because of crooks.'

You should carefully monitor the suspect's reaction as this opening is delivered (Table 7.8).

**Table 7.8**   Most likely reactions to an opening statement

| Reactions indicating innocence | Reactions indicating guilt |
| --- | --- |
| Listens carefully but does not appear threatened | Does not listen carefully |
| Relaxed body language | Moves body into a defensive position |
| Finds the story interesting or even boring | Nervous body language |
| May ask if you are accusing him | Unlikely to challenge the statement |

If the suspect's reaction is indicative of guilt, you should plan to make a soft accusation.

*Example*: 'The trouble is that the employee involved may believe he can succeed by not telling the truth, and that the outsiders will cover for him. The fact is that this investigation will look into everything and we are determined to get to the truth. If the employee concerned is not prepared to tell the truth when we give him the chance, so be it. He must know that the game is up.'

If the suspect's reaction continues to be passive, you should continue with a bridging statement, which moves from an indirect accusation to the specific.

> *Example*: 'The trouble is, Tom, I think you are involved in this and it is important that we work together to clear it up.'

The suspect will either move into an acceptance position (in which case plan your approach as a nurturing parent in line with page 277 or make a denial. In the worst case, you can continue, from any point, with a factual approach or revert to a safe haven (see page 246). If the suspect launches an attack, remain cool:

> *Example*: 'Bill, I have been very fair with you and I have told you exactly what I believe the evidence shows. But I have an open mind, so please explain x [deal with one of the key points].'

## OPTION 4: DIRECT CONFRONTATION

In rare cases, where the evidence is already overwhelming you may use an assumptive opening (i.e. that the suspect is guilty beyond doubt) and ambush him. This gives him minimal time to compose himself, although it may result in an angry outburst that you will have to control, probably by reverting to a safe haven.

The suspect should be kept waiting in the interview room and should ideally be seated. You should enter holding a file, stand within the suspect's personal space and deliver a direct accusation. For example, where the objective is criminal prosecution and the suspect is believed to have stolen a number of PCs from the company, the opening might be as follows:

> *Example*: 'Good morning, Mr Smith. I am Bill Jones from the Audit Department. We are investigating a case of theft of computers from the sales office. [Caution] The evidence we have makes it clear that you are responsible and I want to give you the chance to tell me about it and to work with me to get our property back.'

You should then sit down and wait for the suspect's response. From this point onwards, you are on your own, but remember the principles and the fact that you can always revert to a safe haven.

## OPTION 5: THE FORMALITY

This approach can be used where the evidence is already overwhelming, and the main objective of the interview is to give the suspect the opportunity to give his explanation. This is usually essential if disciplinary proceedings are intended.

> *Example*: 'Bill, we have been investigating an allegation that you have been taking kickbacks from vendors. I want to give you the chance of putting your side of the story. To be fair, and to enable you to give your side of the story, I have to advise you …[Caution].'

You then cover the key points, committing the suspect to detailed replies and more and more indefensible lies. You may, or may not, decide to try to reach the pivotal point and the turn.

## THE BUSINESS MEETING

You eventually get Bill Smith off the golf course, sit him down in a nice quiet room and then get into your introductory statement:

'Bill, as you know, we have been trying to see you for some weeks to get your explanation. My name is Tom Williams and I am a barrister and psychiatrist [but only if this is true!]. This is Jane Marshall and she is from Human Resources. The purpose of this interview is to give you the opportunity of explaining why you have been absent from work for so long, failed to appear when asked, abandoned your job …'

Bill tries to interrupt, but you continue: 'Please let me finish: abandoned your job and been less than frank with us in telling us that you were in hospital today when in fact you were playing golf. So that there can be no misunderstanding, we intend to get to the truth, however long it takes and costs. Why did you tell us you were in hospital today?'

With such an opening, Bill Smith is in a very unenviable position, from which he is unlikely to recover.

## Probing and testing questions – Phase B

### INTRODUCTION

The structure of this phase obviously depends on the success, or otherwise, of the opening but it is generally applicable when you are not certain whether the suspect is responsible or not and want to test his honesty. In effect you become a human polygraph machine. If you are already certain that the suspect is responsible, you may skip this stage, although it can be used to steadily increase anxiety.

The following paragraphs describe the questions and possible responses, but you should always keep an open mind because there is an exception to every rule.

### PROFILE OF DECEPTION QUESTIONS

Experience shows that the way liars answer questions can be profiled. For example, they tend to minimize the seriousness of the case, fail to make committed first person singular, past tense denials and use subjective truths and evasion. Questions based on these profiles are especially relevant to elimination interviews and are discussed in Chapter 9. You can adapt this approach for any interview when there are a number of suspects and you wish to eliminate the innocent and identify the guilty.

### BLOCKING QUESTIONS

Blocking questions, which are usually asked early in an interview, are intended to 'block off' an exculpatory, but untrue, explanation later on. A suspect's denials, when given the opportunity to volunteer information, go towards proving his guilty intent. On the other hand, honest answers to blocking questions can quickly clear an innocent person of suspicion.

Probably the most common blocking question of all is used by customs officers when you arrive in a country.

---

*Example*:
Question:   'Have you anything to declare?'
Answer:     'No, (because) I spent all of my money before I got to the duty free shop.'
Block:      'Have you read this notice which shows what you are allowed to import duty free?'
Answer:     'Yes, but obviously I have not read every word.' (*Lack of commitment*)
Block:      'So you are telling me you have nothing with you in excess of those allowances.'
Answer:     'That's right. I never buy duty free stuff.' (*Generalization*)
Block:      'And is there any possibility that you may have forgotten something you have bought while overseas?'
Answer:     'No, not unless Father Christmas got into my case.' (*Misplaced humour*)

When the passenger's bags are subsequently searched and expensive jewellery and a credit card voucher for its purchase discovered, he is left with no plausible excuse. His answers have established guilty knowledge and pinned him into a corner.

---

You may use blocking questions to test to what extent the subject is going to volunteer information.

---

## PRE-EMPLOYMENT

'Have you ever used narcotic drugs such as cocaine, crack or heroin?'
'No.'
'Or cannabis, LSD or ecstasy?'
'Not that I can recall.'
'But you have experimented with them?'
'Yes, but I did not inhale.'
'Then why didn't you volunteer that information when I first asked you?'
'Because you only asked about cocaine, crack and heroin.'
'I used the words narcotic drugs and gave them as an example to see how honest you were. I think you were playing on words. Now I want to ask you a very serious question about [important topic].'

---

You should consider using blocking questions when you have incriminating evidence, which – under the deception theory – the suspect may be able to explain with a plausible, but false, excuse. The suspect's responses to blocking questions are very important (Table 7.9).

Blocking questions should be asked in a low-key way so that you do not alert the suspect to their real significance. If he fails to volunteer the truth, this omission should be used later to increase his anxiety.

---

*Example*: 'A few moments ago I asked you if you had ever claimed expenses to which you were not entitled and you said that you had not. I asked the question again and you gave the same reply. I am now going to show you this claim. It is false, isn't it?'

**Table 7.9**   Possible responses to blocking questions

| Reactions indicating innocence | Reactions indicating guilt |
|---|---|
| Will usually make a full and honest disclosure and thereby clear himself of suspicion | Will fail to make an honest disclosure when given the opportunity<br>May seek clarification of the question<br>His response is most likely to avoid commitment |

If the suspect admits to being less than open in response to a blocking question, you should press home your advantage by pointing out the seriousness of the attempted deception and then ask an important question to which the answer is not already known.

> *Example*: 'Your attempt to mislead me was very unfortunate. I am now going to give you the opportunity to tell me all about [another important topic]. Please take great care over this. You don't want to make the same mistake twice, do you?'

*Blocking questions are very difficult for the liar*

## INVITE THE SUBJECT TO VOLUNTEER

Ask the suspect whether there is anything he would like to tell you, and that this is his opportunity to come forward with any honest explanation. Warn him if he does not take this opportunity, the evidence will come out and the fact that he has not offered the truth, when given this chance, will obviously add to his difficulties. The guilty person will be stretched by this question and will normally be very careful over the answer he gives (Table 7.10).

**Table 7.10**   Most likely reactions to an opportunity to volunteer information

| Reactions indicating innocence | Reactions indicating guilt |
|---|---|
| Volunteers facts, some of which may be against his self-interest (e.g. that he had made a mistake) | Prevarication and failure to volunteer information or *'What do you expect me to say?'* |

## QUESTIONS TO WHICH THE ANSWERS ARE KNOWN

In addition to preparing visual summaries of the key points (see page 190) you should also make a special note of the evidence or intelligence that the suspect may not know you have. You can then pose questions, based on this knowledge, to test the accuracy of his replies (Table 7.11).

**Table 7.11**   Most likely reactions to questions to which the answer is known

| Reactions indicating innocence | Reactions indicating guilt |
|---|---|
| Answers that accord with known facts | Answers that do not accord with known facts |

## THE GOLFING HOLIDAY

For example, if you have conclusive evidence that the suspect went on an expensive golfing holiday paid for by a vendor, you may casually ask:

| | |
|---|---|
| Interviewer: | 'Have you ever been paid cash by a vendor?' |
| Suspect: | 'No' (Single word, binary answer: probably truthful) |
| Interviewer: | 'Been given cars, watches, expensive jewellery?' |
| Suspect: | 'No' (Single word, binary answer: probably truthful) |
| Interviewer: | 'Received any other direct or indirect benefit from a vendor?' |
| Suspect: | 'No, except for a few golf balls' (Note the qualified denial: untruthful) |
| Interviewer: | 'Had holidays paid for or anything like that?' |
| Suspect: | 'No. Why should I do that?' (Qualified denial with a question answered by a question and probably hiding responsibility) |

Dishonest replies must be challenged and the subject made to face the truth. You should immediately follow up all instances where the suspect has been caught in a lie or evasion with an important question to which the answer is not known.

## THE TRIP TO PRAGUE

You know that the suspect downgraded his business-class ticket and took his girlfriend with him on an all-expenses paid trip to Prague. You have obtained a copy of the voucher from the travel agency. You do not know whether he did the same thing on a business trip to New York.

| | |
|---|---|
| You ask: | 'Did you travel by yourself to Prague?' |
| Suspect: | 'Why are you asking that?' (Question with a question: probably deceptive) |
| You say: | 'Because I want to know.' |
| Suspect: | 'Yes. I always travel by myself.' (Generalization: probably deceptive) |

You show him the voucher.

| | |
|---|---|
| He responds: | 'OK. I took Janet with me. So what? It did not cost the company any more money and everyone does it. I did nothing wrong.' (Rationalization) |
| You say: | 'And you took her with you to New York in July?' (Assumptive question) |
| Suspect: | 'Yes.' |
| You say: | 'Now please be very careful answering this. On what other occasions have you downgraded your ticket, taken the cash or taken someone else with you on a business trip?' |
| Suspect: | 'I have never taken cash.' (Partial denial.) |
| You say: | 'OK, on how many other occasions has someone else travelled with you?' |

Suspect hesitates while thrashing for an answer.

| | |
|---|---|
| You interject: | 'Twenty or thirty times?' (Interjection) |
| Suspect: | 'No, less than that ... Maybe five or ten times.' (Admission) |

The suspect thinks and gives details of five other trips.

| | |
|---|---|
| You say: | 'Are you absolutely certain this is everything?' |
| Suspect: | 'To the best of my recollection, yes it is.' (*Lack of commitment*) |
| You say: | 'If you believed that you had done nothing wrong, why did you tell me that you always travelled by yourself?' |

You continue to press the point and the suspect admits that he knew he was breaking the law. Now you turn to the deep truth and ask him to tell you who else does the same thing.

*An answer that is already known can be used to test the subject's honesty*

This sequence can be regarded as the 'naughty puppy rule': the suspect does not want to get immediately found out in another lie and is likely to answer honestly or, if he does not, he is likely to push his anxiety further up the scale.

*Example*: 'Bill, we have got off to a bad start and you tried to mislead me over [x]. I am now going to ask you about [y] and I want you to think carefully before you try to answer it. Now what did you do with the money?'

## QUESTIONS ON THE KEY POINTS

You should ask questions on the key points and seek the subject's detailed responses to them. Specific indicators of guilt and deception – *in addition to those explained in Chapter 4* – are usually as follows (Table 7.12).

**Table 7.12**   Most likely reactions to questions based on key points

| Reactions indicating innocence | Reactions indicating guilt |
|---|---|
| Clear answers with consistent detail | Evasion, subjective truths and inconsistent detail |
| Commitment | Lack of commitment |
| Quick responses | Slow, censored replies |
| Refusal to change an explanation in the light of new evidence | Changes story to fit emerging evidence |
| Positive non-verbal clues | Negative non-verbal clues |

## RELUCTANCE TO PROVIDE DETAIL

Ask control and relevant questions to test the subject's memory and recall of detail. Do not permit him to deceive you through concealment lies. When in doubt push for more and more detail and take your time (Table 7.13).

**Table 7.13**   Most likely reactions to requests for detail

| Reactions indicating innocence | Reactions indicating guilt |
|---|---|
| Consistent, free-flowing detailed answers to both control and relevant questions | Evasion and inconsistent detail |

## UNWILLINGNESS TO COMMIT

Ask questions that require the suspect to commit to detailed, unambiguous answers and, for very important points, confirm this commitment with him (Table 7.14).

**Table 7.14**    Most likely reactions to a requirement to commit

| Reactions indicating innocence | Reactions indicating guilt |
| --- | --- |
| Committed responses | Evasion, subjective truths and lack of commitment |

## ENTICEMENT QUESTIONS

Many suspects will tell you only what they believe you can already prove and will hold back damaging information if they can. You may do the same, obtain a denial or prevarication and then confront him with the contradictory evidence (Table 7.15).

**Table 7.15**    Most likely reactions to enticement questions

| Reactions indicating innocence | Reactions indicating guilt |
| --- | --- |
| Will usually be reluctant to change an earlier explanation | May ask 'fishing questions' (see page 243) and then change his explanation to fit the new facts |
| May dispute the newly produced evidence | |

The suspect's confidence is eroded every time he has to change an explanation or agree that he has not told you the whole truth. After such admissions, you should ask questions to which the answers are not known and press for detailed answers.

## ASK HIM TO REPEAT

At appropriate times say: 'Would you please repeat that, I am not sure I heard you correctly.' Your tone should imply that you heard, but did not believe what was being said (Table 7.16).

**Table 7.16**    Most likely reactions to a request to repeat

| Reactions indicating innocence | Reactions indicating guilt |
| --- | --- |
| Will repeat the answer with consistent levels of detail | More likely to prevaricate, feigned anger, reluctant to repeat |

## REPEAT IMPORTANT QUESTIONS

You may repeat important questions, each time pressing for more detail (Table 7.17).

**Table 7.17**   Most likely reactions to repeated questions

| Reactions indicating innocence | Reactions indicating guilt |
|---|---|
| Will usually answer the question then point out you have asked it before | Will object to being asked the same question, but then may answer |

## ASK IF THERE IS ANY REASON

Ask the subject if there is any reason why the evidence makes it appear that he is responsible (Table 7.18).

> *Example*: 'Tom, I have already explained some of the evidence to you and you have to admit it does not look good. Bill Jones, your manager agrees. What do you want to tell me about this?'

**Table 7.18**   Most likely reactions to strong evidence

| Reactions indicating innocence | Reactions indicating guilt |
|---|---|
| Deny that the evidence points his way | May give a reason which is usually facile or say 'I don't know' |

## GET HIM TO HANDLE INCRIMINATING EVIDENCE

Hand the subject documents or other incriminating evidence and ask him to explain them: *'Can you explain this?'* (Table 7.19).

**Table 7.19**   Most likely reactions to incriminating evidence

| Reactions indicating innocence | Reactions indicating guilt |
|---|---|
| May ask for clarification on what the documents mean | Will make abnormal assumptions and not ask for clarification |
| Will examine carefully and reply | May not examine carefully |
| Will retain the documents within his personal space | Will push the documents out of his personal space |

## ASK HOW HE WOULD HAVE DONE IT

Ask the suspect to tell you how he would have committed the act in question. Get him to go through exact details step by step, and watch for disclosure of facts that only the perpetrator would know. Then ask direct, admission-seeking questions (Table 7.20).

**Table 7.20**    Most likely reactions to possible commitment of the act

| Reactions indicating innocence | Reactions indicating guilt |
| --- | --- |
| He would not commit the act | May explain<br>May reveal detail known only to the perpetrator<br>May suggest a stupid method as a diversionary tactic |

The fact that a person will admit that he has considered the possibility of committing fraud is significant indication of guilt. You should remain on the lookout for obvious diversionary tactics. For example, the suspect may suggest a method that is obviously unworkable in the hope that he can demonstrate his ignorance of what actually happened.

## ASK IF HE WOULD ADMIT

Ask the subject if he had done the act in question, whether he would admit it (Table 7.21).

**Table 7.21**    Most likely reactions to the possibility of admission

| Reactions indicating innocence | Reactions indicating guilt |
| --- | --- |
| Pausing and then probably 'no' or 'would depend on the circumstances' | Most likely 'yes', but answered without thinking |

## RESPONSE TO ACCUSATIONS: FAILURE TO DENY

You should make a direct accusation (Table 7.22).

> *Example*: 'Tom, I think you did it for the following reasons.' Then explain the deception theory and key points.

**Table 7.22**    Most likely reactions to a direct accusation

| Reactions indicating innocence | Reactions indicating guilt |
| --- | --- |
| Committed first person singular, past tense denial | Pseudo-denial (see pages 98, 235 and Table 4.3) |
| Anger | Feigned anger |

## RESPONSE TO REPEATED ALLEGATIONS

You should repeat the allegations throughout the interview (Table 7.23).

**Table 7.23**    Most likely reactions to repeated allegations

| Reactions indicating innocence | Reactions indicating guilt |
| --- | --- |
| Denials increasing in strength | Pseudo-denials decreasing in strength |

## REASONS FOR LYING

If you believe the suspect is being deceptive, you should ask him if there are any reasons, other than the obvious, why he is not telling the truth (Table 7.24).

*Example*: 'Joe, it is obvious to both of us that you are not telling the truth. I think it is because you [took the money], but is there any other reason why you are not being truthful with me?'

**Table 7.24**   Most likely reactions to being asked the reason for lying

| Reactions indicating innocence | Reactions indicating guilt |
| --- | --- |
| Committed response that he is telling the truth | Hesitancy then a pseudo-denial that he is lying |

## PREVIOUS TROUBLE

Ask if the suspect has been in trouble before (Table 7.25).

**Table 7.25**   Most likely reactions to being asked about previous trouble

| Reactions indicating innocence | Reactions indicating guilt |
| --- | --- |
| Will deny that he is in trouble | Probably 'yes' or 'no', but he accepts that he is currently 'in trouble' |

## ASK WHOM HE CAN CLEAR OF SUSPICION

Ask the suspect to give the names of people he is sure are not responsible for the act in question (Table 7.26).

**Table 7.26**   Most likely reactions to being asked who is not responsible

| Reactions indicating innocence | Reactions indicating guilt |
| --- | --- |
| Will immediately name himself | Will not immediately name himself |

## ASK TO PROVIDE ELIMINATION SAMPLES

In forgery cases, ask the subject to provide a specimen of his normal handwriting and ask him to copy the forged signature, 10 or 12 times (Table 7.27).

**Table 7.27**   Most likely reactions to being asked to provide elimination samples

| Reactions indicating innocence | Reactions indicating guilt |
| --- | --- |
| Will look carefully at the forgery and make a genuine attempt to copy it | Will not look closely at the forgery and will make a poor attempt |

The guilty subject may try to confuse the handwriting expert by giving poor samples and by making no attempt to copy the forged signature.

## ASK IF HE WILL TAKE A LIE DETECTOR TEST

You may ask if the suspect would be prepared to take a lie detector test (Table 7.28).

**Table 7.28**    Most likely reactions to a possible lie detector test

| Reactions indicating innocence | Reactions indicating guilt |
| --- | --- |
| May not agree<br>Will agree and will go | Will normally agree, but then prevaricate |

If he agrees, ask if it can be done later the same day (Table 7.29):

**Table 7.29**    Most likely reactions to an imminent lie detector test

| Reactions indicating innocence | Reactions indicating guilt |
| --- | --- |
| Will usually think and make a reasonable effort to get the matter cleared up | Without thinking, will find a reason why the test cannot take place (i.e. a typical 'stalling' routine) |

## ASK WHY THE PROBLEM OCCURRED

Ask the subject whether he believes the losses are the result of deliberate and premeditated theft (Table 7.30).

**Table 7.30**    Most likely reactions to being asked if the act was probably premeditated

| Reactions indicating innocence | Reactions indicating guilt |
| --- | --- |
| Possibly 'yes' or 'I don't know' | Probably 'no' |

## SENSORY AND REVERSE QUESTIONS

These questions are useful in jogging a person's memory and for testing whether a reply is from memory (probably true) or imagination (probably false). Sensory questions can also be used to get a witness to examine his memory from an entirely different angle and access important information through another 'cue'.

For example, in a robbery, the witness might be asked:

*Example*: 'If you had been standing outside the bank looking in through the window what do you think you would have seen?' or 'Did the robber remind you of anyone you know?' or 'what smells did you notice?'

Reverse questions require the subject to recount an event from other than what he claims was the starting position.

---

*Example*: 'You say the robber ran out of the bank at around 2.03 pm. Starting from here, take me backwards through your memory to the point at which you first saw him come into the bank.'

---

Deceptive suspects have far greater difficulty in dealing with such questions and often make serious mistakes when recounting something in reverse order or starting halfway through a sequence.

*Changing the order of events makes liars uncertain*

## PARAPHRASING AND SUMMARY STATEMENTS

Summary statements can be used throughout all interviews to reinforce earlier statements or admissions made by the subject and, where possible, should be supported by visual input covering the 'key points'.

---

*Example*:
- 'So far you have told me that ...'
- 'You have agreed that ...'
- 'Let's see if I have understood you correctly ...'

---

They can also be used to backtrack to a safe point if an interview goes off course. You may reinforce summary statements by agreeing and writing down bullet points with the subject.

---

| | |
|---|---|
| Interviewer: | 'You have told me: |
| | Point 1: That you were on duty at the time this happened. Is that correct?' |
| Subject: | 'Yes' |
| Interviewer: | 'Point 2: That the supervisor was asleep. Is that correct?' |
| Subject: | 'Yes' |

And so on.

---

The suspect's anxiety will increase as the process moves forward, again leading him towards the pivotal point.

## DECISION POINT

At the end of this phase you will have reached a conclusion on whether the suspect is lying or not. If you believe he is being deceptive you must move on to Phase C and put the monkeys on his back. If you think he has told the truth, carry on with the interview, treating him as a potential witness.

## Anxiety inducing questions – Phase C

### INTRODUCTION

The objective of this phase is to increase the suspect's anxiety to the point where he loses confidence in his ability to succeed, thus bringing him to face reality at the pivotal point.

The suspect's anxiety will increase and the chatter from the two monkeys will become unbearable every time he has to:

- admit that he has not told the truth;
- admit he has done something wrong;
- falsify an answer (rather than to conceal);
- acknowledge that he tried to mislead you through a subjective truth or some other deception;
- change his story to fit new facts presented to him;
- make a denial.

It will also be increased every time he is confronted with evidence indicating his guilt, or discrepancies in his explanations. You should remember that anxiety becomes intolerable, usually not because of one knockout blow but through an accumulation of small points.

You should concentrate on the mechanics, or the 'how' of the case, and on minor wrongdoings; emphasize the evidence you believe you can get and adopt a professional, relentless and critical parent role. This phase has to raise the temperature but you can easily stay in control:

- remain totally committed in what you say and how you say it;
- don't panic in the face of counter-attacks but move on quickly to the next question.

If the interview goes off track, revert to a 'safe haven' and continue as seamlessly as possible.

### TOPIC COVERAGE

In most interviews there will be a number of topics of interest, each with its own key points. *For example, you may have intelligence (and thus a deception theory) to suggest that the suspect took bribes, falsified his travel expenses, downloaded pornography from the Internet and so on. Each one can be regarded as a separate topic and you should summarize the key points for each one.* You may decide to deal with each topic in a self-contained portion of the interview, or you may deliberately decide to jump rapidly from one topic to another to make it more difficult for the suspect to plan ahead (Table 7.31).

**Table 7.31**    Most likely reactions to changes in topic

| Reactions indicating innocence | Reactions indicating guilt |
| --- | --- |
| Will usually accept the change of topics without objection | The deceitful suspect will find topic changes difficult to handle and may object to them |
| Answers will be spontaneous | His delivery of responses is likely to be slow and cautious |

Rapid switches from one topic to another are particularly relevant in Phases B and C to increase the suspect's anxiety.

The order in which you will deal with topics should also be carefully planned. You may leave the strongest until last, thus building up increasing anxiety throughout the interview, or hit him hard with it from the start. Your approach will be dictated by the circumstances, with the ultimate objective of bringing the suspect to the pivotal point on all topics.

## SURPRISE QUESTIONS

Think of unusual questions that the suspect is unlikely to have anticipated and pop them in from time to time. For example, the suspect had given a brilliantly detailed description of a man he had seen supposedly running off with a bag of money and had an outstanding 'memory'[2] of the event.

### LOOKING OUT OF THE WINDOW

| | |
|---|---|
| Suspect: | 'As I said, I was standing looking out of the window and saw this man ...' |
| Question: | 'What was the window frame like, was it plastic or metal?' |
| Suspect: | 'I don't know ... I can't remember.' |
| Question: | 'Was the window a single pane or multiple?' |
| Suspect: | 'I haven't the foggiest idea.' |
| Question: | 'Was there anything on the window ledge, a pot, flower or anything?' |
| Suspect: | 'I don't know.' |
| Statement: | 'Given that your memory is so good in other areas, how come you don't' remember any of this?' |
| Suspect: | [Silence] |
| Statement: | 'It didn't happen that way, did it?' |
| Suspect: | [Long pause] 'I thought it had.' |

He later went on to admit that his story was a sham and that he had taken the money.

*Jump from topic to topic.*
*Ask surprise questions*

## EXPLAIN THE DECEPTION THEORY AND RESOLUTION PLAN

Explain the mechanics of the fraud exactly as you believe it happened, pointing out what evidence is available to prove the case. Confront the suspect with visual stimuli relating to the key points and keep incriminating evidence in his personal space. Explain how the investigation will be conducted – that there is limitless time and resources to do so and that cooperation will be forthcoming from third parties and witnesses. The guilty suspect is unlikely to interrupt and will listen closely to what you have to say. He is extremely unlikely to make committed FPSPT denials.

---

[2]  It was actually far too good, suggesting rehearsal

## EXPLANATIONS OF INCRIMINATING EVIDENCE

Hand the suspect pieces of incriminating evidence (the key points) – documents, photographs and summary statements – and ask for his explanation. You may express an opinion that you believe they prove his guilt. Again the untruthful subject will try to avoid becoming committed to detail. His denials will usually become weaker when allegations are repeated (Table 7.32)

**Table 7.32**   Most likely reactions to key point evidence

| Reactions indicating innocence | Reactions indicating guilt |
|---|---|
| The subject may ask for an explanation about the context in which the exhibits were produced and what they mean | The guilty person may make assumptions about the exhibits without asking questions about their context or meaning |
| He may examine the exhibits carefully and may retain them in his possession | After a cursory view he may push the exhibits away, wishing to distance himself from them |

You can increase anxiety by repeatedly pushing the exhibits in front of the suspect and making him handle them. Generally, the more you can make him keep them within his personal space, the better.

## MINOR TRANSGRESSIONS

Getting the subject to admit to breaches of company procedures and to small fiddles on his expenses is also important. Each admitted breach, and an acceptance of the potential censure involved, is a step nearer to a full confession on more important matters. You can point out that the small admissions he has made are sufficient to result in his dismissal and prosecution, and that he cannot worsen his situation by helping to resolve other matters.

## REPROVING STATEMENTS

You should remain consciously alert to evasions, subjective truths, failures to volunteer etc. and chastise the subject for trying to mislead you.

| | |
|---|---|
| *Example*: | |
| Interviewer: | 'Do you use narcotic drugs?' |
| Subject: | 'I don't use drugs.' (Note the normal honest response would be a binary 'no'.) |
| Interviewer: | 'But do you take them?' |
| Subject: | 'Yes, sometimes, but I don't use them.' |
| Interviewer: | 'Come on, Bill, you are playing with words. This is not the way we are going to clear this up. What drugs do you take?' |

The subject's anxiety is increased every time he is caught out in this way. From time to time, you may plan to ask questions that give the subject the chance to use subjective truths and then chastise him for doing so or give him credit for precise, full answers.

## INTERRUPTIONS AND AVOIDING DENIALS

Wherever possible you should try to intervene every time a suspect starts to tell a lie or wanders off the point. You can do this by oral statements.

---

*Example*:
- 'Hold on, Bill, that cannot be right, can it?'
- 'I think you should stop just there.'

---

Or by non-verbal intervention such as holding your hand up much like a traffic policeman and at the same time shaking your head left to right (Table 7.33).

**Table 7.33**   Most likely reactions to interventions

| Reactions indicating innocence | Reactions indicating guilt |
|---|---|
| Will usually insist on completing his statement | Will usually defer to the interruption |

There are obviously exceptions to every rule, but liars tend to be more passive, less assertive and less committed than truthful people. Stopping false explanations and challenging lies creates anxiety in the mind of the suspect.

*An innocent person usually objects to being interrupted*

## ENTICEMENT QUESTIONS

The object of these questions is to get the suspect to change an explanation or alibi he has already given. They may be asked at any point in an interview, but should usually be asked when:

- the subject is committed to an untrue explanation, or deliberate concealment, probably through blocking questions;
- he can be confronted with a new and important piece of incriminating evidence;
- he has admitted to making an error in an explanation;
- he is at the pivotal point.

If you can get him to change his explanation, the chances are that a confession will follow. Even the approach, by itself, will increase his anxiety.

---

*Example*: 'You have told me that you were not in the supermarket that day. As you know, the security office makes video recordings. Do you want to reconsider what you have told me?'

---

If the subject sticks to his explanation and adds detail to support it, you should add points to the list suggesting innocence.

*Interviewing is not just about exposing the liar; it is also about clearing the innocent*

## ADMISSIONS OF LYING

Anxiety is greatly increased every time the suspect has to admit he has lied or concealed the truth. You must punish deception, taking the role of the critical parent and saying something along the lines:

---

*Example*: 'I am very disappointed with you, Mr Smith. Please be very careful how you answer this question: [Was Tom Jones involved in this?]'

---

## NON-VERBAL COMMUNICATIONS

Observe the subject's body reactions generally and his eye contact in particular. You must deprive him of the comfort of manipulators. You can most easily do this by quietly mimicking them or looking closely at them. Either way, he will usually stop, again increasing anxiety.

## INTERJECTIONS

Interjections are some of the most important tools for finding the truth. The right time to interject is when it is clear that the suspect's memory, imagination, conscious and subconscious states are in conflict and thrashing around trying to contrive a plausible response. At such points the liar is directly connected to his subconscious and memory monkeys and is thus vulnerable to making admissions, Freudian slips and other mistakes.

---

*Example*:
| | |
|---|---|
| Question: | 'Did you go to the office to collect the cheque?' |
| Response: | [Silence and deep thought by the suspect – looking down and to the right] |
| Interjection: | 'Have you been ten times in the last month or less than this?' |
| Response: | 'Well, no, not 10 times.' |
| Question: | 'Then what about 50 times in the last year?' |

---

The key is to interject with an alternative every time the suspect's brain is thrashing for an answer.

In one case the managing director of a computer company, accused of pirating operating systems and exporting high technology to embargoed countries, made an angry outburst:

MD:                        'I am really pissed off with your allegations that we have smuggled thousands of boards and programs to the Soviet Union, inside jukeboxes.'

The investigator interjected:

                           'Well how many boards did you ship inside jukeboxes?'
MD:                        'Well … er.' [Pause for deep thought]
Investigator:              'Was it ten, a hundred, two hundred or what?'
MD:                        'Not as many as a hundred.'
Investigator:              'But you did ship boards in jukeboxes?'
MD:                        [Silence. He could have bitten his tongue off and his lawyer glared at him]

In the cold light of day people find it incredible that suspects make such mistakes but fortunately they do. The reason simply is that the two monkeys are very dangerous creatures, especially when the suspect's anxiety is stimulated.

*Interjections lead to unintentional admissions*

## REGRESSIVE QUESTIONS

Regressive questions, which return phrases from an answer parrot fashion, can be irritating and anxiety inducing.

Response:     'Then I threw the papers into the bin.'
Question:     'You threw the papers into the bin?'
Response:     'Yes.'
Question:     'Why?
Responses:    'Because I thought they were useless.'
Question:     'Because you thought they were useless, you threw the papers into the bin?'
Response:     'Yes.'
Question:     'Why did you think they were useless?'
Response:     'Because I just did.'
Question:     'Because you just did. You threw the papers into the bin because you thought they were useless?'

If you do not believe regressive questions generate emotion, try using them on your spouse or boss, but watch out! Consider using them at any phase in an interview with an overconfident subject to irritate and unbalance him.

## LEVERS AND PROVING THE SUBJECT WRONG

Few people like to be proved wrong, even when the error is in relation to unimportant matters. Every error the subject has to admit to, forced changes to a previous explanation or lie exposed increases anxiety and is a step towards finding the truth. Thus, inconsistencies and untruths in the suspect's responses *must* be brought to his attention and detailed explanations sought.

---

*Example*: 'I don't have to remind you, Bill, that you have just admitted to trying to mislead me and I am not happy about that. Now I want you to take your time and think very carefully about the next question.'

---

He can also be asked enticement questions, but it is important to press home the advantage you have obtained because after being caught out in a lie, the suspect is very vulnerable.

*A liar is vulnerable when he has been caught in a lie*

## WEAKNESSES WITH CONSPIRATORS

It may be possible to drive a wedge between a suspect and his co-conspirators; point out that they will not protect him.

---

*Example*: 'Bill, you know my colleagues are interviewing x and y at this very moment. You know they're going to save their own skins, don't you?'

---

## I KNOW WHAT YOU ARE THINKING

This statement is always worth a try. Some suspects seem to react very strongly to it and it definitely makes them anxious, while others ignore it.

### MORE ON ARTHUR

Arthur, whose exploits were partly described on page 241, was initially extremely confident and domineering until the interviewer said: 'Arthur, I know exactly what you are thinking.' Arthur responded: 'There is no bloody way you know what I am thinking: my mind is my own. You cannot possibly know. You cannot f****** know.'

The interviewer responded: 'I knew you were going to say something like that. I can read you like a book. Your body language keeps giving the game away. You know you cannot go through with this. You made a mistake, OK, now tell me how this all started.' This is precisely what Arthur did.

## 'WHY', FEELINGS AND REASONS QUESTIONS

These open or closed questions focus on the suspect's emotions, feelings and the reasons why certain things happened or did not happen. They are especially relevant when you believe the suspect is delivering a prepared, deceptive answer.

## MISSING FEELINGS

| | |
|---|---|
| Interviewer: | 'You have told me that Mr Smith told you to complete the form the way you did. Is that correct?' |
| Suspect: | 'Yes.' |
| Interviewer: | 'But you knew it was misleading, wrong or false?' |
| Suspect: | 'Not false, no.' |
| Interviewer: | 'But misleading?' |
| Suspect: | 'Yes, a little, but he was my boss.' |
| Interviewer: | 'How did you feel when he told you to do this?' |
| Suspect: | 'What do you mean?' |
| Interviewer: | 'How did you feel about your boss asking you to complete a false form?' |
| Suspect: | 'Well, to be absolutely truthful, I do not remember feeling anything. He was my boss.' |
| Interviewer: | 'Didn't you feel really worried, concerned or upset that he was telling you to do something you knew was wrong, if not criminal?' |
| Suspect: | 'Not that I remember.' |
| Interviewer: | 'I think if he had told you to do this, you would have been very angry, wouldn't you?' |
| Suspect: | 'Possibly.' |
| Interviewer: | 'But you were not angry, were you?' |
| Suspect: | 'Not that I recall, no.' |
| Interviewer: | 'But you would remember being angry, wouldn't you?' |
| Suspect | 'Probably.' |
| Interviewer | 'I have to tell you, Mr Jones, that I think you are mistaken. Maybe you are confusing this incident with another occasion and that you completed this form by yourself. Isn't that correct?' |
| Suspect | 'Maybe.' |
| Interviewer: | 'And that your boss was not involved at all.' |
| Suspect: | [Silence] (The pivotal point) |

Again, the exchange proves nothing, but it has forced the subject to change his prepared story, and thus increases his anxiety and takes him a step further towards the pivotal point.

*Truthful people are more likely to admit their emotions*

## FUTILITY OF ENDGAME STATEMENTS

Most liars do not plan their endgame, possibly assuming that the consequences of their dishonesty will naturally go away. Thus some questions and statements should be directed towards this vulnerability.

*Example*: 'Mr Jones, you know that this is a very serious matter and that we will find the truth. How did you expect all of this to come to an end? You didn't think this through, did you?'

The responses to such a question are likely to be along the lines shown in Table 7.34.

**Table 7.34**   Most likely reactions to endgame questions

| Reactions indicating innocence | Reactions indicating guilt |
|---|---|
| The question is irrelevant | Delayed response and careful thought |
| Committed denial | 'I don't know' |
| Possible anger at an implied accusation | |

Exploring the endgame weaknesses is likely to increase anxiety with a guilty suspect.

*Talking about the endgame forces the liar to face reality*

## SILENCE

### Misconceptions

The steely eyed television detective who stares down the silent suspect would be a failure in real life and silence has to be very carefully handled because it can increase anxiety for both the suspect and the interviewer.

### Causes of silence in an interview

Silence can be the result of a number of factors:

- Created by you:
  - deliberately introduced to increase the suspect's anxiety either in relation to a relevant question or at the pivotal point;
  - while preparing for your next question or considering an earlier reply.
- Created by the suspect:
  - after a question to give him time to plan the next response;
  - at the pivotal point when he is considering whether or not to make an admission;
  - generally, such as by crying or through any other emotional collapse, in the hope that the interview will be terminated.

In all cases plan your response to silence and make sure you deal with it effectively.

*Silence is not golden*

### Deliberately creating a silence

You may deliberately induce an anxious silence by saying something along the lines of:

*Example*: 'I want you to pause for a minute and think very carefully about the next question. If you are not prepared to tell me the truth, I suggest we stop the interview, right now.'

If you use this approach you *must* wait for the subject to respond and under no circumstances should you break the silence. It is unheard of for a suspect to walk out at this point: the reason being that it requires a very high level of commitment to do so.

## Silence created by the subject

Silence by the suspect in response to a relevant question usually means the following (Table 7.35).

**Table 7.35**    The sound of silence

| Meaning of the silence | Your reaction, depending on the context and the phase of the interview |
|---|---|
| He is deciding whether to fight or flee | You should present him with the most detailed evidence you have and require him to commit himself to responses |
| He is playing for time to prepare an answer *(and fighting the two monkeys on his back)* | Assume the silence is an admission. *Interject* with a phrase such as: 'This is too much, Joe, isn't it?' |
| He is confronting himself with the critical decision whether or not to tell the truth: *the pivotal point* | |

An important fact to remember is that when the subject has created a silence to give him time to plan his next response, you must interject (see page 266).

## WRITING IT ALL DOWN

As Spot kindly mentioned in the foreword to this book, it was one thing Mr Staples saying something nice about the elderly ex-guru and quite another committing it to writing. This is true in both trivial and serious cases of deception. If you cannot understand an explanation or don't believe it, consider asking the subject to write down the important facts on a single sheet of paper. Liars don't like doing this because it commits them to barefaced lies.

## THE FIRE EXTINGUISHERS

An accountant, working for a small company, asked the managing director to approve a purchase order (of £10 000 addressed to X Limited) for fire extinguishers, which he said were urgently needed to conform with new fire regulations. The MD believed his company already complied fully with all regulations, but his questions were answered with a load of technical waffle and evasion, which concluded with 'Believe me, we will be in trouble if we don't buy this stuff this week'. The MD said, 'Well we have a few days, so put your case down on a single sheet of paper and tell me all you know about X Limited.'

A few days later, the MD bumped into the accountant and asked him what was happening. 'Oh,' said the accountant, 'I checked and found we were OK, after all.' What he did not admit, as the MD subsequently found out, was that his son-in-law owned X Limited.

*When in doubt, get it in writing*

## THE ULTIMATE STATEMENT

If you believe the liar has no intention of telling the truth, you may seriously excite the subconscious monkey by making a statement along the lines:

---

*Example*: 'Bill, you have told me x and I have explained to you that I do not believe you. I want you to confirm that there can be no misunderstanding about this. If what you have told me is untrue, it must be a barefaced lie, mustn't it? You can have no excuse whatsoever, can you?'

---

Experience shows that liars hate this question because it commits them to a barefaced lie (Table 7.36):

**Table 7.36**   Most likely reactions to the ultimate statement

| Reactions indicating innocence | Reactions indicating guilt |
| --- | --- |
| A direct, short and committed answer such as 'no' | The liar will try to reduce the anxiety within his response by softening the 'no' with additional and unnecessary words |
| Becomes angry | Becomes cautious |
| | Asks for clarification |

Questions of this nature can be asked at any point in an interview, but are particularly relevant in Phases C and D (probing and raising the pavement). In over 40 years of dealing with liars, we have never once known a person whose guilt was subsequently proven to simply say 'no'.

## RIDICULOUS LIES

If the suspect is totally determined not to tell the truth, no matter what, ask detailed questions then explain how his answers can be disproved. If the suspect continues to deceive, he should be asked to sign a witness statement containing all of his lies in the finest detail. Subsequently, these will act against him. After the statement has been completed, you may point out that it is obviously untrue, makes the suspect look foolish and ask him if he wishes to change it. If he does, keep the original.

# Accusatory questions and statements – Phase C (continued)

## INTRODUCTION

It is critical in all interviews with people suspected of deception that you tell them precisely what you believe to be the truth based on your deception theory, i.e. that they did it. However, a statement such as: *'I know you stole the cash, you cheating ratbag,'* is likely to result in a denial, stalemate or worse. You must always treat even the nastiest villain with respect and carefully plan the way in which you make the first accusation:

- a suitable war story, or drawing a parallel in a current news event;
- assumptive questions;
- hypothetical questions;
- a direct accusation prefaced or followed immediately by a rationalization statement.

These questions and statements are particularly relevant in Phases C and D.

*You must politely accuse the liar*

## WAR STORIES AND GOLDEN NUGGETS

War stories (akin to Biblical parables!) are especially useful in making soft accusations.

> *Example*: 'There was a case just like this a few years ago, involving a senior manager just like you. He got caught up in something and got into trouble over his head. He had been a good employee for many years but all of a sudden, through no fault of his own, it all got too much and he took money, which I am sure he intended to repay. Then things went from bad to worse – do you know what happened to him?'

The subject's reaction to a story such as this can be very revealing (see Table 7.37).

**Table 7.37**   Most likely reactions to war stories

| Reactions indicating innocence | Reactions indicating guilt |
| --- | --- |
| Will listen carefully, but will not hear the story as being applicable to him | Will normally take the story very personally |
| Will usually appear relaxed and show a confident interest | May show non-verbal signs of anxiety |
| | May ask: *'Are you accusing me?'* |

If the subject's reaction is indicative of guilt, you may make a direct accusation.

> *Example*: 'The problem is, I believe the same thing is happening to you.'

When planning tough interviews, you may wish to consider developing one or more war stories to fit important elements of the deception theory.

*People like stories and relate to them*

## ASSUMPTIVE QUESTIONS OR CLOSED ALTERNATIVES

These, which can be open or closed, are constructed around an assumption which you may or may not be able to prove (Table 7.38).

In planning tough interviews, you should review the deception theory and list the main assumptions and plan questions to cover them. These can be asked at any stage, but are particularly relevant when the subject is at or near the pivotal point. Wherever possible try to phrase assumptive questions with one soft alternative.

> *Example*: 'Did you accept a personal payment from ABC Limited because you believed you had earned it, or was there some other reason?'

*Guilty people are more likely to accept assumptions*

**Table 7.38**   Examples of assumptive questions

| Example of assumptive question or alternative | Assumption that could result in a denial if posed in an open question |
|---|---|
| 'When did you stop beating your wife?' | That he beat his wife |
| 'How much money did you make from this?' | He did 'this' and made money |
| 'Did this all start because you needed money for your wife or for some other reason?' | That this started |
| 'What time did you leave the office with Bill?' | That he was with Bill |
| 'Did this start because you were short of money or because you saw everyone else getting away with it?' | That this started; everyone is doing it |

## HYPOTHETICAL QUESTIONS

These can be used to challenge, accuse or to deal with any other significant matter where you do not want to confront the suspect directly.

> *Example*:
> - 'If someone said you had taken the money, how would you feel?'
> - 'If I could prove to you that what you just said is not true, what would you say?'
> - 'If you had taken the money, do you think we could prove it?'

The suspect's reaction should be carefully monitored (Table 7.39).

**Table 7.39**   Most likely reactions to hypothetical questions

| Reactions indicating innocence | Reactions indicating guilt |
|---|---|
| Will not normally see the question as applying to him | Will take the question personally |
| Will not normally enter into conjecture or may take a hard, judgemental line | Will discuss the possibilities but will normally take a non-judgemental line |
| Will take a strong committed position | May challenge your proof or evidence with statements such as: *'If you can prove it, then I will have to go to prison'* |

The bottom line is that guilty suspects and liars are usually much more prepared to consider hypothetical questions: possibly because they do not understand how an honest person would react.

## DIRECT ACCUSATIONS

There is no legal or other reason why you cannot simply say what you believe the subject has done. On the contrary, from a technical, truth-finding standpoint you must say this and repeat it. For example, 'I believe you have taken bribes and passed business to X Limited', or, 'you have told me that your product turns water into wine and I don't believe you'.

You may soften the accusation through a rationalization statement.

---

*Example*:
- 'I can understand why this happened and we must sort it out together, but there is no doubt that you ...'
- 'The evidence is overwhelming that you took the money: I can understand how it happened, but it has now got out of control and we have to sort it out.'

---

There is no doubt that accusations stir up anxiety, and the reaction to them tells you a great deal. If they are not denied with a strong negative response or a FPSPT denial (see page 95), the chances are you are correct and you should proceed on that basis. When accusations are repeated, the reaction of the guilty suspect will usually soften, whereas that of an innocent person will stay consistently strong or harden (see pages 96 and 109).

*Reactions to accusations are critical*

## INNOCENCE, BARGAINING AND ACCEPTANCE

If Phase C has gone to plan, you will either have concluded that the suspect is innocent or brought him to the pivotal point. If you are convinced of his innocence, you should say so and, if necessary, apologize. You should explain why it was necessary to ask probing and difficult questions. In most cases, the subject will understand and accept the apology and no permanent harm will have been done, especially if you ask him out for a game of golf.

It is much more likely that the suspect will be brought to the pivotal point where he is deciding whether or not to tell some or all of the truth. He will usually:

- become passive, very thoughtful and possibly tearful;
- will look downwards, with closed or fluttering eyes;
- sigh deeply;
- slump in his chair, possible in a foetal position;
- his legs may move forward, away from his chair;
- often appear to get smaller.

He may ask questions such as:

- 'I didn't do this, but if I admit it, can we get this over ...?'
- 'Can we speak off the record?'
- 'What would happen if ...?'
- 'Would it be possible for me just to resign ...?'
- 'Couldn't I just withdraw the claim ...?'
- 'Would the police have to be involved ...?'

These are all acceptance signals and you know the suspect is at the pivotal point (see Figure 7.2). *You must then switch to the transactional role of a nurturing parent.*

## Empathetic questions – Phases D and E

### PRINCIPLES

People usually confess because they cannot continue with the anxiety caused by deception: in short, because they have internalized that 'the game is up' (see Chapter 3, page 76). At this stage, which will be repeated throughout a 'tough' interview, the suspect is faced with what are usually unbearable conflicting pressures. The first is that he has recognized the futility of further deception; lost confidence in his ability to succeed and wants to confess. The second is that he is fearful of the *immediate* consequences of telling the truth. The monkeys are really on his back.

---

### THE PIVOTAL POINT

The suspect was at the pivotal point and had gone very quiet. He was considering a confession and asked: 'What could happen over this?' The interviewer replied:

'You will go to prison for eight years, you bastard'. Unsurprisingly, there was no confession.

---

Your approach is to work *with* the suspect to help him resolve this dilemma by:

1   *Stressing his inability to succeed with deception –*
    - the absolute *inevitability* that the facts will be established;
    - that you have *limitless time* and resources to find the truth;
    - the *weaknesses* in and hopelessness of his explanations.
2   *Stressing that the consequences are tolerable –*
    - how *you and he* can resolve the problem together and what the future could hold;
    - *why* the problem occurred and a rationalization for it.

This stage is likely to be emotional and you must take your time. You must make a conscious move to adopt the transactional role of a nurturing parent. In the cold light of day, the sug-

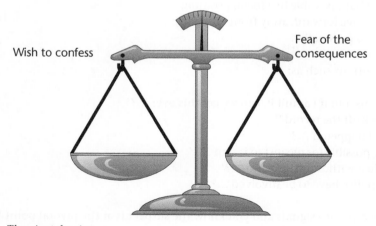

**Figure 7.2**   The pivotal point

gested approach may sound trite,[3] but it works simply because at this stage the guilty subject is overburdened by anxiety in a world that has closed in around him.

## CONSCIOUSLY BECOME A NURTURING PARENT

Push incriminating and other exhibits to one side, implying that the formal interview is over. Address the suspect by his first name, reduce the tone, speed and volume of your voice and:

- if you have been sitting behind a desk move slowly around to sit alongside him within arm's length and to his left;
- address him by his first name;
- as far as possible, mirror his posture and eye movements;
- use slow, positive palms upwards demonstrators;
- talk about his feelings ('I know how you feel');
- emphasize the word 'we' and how the problem can be resolved;
- drop the tone, volume and speed of your speech;
- avoid being judgemental: 'No one could say how they would have reacted in your circumstances.'

However, under no circumstances make promises you cannot keep, and do not mislead the suspect. You must genuinely feel for him and try to put yourself in his place.

*To move into the role of a nurturing parent imagine you are speaking to a loved child who is unwell*

## EMPATHY AND WORDS OF CAUTION

One of the most common failings is that interviewers do not understand that crooks and liars don't share the same values as honest folk. Most have seriously distorted values, so don't go overboard on suggesting that someone that you know is a right villain is really an angel of unconditional virtue who has just temporarily strayed from the heavenly path. For what it is worth, most liars are self-centred and selfish and, at the end of the day, confess because it suits them. So forget about rationalizations like, 'you owe it to your boss' or 'to the company', as these will not work. Very few crooks say they are sorry for what they have done, though many are sorry that they have been caught.

Suggest highly moralistic or religious rationalizations and the suspect will regard you as a gerbil and you will fail. You must put yourself in his shoes and try to hit the right empathetic buttons. Does he seem responsive to the rationalization that he did what he did by accident, because he had been unfairly treated, wanted better things for his family, or because he was in serious financial trouble? You can identify the right 'hot buttons' through trial and error. But, again, take care. For example, if the suspect is a serial philanderer, rationalizations about his wife and family may not go down too well. This is where your background research – and knowing what makes the suspect tick – should pay dividends.

---

[3]   This may be why academics are so reluctant to address the solutions!

## RATIONALIZATION STATEMENTS

You should never, ever attack or criticize a suspect's character by, for example, calling him a 'liar' or a 'crook'; it is always important to allow him to save face, possibly by suggesting a reason why he wandered from the path of honesty.

| A TYPICAL RATIONALIZATION STATEMENT |
|---|
| 'Bill, I know this is very difficult for you and that you are, at heart, a decent person. We all make mistakes and can get over them. Let's try to work this out. Now why did all of this start?' |

You can often identify the right rationalization button by carefully listening to what the suspect says and testing his reaction to a menu of options.

*Example*:
- *Financial pressure*: 'I can understand when people get so financially stretched, they are tempted. Probably you thought you could pay it back. Am I right?'
- *Family problems*: 'I know you have worked hard for your kids, but sometimes hard work is not enough. Am I right?'
- *Being treated unfairly*: 'I know things have been tough at work and have gone against you. Maybe you thought this would solve your problems, but you know it won't. Am I right?'
- *Everybody else is doing it*: 'Everyone seems to have to fight for every penny these days and it is easy to overstep the line. Am I right?'
- *Blaming the victim*: 'Sometimes [the victim company] does not seem to care and leaves temptation in the way of people. That's how it all starts. Am I right?'
- *Any other reason you think might be appropriate*: '... am I right?'

If the suspect shows an interest, the rationalization offered should be developed and repeated (Table 7.40).

Generally, all rationalization statements should be delivered from the position of a nurturing parent and through an emotional channel of communication.

*Guilty people like rationalizations*

**Table 7.40**  Most likely reactions to rationalization statements

| Reactions indicating innocence | Reactions indicating guilt |
|---|---|
| Will normally hear the rationalization as an accusation: may interject | Will usually listen carefully without interruption |
| Will usually dismiss the rationalization as being inappropriate and may become genuinely angry | May dismiss inapplicable rationalizations, but usually in a low-key way |
| | May accept the rationalization |

## COMPLIMENTS

You should be prepared to compliment the subject when he makes an admission.

> *Example*: 'Sam, it took real courage to admit that. Let's see if we can clear up [another important topic].'

You may use positive hand and body movements to reinforce a nurturing parent role.

*Small compliments reward the liar for telling the truth*

## ASK WHY AND GIVE AN ACCEPTABLE ALTERNATIVE

Ask the suspect why he committed the crime, but give him at least one acceptable alternative.

> *Example*:
> - 'Did this start by accident, or did you feel you had no alternative?'
> - 'This started on the spur of the moment, didn't it? I am sure you didn't plan for it to turn out like this, did you?'

Again, the principle is to allow the suspect to save face.

## POINT OUT THE CONFLICT YOU KNOW THE SUSPECT IS FACING

Point out that you know the conflict that the suspect is facing.

> *Example*: 'I have seen many cases like this and I know that it calls for enormous courage to admit you have gone off the rails. People sometimes believe that they can escape by being evasive, but this is never the case. The evidence in this case is overwhelming – you know that – and the facts will come out anyway. Let's try to clear this up now.'

## LOOK TO THE FUTURE

Describe the advantages of telling the truth and focus on the future.

> *Example*:
> - 'Everyone deserves a second chance, but let's see if we can sort out ...'
> - 'This is not the end of the world. With all of this behind you, you can get off to a new start, but first we have to sort out ...'
> - 'This is a temporary setback, but you have the rest of your life before you. But first we have to sort out ...'
> - 'If we can get most of the money back, the problem will not be as bad. Am I right?'

You should also remember that the suspect is probably thinking about two immediate concerns. The first is his wrongdoing and the second having to tell his family and pals that he has admitted to it. Often the second it more important than the first.

> *Example*: 'It takes real courage to admit we have done something wrong … but people will think better of you if you help.'

## OFFER THE SUSPECT YOUR ASSISTANCE

Offer the suspect your assistance. Tell him you are independent and, like a doctor, used to hearing about people's problems and that you have seen it all before. Suggest that you can solve the problem by working together.

> *Example*: 'There are things we all would have done differently, and until you are in that position, you never know how you will react. I can understand why this happened. Now can *we* clear it up?'

## ASK WHAT IS HOLDING HIM BACK FROM TELLING THE TRUTH

Ask the suspect what is holding back his admitting the truth. Establish what his fear is. Downplay the motives for the crime, suggesting that it may have started off as borrowing or as a practical joke.

> *Example*: 'You are a sensible bloke, you know this is all going to come out. What is holding you back from getting this sorted out now?'

Also point out that it does not matter to you whether he tells the whole truth or not. Explain the resolution plan, how evidence will be obtained and that his refusal to accept reality may force the company to take legal action.[4]

## NOTHING TO LOSE

If the suspect has admitted to minor violations (or they can be proven), you may suggest:

> *Example*: 'Geoff, you know that if the company wants to throw the book at you for [the minor offence] they can. If we can help them sort out this [more serious matter] I am sure that will influence any decisions they take. You know you have nothing to lose by getting all this out of the way, don't you?'

## THE LIMITED WINDOW

Emphasize that the suspect does not have unlimited time.

---

[4]    But don't make threats or promises you cannot keep

*Example*: 'Our investigations will be completed in a couple of days and I will not be able to see you again. This is your best chance of getting this sorted out now … so how can we get some of the money back?'

## DEALING WITH ADMISSIONS AND CONFESSIONS

Now comes the really tricky bit. Your initial reaction to an admission of a deep truth may be one bordering on euphoria, but this is the last thing you should show. You must treat even the most damning or dreadful admissions and confessions in a low-key and unemotional way and then probe, as a nurturing parent, for corroborating detail. The more detail you can get, the less likely it is the confession will be withdrawn or that you will be attacked in the witness box, or elsewhere, for giving a misleading account of what was said. Corroborating detail may include why the person did something one way rather than another; how he felt at the time; by recovering tangible evidence; or by noting something known only to the perpetrator. You must take your time obtaining this detail and getting to the deep truth. It is always time well spent.

*Always probe for more detail of the worst case*

You may also invite the suspect to make a written statement, apologize to his manager, or write a letter: again this will serve as corroboration of his confession. Finally, you must handle the suspect fairly. He has placed a great deal of trust in you by telling you the truth and you must not betray it.

# Getting to the deep truth – Phase F

## PRINCIPLES

This phase is where the really good interviewers earn the pittances they are paid. It is all about getting to the deep truth and finding out everything that could be relevant. Both you and the suspect should be totally on the same wavelength and you must take limitless time.[5] You have three objectives:

- to obtain a detailed, accurate confession which the suspect will find impossible to retract;
- to find out about other matters;
- to identify ways of getting your money back.

It is critical that you do not rush or become judgemental or assertive. You are now in the role of a nurturing parent and the suspect an adaptive child and you must really believe this and become totally empathetic.

## CONFIRMING THE CONFESSION

There is no doubt that some people (although it is fairly rare) confess to things they did not do. There are various reasons for this including attention-seeking, the Freudian *thatanos* death

---

[5]  If criminal prosecution is an objective and you have not already cautioned the suspect it is far too late, you have destroyed the case and your only option is to apply to become an accountant

wish, bravado etc., but the most dangerous and unfair is where a false confession is made simply to bring a fear-ridden interview to a close. Thus you should make every effort to confirm every aspect of the confession by:

- trying to identify and recover documentary and other corroborative evidence;
- trying to confirm information known only to the perpetrator;
- establishing how the suspect felt at the time the offences were committed and his motivation;
- any other detail that supports the confession.

If you have even the remotest suspicion that the confession is untrue, you must discuss this in depth with the suspect. This is a very rare and difficult position and you must balance the possibility of encouraging a guilty suspect to withdraw a true confession with the interests of justice. Any doubt should be in favour of the suspect.

## HELPING THE SUSPECT

In this phase it is not unusual for the suspect to ask what might happen to him. This is a very serious and important question which you must answer truthfully. You should list the options and (hopefully, you may genuinely feel this way) say something along the lines of:

> *Example*: 'I don't know what will happen. We both know this is a serious matter, but I can see why and how it happened. It is difficult to see how facing up to your responsibilities can make matters worse and you have been brave enough to do this. I am quite prepared to state on your behalf that you have been frank with me and have genuinely tried to minimize the company's losses, but I need to know x.'

You should continue with any outstanding matters and, in due course, bring the interview to a natural close. You must stick to your word.

## AGREE THE SIZE OF THE PROBLEM

In general and very low-key conversation, ask the suspect to:

- agree to when the offences started;
- agree to the average frequency of the fraud;
- agree to where the fraud started;
- agree to the average amount stolen each time.

You should also try to establish detail that only the guilty person would know.

## LETTER OF APOLOGY

Consider asking the suspect if he would like to write a letter of apology to his manager. This makes withdrawal of the confession less likely.

## OFFER THE CHANCE OF MAKING A WRITTEN STATEMENT

When all aspects of the fraud have been covered, ask the suspect if he would like to make a written statement. You may say: 'To avoid any misunderstanding over what you have told me, I would like to record the main points in writing. Would you like to make a written statement?' The statement should then be taken down at the suspect's dictation; he should not be prompted, although questions to remove any ambiguities may be asked. He should be asked to read through the statement and should initial all alterations.

The suspect should write and sign the following declaration at the end of the statement:

*Example.* 'I have read the above statement and I have been told that I can correct, alter or add anything I wish. This statement is true, I have made it of my own free will.'

If the suspect refuses to sign this declaration, a note should be made of the circumstances surrounding the refusal. The note should be signed by you and by any witnesses to the interview.

## OPEN QUESTION ON ANYTHING ELSE

Compliment the suspect on his courage in admitting to his mistakes, then ask:

*'Is there anything else that we should get cleared up now?'*

Emphasize that all sympathy for the suspect will be lost if he is not totally honest.

*Example*: 'Bill, I know this has been very difficult and I appreciate your being frank with me. I have to check out some of the things you have told me and we may need to meet again. Will that be OK? You can also telephone me at any time if there is anything else you want to say or if you have problems.'

## FURTHER INTERVIEWS

You should plan to close the interview with an agreement that you might wish to see the suspect again.

This sort of agreement will make it less likely that the suspect will refuse to see you later on. Also, always try to leave the suspect some small task to do, like finding papers, or returning property. This will provide a good reason for keeping your communications channels open.

# Things to avoid at all costs

## INTRODUCTION

There are a number of things that you must avoid at all costs. There are two reasons for this. The first is that they are improper and may lead to the creation of fear and false admissions. The second is that you will not be able to defend them honestly if the case comes to court.

## THREATS, BLACKMAIL, PROMISES AND AMNESTIES

It is critical that no threats or promises are made which could render admissions and confessions improper and thus inadmissible. Ultimately, a trial judge may decide what is fair and what is not, but statements and questions such as the following are dreadful.[6]

---

- 'If you don't tell the truth you will go to hell and your soul will be forever damned.'
- 'I suggest you get down on your knees and pray to God for forgiveness.'
- 'If you don't tell the truth, I will give you a good spanking.'
- 'Tell me the truth and we can then forget it.'

---

They and statements like them must be avoided at all costs. The rule is 'if you have the slightest inkling that what you are thinking of doing could not be admitted without fear in the highest court in the land: don't do it.' This still leaves all of the techniques described in this book at your disposal, and even if you apply them fairly and honestly, you must still anticipate getting your ass kicked in court: this is life (see Chapter 10).

## WINGERS AND VERBALS

These are admissions and confessions falsely attributed to the suspect by a dishonest interviewer. In days gone by, 'wingers' and 'verbals' were far too common for comfort, especially in criminal prosecutions. Most times they varied from the totally unsubtle, such as: 'It's down to me, Mr Smith. I was the one what did it and you are the only person clever enough to catch me. You should get a pay rise for this', to the case where a bank robber, who, during a five-hour interrogation, denied everything, was reported as saying: 'I have told you I did not do it. But if I am picked out at an identity parade, I will grass on the others'.

Today the pendulum has swung towards rampant suspicion and opposing barristers will challenge (quite rightly) any alleged admissions by their clients, possibly arguing that they have been 'winged' or 'verballed'. They overlook the fact that people regularly confess and find their bursts of honesty cathartic.

---

### THE FORGIVENESS COMPUTER

Professor Greg Harvey from Concordia University, Montreal, has developed an interactive computer called the 'Automatic Confession Machine' which can replace the more conventional confessional. The not-for-profit system requires the penitent to type in the customary 'Bless me father for I have sinned'. It responds by getting details and then churns out the penance.

---

The bottom line is to ensure that all interviews are professionally conducted, accurately recorded, and that evidence of them is given honestly and openly. If, by chance, someone does confess by saying: 'It's down to me, Mr Smith. I was the one what did it and you are the only person clever enough to catch me. You should get a pay rise for this', best get some ass protection as no one will believe you.

---

[6]  Believe it or not these statements were made and given in evidence

## Rehearsing the interview

You should carry out a practice run with a colleague acting as the suspect. In a second trial, you should take the role of the suspect. Often the rehearsal in which you *play the role of the suspect* is the most important. You will understand where the evidence is the strongest; you will be able to anticipate, and then defeat, false excuses. Rehearsal will make you more confident. When an interpreter is to be used, he must be involved in the rehearsals.

## Conducting the interview

If your planning and rehearsal have been completed properly, conducting the interview should be a cinch but:

- Have a good night's sleep before the interview is due to take place: keep off alcohol and vindaloos and, ideally, remain celibate.[7]
- Make sure you dress professionally and settle in the interview room before the suspect arrives. Check everything.

Stick to your plan and don't panic. You can overcome any nervousness (which is entirely justified in important cases) by taking a few deep breaths before the interview starts and by really concentrating on the suspect throughout. He has far more to lose than you have and the cards are stacked in your favour.

*When you are feeling nervous concentrate on someone else*

## Follow-up – Phase G

As soon as possible after each interview, complete your notes and secure all of the other evidence. Update the resolution plan, diary of events and deception theory and carry out further investigations and interviews as quickly as you can. In the days and weeks following the interview you should keep in regular contact with the suspect until asked to do otherwise.

Before the case goes to court, it is possible that the suspect's attitude towards you will become hostile: this should not affect your position. You should continue to deal properly with him and be abundantly fair in the way you act and give your evidence. Always remember that what goes round, comes round.

## Checking your performance

Tiger Woods says he only hits one good shot a round, but he analyses every one and learns from his mistakes. We can do the same with interviews: think what you did well and what went badly and learn your lessons.

---

[7]  This is why elderly investigators are to be preferred because they no longer bother with such trivia

*Some investigators have 40 years' experience: others have one year's experience repeated 40 times*

## Conclusion

Despite what the smelly socks say, even the worst of malodorous villains confess, as do a lot of basically good people and both types feel better for it afterwards. If an interview with an obviously guilty suspect fails (and in reality not many do) you must go back to basics and try to prove the case by other means, through witnesses, documentary, forensic, technical and other evidence. But remember, a clear confession speeds up the wheels of justice and saves taxpayers' money.

*Never give up.*
*The last person left standing is the winner, or his lawyer*

'WELL, MR JONES, THE MANUSCRIPT IS GOOD, BUT AN ADVANCE ON ROYALTIES IS OUT OF THE QUESTION'

# 8 *Dealing with Deception in Writing*

*An oral statement isn't worth the paper it's written on*

## Background

Both achievement and exculpatory lies can be conveyed in written 'stories' which may be freestyle or guided. In freestyle the writer has total control over the topics he chooses to include and the words selected. Stories may also be guided by a template, based on legal advice or determined by specific questions:

**Table 8.1**  Lies in written stories

| Type | Achievement or exculpatory or both | |
| --- | --- | --- |
| | Historic (past events) | Future (events) |
| Free style | Correspondence | Correspondence |
| | CVs | Offer documents |
| | Statements and affidavits | Proposals |
| | Depositions | Marriage proposals |
| Structured | Reports and surveys | Forecasts |
| | Statements | Business plans |
| | Insurance claims | Application forms |
| | Accident reports | Business proposals |

Freestyle stories are usually the most revealing, but the rules for detecting deception can also be applied to guided stories, especially interview transcripts.

The nature and purpose of the story both have a bearing on the nature and number of clues that can be expected usually depending on the degree of jeopardy – and thus anxiety – involved if deception is detected. Also whether the writer is recalling something from the past or is making promises about his future intentions affects his anxiety levels and thus the structure, content, syntax and other clues in the story.

*Lies about intended future performance are usually less stressful, because someone else can be blamed*

Most of the principles of deception described in Chapters 2, 3 and 4 apply to written lies, even though the liar has had time to plan every word, to edit and maybe even take legal advice before committing himself to paper. This chapter outlines the ways in which lies in writing can be identified and then resolved in what we will refer to generically as the Structured Analysis of Stories (SAS).

# Structured analysis of stories

## ORIGINS AND FURTHER DEVELOPMENT

The origin of SAS can be traced to the mid 1930s and the work of Dr Udo Undeutsch of the University of Cologne. He developed a methodology called 'Statement Reality Analysis' (SRA) for assessing the credibility of rape victims. For years the work was confined to academic circles but in the 1980s spread to the USA, Canada and Israel and into the commercial world.

Avinoam Sapir, of the Laboratory for Scientific Interrogation (LSI) (www.lsiscan.com), and Don Rabon (www.donrabon.net), of the North Carolina Justice Academy were among the prime movers in the promotion of statement analysis, primarily focused in the US criminal justice areas and on exculpatory lies in single incident cases

Mr Sapir's work, especially, has triggered others into action and now scores of people are offering similar techniques. Many are no more than gimmicks which produce sound and word bites. These undermine the value of statement analysis.

## AVINOAM SAPIR AND SCAN

### A mathematical equation

Avinoam Sapir's excellent website at the LSI should be the starting point for anyone interested in digging deeper into 'pure' statement analysis. His approach is called Scientific Content Analysis (SCAN) and it has become the standard among American law enforcement agencies, including the FBI.

---

### SCAN AND SAPIR

Mr Sapir's definition of SCAN is as follows:

'SCAN looks upon a statement as a **mathematical equation** ... We are not interested in the content of the statement, but in the relationship between:

- The different links of the statement (i.e. the positioning and connection between topics)
- The subjective meaning the writer attributes to each word
- The different locations in which a certain word is used
- The relationship between the different words

The end result of a SCAN analysis is to know the background information which generated the subject's vocabulary or dictionary (i.e. his linguistic code) ... In other words we would discover the full story that the subject didn't want to expose openly in the content of the story.'

Our experience, since 1990, of using SCAN type techniques has been very positive, but with some important provisos. First, like any alternative method, it is very time-consuming and thus expensive. For example a 30-page statement, which is fairly modest by corporate fraud standards, may take an expert four or five full days to review effectively. The second point is that the reviewer must be properly trained and exercise his skills regularly. Finally, statement analysis is not an end in itself but merely a guide to questions that should be asked or lines of further investigation.

*SAS is not an end in itself*

## Detractors from SCAN

The Skeptic's Dictionary (skepdic.com) has been critical of SCAN and its website on 'Too Good to be True' states:

> The { LSI } letters stands for Laboratory for Scientific Interrogation Scientific Content Analysis. It also stands for gullibility and wishful thinking. Its market is the same as the Quadro Tracker and the polygraph: law enforcement, including the FBI. L.S.I. claims that a linguistic analysis of a written statement by a suspect will reveal
> – whether the subject is truthful or deceptive
> – what information the subject is concealing, and
> – whether or not the subject was involved in the crime
> L.S.I. boasts that 'while others are out searching for physical evidence, you have already solved the case – using only the subject's own words.' Furthermore, anyone can learn the technique in 32 hours for only $600.
> The SCAN technique is now being used by the FBI and other federal agencies; by law enforcement agencies and military agencies throughout the U.S., Canada and Australia; by bank and insurance investigators; and by private industry.
> How does SCAN work? You begin by having the subject write a statement such as the following:
>
> **Can you find the confession in this statement**
> 'On February 22, 1989, a bundle of 10's totalling 5000 dollars was found in locker #3, where my cash drawer is kept. The date stamped on the straps of the bundle is that of the 31st of January 1989, on this day as on most Tuesdays I am responsible for balancing the vault. At approximately 2:00 p.m. I balanced the vault. The currency is then placed in vault locker #5. If #5 is locked then the currency is placed in any open locker and locked, if I am doing the vault then I will put it in locker #3. I did not have a chance to find someone to tell them before they went to the vault. If I placed the bundle in locker #3 then it was there from the 31st of January until it was discovered on the 22nd of February. I had no knowledge of the missing money. I've been with this bank for more than two years and if in that time you are unaware of my trustworthiness then I suggest we need to come to some sort of agreement so this does not happen again.'
> You then solve the case by applying special scientific linguistic techniques to the statement. For example, you will learn that;
> People who work in banks work with 'currency', 'bundles', etc. They do not work with 'money'. People cannot spend 'currency' or 'bundles'. They can only spend 'money'. When the teller referred to the 'missing money', she incriminated herself.

It's really that simple. An untrained investigator might think that more evidence would be needed before going to trial. In fact, SCAN makes trials unnecessary. Guilt or innocence is so much easier to discover by analysing words than by the old fashioned method of having to prove guilt beyond a reasonable doubt.

Sapir claims to know that John Ramsey is 'an abuser and knows who killed his daughter [Jon Benet].' He analysed the CNN interview of the Ramsey's done about a week after the murder of their daughter. He knows this by Mr. Ramsey's choice of words. Sapir also claims that Magic Johnson got infected with HIV in a bisexual encounter. He knows this because Johnson never said he wasn't a bisexual, only that he wasn't a homosexual, and he said he was certain he got HIV from a woman. According to Sapir, using the word 'certain' indicates 'a lack of certainty'.

I wonder if he's certain of that?

It doesn't do much to instil faith in law enforcement when we see law enforcement officers taking classes from people they should be investigating. In their defence, law enforcers claim that things like SCAN, the polygraph and the voice stress analyzer 'work.' It helps them catch the bad guys because some of the bad guys are ignorant and think these things can really detect lies with some provable degree of validity. Some of the ignorant are intimidated into confessing. They 'work' in the same sense that torture or extortion 'work'. They get the result you want some of the time.

### In the name of science

Apparently, the only thing scientific about Scientific Interrogation and Scientific Content Analysis is in the names. The patterns that Mr. Sapir thinks he sees are not supported by any scientific studies. His folly has been seen before in cases like Judge Edward Jones and personology.

Given that the Skeptics Dictionary holds itself out as the citadel of unbridled truths it is a shame that it should misrepresent the facts and overlook the truth that SCAN is effective and a very good tool for dealing with deception.

Mr Sapir's analysis of the story referred to by the Skeptic's Dictionary may be summarized as in Table 8.2.[1]

---

[1]  He does his analyses in a simple text, rather than tabular, format

**Table 8.2**  Mr Sapir's analysis

| No. | Extract from the statement | Comment | Labels and actions |
|---|---|---|---|
| 1 | On February 22, 1989, a bundle of 10's totalling 5000 dollars were found in locker #3, where my cash drawer is kept. | Was found = passive | Bundle |
| 2 | The date stamped on the straps of the bundle is that of the 31st of January 1989, on this day as on most Tuesdays I am responsible for balancing the vault. | | Bundle |
| 3 | At approximately 2:00 p.m. I balanced the vault. | FPSPT = committed | |
| 4 | The currency is then placed in vault locker #5. | Is placed = passive and lack of commitment | Currency |
| 5 | If #5 is locked then the currency is placed in any open locker and locked, if I am doing the vault then I will put it in locker #3. | | Currency |
| 6 | I did not have a chance to find someone to tell them before they went to the vault. | Out of sequence statement | |
| 7 | If I placed the bundle in locker #3 then it was there from the 31st of January until it was discovered on the 22nd of February. I had no knowledge of the missing money | Bundles and currency become 'money' when it is available for the cashier to spend | Bundle Money |
| 8 | I've been with this bank for more than two years and if in that time you are unaware of my trustworthiness then I suggest we need to come to some sort of agreement so this does not happen again. | | |

Mr Sapir's conclusions were:

## THE SOLUTION

Please note the following:

- Passive language + present tense = 'currency'.
- 'I' + past tense = 'bundle'.
- Missing = 'money'

People who work in banks work with 'currency', 'bundles', etc. They do not work with 'money'. People cannot spend 'currency' or 'bundles'. They can only spend 'money'. When the teller referred to the 'missing money', she incriminated herself.

This is a good example of the change in labels[2] which is typical of deception, but Mr Sapir is not claiming it proves anything, nor even suggesting what should be done about it.

However, if you study the story in even more depth you will find – in addition to Mr Sapir's conclusions – a glaring unconscious mistake, of the Freudian slip variety, revealing that the suspect *knew* the missing money was in her locker before it was discovered by others. The suspect would find her own statement difficult to explain in an interview. Can you see what it is? The answer is given at the end of this Chapter.

---

[2] Nouns and pronouns

## OTHER SCAN TYPE METHODS

Don Rabon has developed an alternative method to SCAN, usually called Discourse Analysis. Mr Rabon is a brilliant teacher and his courses are highly recommended. Also the Internet site www.theirwords.com is becoming a useful source on the subject and for US$50 you can buy a macro for Microsoft Word® that is an excellent tool for statement analysis.

## LIMITATIONS IN THE FRAUD AREA

In fraud cases, in which there may be thousands of pages of affidavits, statements and exhibits, conventional SAS approaches are not appropriate and in fact, are often a waste of time because most of the documents available for analysis are not freestyle versions. However, there are usually some documents in every case, probably written by the suspects to achieve or excuse their deception, which can be revealing. Selecting what is worth analysing is the key.

*SAS means being selective*

## WHAT IS NEEDED IN THE FRAUD AREA

Going back to basics, the objectives of statement analysis are to identify specific areas of possible deception to enable suspects to be more effectively interviewed or to direct external investigations. The analysis should also assist in the development of an accurate fraud theory and diary of events (see pages 189–90).Thus the content, background, external evidence etc. has to be interwoven with the pure analysis to give the optimum results.

*More than a 'pure' type of SAS is needed*

The structure of written, exculpatory, stories can be represented as in Mind Map 10.

Mind Map 10 represents the fact that in most truthful exculpatory stories there is background detail, clarification and emotional overtones that affect everything that happened. This background, or scene setting, is critical to interpreting the individual topics, scenes or activities which should normally appear in sequential order and with consistent detail. One or more of the topics may be regarded as the 'critical issue' and the way the subject leads to this though a prologue (which may be in the general background or within the scene or topic) and closes it through an epilogue can be very revealing. In most deceptive stories the prologue is extended while the liar prevaricates (see page 30)

Each element of background and individual scenes or topics can be separately analysed, in ways described later, to produce useful output The differences between a pure and holistic approached to statement analysis can be demonstrated by the following example.[3]

---

[3] Mr Sapir's excellent work on this case is acknowledged

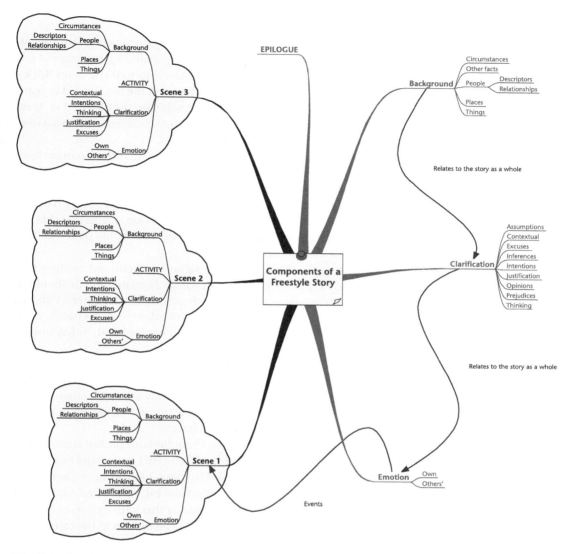

**Mind Map® 10**   Structure of written exculpatory stories

# The dingo case

## BACKGROUND

### The tourist centre

The Ayres Rock is in the Uluru National Park in Central Australia, around 478 km from Alice Springs and is one of the country's main tourist centres. Steeped in aboriginal mythology, the sandstone outcrop is the largest monolith in the world and rises some 348 m above the surrounding plains and is 9 km around its base. There are many points of interest on Ayres Rock including The Climb, Maggie's Springs, the Kangaroo Trail, the Fertility Cave, the Maternity Cave and the Brain.

## The Chamberlain's trip

On 13 August 1980, Michael Chamberlain, a pastor in the church of the Seventh Day Adventists,[4] set off from his home at Mount Isa with his wife Alice Lynne ('Lindy'), six-year-old son Reagan, four-year-old son Aiden and ten-week-old daughter Azaria to tour the Ayres Rock – Alice Springs area. They drove off in their car packed with a tent and the usual holiday gear.

On 16 August 1980, which was a Saturday and for them a sabbath, they arrived at Ayres Rock. They found a camp site – which was almost full – and pitched their tent near to a barbecue area and backing on to a patch of rough, bushy ground.

At breakfast on Sunday 17 August 1980 external evidence proved that the Chamberlains discussed dingoes and how dangerous they are with Mr and Mrs West, fellow campers. The Wests explained that their 12-year-old daughter had been grabbed by a dingo at the campsite. The area in which the Chamberlains had parked was littered with dingo trails. Mrs Chamberlain did not reveal this conversation in her statement, but she did others, suggesting that she was fully aware that dingoes were dangerous creatures and that her baby could be at risk. This makes her subsequent actions even more incredible.

The Chamberlains went to see Ayres Rock and other sights and returned to their tent just after dark. Mrs Chamberlain had a long conversation with a Tasmanian man about the dangers of dingoes and warned him to be watchful for his 18-month-old daughter. With this conversation fresh in her mind, Mrs Chamberlain put Azaria into their tent, dressed in a singlet, jumpsuit, bootees and a matinee jacket and returned to join her husband, Aiden and the Tasmanian couple at the barbecue.

A short while later, Michael Chamberlain said he heard Azaria cry and Lindy returned to the tent to see a dingo trying to get out with something, that she could not identify, in its mouth. Azaria had disappeared, although Reagan remained soundly asleep throughout. The case grabbed the headlines, worldwide, and the story was made into a film, called *A Cry in the Dark*, starring Meryl Streep. Twenty years later it is still a mystery.

After an extensive, but abortive, search for Azaria, the Chamberlains packed their possessions and drove to a local motel where they stayed overnight. A district nurse, who had helped with the search, went in their car with them. She saw Michael Chamberlain's camera bag lying on the floor alongside his seat and suggested she should move it. He resisted, saying that it was always kept in the car in that position. Her recollection of this journey was to become important later, because it was alleged that Azaria's body had been hidden in the camera bag and removed from the scene.

On Monday 18 August 1980, the family returned to their home in Mount Isa. The loss of Azaria led to a major police enquiry, but her body has never been found.

## Clothing found

Ten days later on 23 August 1980, a Mr. Goodwin found Azaria's singlet, jump suit and bootees just off the road in dense foliage some 10 miles away from the campsite. Although the baby's body was missing, only four studs on her jump suit had been undone and her bootees were still inside the leggings. The forensic examination of this clothing became a central feature of the case.

---

[4] Merely mentioning this position can create unjustified prejudice

## Police interviews

On 1 September and 1 October 1980, Mr and Mrs Chamberlain were interviewed by the police and gave their explanations. An extract of Mrs Chamberlain's statement, which was an exhibit at the subsequent inquest, is set out below in Table 8.4. It is not a full transcript nor a fully freestyle version.

## The first inquest and follow-up

On 20 February 1981 the inquest was held into Azaria's death. Forensic evidence indicated:

- the damage to Azaria's clothing had *not* been caused by an animal but by sharp instrument;
- there was a distinct possibility that the clothes had been buried, dug up and placed in the position where they were discovered by Mr Goodwin.

The coroner concluded that the baby had been killed by a dingo, but incredibly continued to say that:

- the clothing had been removed, buried and later dug up;
- the body had been disposed of by a person or persons unknown.

This seemed to be the end of the case, but media interest continued and many people suspected – often built on prejudice – that Mr and Mrs Chamberlain had murdered their daughter. The police felt the same way and sent clothing and other exhibits to the UK for examination by the eminent pathologist Professor James Cameron. This and other enquiries led to a second inquest.

## The second inquest

On 14 December 1981, the coroner found that Mr and Mrs Chamberlain had murdered their daughter. His finding was based on what appeared to be overwhelming forensic evidence, from Professor Cameron and other experts, who stated that:

- Azaria had been decapitated by a human. The bloodstains on her clothing were consistent with one deep cut rather than a number of tooth marks as would have been the case in a dingo attack.
- There was no animal saliva on any of the clothes.
- There was no evidence that the body had been dragged, as would have been the case had the baby been carried away by a dingo.
- Blood stains on the singlet showed that it had been worn the right way around during the attack but had been reversed inside out when the cut marks were made.
- Professor Cameron had identified bloodstained finger and thumb prints on the right shoulder of Azaria's clothing, suggesting that she had been held in a vertical position in someone's left hand while being killed with the right.
- The body had been buried fully clothed sometime after death and subsequently dug up when the clothing had been removed.
- Cuts to her clothing had been made by scissors rather than by canine teeth.
- From an analysis of the bloodstains on the clothing, the wounds could not have been inflicted by a dingo.

Joy Kuhl, a forensic biologist from New South Wales, examined the Chamberlain's car and found extensive bloodstains and arterial sprays on the seats, in the floor well, under the dashboard and on a pair of scissors. All of the blood contained foetal haemoglobin which is only present in young babies.

Ms Kuhl also found bloodstains and small fabric scraps, cut from Azaria's jump suit, in Michael's camera bag. This led to the conclusion that, at some stage, her body had been hidden in the bag

## The criminal trial

On 13 September 1982, the Chamberlains were charged with murder and appeared before the Darwin Supreme Court. Enormous forensic evidence was produced by both the prosecution and defence. Unusually, the prosecution made no attempt to explain the motives for the alleged murder.

In summing up, the prosecutor said that if the Chamberlains were to be believed:

- the dingo went to the tent;
- pulled the baby from its cot;
- ran away, while being chased by a posse of followers with the baby in its mouth;
- buried the body, still fully clothed;
- disinterred it later;
- ran a further 14 km with the body;
- took the body from its clothing, without opening all of the studs or leaving any saliva;
- turned the singlet inside out and then bit it;
- left the booties inside the jump suit;
- placed the clothing down carefully in one neat pile, near a main road.

He concluded that it had to be a very clever and tidy dingo.

On 29 October 1982 the Chamberlains were convicted. Mrs Chamberlain was sentenced to life imprisonment with hard labour and Mr Chamberlain to 18 months imprisonment, suspended so that he could look after the children. All appeals were rejected. Here, again the matter rested until ...

## New discoveries

On 2 February 1986, the body of David Brett, a British citizen who had a history of mental illness and believed he was to be sacrificed at Ayres Rock in a black magic ceremony, was discovered in Uluru[5]. About 50 yards away from his body, which had been partially eaten by dingoes, police found Azaria's missing matinee jacket. The case was again front page news and inexplicably the discovery of the matinee jacket was viewed as corroboration of the Chamberlain's innocence.

## The Royal Commission

In 1988, a Royal Commission was set up, and some of the forensic evidence was discredited. In particular, the German manufacturers of the chemicals used by Miss Kuhl wrote a letter to the court suggesting that the tests could produce unreliable results and that what she believed to be arterial blood stains could have been a rust prevention chemical. The court stated: 'This is

[5] Not far from where the other clothing has been discovered six years earlier

a sobering example of injustice stemming from prejudice, incompetence, misplaced zeal and excessive confidence in the certitudes of science'. The Chamberlains were released.

## AVINOAN SAPIR'S ANALYSIS

In 1990, Mr Sapir published a clever analysis of Mrs Chamberlain's statement and concluded that police theories were based on two propositions. The first was that the murder was a conspiracy by the husband and wife for reasons unknown. The second was that the wife, acting alone and without extensive premeditation, murdered Azaria and that her husband helped conceal the crime.

Mr Sapir concluded, primarily from the 'mathematical equations' in her statement, that her relationship with her husband was not amicable and that a pattern could be seen in the way she referred to him, sometimes as 'Michael' or 'husband' or 'their father'. Mr Sapir's drift was to the effect that when Mr Chamberlain was doing something that pleased her, she referred to him as 'Michael' and when not as 'my husband' or 'their father'.

He also noted a possibly strained relationship between Mrs Chamberlain and Azaria: only once did she refer to her daughter by her given name. More usually she labelled Azaria as 'the baby' or 'it'. Even more significantly, Mr Sapir noted, that after Azaria's disappearance, Mrs Chamberlain only referred to her husband as 'Michael'.

Mr Sapir's conclusion was that: 'before the baby vanished there was tension between the couple and after it vanished the crisis brought them together. This causes the prosecution's first scenario to fall down because if there was no way that the couple could have had a meeting of minds before the baby vanished, how could they reach a decision to kill their baby?'

During the search for Azaria, Mr Sapir continued, Mrs Chamberlain rated her husband's performance badly and effectively accused him of incompetence. He concluded: 'And if we feel that Mrs Chamberlain feels that her husband didn't search properly after the baby, can we say that the prosecution's second scenario (that the husband was an accessory after the murder) has any validity?' The bottom line, therefore, was that Mr Sapir concluded that Mrs Chamberlain's story was consistent with her innocence.

We do not agree with all of Mr Sapir's conclusions, but before presenting the edited transcript, for you to review, there are two points to note. The first is that Mr Sapir's analysis was made over 12 years ago and his methodology has made great advances since then. The second point is that SCAN treats the narrative as a self-contained object and disregards content and all external factors. To that extent it is a 'pure' method or, as he says, a 'mathematical equation'. Our approach is much more holistic and incorporates content and other case facts.

## THE INTERVIEWS

Lindy Chamberlain and her husband were questioned separately on the night of Azaria's disappearance, but unfortunately the police kept no notes, which was a critical omission. Mrs Chamberlain was formally interviewed in the Mount Isa Police Station on 30 September 1980 and on 1 October 1980 by three officers.[6]

Detective Sergeant Charlwood did the questioning, while Detective Sergeant Morris typed the answers and Detective Constable J.E. Scott observed. In total the interviews lasted around six hours.

---

[6] This is not something we would recommend

Table 8.4 sets out some of the questions and answers in column 3. Some of Mr Sapir's comments are shown in shaded cells in column 4. Our comments are also made in column 4, but in clear cells. Comments which are derived from external evidence or are not based only on the wording within the transcript are in italics. Column 5 contains a list of the labels (nouns and pronouns) used in column 3 and important verbs. These words were highlighted and used under Word's 'identify' command to find repetitions.

Mrs Chamberlain's story falls naturally into nine divisions as shown in Table 8.3.

**Table 8.3**   Arbitrary divisions in the dingo case story

| Segment | Detail | |
|---|---|---|
| Introduction | Background<br>Clarification and emotions | Prologue |
| Scene 1 | Leaving their home in Mount Isa and travelling | |
| Scene 2 | Arrival at the camp in Ayres Rock | |
| Scene 3 | Morning of 17 August 1980 | |
| Scene 4 | At Ayres Rock | |
| Scene 5 | Back at the camp and out again | |
| Scene 6 | To and from Sunset Strip | |
| Scene 7 | Back at the camp | |
| Scene 8 | The critical issues: Azaria disappears | |
| Scene 9 | The search and epilogue | Epilogue |

The transcript of the interviews follows[7] in Table 8.4.

**Table 8.4**   Extracts from Mrs Chamberlain's statement

| No. | Topic | Question or response | Comment | Labels and actions |
|---|---|---|---|---|
| Q | | Can you tell me the date you and your family departed Mount Isa to travel to Ayres Rock? | *Permission phrase by the interviewer … a bad approach. She could have simply answered 'Yes'* | |
| 1 | | Have you got a calendar? (Refers to calendar). Yes the 13th day of August. | *Question with a question. The date that she lost her daughter is something she is unlikely ever to forget* | |

[7] Highlighting in column 3 is a guide to the comments in column 4 and labels in column 5. The division into frames 1 to 161 is for analysis purposes only. Backtrack and a vertical arrow in column 2 shows out of sequence (ie non-memory) statements. 'Q' indicates a police question

| No. | Topic | Question or response | Comment | Labels and actions |
|-----|-------|---------------------|---------|--------------------|
| Q |  | Can you tell me the names of the persons that travelled with you? | *Permission phrase by the interviewer ... a bad approach* |  |
| 2 |  | My husband, Michael Leigh, my six year old son Aiden Leigh and my four year old son Reagan Michael and my nine week old daughter Azaria Chantel Loren CHAMBERLAIN. | *Refers to her sons and husband as 'my' and refers to Azaria as my daughter. This is the only time she does so* | Husband Aiden Reagan Azaria Daughter Son My |
| Q |  | Can you tell me how you made that trip? |  |  |
| 3 |  | In a yellow Holden hatch back V8 Torane |  |  |
| Q |  | Could you just outline the trip after departing Mount Isa and arriving at Ayres Rock? |  |  |
| 4 |  | We went from Mount Isa to Devils Marbles, we camped the night, Devils Marbles ⇒to Alice Springs, ⇒camped at Heavy Tree Gap Caravan Park. We just looked around Alice Springs and camped at the same place the next night. ⇒To caravan park at Ayres Rock. | *We= entire family* ⇒ *= missing pronoun normally an indication of lack of commitment* | We Caravan |
| Q |  | What time did you arrive at Ayres Rock? |  |  |
| 5 |  | Well a short time after sunset maybe an hour. |  |  |
| Q |  | Could you tell me what occurred after you arrived at Ayres Rock? | *Note question 25 below and her broken watch strap* |  |
| 6 |  | We registered at the rangers office, then drove around looking for a camping site, it was crowded, only two spots available. We chose the back one where it was quieter near the sand hills. | *We= entire family See site map ... not a desirable area and adjacent to dingo runs = WHY did they do this? The area was covered in dingo tracks* | Husband The baby I Her |

| No. | Topic | Question or response | Comment | Labels and actions |
|---|---|---|---|---|
| 7 | | ⇒Unpacked and pitched the tent, ⇒fed the baby while my husband got the tea. Ah ⇒ate tea ⇒talked to a group of hitch hikers or tourists or what ever you like to call them. | *Missing pronouns⇒* *Husband= getting tea ++* | The baby |
| 8 | | ⇒Put the children to bed and went to bed. | *'Children' does not include Azaria* | Children |
| 9 | ⇑ **Back** | There was something I should have added in there, the baby slept in the car after its feed, until I retired myself then I transferred her to the tent. | *Backtrack = out of sequence* *The baby = slept* Note she left the baby sleeping in the car until she 'retired' Had Azaria done that on the following night, she would have been safe from dingoes | The baby **Its** ... Her |
| Q | | Could you describe the tent you had at Ayres Rock? | | |
| 10 | | It's a four man pup tent with twelve inch walls, Ah green and gold colour with zip front a tear beside the zip about a foot long. The tear is on the left hand side of the zip facing the tent about six inches up from the bottom in the fly screen. It has a small window at the back with stitched in fly screen over it. That's about it I think. | *'That's about it' usually means there was other relevant information but that it has been omitted. Possibly there were other weaknesses in the tent* | |
| Q | | Where was everyone sleeping in the tent? | | |
| 11 | | Facing the tent Reagan was on the right, I was next, then my husband, Aiden on the left with our heads facing the door, the baby across the back right hand corner in a carry basket at Reagan's feet. | *Please notice the order in which the family members are mentioned – first Reagan, then the subject, her husband, Aiden and the baby. The husband and the baby are the only ones who are described not by their names but by their position in the family* | *The baby* |
| Q | | Could you tell us what you did the following day? | This is the day Azaria died | |

| No. | Topic | Question or response | Comment | Labels and actions |
|---|---|---|---|---|
| 12 | | My **husband** got up half an hour before sunrise and photographed the sun rise. He came back and went off again for a walk. | *Husband = leaving –* | |
| Q | | Had you got up by that stage? | | |
| 13 | | I was **feeding** the baby. I was actually up and around the tent but **I didn't go away from the tent.** | *Unsolicited denial … why did she say she 'didn't go away from the tent?' This means she was still in the tent when Michael came back from his first walk. Did this lead to an argument? Did Michael criticize her?* *Baby feed number 1 @ 8.00* *No nappy change?* | Feeding The baby |
| Q | | What time did your **husband** return from his walk? | | |
| 14 | ⇑ **Back** | The other half of that sentence was that he was going for a walk to photograph from another direction near the rangers residence. He probably returned to the tent around eight. | *Out of sequence* *When Michael returned for the first time, she was in the tent?* | |
| Q | | Could you tell me what occurred next? | | |
| 15 | | I dressed the **children** and **started** getting breakfast. I took **the baby** in the carry cot to the barbecue stove with me, sat **her** on the seat while I was preparing breakfast. She was in the carry cot. The **boys** were playing in the area with me or around me. . | *She did this while Michael was away. She had not finished preparing breakfast when he returned and was possibly interrupted by him. Hence the use of 'started'* | Children Started Boys |
| 16 | | **Michael** came back **we** had breakfast spent some time **talking** to the lady from Esperence, she was using the other stove. | *Michael back = ++* *Other evidence shows that this lady is a Mrs West and that they had a conversation about the danger of dingoes… OMITTED* | |
| Q | | The area that you were camping in, is that the same area that you indicated to me earlier on the map? | | |
| 17 | | Yes. | | |

| No. | Topic | Question or response | Comment | Labels and actions |
|---|---|---|---|---|
| Q | | What occurred after you had breakfast? | | |
| 18 | | We talked to the lady for a while longer and cleaned up the dishes, ⇒got in the car and went sight seeing around the rock in the direction of the brain. We went back to the airport had a look at the planes and slowly around the base of the rock to the climb. | *Took around two hours to get breakfast and then on the road ⇒ No pronoun = possible argument getting into the car? 'Back to the airport', she has not mentioned going there OMITTED* | Talked |
| Q | | Can you tell me what time you started your sight seeing? | | |
| 19 | | Maybe about ten. | | |
| Q | | Can you tell me what time you arrived at the base of the climb? | | |
| 20 | | Possibly about eleven thirty that's a guess. | | |
| Q | | What occurred after you arrived at the base of the climb? | | |
| 21 | | The baby was asleep in the car and I told a woman that the baby was asleep and to keep an ear out if she cried. I was taking the two boys to the start of the chain for photographs with their father before he did the climb. | *Told the woman and not asked her … to look after the baby. Would most mothers leave a ten-week-old baby in a car in the heat with a stranger?* Two points are important here: he is the 'father' when leaving her with the boys and 'Michael' when he returns | Told Talked |
| 22 | ⇑ **Back** | She waved to me from the car that the baby had woken and went and talked to her while I brought the boys straight back down to the car, where I fed her and the boys played, then we had lunch while waiting for Michael to come back. | *Out of sequence … unless she returned to the baby and then went back to collect the boys ⇒ Missing pronoun Michael = away but waiting to come back ++* They had lunch without him | |
| 23 | | He then had lunch and took the two boys up the climb | He had lunch by himself | |
| Q | | What time did he return from his first climb? | | |
| 24 | | Between one thirty and two, possibly he timed himself and would know the exact time. | | |

| No. | Topic | Question or response | Comment | Labels and actions |
|---|---|---|---|---|
| 25 | ⇑ **Back** | My watch band broke on the way down to the car | *Irrelevant information about broken watch strap. Why was this significant to her? The broken strap was kept in the glove compartment of the car. Could it have been broken in an attack on Azaria?* | Watch |
| Q | | What did you do while your husband and the two boys climbed the Ayres Rock? | | |
| 26 | | There was several bus tours climbing the rock and I, the baby was awake, and I sat on one of the stools at the bottom watching them climb along with an elderly couple that were eating their lunch and a family of four who had binoculars and were reporting the progress of my husband and boys. | *Extended prologue* *Hanging sentence 'and I, the'* *Note 'I' not 'we'* *Baby was never included in 'we' group with her mother* *Poor relationship?* | |
| 27 | | I stayed there until they came back. | *Not 'we' to include Azaria* *She was alone with the baby for around 2 hours* | We |
| 28 | ⇑ **Back** | We left the area at around four, after taking three pictures of the baby standing on the rock beside Chicken Rock. | *Out of sequence 'after'* *Why specifically 'three' pictures? Is it significant?* The baby looks older than 10 weeks. In other photographs Azaria appears to have dark hair | Backtrack |
| Q | | What area do you call Chicken Rock? | | |
| 29 | | It's on the maps too, its the end of the rocky section of rock which overlays the rock at the base of the climb. | | |
| Q | | What did you do after you left the area of the climb? | | |

| No. | Topic | Question or response | Comment | Labels and actions |
|---|---|---|---|---|
| 30 | | My husband was tired and wanted to go straight home, I told him that I promised the boys they could see Maggie Springs where there was real water and as we were planning to go onto the Olgas the next day. It was the only major attraction we had not yet seen and wouldn't have time for it the next day. | *Azaria's clothing found not far from Maggie Springs after her death but, in the end, they did not go there*<br>*Husband = with her but tired and they disagreed – she 'told' him*<br>*Justification for her argument* | |
| 31 | | We waved to tourists hiking around the base of the rock, a family of four with two early teen children. | | |
| 32 | | My husband agreed to stop at the springs, I went ahead with the three children. | *The 'husband' 'agreed' (meaning that they disagreed before that)* | |
| 33 | | The baby being awake and carried in my arms. | *Mixed tense = being* | |
| 34 | | My husband stayed behind to change his camera gear a film or something then catch us up. We walked to the fertility cave and through it out the back entrance where we met the family of four that we had previously waved to and started speaking to them. | *Husband = stayed behind*<br>*They were apart for a considerable time. Was the relationship poor?*<br>*The use of 'started' is consistent because the speaking was interrupted by the dingo* | |
| 35 | | I sensed something watching me and I looked up to see a young dingo head and shoulders down about where legs start. It was looking down at us over the top of a boulder. I remarked on it and we all stood watching it for several minutes. | *Something watching 'me' but looking down at 'us'*<br>*Michael not with them for several minutes*<br>*Notice just the head and shoulders and a young dingo just like at the camp later on* | Sensed |
| 36 | | My husband arrived with his camera just after it had left. | *Husband = arrived +++ after a considerable delay* | |
| Q | | How far away was the dingo from you? | *'The' dingo is consistent, following the description of 'a' dingo* | |
| 37 | | A distance of about seven to nine feet. | | |

| No. | Topic | Question or response | Comment | Labels and actions |
|-----|-------|----------------------|---------|--------------------|
| Q | | What occurred after your husband arrived? | | |
| 38 | | We all told him the dingo had been there, he was disappointed he missed it to photograph. The other folks left. | In Q30 the 'husband' became 'Michael' – when he took some photographs of the cave drawings | |
| 39 | | The bus tour had caught up to us and had climbed to what I believe is called the cut throat. The children and I followed them up, while Michael photographed some of the cave drawings. He took some photographs of us along with the other people on the rock, then came up too. | Michael = stays behind – – – photographing but took some photographs of us +++ | |
| 40 | ⇑ **Back** | Stop for a minute. A couple of young people on the bus tour came up and spoke to me, asked me how old the baby was and what her name was. | Out of sequence … to prove Azaria was alive? Spoke to 'me' was Michael not with her? | Backtrack |
| 41 | | They told me a little of the aboriginal legend of the fertility cave and cut throat. | Never asked to explain what this was | |
| 42 | | My husband was very tired and wanted to go straight home. We decided not to walk on to the springs. | Husband = **very** tired – She was agreeable to going home Did not go to the springs | |
| 43 | | The children and I went back through the cave, I can't remember whether Michael did nor not, I think he went around the part on the outside. We met near the front entrance. | Children = 2 boys plus baby? Michael = away – Strange not to remember Why is this information relevant: unwanted detail? | |

| No. | Topic | Question or response | Comment | Labels and actions |
|-----|-------|----------------------|---------|--------------------|
| 44 | | We went back to take another photograph of a rock drawing he missed. | *From this it appears that she did remember that Michael walked outside the cave. If Michael had been with them on the walk back through the cave he would have taken the missing photograph at that time. The use of the pronoun 'we' may be misleading. Michael appears to have gone back by himself, hence the delay in catching them up* | |
| 45 | | The children and I walked slowly back to the car, Michael caught us up, we left just before the bus tour party got back to the bus. | *Michael = away –*<br>*If they walked slowly back Michael must have stayed behind or walked even more slowly* | |
| 46 | ⇑<br>**Back** | We went straight back to our tent, I bathed the children, the baby first and then the two boys, it was just on sunset, | *Note about bathing the baby is slightly out of sequence* | |
| 47 | | My husband told me to hurry or we would miss the photography. We came straight from the shower block to the car and drove out to sunset strip where we parked near another young couple who were also photographing, we both, they also had a wide angled lens and so we were closer to the rock than any of the buses or other cars. | *My husband = told –*<br>*Hanging sentence…* | |
| 48 | | I fed the baby while my husband photographed. The boys stayed in the car too in order to stay clean. Reagan went to sleep. I got out of the car and spoke to the other young couple. We wanted to stay for the after glow, there didn't seem to be one that night. | *Husband = away* | Fed |
| 49 | | The buses started leaving and made clouds of dust so we packed up and went straight back to the camp | *Is this a justification for leaving early? 'Started' = because not all had left* | |

| No. | Topic | Question or response | Comment | Labels and actions |
|-----|-------|----------------------|---------|--------------------|
| Q | | Do you know the names of the people that you spoke to out at Sunset strip? | | |
| 50 | | They may have said their Christian names but I can't remember, I wondered if they were on their honeymoon, because she was the photographer and he was extremely patient, they were in a four wheel drive cream and bone long wheel base I think. | 'She compares her relationship with her husband, the photographer, to the relationship between another couple. Actually the subject is saying something like: "We were not on our honeymoon because he (my husband) was the photographer and I was extremely impatient". | |
| Q | | Can you tell me what occurred after you returned to your camp from sunset strip? | | |
| 51 | ⇑ *Back* | I forgot to mention the children were also wearing army green quilted parkas. | Out of sequence... why is this relevant. She did not describe anyone else's clothing | Backtrack |
| 52 | | The baby had wind so I nursed her and patted her back. | Wind is normally after a feed, but she does not say the baby was fed except at Sunset Strip | |
| 53 | | Aiden held the baby. | Still in the car? The baby was in the car with Aiden and not asleep (see 57) | |
| 54 | | while I lifted the sleeping Reagan from the car ⇒took (off) his parka while sleeping, placed him down in his sleeping bag, zipped it up and covered him with his half of the space blanket. | ⇒ Missing pronoun Reagan went to bed with no tea | |
| 55 | | I folded my side of it back across though not folded so I had a clear track to the back of the tent and put my sleeping bag on top of my husband's. | Hanging sentence "though not folded' Why did she want to have a 'clear track to the back of the tent'. Why did she put her sleeping bag on top of her husband's. Forensic evidence showed blood on his bag but not hers. | |

| No. | Topic | Question or response | Comment | Labels and actions |
|---|---|---|---|---|
| 56 | | I then put the baby's carry cot from the car into the tent, put the children's towels and dirty clothes away. | *Put = took*<br>*Then= discontinuity = omitted detail*<br>*Put the clothes away in the back of the car* | |
| 57 | | I then took the baby back from Aiden who had been sitting in the car with her. | *But did not feed her or change her nappy? The baby must have been awake*<br>*Then= discontinuity = omitted detail* | |
| 58 | ⇑<br>**Back** | My husband had been making tea preparations while I was doing this. I zipped the tent up and walked to the cooking area with Aiden and the baby. | *Husband = making tea*<br>*Zipped up the tent with Reagan inside*<br>*Out of sequence: she must have gone from the car to the tent, but does not say so* | |
| Q | | What time did you get to the camp from Sunset Strip? | *She does not answer this question* | |
| 59 | | My watch was in the glove box of the car, it was dark. | *Seems reluctant to give times* | Watch |
| Q | | When did the boys put their parkas on? | | |
| 60 | | In the car on the way to Sunset Strip. | Because it was cold | |
| Q | | The carry cot that you put in the tent, is that the carry cot that you gave me earlier today? | | |
| 61 | | Yes. | | |
| Q | | Where did you put the towels and dirty clothes? | | |
| 62 | ⇑<br>**Back** | In the back of the car. We had a laundry bag in there. | *She went to the car after arriving back at the camp* | |
| Q | | Can you continue with what happened when you went down to the cooking area? | *The next stage would be putting Azaria to bed. She does not say that she fed the baby or when she dressed her for bed* | |

PREVARICATION IN ADDRESSING THE CRITICAL ISSUE

| No. | Topic | Question or response | Comment | Labels and actions |
|-----|-------|---------------------|---------|-------------------|
| 63 | | Before I do that do you want a description of what the baby was wrapped in? | *Responds to a question with a question. Why is it relevant? Prevarication before getting to the critical issue?* | Backtrack |
| Q | | Now if you like. | | |
| 64 | | Alright, she had a blue bunny rug which I had made plain blue on one side with blue kittens and grey balls of wool on a white background on the other side edged in blue satin ribbon wrapped next to the clothing. Then a pent house blanket mulberry one side and a bright pink the other edged in matching mulberry satin ribbon doubled around her with a slightly smaller matching blanket on the side the wind was coming from. | *Note this is not a description of her clothing … Simply the blankets … etc. There were no bloodstains on the blankets?? This suggests there were four layers of blankets … later she says there were six The baby must have been wrapped in this way when the man from Tasmania saw her* | |
| 65 | | She went to sleep in my arms while Michael and Aiden were finishing cooking and eating their tea. | *Michael = cooking ++* | |
| 66 | | There was another young couple from Tasmania with an eighteen month old daughter cooking tea on the other side. I sat on the railing and talked to the husband while my husband and his wife joined in occasionally during the preparations or while they were working. He was drinking a stubby no wrong it was a can in a stubby cooler. | *Husband = talking to woman –* | |
| Q | | What is a pent house blanket. | | |
| 67 | | Its the brand of a double thickness blanket which takes the place of two ordinary blankets and may be used in place of a bed spread, I had bought a queen size bed one and cut it down to make the smaller ones myself. | | |
| Q | | Do you know the names of the couple you were speaking to at the barbecue area? | | |

| No. | Topic | Question or response | Comment | Labels and actions |
|-----|-------|----------------------|---------|--------------------|
| 68 | | No. They did tell us their Christian names. What happened the rest of the night made me forget them. | *Emotionally consistent* | |
| 69 | | If you are agreeable we will terminate the interview now until tomorrow morning. | *What a bad time to end* | |
| 70 | | OK | | |
| Q | | Do you recall the conversation we had in this office yesterday? | *Silly question* | |
| 71 | | Yes. | | |
| Q | | Is there anything further you would like to tell us in relation to that conversation? | | |
| 72 | | Yes. I've been thinking how my husband came to be wearing socks and had none on. He was wearing socks for the first half of the day, he took them off after he climbed Ayres Rock because they were giving him blisters, cut his toe nails and put his shoes on again without them before he climbed the rock again with the children. Aiden got ahead of Michael and Reagan, Michael brought Reagan down again while Aiden continued climbing with a party. Michael then climbed up a third time and met Aiden, three quarters of the way up and came back with him. I made a mistake in the shirts the boys were wearing. Reagan had a blue one with stars on the front, Aiden had a white one with his name on the front. | *Husband =*<br>*Michael = climbing with the boys ++*<br>*Michael = brought Reagan back ++*<br>*Michael = climbed again –* | |

| No. | Topic | Question or response | Comment | Labels and actions |
|---|---|---|---|---|
| 73 | | Reagan was also wearing a bottle green crocheted cardigan. Michael removed his shirt during his climb and tied it around his neck. I noticed a man on the climb who sat down most of the way and skidded down on his bottom. The tour director had to go and meet him. The elderly lady next to me told me he was a maths teacher who had a nervous break down. They had told him not to go but he insisted, he had steel caps on his heels and toes. They had had trouble with him right throughout the tour. They were waiting for him and her husband. The rest of the tour went for their scenic flights and had to return to pick up her husband who was slower due to a heart condition and had frequent rests during the climb. The bus came back to collect him. | *Michael = on climb* | Noticed |
| Q | | Do you recall what stage you got up to yesterday relating to the incident at Ayres Rock? | | |
| 74 | | I just mentioned the Tasmanian man was drinking beer. | *But she had not described how she had put Azaria to bed* | |
| Q | | Could you go on from that please? | | |
| 75 | | We were talking about the effects of drinking and smoking on physical health of a person and the relationship to life expectancy between that life style and an abstainer. He said when it was time to die you would die anyway. He didn't want to be old and decrepit. He told us he was a part time student at Hobart Tech or Uni, he did something in the building trade, I can't remember what. They lived in a small place which I remember thinking at the time was Southport. | | |
| 76 | | They mentioned Hughenville, my husband thought it was Maydena. | *Husband = disagreement* | |

| No. | Topic | Question or response | Comment | Labels and actions |
|---|---|---|---|---|
| Q | | How long did the conversation with these people last? | | |
| 77 | | Between half an hour and an hour. We were still talking when our attention was drawn to the baby. | *Out of sequence she has not mentioned putting the baby to bed. 'We were still' is an odd phrase. 'Our attention was drawn' is strangely passive. One would expect her to have said 'When Michael heard the baby'* | |

**PREVARICATION IN ADDRESSING THE CRITICAL ISSUE?**

| No. | Topic | Question or response | Comment | Labels and actions |
|---|---|---|---|---|
| 78 | | I hadn't finished can I carry on? | *Question with a question and a diversion* | |
| 79 | ⇑ **Back** | Did I mention yesterday in the statement about the dingo? | *She is referring to the statement with the Tasmanian couple the officer believes she is referring to the dingo conversation at the Fertility Cave* | |
| Q | | Yes before we started the statement but not in the statement, you did mention the dingo at the fertility cave. | | Dingoes are dangerous |
| 80 | ⇑ **Back** | The people had only arrived that night. | *SHE DOES NOT CORRECT THE MISUNDERSTANDING* | |
| 81 | ⇑ **Back** | They had an eighteen month old daughter. | *This is the Tasmanian couple who arrived on 17 August 1980* | |
| 82 | ⇑ **Back** | We told them to keep their food under cover as there were dingoes in the area which we had seen the night before only a few yards away. | *She knows dingoes are dangerous and in the area. This conversation took place minutes before she put Azaria to bed* | |
| 83 | ⇑ **Back** | Aiden was interested in a mouse and wanted to know what sort it was. | *This is referring to another dingo incident on 16 August 1980* | |
| 84 | ⇑ **Back** | During the evening the gentleman thought it came by our feet | *Note 'gentleman'* | |
| 85 | ⇑ **Back** | and told Aiden to bring the torch over. | *Was the torch working then?* | |
| 86 | ⇑ **Back** | Before he got there a mangy dingo had pounced on the mouse which was between our feet | *Note 'a' dingo came between their feet. It is 'a mangy dingo' not a 'dog'* | |

| No. | Topic | Question or response | Comment | Labels and actions |
|-----|-------|---------------------|---------|--------------------|
| 87 | ⇑ **Back** | We were sitting about three feet apart. | | |
| 88 | ⇑ **Back** | We were unaware that the dingo was there. | | |
| 89 | ⇑ **Back** | It was very silent and disappeared quickly into the darkness with its prey. | | |
| 90 | ⇑ **Back** | We told them the dingoes bit and they endeavoured to keep their daughter away. | *This is reverting to the conversation on the morning of 17 August 1980 with the Tasmanians* | |
| 91 | ⇑ **Back** | She was toddling about. | | |
| 92 | ⇑ **Back** | Aiden asked me if the dingo would take our baby. I told him no mummy wouldn't let him she was safe with us. | *This should have alerted her, more than ever, to the dangers for Azaria* | |
| 93 | ⇑ **Back** | They wouldn't come close or in our tent. He was afraid of them. | *She knew they had come close i.e. between their feet and what she was telling Aiden was incorrect* | |
| 94 | | After Aiden and Michael had finished the bake beans and mushrooms. Aiden said he was tired | *Disconnect word 'after' indicates something has been left out between the time that they started and finished eating. Aiden does not complain that he is still hungry* | Backtrack |
| 95 | | Michael suggested I should eat tea even though I said I wasn't hungry. I agreed. | *She only 'said' she wasn't hungry* | |
| 96 | ⇑ **Back** | Azaria had been asleep for some half hour and seemed to have got over her wind trouble. She was now sleeping peacefully instead of wriggling. | *Only mention of 'Azaria'*<br>*Still no feed or nappy change*<br>*Out of sequence had not previously mentioned 'wind trouble'* | |

| No. | Topic | Question or response | Comment | Labels and actions |
|-----|-------|---------------------|---------|--------------------|
| 97 | ⇑ **Back** | The Tasmanians had asked her name and its meaning, her age and the husband had had a look at her and remarked on her being beautiful. | *Out of sequence but 'proves' baby was alive at this stage. However the Tasmanian could not have seen her as she was 'almost invisible'* | Backtrack |
| 98 | ⇑ **Back** | He had not realized she was so small due to **being almost invisible down the** blankets I was holding her in. | *This witness evidence was pivotal in the police theory that Azaria was alive at bedtime on 17 August 1980* | |
| 99 | | I walked from the barbecue back to the tent, unzipped the tent. and crawled in. | *Not 'we' Does not say she took the baby with her Aiden went into tent at this time or sometime later* | |
| 100 | | Aiden followed me. | *She does not say how long it was before Aiden followed her Witnesses say this was a ten minute period* | |
| **The police theory was that in this period she killed Azaria in the car** | | | | |
| 101 | | I put the baby down lying on her tummy. She had both arms up beside her head with her face towards me. She stirred slightly and turned her face to the back of the tent. I tucked her in with a loose blanket securely. | *This is an odd way to put the baby down ... normally it would be on its back. On the previous night she had put the baby in the car until she 'retired'* | |
| 102 | | The blankets came up to within half an inch of the crown of her head. She had effectively six layers of blankets over her with a bunny rug wrapped around her on the inside. These are the ones in the possession of the police. | *Blankets were covering her face: again unusual Six layers yet previously only four were described* | |

| No. | Topic | Question or response | Comment | Labels and actions |
|-----|-------|---------------------|---------|--------------------|
| 103 | | I then turned to Aiden who was now sitting up in his sleeping bag. He asked if that was all the tea he was getting. I said 'Are you still hungry?' he said 'Yes'. I said I would give him some more tea. I asked him what he would like. He said he didn't know so I suggested some more bake beans. He agreed. I climbed out of the tent and walked around the tent to open the car door which hit the tent as it opened. I got out the tin of bake beans and then climbed back in the tent. | *'I then' = discontinuity phrase = something omitted?* *Got out of the tent, into the car and opened the door on the off side. Were the beans in the car or in the boot?* *Excessive detail = means this is very important to her* | |
| 104 | | I asked Aiden if he wanted it in the tent or wanted to eat with me. He said in the tent but I wasn't sure which was his plate and he had a habit of spilling beans. I told him to come with me back to the stove and show me his plate. | *A very strange reason for getting Aiden out of the tent, especially in his pyjamas on a cold night. A possible reason for not putting his Parka on was that it was already bloodstained* *There were only two plates: Michael's and Aiden's. Michael who was at the barbecue could easily have answered this question* SHE DID NOT ZIP UP THE TENT | |
| 105 | | He went one way I went the other around the bushes and we had a race to the barbecue area. | *'Race' is the only time she had fun with the kids. Aiden was in his pyjamas!!* | |
| 106 | | Michael was talking to the Tasmanian man who wanted to go and try the local bar after tea. | | |
| 107 | | I climbed the rail and walked around the gas bottles to the stove we were using. I put the beans down and picked up the can opener. | | |

| No. | Topic | Question or response | Comment | Labels and actions |
|-----|-------|----------------------|---------|--------------------|
| 108 | | The lady walked across she started to speak. Michael said he heard the baby cry: she had not settled. I said I think so are you sure | *Lindy did not hear the baby*<br>*If the baby was dead, Michael could not have heard the cry and thus was either mistaken or involved at that stage*<br>*Note 'Michael **said** he heard'* | |
| 109 | | I had not heard her. He affirmed he had and the other man agreed. | *The mother would normally be much more attuned to a baby's cries. Perhaps suggesting that Michael was already involved in the murder and had received a pre-arranged signal to report a cry. 'Affirmed' is a strange word and a possible breach of her linguistic code* | |
| 110 | | I said I'd go and check. I put the can opener down walked back past the gas bottles | *Walked* | |
| 111 | | climbed the rail and walked towards the tent. Half way back I saw the head and chest of a dingo trying to get out of the tent. | *Missing conjunction = suspicious profile, Missing pronoun*<br>*…'Climbed'. Why did 'a' dingo have difficulty when the tent was wide open?.*<br>*Same image of a dingo as seen at the Fertility Cave* | |
| 112 | | It was shaking its head from side to side with its nose down. The way it was shaking it looked like it was trying to get something through the tent fly. | *Yet, supposedly, the tent was open*<br>*Something = baby*<br>*Animals would normally drop an object if they were being chased* | |
| 113 | | Our shoes were all along the inside of the tent. | *This is a very strange (inconsistent) thought in giving priority of shoes over the baby and Reagan and why did she assume it had taken her husband's shoes?* | |

| No. | Topic | Question or response | Comment | Labels and actions |
|-----|-------|----------------------|---------|--------------------|
| 114 | | Whatever it was the dingo was having difficulty getting it out. I thought it may have had my husband's shoe and it was swinging by the laces. I yelled 'go on get out'. Thinking it would drop it and run | *She could hardly mistake a shoe for a baby = not consistent* *Why did she think it was her husband's shoe when all of the family's shoes were in the tent?* *Yelled = emotionally consistent but only 'yelled' at the dingo and not for help* *'It' = baby* | Yelled |
| 115 | | The thought crossed my mind that it may have still been a puppy nine to twelve months old and bent on mischief | *The profile is that 'mind' has to be regarded as an imagination and not a memory* *Puppy = small* | |
| 116 | | I wondered if it was the same dingo we have seen by the fertility cave earlier but thought it was too far away. There were numerous dingoes in the area and that seemed too coincidental. | *Emotionally inconsistent. There would be little time for conscious thought or 'wondering'. She would have been in a blind panic* | |
| 117 | ⇑ **Back** | I had paused when I first saw the dingo after I yelled I started running towards the tent. | *Why pause= not consistent and mentioned out of sequence* *After = discontinuity word suggesting something is missing between seeing the dingo and 'yelling'* *'First saw' – wrong tense* *No further 'yelling'* *Ambiguous sentence does she mean 'I had paused. When I first saw the dingo after I yelled ...'* *or 'I had paused when I first saw the dingo. After I yelled ...' The meanings are totally different* | Yelled |
| 118 | | glances back over my shoulder and noticed Aiden following me, about six feet away. | *Note 'glances' = present tense = suspect* | |
| 119 | | I called there was a dingo in the tent. | *Called = not emotionally consistent after previously 'yelling'. Note dingo in the tent. She does not explain how or when the dingo succeeded in getting out of the tent, but she was only feet away* | Called |

| No. | Topic | Question or response | Comment | Labels and actions |
|---|---|---|---|---|
| 120 | | I remembered I was going to the tent 'cause the baby had cried. I felt sick. It occurred to me dingoes are wild animals. If she had cried she had been disturbed when she first went to sleep she was hard to disturb and therefore may have been attacked. This all flashed through my mind in a matter of four or five seconds. | Remembered = always a suspicious word. How could she have forgotten? 'Occurred' = she fully understood the dangers of dingoes | |
| 121 | | I thought she may need immediate first aid. I'm a first aider with a St John's certificate. | Again a reference to 'mind' | |
| 122 | | When I got to the railing I could see her blankets were scattered between the carry cot and the door. They were in three different places. Reagan was sleeping peacefully with his sleeping bag hood on and his face buried in the pillow. There was no visible flesh anywhere. | 'When I got to the railing and I could see' is a very odd phrase, suggesting she already knew what to expect inside the tent. A truthful statement would be 'I got to the railing and saw ...' This means that the tent was wide open. Therefore why did the dingo have trouble getting out = inconsistent 'Visible flesh'?? | |
| 123 | | I dive straight to the back of the tent. Instinct told me she was gone. Reason told me it was not possible | 'Dive' = present tense = suspect. Again excessive conscious thought | |
| 124 | | I felt in the carry cot to make sure she was not there even though I could see she wasn't. I scrambled back to the door backwards feeling as I went the blankets to make sure she was not unconscious and lying under one of the blankets. | But note no further 'yelling' | |
| 125 | ⇑ **Back** | She was very tiny approximately nine pound four ounces bare weight. | | |
| 126 | | I felt Reagan as I went past to make sure he was really still there | | |

| No. | Topic | Question or response | Comment | Labels and actions |
|---|---|---|---|---|
| 127 | | as I backed out the tent I called to Michael 'The dingo's got my baby' | 'The' dingo has got my baby and not 'a' dingo<br>Called not 'yelled' again emotionally inconsistent<br>This only time in the whole transcript that she refers to the baby as 'my baby' not 'our' baby. Was it Michael's baby? | Called |
| 128 | ⇧ **Back** | When I had previously yelled at the dingo it had run out of the tent across the front of the car and into the shadow. As I was calling to Michael I was running in a direction the dingo had gone around the front of the car. | 'Calling' is not the same as 'yelling' Not emotionally consistent. She must have had a good frontal view of the dingo. Its exit from the tent is out of sequence = suspect | Backtrack |
| 129 | | Michael said 'What'. | 'Said' not emotionally consistent: she had 'yelled' and 'called' | |
| 130 | | As I reached the front corner of the car left hand corner at the time Michael answered | Still no yelling or panic attack | |
| 131 | | I noticed the dingo standing motionless and slightly behind the rear of the car in its shadow approximately the middle of the distance between the two railings. It had it's back to me but at a slight angle with its whole body visible its head was turned slightly as if listening | Noticed is far too soft a word under the circumstances<br>Of course there may have been more than one dingo | |
| 132 | | I did not see anything in its mouth | LACK OF COMMITMENT??? | |
| 133 | | My mind refused to accept what was happening I'm glad I did not | The normal emotional reaction at this point would be blind panic. Again a reference to 'mind' | |
| 134 | | As I appeared it ran swiftly on an angle to the right into the scrub towards the sand hills. I did not hear it move the night was very quiet | Please note that after the dingo disappeared the subject refers to her husband only as 'Michael'. No more 'my husband'. | |
| 135 | | I cut across the angle to where it was heading | | |

| No. | Topic | Question or response | Comment | Labels and actions |
|-----|-------|----------------------|---------|--------------------|
| 136 | | I answered Michael's question as I ran I repeated 'the dingo has got the baby'. | *Merely 'answered' and 'repeated' not 'yelled' and thus emotionally inconsistent.*<br>*Got 'the' baby not as she said earlier 'my baby'* | |
| 137 | | As I reached the edge of the road the dingo had disappeared. There was dead silence I could not hear it or see it was as if it had vanished. | *'it was if it had vanished' = imagination? It had, in fact vanished* | |
| 138 | | It was very dark here the low bushes made very dense shadow | *Here not there* | |
| 139 | | Michael had run straight from the cooking area He called 'which way' as he ran I pointed and said in there. He ran straight into the scrub several yards away with no torch. | *She had told Michael that the dingo was in the tent. Was Michael's a **guilty assumption** indicating prior knowledge. Lindy never said the dingo had run away from the tent with the baby.* | |
| 140 | | I called it's no good you can't see you'll need a torch. We had looked for our spare torch earlier it was the big one the big 'Jim'. Something had been packed on top of it turning it on. The new battery was flat. | *Is it possible that they planned to make sure no torch was available? The effect was that Michael was able to return to the tent while the others searched in the bush* | Our |
| 141 | | Our other torches needed new batteries I knew they weren't good enough. I yelled as loud as I could 'Has anybody got a torch'. 'The dingo has got the baby has anybody got a torch'. | *'Yelled' as loud as I could for a torch. Contrasts with 'called' and 'repeated'* | |
| 142 | | I prayed they wouldn't think I was drunk or joking Three men with torches came almost instantly. One from the right and one from the left hand tents near us. I can't remember whether the third man came from the right or the left. They were running with their torches on and called 'Which way' I pointed and said in there they called to one another to spread out and went three different directions from the spot. | | All to do with the torch |

| No. | Topic | Question or response | Comment | Labels and actions |
|-----|-------|----------------------|---------|--------------------|
| 143 | | Michael called to them to help him .I called come back and get a torch Michael you can't see. He started to come back. The man we were having tea with had got his torch and met us near the car as I was coming back with Michael, back to meet Michael. | 'Michael' = pleased with him Michael already had a torch but came back | |
| 144 | | He spoke to us I can't remember what except telling him which way to go. He went straight. the Western Australian lady had come round by the car. and asked me had we gone for the Police. I said 'No' and she said would you like my husband to go | | All to do with the torch |
| 145 | | and I said Yes and Michael hasn't got a torch our torch is no good and the battery is flat. She loaned us a torch. | Michael now had a torch but appears reluctant to leave the immediate scene. She said earlier simply that the battery was flat = inconsistency | |
| 146 | | Michael by this time had got back to the car We tried to give him a torch it was a fluorescent one about a foot long like those trouble lights. He wouldn't take it He seemed to be in shock He kept looking for ours. He used our small one. | Michael at the car. He already had a torch … but searches for more. He kept coming back to the car and tent | |
| 147 | | Did you see anything in its mouth when it ran into the scrub? | LACK OF COMMITMENT? | |
| 148 | | I have already stated that I didn't, my mind refused to entertain the possibility. It was like a mental block. I tried to recapture the picture. I can see the dog in my mind, its mouth remains a blurred blank. | Referral statement = possibly untrue. Only 'like' a mental block = imagination. The use of the non-threatening label 'dog' at this point is very strange. 'In my mind' is not reality = imagination | DOG |
| Q | | You have related so far up to the time when neighbouring campers commenced searching. Could you go on from that point? | | |

| No. | Topic | Question or response | Comment | Labels and actions |
|---|---|---|---|---|
| 149 | | A number of people appeared and asked if they could help. Michael asked people for torches and told them if they were Christians to pray. | *Told = assertive* | |
| 150 | | He kept looking for the torch and found it. | *Where was he looking? In the car or camera bag? At this point Michael would have had three torches* | |
| 151 | ⇑ **Back** | I should back track here I don't recall where Aiden was when I was searching the tent but around about the time the Western Australian lady came he met me near the back of the car and put his arm around me and said 'Mummy don't let the dingo eat our baby, we've got to find her quick. He was still in his pyjamas he had taken his parka off when he had previously prepared himself to get into bed. | *The last time Aiden was mentioned was when he was eating beans ... at the barbecue Out of sequence but very important to her. It explains why Aiden's parka was later found in the tent with bloodstains. However, why did she allow her four year old son to stay out in the cold in his pyjamas = possible reason is that the parka was already bloodstained and that she stopped him putting it on when she got him out of the tent to give him more beans* | |
| 152 | | It was lying with Reagan's at the door of the tent I cuddled him and told him we were trying to find her and Jesus would look after her. | *The phrase 'Jesus would look after her' could indicate that the subject already knew that the baby was dead.* *Told = assertive* | |
| 153 | | Michael found the torch. | *He already had 3 torches* | |
| 154 | ⇑ **Back** | I'm going on with where I left off now. And went out to look again the West Australian lady went to see her husband. He went for the Police. Michael had gone somewhere and now reappeared. | *Where had Michael gone. His search for the torch would have given him a good excuse to rummage around the car* | Backtrack |
| 155 | | The sequence from here on gets a little hazy. I may get some things back to front things were happening quickly. | *Out of sequence* | |

| No. | Topic | Question or response | Comment | Labels and actions |
|-----|-------|----------------------|---------|--------------------|
| 156 | | People were asking what they could do to help We asked them to round up as many people with torches as possible and start searching. There were already between twenty and thirty out. | | |
| 157 | | We told them to try and keep the dog on the move so that it would either drop it and run or keep carrying her so we could catch it and get her back. | *Told = assertive*<br>*Note again 'dog' If she had believed the dingo had taken her baby she would have said 'so that it would either drop her and run …' The inconsistent use of the pronouns 'it' and 'her' may indicate that she knew the dingo did not have her baby. Why use the non-threatening noun 'dog' instead of 'dingo'?* | |
| 158 | | Michael asked me was I sure she wasn't in the tent I said I was positive but to come with me she wasn't there before the Police arrived. | *Revisiting the tent … before the police arrived is an odd phrase. Possibly suggesting that they had tidied the scene* | |
| 159 | | as we were coming out of the tent we checked it together. | *Ambiguous sentence …. Does it mean they only checked for Azaria as they were coming out of the tent. If so, they went in there for another reason 'before the police arrived'* | |
| 160 | | Michael lowered his torch and it fell on drops of blood on the bottom of his sleeping bag. | *But Michael's sleeping bag was under hers. The torch was not 'his', but had been given to him by the lady (see frame 145).* | |
| 161 | | We didn't notice any other blood at the time. We knew she was bleeding. We looked for a trail of blood in front of the car in the sand. but could not find any with our torch. | *Excuse … if they had a better torch would they have seen blood?* | |

Mr Sapir's comments are extracted from *The View Questionnaire – Manual,* © LSI 1990 Laboratory For Scientific Interrogation

## THE OFF THE RECORD CONVERSATIONS

On 19 September 1981 (that is a year after the interviews set out above), Detective Charlwood drove Lindy Chamberlain to the police station, following a search of her home. Their conversation – which was supposedly 'off the record' – was not admitted into evidence at the criminal trial, but according to the Australian book *The Crown Versus Chamberlain* by Ken Crispin (p. 84)[8] was as in Table 8.5:

**Table 8.5**   The off the record interview

| No. | Question or response | Comment |
|---|---|---|
| Q | 'Did you kill your child?' Charlwood asked. | |
| 1 | *'You've asked me before'*, Lindy replied. | Not a denial |
| Q | 'I've never asked you that before. I've asked you if you knew what happened to her.' | |
| 2 | *Lindy was getting angry. Besides she had been advised by her solicitor that she should not take part in any interview unless he was present. She was uncertain whether she could answer some questions without waiving her right to decline to answer others* | Implies that she was not genuinely angry |
| 3 | *'What are the implications if I tell you?' she asked* and then added with a touch of sharpness, *'You've broken your word before.'* | Fishing question = negotiation = suspect |
| Q | 'What do you mean?' Charlwood asked. | |
| 4 | *'Last time we spoke like this, it was about hypnotism. Then you got to the inquest and threw it up at me. What guarantees have I got that you won't throw this up at me in court?'* | She had refused to submit to an examination under hypnosis |
| Q | 'It depends on your answer,' Charlwood responded candidly. | This was effectively a caution |
| 5 | *'You don't think if I did, I could have carried out this charade all this time?'* | Again no denial. Note '**this** charade' indicating that her present action was a specific charade |
| Q | 'You are selling yourself short.' | This was a very bad response = non empathetic. He should have adopted the role of a Nurturing Parent ... |
| 6 | *'Oh, come on!' Lindy snorted. 'You are crediting me with the brains to commit the perfect murder and get away with it.'* | Fishing question for flattery? |
| Q | 'I mean it', Charlwood said. 'You are an intelligent woman. Don't sell yourself short.' | The response was a sort of flattery, but inappropriate |
| 7 | *'Ask my friends. They'll tell you I can't tell lies.'* | Referral and therefore suspect |

[8] *The Crown versus Chamberlain 1980–1987*, Ken Crispin, Albatross Books Pty Ltd, out of print

| No. | Question or response | Comment |
|-----|----------------------|---------|
| Q | 'You haven't answered my question.' | |
| 8 | *'No, I haven't have I?'* | |
| Q | There was a pause as Charlwood brought the car to a halt in the police driveway and Lindy got out. Meaning there was a significant delay before she responded | |
| 9 | 'No, of course I never killed my child!', Lindy said with feeling. | A profile of murderers is that they seldom refer to their family relationship with the victim. It would have been more convincing if she had said 'daughter' or 'Azaria'. However, her choice of words may have been influenced by the detective's question when he used the word 'child' |

On the face of it, this is a very telling conversation, but Detective Charlwood was never subject to cross-examination on it and therefore its reliability has not been tested. For our purposes, however, it is useful background information; no more and no less.

## COMMENTS ON MR SAPIR'S 'PURE' ANALYSIS

Mr Sapir's finding that the relationship between husband and wife was fractious is a smart conclusion. In fact, the syntax suggests that they may have had an argument at breakfast (because she was still in bed when he returned from his first walk) that continued through the rest of the day. The fact that he went off by himself, leaving her behind with the baby, is understandable, but their separation while he changed films, walked by himself around the outside of the Fertility Cave and so on could indicate that they were barely on speaking terms and did not want to be in each other's company. An alternative explanation, if they planned to kill their baby, possibly for what they had agreed was a good reason, is that Mr Chamberlain simply wanted time and space to think.

Also Mrs Chamberlain's relationship with Azaria appears poor. Most mothers of ten-week-old babies are preoccupied with two tasks and their day centres around them: these are feeds and nappy changes. Her account includes only three feeds during the day of 17 August 1980 and no nappy changes. Given the stress Mrs Chamberlain was under in recounting the tragic events, it is possible that she failed to recall these motherly tasks. But the fact that nothing is mentioned about Azaria being fed immediately before being put to bed on 17 August 1980 may be very significant: especially if the intention was to murder her or if she was already dead.

We have highlighted where Mrs Chamberlain refers to 'Michael' or 'husband' and where he is doing something that she should like we have inserted the symbols '+++'. You will see that the correlation of labels for, and her happiness with, her husband are not linear and we can find no pattern in them. The one exception, as Mr Sapir correctly identified, is her consistent reference to him as 'Michael' from the moment Azaria went missing. Mr Sapir appears right in his conclusion that the tragedy drew them together but we seriously question his second conclusion.

This is that Mrs Chamberlain was not happy with the way her husband conducted the search and therefore he could not have been involved. Her explanation about the torches and her husband's clamour to get back to the car and tent is incredible. But during and after the search she only refers to him as 'Michael' indicating that he had been in her favour at this time. This would, of course, be understandable if she had murdered her baby and did not want the body found, because under such circumstances the more useless the search, the better.

## 'HOLISTIC' CONCLUSIONS

### Possible limitations and benefit of the doubt

Any analysis of Mrs Chamberlain's discourse is limited because it is not a true freestyle version although there are freestyle elements within it. We also have to give her the benefit of any doubt and no-one could really profile how they would react in the face of her tragedy.

### Three areas of concern

That aside, we are concerned about three areas. First, the things that Mrs Chamberlain did not say, her attitude and the absence of any explanation of the things she and her husband did that put their daughter's life at risk. Secondly, the emotional and factual inconsistencies in her reactions and, finally, the syntax of her replies.

### Things not said and attitude

Imagine yourself in the position of an innocent parent whose baby had been killed by dingoes because of your negligence. You would be burdened with remorse and are likely to express this and try and justify or rationalize your actions at almost every opportunity. In this case this might include why:

- it was necessary for you to take a nine-week-old baby into the wilderness;
- you pitched your tent in an exposed area that was obviously on a dingo run and adjacent to sand dunes where they hunted;
- you had specifically assured your four-year-old son that the baby was safe: that dingoes would not come near, when you fully believed the opposite;
- minutes after giving warnings about dingoes to the parents of an 18-month-old child you left your tiny daughter exposed in a flimsy tent, which you carelessly did not close;
- on 16 August you fed the baby and put her safely to bed in the car, yet on the following day you did not feed her at bedtime and laid her down in a tent which you had failed to secure.

Mrs Chamberlain made no attempt to explain any of the above and her omissions are suspicious unless, for some reason she felt the baby's death was justified.[9]

### Emotional and factual inconsistencies

Mrs Chamberlain's inconsistent emotional reactions and factual recollection when supposedly discovering the dingo coming out of the tent with something in its mouth are also disturbing:

---

[9] For example, if the baby was seriously ill or deformed

- She knew dingoes were dangerous and attacked people yet her first reaction was that it was a pup which may have taken shoes.
- When she first saw the dingo 'trying' to get out of the tent she 'yelled' at it: she did not 'yell' at her husband for assistance, nor did she continue 'yelling'.
- She paused before running towards the tent and then merely 'called' her husband that the 'there was a dingo **in** the tent'.
- She again refers to 'calling Michael' and 'answering' his question when the natural reaction would be to scream blue murder.
- How could the dingo have had difficulty trying to get out of the tent when, seconds later, it was so wide open that she was able to see right into the back of it from railings some eight to ten feet way?
- Why did she say nothing – except for one short backtrack – about how and when the dingo got out of the tent: she saw it trying to get out and then standing outside. She had been watching it the whole time and had only been feet away; this is a significant omission especially as she must have seen the dingo face on, when it would have been clear if it had anything in its mouth.

The phrasing of her answers appears to reveal decreasing levels of anxiety when in truth anxiety would have escalated off the scale. Her emotions appeared to operate in reverse of those that would be natural if the dingo story was truthful. Also throughout the passage (frames 114 to 139), she reports far too much conscious thought to be consistent with the emotional turmoil she was facing. At such a time the lower brain would take command and by-pass most, if not all, higher brain considerations.

## Clues in the syntax
### Overall construction
We cannot read anything into the division between prologue–critical issues and epilogue because the structure of the interview was driven by Mr Charlwood's questions. However, as indicated in column 2, Mrs Chamberlain backtracked in her replies giving out of sequence information on:

- recurring problems with and conversations about dangerous and 'mangy' dingoes;
- the baby: most of statements appear to indicate Azaria was not important in her life: she never once said she had loved her or missed her, nor shared any guilt for her death;
- the damage to her watchstrap;
- people asking about and looking at Azaria (again either as an afterthought or to suggest that she was alive until being put into the tent on the evening of 17 August 1980);
- the location of the boys' parkas;
- how the dingo got out of the tent;
- her pause when first seeing the dingo.

These are all important issues, because facts recalled from memory are normally in sequence and are not backtracked.

## Dog instead of dingo

As far as the syntax is concerned, among the most worrying sentences are those that relabel the threatening 'dingo' as a 'dog' (see frame 148) and these are both where the dangerous animal is supposed to have her daughter in its mouth. Her terminology is in stark contrast to the way she described the 'mangy dingo' when one had run off with a mouse the previous evening. The change to a 'soft' label at the point of maximum anxiety is highly suspicious.

## 'In the tent' or 'where'

The sequence at frames 114 and following is interesting:

- She **yelled** 'go on get out' at the dingo: she did not yell for help from Michael.
- She **paused** then ran towards the tent.
- She **called** 'There is **a** dingo is in the tent'.
- She '**dive**' into the tent but did not shout or yell and searched for the baby without yelling for help. The change to present tense, at this precise point, is suspicious.
- As she backed out of the tent, she **called** to Michael '**the** dingo has got **my** baby'.
- Michael **said** 'What?'
- 'I cut across to where it was heading'.
- 'I **answered** Michael's question and said "the dingo has got **the** baby".'
- 'Michael had run straight from the cooking area. He called "which way?" as he ran I pointed and **said** "in there".'

If Michael had heard the call that the dingo was 'in the tent', his immediate assumption 'which way' would indicate prior knowledge and a plan to distract searchers away from the tent and car.

## Is Azaria an 'it' or a 'her'?

Also the sentence (frame 157 and following) appears very significant. Mrs Chamberlain said 'We told them to try and keep the **dog** on the move so that it would either drop **it** and run or keep carrying **her** so that we could catch it and get her back.' This could be rephrased without altering the meaning ... 'try to keep the dingo on the move so that it would either drop [the inanimate object it was carrying and run away] or keep carrying [my daughter, which would slow it down] and we could catch it and get her back.' You can take different views of this sentence, but the inconsistent use of pronouns appear to suggest that she knew the dingo had not got her baby. It may have removed something else, like her husband's shoe, with the baby lying dead in the tent or in the camera bag. It is also possible that the baby could have been murdered and the tent left open to encourage a dingo to enter; thus supporting the false story.

## Before the police arrived

Note the statement at frames 158 to 159 to the effect, 'Michael asked me if I was sure she wasn't in the tent. I said I was positive but come with me. She wasn't there **before the police arrived. As we were coming out of the tent we checked it together.**' This suggests that the reason for going into the tent was not to check for Azaria, because they only did this as they were coming out. Is it possible that their reason for going into the tent – 'before the police arrived' – was to remove Azaria's body into the camera bag or to clean the scene?

*Aiden left in the cold*

Her explanation for Aiden's leaving the tent (frame 103) contains what must be viewed as excessive and apparently unimportant, detail. The sequence was obviously very important to Mrs Chamberlain, otherwise she would not have covered it in such detail. She says that Aiden, just having eaten his tea, was in the tent with her and that she raced him to the barbecue area to give him some more beans. Her explanation is unconvincing and she does not clarify why, on a very cold night, he was dressed only in his pyjamas. The possible answer is that his parka, which was in the tent, was already heavily bloodstained and that she stopped him from wearing it or did not tell him to put it on.

*Didn't see the baby in the dingo's mouth*

Of course, the big question is, if she was a murderess, why didn't she say that she had seen the baby in the dingo's mouth? Nearly every time questions were leading to that point she prevaricated or backtracked, possibly unconsciously, to avoid addressing the critical issue. We can draw no conclusions from this, because prevarication would be justified whether she was guilty or innocent. However, if she did kill her daughter, the only explanation for Mrs Chamberlain not claiming to have seen her daughter in the dingo's mouth was that it was a step too far, requiring too much falsification. If she had said she had seen the baby in the dingo's mouth she would have been open to detailed further questions and required to tell barefaced lies, like how the baby was being held, was she crying, etc. If she was the killer, her safe course was to answer as she did, blaming emotional turmoil for the lack of recollection. However, such an emotional blackout is not consistent with the raft of conscious thoughts supposedly going through her mind at the time: a classic example of incongruency.

## THE POLICE THEORY

The police theory put forward during the criminal trial was that:

- Mrs Chamberlain killed Azaria in the car in the 6 to 15 minute gap between leaving the barbecue area (frames 101 to 108).
- She hid the body in the camera bag or cot and returned to the barbecue area to give Aiden his second helping of beans.
- She (and not Michael) raised the alarm and encouraged people to search well away from the tent and car.
- She told her husband what she had done sometime later. He agreed to help her with the cover up.
- During the search one of them buried Azaria's body.
- On Monday 18 August 1980 they dug up Azaria's body and removed the clothes (including the matinee jacket), accidentally turning the singlet inside out before cutting it with scissors to simulate canine teeth marks.

The prosecution made no attempt to offer a motive for the murder, but there was a great deal of speculation and prejudice including:

- A religious sacrifice ('Azaria' was falsely said to mean 'death in the desert'), based on a complete misunderstanding of Seventh Day Adventists.

- The idea that Azaria had been born brain damaged or had been injured and was killed to save her further pain (there was no evidence of either).
- They did not want the baby, possibly because Michael was not the father. This theory was 'supported' by the fact that she referred to Azaria as 'the baby' or 'my baby' but never 'our baby'. Under this theory, is it possible that the baby was deliberately exposed to danger and that dingoes were selected as the murder weapon?.
- She was killed in a momentary panic attack, following a difficult day.
- She had been injured or killed by Aiden or Reagan and the parents covered up.

We are unlikely ever to know the truth, but in fairness to the Chamberlains they have borne themselves with great dignity and have been reasonably consistent in their denials. In the end there is still reasonable doubt.

## CONCLUSIONS

Before leaving this fascinating and tragic case there are three points worthy of note. The first is the compromising of the crime scene. This case happened in 1980 when procedures were not as well defined as they are today but over and over again – such as in the OJ Simpson case – early mistakes are made from which the prosecution never recovers. The same is true in fraud cases, where computers are improperly searched, documents and other exhibits compromised. This makes it imperative that investigators are trained and work to specified processes.

The second point is that the police interviews stood no chance of getting to the deep truth. This emphasizes the need for a sound methodology, both in terms of process and interviewing skills.

The third point, which we have mentioned before but is worth repeating, is that statement analysis is interesting, but does nothing other than to act as a guide to further questions or investigations: it is not an end in itself and proves nothing. It is easy to see from our analysis what questions should have been asked of Mrs Chamberlain at her next interview.

# SAS in fraud cases

## APPLICATION AND SPECIFIC OBJECTIVES

Structured Analysis of Stories (SAS) can be a useful support tool in most fraud cases, but the art is to:

- be selective and only spend time on potentially important documents that are more or less freestyle versions;
- only analyse long documents if they are in electronic form (this may mean scanning or keying in).

Even then the analysis should have a specific purpose and the time involved justified to prepare for an important interview, to refine the fraud theory or investigations plan.

## RECOMMENDED STEPS

### Two heads and brainstorming

The analysis can be conducted in a number of steps, but we always recommend that two people should analyse every important story separately and brainstorm to produce an end result.

### Work on the deception theory

Write down a fraud or deception theory:

- what you believe happened (and not just what the subject is currently suspected of doing);
- how you would explain it if you were in his position;
- what emotions and thoughts might be involved;
- how an innocent person could react under the circumstances.

This will give you a good idea of what adverse information the subject might try to conceal or falsify.

### Import the text into Word

Import the file into Microsoft Word and select 'Text to Tables' from the Table menu. For example,

---

**Text (in practice this could be a very large number of pages)**
On 11th May 1983, three telexes purporting to have been sent by machine 45 407 in the Banco de la Republica were received by Chase Manhattan Bank in London. These instructions which were not authenticated by a test key, appeared to authorize the transfer of US$13.5 million from an account maintained by Chase for the Ministry de Hacienda to the account of the Republic of Colombia with Morgan Guaranty Trust Company of New York. Prior to this, all instructions from Banco de la Republica to Chase had been authenticated and test key arrangements between the two banks had been in force since 1952.

---

### Convert the text into a table

Reduce the font to 9 point, narrow the column width or alter the page setup to landscape.

---

On 11th May 1983, three telexes purporting to have been sent by machine 45 407 in the Banco de la Republica were received by Chase Manhattan Bank in London. These instructions which were not authenticated by a test key, appeared to authorise the transfer of US$13.5 million from an account maintained by Chase for the Ministry de Hacienda to the account of the Republic of Colombia with Morgan Guaranty Trust Company of New York.
Prior to this, all instructions from Banco de la Republica to Chase had been authenticated and test key arrangements between the two banks had been in force since 1952.

---

For complicated cases, a landscape layout is recommended as it provides the opportunity to add additional columns for sorting key words and entering follow-up actions.

## Insert columns and headings

Use the Insert Columns from the Table menu to add columns, resize them and enter titles:

| No. | Topic | Statement | Comment | Labels and actions |
|-----|-------|-----------|---------|--------------------|
|     |       | On 11th May 1983, three telexes purporting to have been sent by machine 45 407 in the Banco de la Republica were received by Chase Manhattan Bank in London. These instructions which were not authenticated by a test key, appeared to authorize the transfer of US$13.5 million from an account maintained by Chase for the Ministry de Hacienda to the account of the Republic of Colombia with Morgan Guaranty Trust Company of New York. Prior to this, all instructions from Banco de la Republica to Chase had been authenticated and test key arrangements between the two banks had been in force since 1952. |         |                    |

## Read carefully and break into blocks

At this stage the story should be in one column and one row. Read the document thoroughly and identify the critical issues. In the above case it was what happened on 11 May in the wire transfer room. Break the table into frames by cutting and pasting phrases and sentences into new rows: Table 8.4 in the dingo case gives an example of frames. Make sure you do not jumble the sequence of the story.

| No. | Topic | Statement | Comment | Labels and actions |
|-----|-------|-----------|---------|--------------------|
| | | On 11th May 1983, three telexes purporting to have been sent by machine 45 407 in the Banco de la Republica | | 45407 |
| | | were received by Chase Manhattan Bank in London. | | Chase |
| | | These instructions which were not authenticated by a test key, appeared to authorize the transfer of US$13.5 million | | Test Key |
| | | from an account maintained by Chase for the Ministry de Hacienda to the account of the Republic of Colombia with | | Hacienda |
| | | Morgan Guaranty Trust Company of New York. | | Morgan |
| | | Prior to this, all instructions from Banco de la Republica to Chase had been authenticated and test key arrangements between the two banks had been in force since 1952. | | |

## Use the Find and Highlight facilities

At this point, you should not enter the sequence numbers in column 1 because as you get deeper into the analysis you are likely to make further breaks and create new rows. You can, however, start to enter what could be important labels (nouns and pronouns) and verbs in column 5. You can then use Microsoft Word's Find and Highlight facilities to locate and mark every time the labels appear in the text, also highlighting column 5 to show that you have done so. In our example we have searched for all occurrences in the text of 'Chase'. Normally you would not complete this flagging until you have reviewed the text in depth and really determined what labels are important.

## Get into the detail

This is where the detailed work begins and you should go through the text frame by frame, word for word entering your comments in column 3 and highlighting anything of interest as well as flagging labels and actions in column 5. It is a long and difficult iterative process. Initially we recommend you focus on just areas and highlight possibly significant points in yellow and dates and times in red (Table 8.6).

**Table 8.6**    Initial screening

|  | Look for | Comment |
|---|---|---|
| C | **CONTEXT AND BACKGROUND** | Applying to the story as a whole |
|  | Circumstances | Setting the scene |
|  |  | Attitude |
|  |  | Description of people, things and places |
|  | Clarification | Assumptions |
|  |  | Intentions |
|  |  | Justification |
|  |  | Failing to do or say things an innocent person would |
| C | **CONSISTENCY** |  |
|  | Divisions | Prologue – critical issues – Epilogue |
|  |  | Backtracking and out of sequence topics |
|  |  | False boundaries to the statement (start and end) |
|  | Omitted topics | Discontinuity words and phrases |
|  |  | Other clues |
|  | Subjective space v. objective time | Compare the number of lines for each topic (subjective time) with the time taken in real life (objective time) |
|  | Linguistic codes | Breaches of linguistic codes |
|  | Emotions | Failure to act as an innocent person would |
|  |  | False emotions |
|  |  | Fluid or erratic emotions |
| L | **LACK OF COMMITMENT** |  |
|  | Any or all of >>> | Avoidance of FPSPT |
|  |  | Missing pronouns |
|  |  | Passive or conditional phrasing |
|  |  | Subjective truths |
|  |  | Reducing the significance of a topic |
|  |  | Projection and referral |
|  |  | Generalizations etc. |
| L | **LABELS** | Nouns and pronouns |
|  | Any or all of >>> | Inconsistent use |
|  |  | Relationships within sentences |

|   | Look for | Comment |
|---|---|---|
| A | ACTIONS | Verbs and adverbs |
|   | Any or all of >>> | Inconsistent use of tense |
|   |   | Cerebral verbs |
|   |   | Things that didn't happen |
| A | ANXIETY MINIMIZATION |   |
|   | Any or all of >>> | Subjective truths |
|   |   | Projection and referral |
|   |   | Self-deprecation |
|   |   | Prevarication and end softening |
|   |   | Reference to a mental state e.g. 'mind' |
|   |   | Challenging proof or evidence |
|   |   | Avoiding binary answers |
| D | DETAIL |   |
|   | Any or all of >>> | Missing or inconsistent detail |
|   |   | Apparently irrelevant detail |
|   |   | Absence of conjunctions |
|   |   | Abnormal assumptions |
|   | Timelines (dates, times etc. all to GMT) | *Prepare a timeline or diary of events showing objective or real times* |
| D | DENIAL | Failure to deny |
|   |   | Pseudo denials |
|   |   | Declining strength of denials |
|   |   | Unsolicited denials *(of accusations not made)* |

As you go through this process, you will normally have to add new rows and cut and paste. Do not be worried about creating too many rows even if sometimes all they will contain is one word. Keep the labels in column 5 up to date as you encounter important new labels and actions. Enter a bookmark at the starting point and find and highlight repetitions.

## Numbers, topics and word counts

When you have completed your detailed analysis and breakouts you can number the frames and, if appropriate, carry out a word count of the prologue etc. using Word Count from the Tools menu. You can also use Word Count to calculate the subjective–objective time of topics. In most cases you will need a number of iterations before exposing the full story.

## Summarize your conclusions

Ideally, a colleague should have gone through the text and you should conclude with a brain-storming session to identify what action can be taken based on your findings. This may include questions to be asked or lines of investigations. Sometimes the findings are of such importance that they can be extracted as a key point and scheduled in a way that they can be presented to suspects and witnesses.

For example in the cash transaction example we looked at earlier, you may have one single piece of paper with the suspect's phrase:

I did not have a chance to find someone to tell them before they went to the vault.

This proves that she knew the missing money was in her locker and she can be confronted with this 'key point' at the appropriate time.

# Achievement lies and analysing correspondence

Brochures, proposals, letters etc. containing achievement lies can be analysed using the techniques described above, but sequences of correspondence or different types of documents produced by the conman can be used to expose additional clues to deception. These are discussed in Chapter 9.

# Conclusion

SAS is an important tool in the fight against deception. If you have laboured through this chapter and especially the dingo example, you will appreciate it is very time-consuming and you still need a cunning plan to deal with the information you have uncovered, as we will see in Chapter 9.

'BLOODY LIAR! I KNOW HE'S GOT WHISKY!'

# 9 *Other Applications*

*If two wrongs don't make a right, try three*

## Background

The cunning plan can be used anytime you believe you might be told lies and it should become as much a part of your life as your mobile telephone, Filofax, PDA or even your Scotty Cameron putter. This chapter gives examples of how the plan can be applied in dealing with the situations shown in Table 9.1.

**Table 9.1**   Coverage of this chapter

| Types of situations and lies | Examples and *comments* |
|---|---|
| Achievement lies and dealing with conmen (see this page) | Dealing with confidence tricksters or 'conmen', including job candidates |
| Anonymous letters (see page 365) | Resolving allegations made against employees etc. |
| Elimination interviews (see page 369) | Eliminating innocent people from suspicion |
| Witnesses (see page 377) | Obtaining intelligence and evidence from potential witnesses using cognitive techniques |

## Achievement lies and dealing with conmen

### BACKGROUND

#### Types of conmen and modus operandi[1]

The main focus of this section is on achievement lies, involving determined opponents often with large amounts at stake. The subjects, suspects and liars are referred to as 'suspected conmen' or 'conmen' and they come in all shapes, sizes and colours.

The difficulty arises in distinguishing conmen from people who may, or may not, fall into that category. Obviously, once you have determined that a person is a conman, as opposed to merely a suspect, you should have no dealings with him as you will always come out badly.

*Never deal with proven conmen.*
*Don't play with fire*

---

[1]   Just to remind you of the dangers of Latin

Some people who fall into our category of conmen are, in day-to-day life, reputable businessmen, politicians, professional advisers and civil servants. They become tricksters only for a short time, possibly in relation to a specific transaction. The conman may operate alone, in a group or through a company, charity, or some other existing or totally false organization or 'front'. There are a number of conmen who are on the run and operate internationally, away from the scenes of their previous crimes and country of origin. A number use totally false identities (see the Paper Trip www edenpress.com).

*Opportunities always look bigger going than coming.*
*Artificial intelligence is no substitute for natural stupidity.*
*If you must pick between two sins, pick the one you have not tried before*

In all cases, the conman's objective is to obtain an improper advantage by exploiting achievement lies. He succeeds because he knows you, as a potential victim, are facing a dilemma: in fact it is almost a pivotal point, in reverse. On the one hand you want the transaction to succeed and don't want to upset anyone in case you miss the opportunity. On the other, you have nagging suspicions that you are just about to sacrifice your house, dog and Scotty Cameron putter. A good conman will ruthlessly exploit this dilemma, knowing that most victims are unprepared to commit themselves sufficiently to walk away.

## Types of achievement lies

There are thousands of ways in which you may be victimized by conmen in both your business and private life including:

- acquisitions;
- applications for loans or credit;
- discussions, meetings and negotiations;
- investments, *ranging from simple Nigerian 419 scams to complex financial deals with derivatives, prime bank guarantees, investments, venture capital etc.;*
- *job candidates, employment agencies, consultants and advisers;*
- procurement and purchasing involving salesmen from both good and dishonest companies.

The essential feature is that achievement lies are told before you make a decision or part with any money and with the intention that the liar will gain an unfair advantage. They usually have the following characteristics:

- an apparent opportunity for you to make *exceptional profits* or avoid exceptional losses;
- *artificially imposed deadlines* panicking you into making a quick decision before being able to check the facts;
- *alleged secrecy or confidentiality* of the transaction: to the extent that the conman may insist that you don't discuss anything with your family and colleagues;
- *vague promises of future benefits;*
- *penalties or adverse consequences* if you do not meet the deadline;
- *competitors* who are ready to seize upon the opportunity, should you fail to do so.

Once you have committed yourself and have parted with your money or acted in other ways which will turn out not to be in your best interests, achievement lies are characterized by:

- *failure to deliver the benefits promised*, usually for reasons supposedly beyond the liar's control;
- *failure to respond* to your complaints, to return telephone calls or requests for meetings – the liar deliberately remains inaccessible;[2]
- almost limitless *exculpatory lies*, including blaming you for any failure;
- changing the ground rules, *denying earlier promises* by suggesting loss of memory on your part;
- *feigned anger* if you question him, perhaps stating that he is 'sick of your insults'[3] and *claiming the moral high ground* to the extent that he is the injured party.

Finally, the victim usually loses and the liar escapes to fight another day. Often his goals are short term to the extent that he only intends to get your money and run.

*If the deal looks too good to be true, it is too good to be true*

## PRIME BANK GUARANTEES

Over 20 years ago, shady American loan brokers and advance fee scamsters hit upon the idea of Prime Bank Guarantees (PBGs). These fictional 'bank instruments' are supposedly issued by 'prime banks' as a method of raising off balance sheet funds. The scamsters claim to have an inside route for obtaining these for 'self-liquidating loans'. Essentially the scheme is that a person or company that wishes to raise finance (usually in 'tranches' of $100 million) can buy for $85 million a PBG from a leading bank which has a face value of say $100 million, bearing interest at 4% per annum and being repayable in ten years' time. This instrument can then be used as collateral for a loan of $100 million from another bank. This money is then used to immediately liquidate the loan, leaving the borrower with an immediate 'fall out' of say $10 million after all fees have been paid. It all sounds a great idea and many victims have fallen for it, but the logic is fatally flawed[4] and PBGs, in the form suggested, don't exist.

## Tricks of the trade

The most important attributes of a conman are that he is plausible and determined, with an extremely thick skin, ruthlessly exploiting the greed and gullibility of his intended victims. The conman may use fine words and appear to be your dearest friend, but his intention is simply to do or say anything necessary to gain an advantage.

Sometimes the conman will inveigle his victims into illegal acts, in the process knowingly depriving them of any form of redress.

---

[2]  This is often for two reasons: the first is to avoid you and the second because he is busy ripping off new victims
[3]  Conmen seem to use this word rather a lot
[4]  When you look at the instrument in terms of net present value, why should one bank give a value of $85 million and another $100 million?

## OFFSHORE TRANSFER

In a recent merger, one of the negotiators suggested that he could pay the seller for his shares through an offshore tax haven. 'We do not even have to describe the transaction as a share sale. If you set up an offshore vehicle, you can transfer the voting and dividend rights in the shares to us and then invoice my offshore vehicle for goods or services. We can pay it and you will save the tax. We can think about formally transferring the shares later.' What he really meant was if the victim transferred his voting rights through an illegal deal he would never be able to enforce the debt and thus would lose everything.

*Agree to anything illegal and your rights of recovery go out of the window.*
*There is no such thing as a free lunch*

The victim may be sexually compromised or led astray in other ways: again the conman's objective is to deprive the victim of his rights of redress. This is sad, but true, of many achievement lies.

*Never compromise your own position*

The higher-level conmen often retain superb legal advisers who will go on the attack immediately a victim starts to complain. In a process known as 'papering' they flood everyone with threats, letters before action, injunctions, writs, complaints, summonses and subpoenas as diversionary tactics. Conmen know they can outrun their victims in terms of legal costs, especially when they don't intend to pay them.

*Conmen often sting reputable lawyers for their fees: this is the ultimate irony*

Conmen seem to have no difficulty convincing very reputable people and pillars of society to join the boards of their companies or back their schemes. The names of worthy citizens are used to add credibility – and to provide a 'front' – for very shaky deals. Thus the fact that the conman has retained the best lawyers, accountants and advisers and is surrounded by dignitaries means nothing, since it is likely that they have all been deceived. Once one victim or sycophant has been conned, he will be used as a reference or 'bait' for others.

# THE NATO FRAUD

In 2000, a number of large electronic companies were asked by what they believed to be the North Atlantic Treaty Organisation to tender for a multi-billion dollar contract to supply cameras, televisions, video, editing and other electronic equipment. More than 30 potential vendors were required to enter into severe confidentiality and other agreements (with 'The North Atlantic Treaty Organization') and to supply equipment, free of charge, to what they believed were Military Testing Laboratories (MTUs) in Belgium and Italy.

Two American Colonels, Reed and West, represented NATO and over a six-month period – as equipment was being supplied and supposedly tested to destruction – would telephone vendors reporting how their equipment had passed or failed laboratory testing. One vendor spent six months and around $3 million manufacturing a special satellite receiving system which was shipped to an MTU in Belgium. Another had to hire a Boeing 707 to make a special shipment to Brussels.

Both colonels were incredibly knowledgeable and conversations (always on the telephone and usually late in the evening) with the technical and sales representatives from the vendor companies were probing. Most conversations resulted in shipments of further equipment and in Colonel West telling the people he was dealing with that Colonel Reed was a bad man and was trying to steer business to their competitors. Colonel Reed said the same, to the group of vendors with whom he was dealing, about Colonel West.

One vendor became concerned over the delay in any of the contracts being closed and retained investigators to try and establish the truth. This was not difficult. Examination of the confidentiality and other agreements shows that the genuine NATO never used the definite article 'The' in front of its name and spelt 'organisation' with an 's' and not a 'z'. The names of military personnel shown in volumes of correspondence did not exist. The destination of the equipment was not an MTU but a small apartment in Northern Belgium occupied by a black American, using the name of 'Lamar Reed', and his Belgian 'wife'. The corridors and garages of the apartment were stacked with boxes of valuable electronic equipment, and new deliveries, from the UK, Germany, Japan and the USA were being made five or six times a day.

Boxes of equipment removed from the apartment were followed to a commercial video processing laboratory in Paris owned by – surprise, surprise – Dr Lamar Reed. Enquiries revealed that the genuine Lamar Reed was a master sergeant in the catering department of the American Army based in Virginia. Civil search orders were obtained for addresses in the UK, Belgium and France and millions of dollars worth of equipment recovered. The worthy Colonels, Reed and West, were one and the same 38-year-old Jamaican with only elementary level education.

Why did this fraud succeed? The simple reason is that the victims, who always had their worries, did not engage their conscious brains to turn vague suspicions into specific concerns that would require attention. They were also blinded by the potential rewards.

In some instances, conmen are supported by violent criminals who will not hesitate to maim or murder anyone who stands in their way. Sounds dramatic, but it happens.

## SERIOUS AND ORGANIZED

A British company was approached by a group of organized and violent criminals to buy its scrap products, which were virtually worthless. The gang negotiated with Freddy, who was a junior manager in one of the victim's factories, and paid him personally £3000 in cash to ease the deal through. Without consulting his managers, he signed the contract. However, he did not know that other members of the gang who were posing as a competitive bidder had signed a national contract to buy the scrap with another manager. The gang then sued the victim company for breach of contract and produced false affidavits to show losses of £5 million. They put pressure on Freddy to support their claim and he initially became a witness on their behalf. Coincidentally, when he lost his enthusiasm, Freddy was involved in a serious car crash. Although this had been a pure accident, the gang convinced him that he should take the crash as a warning and his resolve in the gang's favour was quickly reinstated.

*Conmen can be really heavy*

## The hard facts

### The fundamentals

There are some hard facts to remember about achievement lies and conmen. The first is that you will be chosen as a victim not because they like your Hush Puppies and purple flared trousers but because they believe you are a 'soft touch'. You also have to accept that conmen live by different rules from honest people. They are quite prepared to lie and cheat and then to move on to new victims. Very seldom do they have long-term friends or business associates.

*Conmen pick soft, gullible and vulnerable victims.*
*They live for the short term*

### Awareness and counter-surveillance

The second hard fact is that you should never underestimate the skill and determination of conmen. The good ones seem to be able to react instinctively to any situation: or maybe it is just practice. They use counter-surveillance techniques, including bugging the victim's telephone, accessing his computer and picking up trash thrown outside his office or house. They are on the lookout for that tiny bit of information that adds to their advantage or warns them that you are suspicious.

*Good conmen always seem to have their senses finely tuned,*
*whereas the victims are blissfully unaware*

### A numbers game

The third hard fact is that you are likely to be one of many, possibly hundreds, of victims all simultaneously suffering the same fate. The conman may not have a defined endgame but he will know, from experience, that most victims fail to pursue their rights quickly enough or with sufficient determination.

## THE DEAD DONKEY

A truck driver moved to Texas and bought an old donkey from a farmer for $100. The farmer agreed to deliver the animal the next day but he telephoned to say it had died in the night. 'Don't worry,' said the truck driver, 'just deliver the dead body'. The puzzled farmer asked what he intended to do and the truck driver said he planned to 'Raffle him off'. 'You can't raffle a dead donkey', said the farmer. 'I sure can', said the truck driver, 'just watch me. Of course, I won't say it is dead.'

A month went by before the two men met again. 'What happened to the dead donkey?' asked the farmer. 'I raffled him off and sold 500 tickets at $2 a throw and made a profit of $996.' 'Didn't anyone complain?' the farmer asked. 'Sure,' replied the truck driver, 'the winner was really pissed off, so I gave him back double his money and kept the rest.'

Although the conman may have to repay some victims, or deliver some of what he has promised, the majority of losers will fund the few winners, leaving him with a substantial profit.

*Safe money*
The fourth hard fact is that conmen usually put their money in safe havens where the victims have little chance of recovering it. The current classic is to have the proceeds of crime laundered through false identities, nominee companies, international business corporations or asset protection trusts, so that while the villains retain control, their ownership is obscured. Thus the chances of most victims getting their money back without positive assistance from the conman are remote. Even then, one of the characteristics of a good conman is that once his scam has been exposed, he feigns bankruptcy.[5]

## The bottom line
There are classic situations in which conmen operate, and standard profiles. But the bottom line is that – before entering into any significant personal or business transaction – you must consciously examine the fundamentals: take a step back and ask yourself: 'Am I being had over?' This, in more polite terms, is known as remaining alert and it is the first step in the cunning plan.

> *For every credibility gap, there is a gullibility fill.*
> *If they accept your first offer, you gave away too much*

## OBJECTIVES

Your objectives in the area of achievement lies, and suspected and actual conmen, are three-fold. The first is to establish the truth so that you can make a balanced decision based on fact rather than on fiction. This means that you want to avoid bad deals and close those that could be good. The second objective is to decide whether the potential reward from the proposed deal is worth the risk. The third objective is to determine whether or not, by catching the conman with his pants down, you can turn the tables and obtain a far better deal than he ever intended. This is a potentially dangerous and unusual objective, but remember that a person is at his most vulnerable when he has been caught out in a lie.

---

[5]  Although very few are and feigning financial distress is part of the scam

## ANOTHER 419 SCAM

A great example of the Nigerian 419 scam is given (www.scamorama.com) where x convinced the fraudsters that he had murdered his wife (attaching a photograph of her 'dead' in the bath) and needed money from them to escape. He also got another fraudster who wanted to meet him in Amsterdam to dress in an all-yellow outfit and hop on one leg down the main thoroughfare so that he would be able to recognize him. X did not get the money, but he had great fun.

Remember, everything is easier to get into than out of, and attaining your objectives in the face of achievement lies is all about timing.

In most cases, your fervour, gullibility and the fervour of the conman are related.

In the early stages of the scam, he is the most eager; then you get bitten and become more committed than him. If you are not careful, your eyes are closed to reality and all you can see are the benefits. Then, when reality strikes, your enthusiasm hits rock bottom. There are two rules you most follow. The first is to make sure that on the upward curve, you ask detailed questions about everything, keep an open mind and control your enthusiasm.

*If something does not look right, politely question it*

The second rule is that once you have made your decision or parted with your money, you are vulnerable and it is imperative that you take your time and plan an ambush. If, at that point, you act in haste, or let the conman know you have suspicions, he will just walk away and you will lose everything.

*Timing is critical*

## METHOD BEFORE THE EVENT

### Principles
The majority of conmen can be detected or deterred before the event, providing you take a few elementary steps.

### Remain alert
You must remain alert to the circumstances in which you might be deceived and, as usual, elevate your suspicions to a conscious level. Once you have done this, and suspect the conman without his knowing that you have questions about his integrity, you have the advantage and can ambush him in the ways discussed later. However, if you are careless and let the conman know you suspect him, he is likely to fight or flee before you are ready to act. If you are not sure whether you are being told lies or not, get some of your female colleagues, or your wife or mother-in-law, involved. 'Women's intuition' is a fantastic tool (see page 46).

*Get females involved and follow their advice*

### Assessment of risk and reward
Remember, risks and rewards are symbiotic and if you cannot afford the pain of the potential loss, don't chase after the gain. Further, if the suspected conman lies to you at any point about

any important aspect, you know his motives are bad and you must plan to take action at the appropriate time.

## Develop a fraud theory and minimize the downside

Develop a fraud theory and think carefully about the liar's endgame; in most cases it will be to take your money and run or to hide behind a thick legal shield. Pay particular attention to pieces of the jigsaw that don't appear to fit and try to find an explanation for them. Assume everything that happens, and does not happen, is part of the conman's scheme and remember that in deception, there is no such thing as a coincidence.

> *Assume everything happens for a reason and is part of the conman's plan.*
> *Stand back and ask, 'Is it viable?'*

Always try to make sure you owe the conman more than he owes you. You may do this by or through:

- retentions or payments into an escrow account;
- performance bonds;
- personal guarantees;
- agreed performance timetable and penalties.

If he is really a conman (rather than just a suspect) he is likely to protest that you don't trust him and make some sort of emotional attack. Don't panic and, if your requirements are reasonable under the circumstances, don't weaken. Make sure he delivers what he has promised before you part with your money.

## Appoint an ogre

It does not matter whether the deal is being handled with the assistance of a professional team of advisers or not, or if it is in your business or private life. If you believe you may be seriously deceived, you should consider appointing an ogre[6] to your side who will stand slightly off line, be a pain in the neck for the suspected conman and question everything. You can then maintain a friendly relationship with the suspected conman, while blaming the ogre for any difficulties. In extreme cases you can pretend to side with the conman against the ogre, requiring him to convince you of his bona fides.[7] This is a variation of the 'good guy/bad guy' approach suggested in some poor books on interviewing as a method of dealing with fraud suspects.[8]

> *An ogre enables you to take a neutral position*

## Get the background

Obtain as much background as possible on the suspected conman and the proposed transaction. Carry out a full due diligence audit: get bankers' references and speak to his other clients, but remain alert to the possibility that they are part of the scam or have themselves been misled.

---

[6]  Possibly a female
[7]  Comer was right: Latin is just everywhere
[8]  And which we do not recommend except in dealing with suspected and actual conmen

*Check everything*

Make sure you positively identify the conman, for example, by covertly collecting his fingerprints and handwriting and craftily let him realize you have done this.

## THE WINE GLASS

The victim admired the glass that contained the conman's vermouth and asked the waiter in the bar of a posh London hotel if he could buy it to take home for his wife. The conman, realizing his fingerprints would be all over the glass, deliberately knocked it off the table. This raised the victim's suspicions and he pulled out of the deal before he lost his shirt.

Get a detailed written biography of the principal conman and all supporting players[9] and check them line for line, getting as much detail and personal information as you can. Most conmen are garrulous, so whenever you have a spare moment together, find out everything about him, where he has assets invested, his favourite haunts, the countries in which he has lived for extended periods,[11] details of his mother, father, brothers, sisters, children, spouse, ex-spouses, lovers and ex-lovers: his hobbies, interests etc. Write all of this down and note any changes to his story and remember if he gives you any false background, he cannot be trusted.

*One serious lie should be enough to tell you his intentions are not honest*

Also try to identify other people with whom he is working and other potential victims. Note all of this information down. If it all goes wrong, it will be invaluable in both tracing him and his assets.

Get details of the competitor allegedly waiting in the background if you do not seize the opportunity the conman is kindly offering you. Speak to the managing director of the competitor or its bankers or accountants and, if you cannot do this, consider retaining investigators to get the full story. Pin everyone down to detail, preferably in writing. Let the conman know you are taking up these references and ask him to explain any discrepancies but do not burst the bubble until you are ready.

### Get the answers and retain the evidence

Ask the conman detailed questions at every opportunity. You must also carefully document every 'fact' on which you are relying and get the conman's written acknowledgement of it. If he does not put things in writing, you must write to him and retain proof that he has received it. Also consider covertly recording meetings, retaining the tapes and transcripts securely. If things go wrong you must have an overwhelming, watertight case. Make sure your correspondence and computer files are complete and accurate and are kept securely. Keep back-up copies of important documents in a secure location unknown to the conman.

In complex cases, keep a detailed chronology recording meetings, correspondence and promises made but not kept (Table 9.2).

---

9   Especially people in the shadows who may be the real principals
10  If the going gets tough, they will flee to a country where they have connections

**Table 9.2**   Tracking evolving stories

| What I have been told | When and how I was told it | | | |
|---|---|---|---|---|
| RATE OF RETURN | Date | How | | |
| The rate of return would be 80% pa | 1.1.2003 | Prospectus | | Meeting |
| The rate would be 40% | 1.2.2003 | | Contract | |
| The rate would be 8% | 1.3.2003 | | | |
| | | | | |
| HIS BACKGROUND | | | | |
| PhD from Cambridge | 1.1.2003 | Prospectus | | |
| O level in woodwork | 2.4.2003 | | Bill Smith | |

Try to make sure he answers every question and every point in every letter. Don't let him escape with concealment lies.

*Not answering difficult questions is a characteristic of a conman*

## MISSING CORRESPONDENCE

A typical trick of conmen is to say that they never received a particular letter or email and thus their failure to respond did not imply that they agreed. Obviously, you can avoid this problem by sending important communications by registered letter or through a secure courier but this may alert the conman that you have suspicions and cause him to flee before you are ready to pounce.

A less obtrusive way of achieving proof of delivery is to ensure that every important communication also contains something the conman would like to know or have, such as an invitation to the theatre or a golf match. If he reacts to the bit that pleases him, he cannot later deny receipt of the part he would prefer not to acknowledge.

In some cases you may let the conman discover that you are building up a dossier that could 'paper' him if he does not deliver what he has promised. This is akin to 'raising the pavement'. If you are right and he really is a crook, he may divert his attention to another victim and this is to your advantage providing you have not already parted with your money. If he is genuinely honest, he will understand the reasons for your caution. Always try to have the detail at your fingertips.

## Analyse the paperwork

Pay special attention to accounts, proposals, projections, spreadsheets, surveys, brochures, contracts, letters and other documents provided by the conman and on which you are expected to rely. Stand back, and again ask yourself: 'Is the basis of this transaction sound? Is the story believable and consistent?'

## ENRONESQUE DEFINITIONS

*Feudalism.* You have two cows. Your Lord takes some of the milk.

*Fascism.* You have two cows. The government takes both, hires you to take care of them and sells you the milk.

*Communism.* You have two cows. You must take care of them, but the government takes all the milk.

*Capitalism.* You have two cows. You sell one and buy a bull. Your herd multiplies, and the economy grows. You sell them and retire to play golf.

*Enronism.* You have two cows. You sell three of them to your publicly listed company, using letters of credit opened by your brother-in-law at a Luxembourg bank, then execute a debt-equity swap with an associated general offer so that you get all four cows back, with a tax exemption for five cows. The milk rights of the six cows are transferred through an intermediary to a Cayman Island company secretly owned by the majority shareholder who sells the rights to all seven cows back to your listed company. The Enron annual report says the company owns eight cows, with an option on one more and has securitized the income on all 12 cows.

*Pay the closest attention to detail*

If there are important documents of title which are central to the deal, such as share certificates, deeds to gold mines in Clapham, debentures, proof of asset ownership or custodial receipts, inspect the originals and have their authenticity confirmed, possibly through your bankers or professional advisers. Make sure you keep copies securely.

*Remember that vital documents may be forgeries. So check them out*

Over a series of correspondence, the liar may drop the topics he wishes to avoid, perhaps by creating diversions, raising spurious matters or by feigning anger or humour. He may escape if the reader fails to persist.

> *Recommendation*: When involved in prolonged correspondence, list all of the topics in which you are interested. Make sure you get a response to each; note the order in which they are dealt with and the number of words devoted to each one.

At a lower, but equally important level, failure to answer a question or to address the critical issue is a strong sign of deception.

## Don't be tempted

Do not be tempted into doing anything that is illegal and do not compromise yourself in any way. In fact, if you are dealing with a suspected conman, don't let your guard drop for a single moment.

*You can never cheat an honest man, but it is always worth a try*

# Meetings and negotiations

## BACKGROUND

Cynics say that meetings are usually a displacement activity for people who have nothing better to do and that standing committees are the worst of all.

### RED TAPE COMMITTEE

At a recent meeting of the Red Tape Committee it was unanimously agreed (with four dissenting votes) that unnecessary meetings cost the UK taxpayers between £1 and £50 billion per annum. The committee thus reported a mean loss of £25 billion.

*The intelligence of a committee varies inversely with the number of people on it.*
*Never underestimate the power of very stupid people in large groups*

There are many different types of meetings, some of which are more exposed to deception than others, depending on whether they are internal and involve only employees or external with the participation of third parties, and whether they are:

- *decision-related*[11] – when the purpose is to agree on some future action, such as whether a new product should be launched or a new procedure put in place;
- *informational,* – when the main purpose is to advise people on a decision that has already been made, such as announcing the creation of a new department or putting a redundancy program in place;
- *task-related* – to produce a desired detailed output, such as finalizing a legal contract or designing a new brochure.

The possibilities and estimated levels of potential deception, varying from good lies to hot air and outrageous trickery, can be summarized as in Table 9.3.

This section deals with most types of meetings and suggests how you can handle them to minimize the risks of being deceived.

## OBJECTIVES

Your objectives, for most meetings, are likely to be:

- to ensure you take decisions based only on the truth;
- to influence the meeting in a way that achieves your objectives;
- to minimize the amount of time you and your subordinates spend on pointless meetings;
- to ensure that an accurate record is kept of all important meetings.

These objectives can be achieved by a slight modification of the cunning plan and will depend on whether you call (and are thus in charge of) a meeting or are merely a participant.

*Stay neutral in a conflict so you can win whichever way it goes*

---

[11]  Including negotiations

**Table 9.3**  Types of meeting

| Type of meeting Examples | Potential for deception | | | |
|---|---|---|---|---|
| | Decision-related | Informational | Task-related | Other |
| INTERNAL (involving employees) | | | | |
| *Team meetings* | High | | Low | Variable |
| *Annual budget meetings* | | | | |
| *Bid evaluation meetings* | | | High | |
| *Detailed work on legal agreements* | | | | |
| EXTERNAL (involving third parties) | | | | |
| *Negotiations* | High and always remain alert | | | |
| *Assessment of a vendor's quality control procedures* | | | | |
| *Discussion of a customer's warrantee claims* | | | | |
| *Compliance meetings with regulatory agencies* | | | | |

## METHOD

### Background

The steps suggested below are mainly relevant to important meetings where gross trickery or deception is possible. However, they can be adapted to most meetings, including those of the Hush Puppies Appreciation Society.

### Determine your objectives

Before any meeting, decide on your objectives and success criteria by asking yourself 'If I could wave a magic wand, what result would I like to achieve?' Then consider if the meeting is necessary at all or whether the same or better results could be obtained by a telephone call, exchange of memos or by doing nothing. It is usually to your advantage if you can avoid a meeting and play golf instead.

> ## HAVE YOU NOTICED?
>
> When you received the email inviting you to a meeting at your office in Birmingham, you just knew it would be a waste of time. But, being a diligent employee, you cancelled your golf, got up at 5.30 in the morning and returned home at midnight. The day was a total waste of time. You told yourself you would never do the same again, but you will. Why? Because we are all scared of missing something.

*If you believe a meeting[12] is going to be a waste of time, it invariably is*
*Unless you are convinced a meeting is necessary, don't go*

---

[12]  In both your business and private life

However, if a meeting really appears necessary, list your objectives in the left-hand column of a piece of A4 paper (or a Mind Map) and in the right-hand column show the key points that should swing the meeting in your favour.

Also consider the objectives and success criteria of other potential participants and the approaches they might take. Again list these on a sheet of A4 paper, showing their key points. You can extend this sheet so that, in effect, it becomes a deception theory.

Sometimes your position may appear weak or even hopeless and if this is the case, you should:

- list all of the key points in your favour and support them with detailed evidence;
- list how you can defeat the opponent's strong points;
- consider how you can divert attention away from your weak position.

## THE CUSTOMS LAWYER

Years ago most of the worst smugglers and purchase tax evaders would consult an elderly, butter would not melt in his mouth, London solicitor. He was a star. When accompanying his clients at interviews with Customs and Excise lawyers and investigators he would always take a passive role and get them to produce their most dreadful evidence against his clients. From time to time he would make 'tutting noises', look towards his client and shake his head, but say nothing else.

When his turn came he would select the weakest element in the case against his client and build it up into a hanging offence: sometimes haranguing his client along the lines: 'This is much worse than I believed. I did not know that you had done this'. In eight-, ten- or twelve-hour meetings he was able to prevent the officials from asking his clients any meaningful questions about the more serious aspects by interrupting and saying 'No, we must deal with this really important matter first', and then continuing to beat the least relevant issue to death.

## The proposed participants

Take great care over the proposed participants in any important meeting and don't just throw out invitations willy nilly. Think of the participants in three categories, those that:

- are likely to support you (usually around 10 per cent);
- are likely to oppose you (usually around 11 per cent);
- are likely to sit on the fence (usually around 79 per cent).

Your success in meetings and negotiations is likely to depend on having more, or more powerful, people supporting you than opposing you, so plan carefully.

Try to identify the opposing power player – who may dominate the meeting by adopting a critical parent role – and there may be more than one. From the outset you should consider ways in which he or they can be marginalized and the easiest way of doing this is to get someone on your side who is more powerful than him.

*Indecision is the key to flexibility*

If your research indicates that there are other people, supposedly on the power player's side, that don't really agree with him, consider the ways that you can invite them to the meeting even though their presence may not be justified. On the other hand, if there are people supposedly in your team that might subvert you, try to make sure that they are excluded.

*Your chance of success in any meeting varies directly with the number of participants who support your view*

Always consider the cost of the meeting. If it involves lawyers, consultants or even investigators who charge an hourly rate, don't agree to their attendance *en masse*.

*Always consider the cost of meetings*

If you are calling the meeting, you can list the participants and move forward on that basis. If you are a guest, you might suggest rearranging the meeting for a date when you know the power player is not available or try some other ruse to swing the balance in your favour. If you have no alternative but to attend in a minority position, don't panic, as all is not lost.

## Getting the background

If you don't already know it, obtain as much background as possible on the proposed participants, including their career histories and private interests (see page 179). As always, even small details can make the difference and may be used to your advantage.

> If you discover that the opposing power player disappears every Thursday afternoon to play golf, and you want a nice brief meeting, you should try and fix it on a Thursday morning.

You should carefully research the rules of formal meetings and understand the procedures, so that you know more about them than the other participants. Then, if you want to create a critical parent role, you can point out some procedural gaffe and throw your opponents off track.

*Attention to detail pays dividends.*
*The harder you work, the luckier you become*

## Strategy

### Fight, flight or appease

Deciding on your strategy is akin to specifying an investigations plan. You should think about this carefully and there are essentially three options which, as always, are based on the animal instincts of fight, flight or appease. Are you going to swing the meeting in your favour by taking a tough attacking position or by playing possum? You must decide.

*Decide on your strategy*

Be prepared to alter course during the meeting if your approach does not work, but remember, changing from an attacking role to appeasement can be a serious climbdown, so to successfully attack, you must be absolutely sure of your facts and remain committed.

### Strong and weak points

If you are in a very strong position, you may decide to go for a knockout blow using a very powerful opening. Alternatively, you may let your opponents make the running and then shoot them down in flames. If you are in a weak position, consider whether you can hijack the meeting with some diversionary tactic.

If you are in a desperate position, consider how you can avoid the meeting altogether, possibly by submitting a brief note setting out your arguments or defences and then disappearing on an important business trip to Bulgaria. This is much better than getting your ass kicked and if you are not present, and the others ignore your memo, you can claim the Nuremberg defence and live to fight another day.

## Relax time pressures

Many negotiators[13] impose unrealistic deadlines, for example: 'If this deal is not closed by tomorrow, we will have to go elsewhere.' You should weigh up whether the deadline is valid and pin down the reasons. If the timescale is unrealistic and puts you at a serious disadvantage, you must extend it or pull out.

*Never act in panic.*
*When in doubt, pull out*

## Set the agenda

Try to make sure that there is a written agenda (ideally only listing the points you want to cover) for every important meeting: even the most obdurate participant will find it difficult to disagree with this, and you should also try to set a time limit. It is often a good idea to expand the agenda and to state specifically what the objectives are and how decisions will be made.

---

*Example:* 'The purpose of this meeting, which is scheduled to last for 30 minutes, is to decide whether we are going to open a branch in Cheam. The decision will be taken on a vote of the participants and proxy votes will be [if they are in your favour] won't be [if they are not in your favour] allowed.'

---

Also ensure that a chairman is appointed as well as someone who will take the minutes. Ideally you should either be chairman or minute taker and, given the choice, the latter is usually more influential than the former.

*He who takes the minutes, has control*

If you are not in a position to submit an agenda before the meeting, prepare one anyway and produce it immediately the meeting opens. If an agenda has been provided by someone else, don't just accept it. Read it carefully and think how you can swing it in your favour. Also make sure that the topics to be discussed in Any Other Business are listed in full. This will prevent you being ambushed, which is always a bad scene.

*Always pay attention to Any Other Business, charts, tables and appendices because the lie may be disclosed in the back up documentation, which the liar thinks no one will read*

---

[13]   And conmen

## Decide on the venue
### The location
If you are in a position to decide on the venue, so much the better and again think carefully. If you want to impress outsiders, consider holding the meeting in the Presidential Suite of the Ritz. If you want to deflate someone who believes he is the most important person in the world, choose the scruffiest room you can find. In dealing with all forms of deception, small points matter, and your objective may be, in the nicest way possible, to marginalize your opponents and make them slightly anxious.

If you have to hold the meeting in your own office, make sure it gives the impression you want it to give. For meetings with third parties (as well as many internal meetings) the big question is whether you go to their premises or they come to yours. The protocol[14] appears to be that the senior participant, or the most important party, is saved the trouble of having to travel. But you should think about this.

### The timing
If the opposing power player is an owl, fix the meeting for as early in the morning as possible and in a location where he has to get up early to travel but with no justification for staying overnight. Do the opposite if he is a lark. If you know he is a heavy drinker, fix the meeting in the early morning in a posh hotel that stocks every brand imaginable of his favourite drink. Make sure that one of your supporters, who is not critical to the meeting, takes him for dinner the night before and gives him a heavy alcoholic marinating. Remember, everything is fair in love, war, in business meetings and, of course, GOLF.

*There is no such thing as a free lunch*

## Summarize the history
Make sure you know the facts which are to be discussed in the meeting inside out, backwards and forwards. Most participants don't prepare sufficiently and the rule is 'Who knows, wins'. In complex cases, consider preparing schedules of events, correspondence and detailed chronologies. Think about summarizing key facts[15] in a Microsoft PowerPoint® presentation or fancy handout, but make sure that everything you say is accurate.

*The person with the better detail is in command*

Pay particular attention to mistakes, errors or omissions previously made by your opponents and make sure you have them summarized on single sheets of paper or in a PowerPoint presentation that you can thrust under their noses at the appropriate time.

*Having to admit to a mistake may destroy a person's credibility.*
*Being shown to have lied is fatal*

## Watch for dirty tricks
You should remain on the lookout for dirty tricks played by the opposition, including:

---

14   Inherited through evolution
15   Especially those in your favour

- bugging hotel bedrooms and rooms used for pre-meetings by your side;
- glamorous blondes sat next to you on the aircraft while travelling to or from the meeting or in the bar, restaurant or bingo hall;
- briefcases, pens, coats etc. containing tape recorders left behind by the opposition when your side remains in the meeting room during adjournments;
- collection of waste paper from bed and conference rooms (including partly used notepads which will contain ESDA sensitive impressions);
- theft of personal computers;
- arranging social trips for the participants' wives so that they can be pumped for information.

Fortunately, most opponents don't stoop to such tactics, but some do: so don't let your guard drop.

## Preparing the meeting room

You should always be the first to arrive at the venue and, if possible, enter the meeting room before anyone else and generally check it out.

### THE SAUSAGE CASE

A post acquisition meeting was planned with a father and son who had sold their sausage making business to a British listed company at around four times its real value, mainly because assets had been grossly inflated. The listed company's team arrived early in the room and heard shuffling noises which appeared to be coming from a void in the gabled roof of the office. They looked around and found a microphone hidden in an exotic plant connected to a cable going under the carpet and then into a cupboard and up into the roof void.

A vigorous pull on this cable resulted in a scream from the roof void, then a loud crash and the words 'Oh shit!'. Further investigation revealed a young man who had concealed himself in the roof void, wearing earphones connected to the cable. When this sad creature was interviewed he admitted that the father and son had intended to start the meeting, then adjourn it, leaving the listed company's team alone to discuss their position. They then planned to react based on this inside information.

If you have called the meeting, consider setting out place names, putting the opposing power player to your right and as far away as possible from his supporters. If you cannot do this, get your team in their seats before the opposition arrives and try to marginalize them. If you know the power player is deaf in his left ear, sit him to the right of everyone else and preferably near a noisy window.

If you plan to use PowerPoint, video conferencing or any other equipment, check it out because if you are unable to operate it, you look a plonker and are thus put in the role of a child: this is not good news.

## The meeting

*Basic principles*

If you have planned effectively the meeting will be a cinch but you must:

- deal quickly and politely with anything you think is untrue;
- never let anyone conceal the truth but raise the pavement by requiring them to falsify details.

You should also carefully monitor the transactional dynamics of the participants and change your role accordingly. Also remember that the opening and last 20 per cent of a meeting are the most critical.

*Openings and closings are critical*

### Demand equivalent concessions

If you are involved in a hard ball meeting or negotiation, you should only make a concession when an equivalent benefit is obtained.

---

*Examples:*
'We are prepared to reduce the price by two per cent, but need payment in advance.'
'I accept that we should open a new office in Cheam, but [think of something you would like[16]].'

---

In some instances the psychological gains from insisting on a reciprocal concession will far outweigh the financial benefits. However, in financial negotiations, you should make sure that the concessions you make are in the smallest possible increments.

---

*Example:* A builder quotes you £30000 for erecting an indoor driving range at your home. You think this is expensive and should be no more than £20000. Thus you start by offering him £12000 and concede that you will pay him a 50 per cent deposit. He is not prepared to accept, so your first increment is to £12100 and his to £27000. If you are advancing in increments of £100 and he is reducing by £3000, you should come out a winner.

---

*In negotiations, the party that concedes the smallest increments usually wins*

### Watch for legitimization

Negotiators frequently use legitimization statements (see pages 85 and 105) to justify their position, by claiming, for example, that they can only work from a standard price list, that company policy does not permit discounting or that the terms of a contract are non variable. Legitimization also pops up in other meetings with statements such as: 'We cannot do that because of the Data Protection Act/human rights legislation.' If these go against your objectives, you must question them and press for more and more detail. In most cases you will discover that the person concerned is unsure of his facts and that his legitimizations can be dismissed. This also seriously reduces his credibility for the remainder of the meeting.

---

[16]    For example, a new Calloway driver

*Raise the pavement*

Many people are unclear where the line is drawn between trade puffing and criminal deception, but the fact is that a criminal offence is committed if anyone tells lies to obtain a pecuniary advantage and this includes retaining his job.

If you believe that someone is trying to deceive you over an important matter, you should consider raising the pavement with a statement along the lines:

---

*Example.* 'Can we stop there a moment, Bill, because I want you to be absolutely sure of your facts. You realize that if what you have just said is untrue and we rely on it, you could be in very serious trouble [long pause]. If, on reflection, you are not sure and may have made a genuine mistake, then we can start over again and no damage has been done.' [Note the rationalization statement]

The chances are if his statement was untrue, Bill will soften and you can move on from there. If he continues with what you believe is a significant lie you should consider delivering the ultimate statement along the lines:

'If we find out that what you have said is untrue, the only explanation is that you have told a barefaced lie that may amount to fraud. Am I correct in this?'

If the reply is a binary 'Yes' without any unnecessary words before or after it, you can assume you are being told the truth. Any deviation from this and you must remain on your guard.

---

A single exchange along the above lines is likely to keep people far more honest for the remainder of the meeting, but it will raise the temperature, so be careful.

*Closing the meeting*

The way you close any meeting is important and you should summarize the key points and any proposed actions: make sure that everyone present agrees or that their dissenting view is recorded.

## Follow-up action

Accurate and timely minutes should be prepared and circulated after every important meeting and you must check them carefully. If you do not agree with anything, suggest amendments and if these cannot be agreed immediately, prepare a dissenting report, submit it to all of the participants and put it on the agenda for future meetings. If minutes have not been taken, make sure you preserve your notes; they may be very important one day.

*Never agree to minutes which are not totally accurate*

## RAISE YOUR CONCERNS IN A LOW-KEY WAY

As soon as you have specific concerns you must raise them in a low-key way, and commit the conman to more and more detail, which you must document and preserve. However, it is critical, unless this is part of a planned ambush, that you don't frighten him off. You can take an approach much like the fictional detective, Colombo, by saying something along the lines:

## BLAME THE OGRE

'Bill (the ogre) is very concerned that the custodial receipt from the Bank of Credit and Commerce may not be genuine and he is advising me to pull out. I have told him I have total confidence in you. How can we reassure him?'

The chances are the conman will comply with your request (because he still believes you are gullible and on the hook) and this is precisely what you want and will add to your case if the worst happens. He may also approach the ogre to strike a side deal and, again, this will tell you all you need to know.[17]

*The more evidence of gross deception you have, the more likely you are to get your money back*

If you have reached the point where you have serious concerns, don't make the matter worse by parting with more money. As Edward de Bono, the originator of lateral thinking, said: 'You don't dig a better hole by digging the same hole deeper'. This may mean you have to tell a few white lies to keep the conman in play while you plan your ambush.

## CONTRACTS

Good conmen are great at contracts and usually have had years of practice developing subtle phrases that appear to say one thing but mean another. Thus, in important deals, you must get a good lawyer to review every document and assess the significance of every word and phrase. He should also pay very close attention to standard clauses that don't appear. In short, he should continually ask himself the question: *'If I were a crook, how could I weasel my way out of this clause, statement or contract?'* Then he should make sure you are fully protected, either in the contract itself or in some other document signed by the suspected conman. (The compare facility in Microsoft Word is an excellent tool for tracking changes between versions of the same document.)

## PREPARING FOR THE AMBUSH

If the time comes when you are sure the liar is a conman, rather than just a suspect, you must plan your action carefully. Ideally you want him on tape and in writing, telling outright, indefensible lies for which he can have no plausible excuse. This will probably result in the conman being exposed to criminal prosecution under the Theft Act and will give you significant leverage if you decide to negotiate with him or litigate.

## DON'T GIVE REFERENCES

A common conman's tactic is to get one victim to give references that can be used to mislead others. If you are less than 100 per cent certain about anyone, do not give references. If you are asked to do so by a suspected conman, you can quite reasonably say:

*'When our deal has been completed to everyone's satisfaction, we will be more than happy to consider giving a reference. As you know we have not yet reached that stage. Now tell me again, when can we expect completion?'*

---

[17]  Unless he succeeds

Do not waver from this course, under any circumstances, because if you do you may be liable for your own losses, plus those of other victims. This is a bad scene and also, whatever you do, don't join the board of his companies, however flattering that might be, until you are absolutely sure of his honesty.

## METHOD WHEN IT GOES BELLY UP

### The dreadful realization

Let's hope your fears were misplaced and the breathtaking deal comes to fruition, proving that the person you thought was a liar is a pillar of virtue. However, the chances are that sooner or later you are going to take the hit and this is where you must react quickly. There are two things you must remember. The first is that the conman is likely to have scores, if not hundreds, of victims in just the same position as you. If you sit back and wait you will fall to the end of queue and will never succeed: the victim that causes the biggest fuss is most likely to prevail.

*You must become the conman's biggest problem*

The second point is that the conman is likely to have pending deals in progress with other victims and he will not want these upset. This is his Achilles heel. However, as in all cases of deception, you must plan to ambush him with a knockout blow from which he never recovers. This is akin to the *first step* in fraud investigations.

### Objectives and action plans

A victim's initial reaction when the bubble bursts is to panic and rush around like a headless chicken, blaming everyone in sight, especially the innocent. This is a natural reaction, but you must get over it quickly and plan an effective and unemotional reaction.

*Nothing useful is achieved by self-flagellation*

You must also set realistic expectation levels and if you have been stung, the chances of getting all of your money back are remote. Ideally, put someone in charge of the recovery plan who was not party to the transaction concerned and who has no vested interest in covering his ass. He is in a good position to assess the position and whether it is worthwhile devoting time and effort to chasing a lost cause.

Depending on the facts of the case, your priorities might be:

- To prevent further losses and cancel transactions that are still in progress.
- Minimizing your liabilities to others. For example, in some recent banking cases, victims had to pay other victim banks for fraudulent letters of credit that fell due for payment long after the dishonesty was exposed.
- Minimizing your liabilities for legal and regulatory breaches.
- Recovering the amounts that have already been lost.
- Exposing and prosecuting the conman.
- Minimizing adverse publicity.

The first three points are really important, because it is extremely exasperating for any victim to have to continually pay out after the conman has been exposed.

## Possible approaches

You have a number of possible approaches, which are not mutually exclusive, and all are based on the principle that you must ambush the conman with overwhelming force and become the biggest problem in his life. You must convince him it is not in his interest to engage you in a battle.

The options are given in Table 9.4.

**Table 9.4**  Options for dealing with conmen

| Method of approach | Success rate | Examples |
| --- | --- | --- |
| Negotiation | 20% | Using your overwhelming case, you can take the conman by surprise and let him know that unless he makes good your losses he is in serious trouble |
| Legal | 20% | You may mount an ambush through the civil courts by obtaining search, seizure and freezing orders that enable you to enter his premises, car, bank, golf bag etc. and remove evidence that assists your case. The freezing order will also compel the conman to disclose his assets and if he fails to do so, he can be imprisoned for contempt of court |
| Police and regulators | 2% | You may make a report to the police or regulatory agencies concerned. However, even if they are interested action is likely to be slow, allowing the conman to escape |
| Media | 2% | You can report the facts to a friendly journalist and expose the conman, thus frustrating any deals he has in progress |
| Disruption | 20% | You can harass the conman, by having him followed, making it clear to him that any deals he has in progress will be disrupted |

In most cases, you must retain the very best, blood curdling litigation lawyers and set them loose as part of an integrated action plan. All actions are obviously dependent on whether you believe the conman has assets and part of his plan may have been to falsely convince potential litigants that he is penniless. Thus it may be worthwhile for you to retain investigators to see if they can trace his assets.

## Budgets for recovery

Bear in mind that investigation and litigation costs can be crippling and there is no point in throwing good money after bad. A worksheet that may help you decide whether a potential loss is worth pursuing or not can be downloaded from www.cobasco.com.

*Don't throw good money after bad*

If you decide to press for recovery, it is essential that you set a realistic legal and investigative budget. This should be under the control of the person put in charge of the recovery action plan and not line managers who were deceived; this may be you!

## ESCORTS GALORE

An investigation was moving along just fine, driven by a team of external lawyers and consultants under the control of a director of the bank. He had been very positive throughout and the team was confident it would recover many millions of dollars under fidelity insurance. Then, all of a sudden, client support disappeared. Invoices from the lawyers and consultants were not paid and the credit head's deputy nit-picked every line of enquiry and its cost.

Before long the case ran out of steam and then collapsed. The director blamed the consultants for the failure, saying that they were 'too greedy, had lost focus and were going nowhere'. His managers accepted this excuse, since they didn't like paying consultants, either.

A few months later the real reason for upsetting the lawyers and consultants emerged. It appears that one evening the main suspect working for the bank called on the director and warned him that if the investigation continued, some very fruity photographs and tape recordings of his sexual misbehaviour with escorts while he had been travelling overseas on the bank's business might surface. The director was terrified and wanted to comply but did not wish to put his neck on the line by terminating the investigation. However, he achieved the same result by not paying the advisers' bills and by nit-picking, causing them to withdraw.

The bottom line was that preservation of the director's career cost the bank $20 million. But the problem has not really gone away and if the shareholders were ever to discover the truth, all hell would be let loose.

Another normal reaction of victims to gross deception is to join together and pool their resources to share legal costs. Banks do this all of the time and it never produces results. This is because multiple victims are all chasing after the same assets and in the end, fight over them. If you are one of a number of victims of the same scam, you must act alone and stay ahead of the chasing pack. Do this and you might just succeed.

*Joining forces with other victims to save recovery costs is a waste of time*

## CONCLUSIONS

Recovering after you have been victimized is a nasty and costly experience. It is always preferable to avoid getting into bad situations in the first place through effective due diligence and other procedures and by asking the right questions at the right time.

*It is always easier to fall into the crap than to get out of it.*
*Prevention is far better than cure*

# Anonymous letters

## BACKGROUND

In most frauds there are people on the sidelines who know what is going on but are frightened to make a direct report. However, they may do so anonymously through letters, emails or telephone calls. Obviously, some allegations are malicious or improperly motivated by the chance of a financial reward, but these are in the minority. The allegations usually relate to employees, although they may be made against companies, including vendors and customers. Experience shows that most anonymous communications contain at least a grain of truth and therefore must be taken seriously.

## IGNORED ALLEGATIONS

An investigation revealed that a senior manager in a company's treasury department had defrauded over £2 million, by working in collusion with a brokerage firm of which his wife (using her maiden name and her parent's address) was the co-owner. A review of his personnel file showed that four years earlier an anonymous letter had been received setting out the precise mechanics of the fraud and naming the brokerage firm. It had been filed with the annotation 'Rubbish, GG is a senior officer of the company and these allegations are malicious.'

*Never ignore anonymous allegations of wrongdoing*

## OBJECTIVES

When an anonymous allegation has been received, there is an obligation to find the truth in the interests of the victim organization and of the subject. Thus, the objectives are to:

- establish whether the allegations are true or false;
- establish the facts of a possible 'worst case' (see Appendix 1);
- identify the informant, to see if he can provide further information or to censure him for making a false allegation.

Responsibility for investigating allegations should be passed to internal audit, corporate security or to external advisers and handled by trained investigators in strict confidence: under no circumstances should the allegation be handled by managers in the business line concerned. Ideally the company's reporting of incidents procedures should cover anonymous allegations (see page 161). These matters should be covered in a fraud policy. A template can be downloaded free of charge from www.cobasco.com.

## METHOD

### Initial handling
It is critical that the forensic integrity of the physical media on which the allegation is communicated is maintained. For example, anonymous letters and envelopes should not be touched unnecessarily, so that fingerprint and other evidence are not compromised. The originals should be copied and placed in a cardboard-reinforced envelope.

### Try to trace the informant
You should consider having the letter and envelope forensically examined to see if there are any clues that could identify the author. For example, an Electrostatic Document Examination (ESDA) may reveal impressions from writing on other documents.

## HOW ON EARTH DID YOU TRACE ME?

An anonymous letter was subject to an ESDA examination. In the top right-hand corner, the examiner discovered the impression of an address which had been made when the author had used an earlier page in his notepad to write to his mother. From this investigators traced and interviewed him: 'How on earth did you trace me?' he asked.

Also, the syntax of the letter, its layout, the typeface, the precise nature of the allegations made and *not* made, the time frame to which they relate and the possible motivation of the informant should be considered. These may lead to identification of the author.

*Always try to identify the informant*

You should check to see if other allegations have been made about the same person or relating to the area in which he works. If these were fully investigated and proven to be untrue, this will obviously influence the importance you attach to the current information but, even so, don't simply dismiss it.

## Obtain full background on the subject

Without alerting the subject of the complaint, find out as much background information as possible about him, from personnel files, telephone call logs, expense statements etc. Review his authority levels and the transactions he handles. These details may help you decide whether the allegations are true or even feasible.

## Develop a fraud theory

List the allegations which have been made and note alongside each one the evidence that supports or contradicts them, and assess whether they are credible. In the first instance, assume the allegations are true.

*Do not dismiss allegations without investigating them carefully*

If possible, you should review audit and performance reports for the area in which the subject works. Develop a fraud theory of the 'worst case' and assemble any 'key points' (see page 190) that support or rebut the allegations. In some cases it may be possible, without alerting the subject, to review transactions for which he is responsible. Again the objective is to test the accuracy of the allegations.

Prepare a brief investigations plan and consider actions you might take (see Appendix 1), including test purchases or sales, interception of communications, examination of telephone call logs, personal computers etc. prior to interviewing anyone. However, remember that the action you take must be proportionate to the seriousness of the allegations concerned.

## TAPE RECORDING

It would be proportionate to intercept the communications of an employee where massive corruption was potentially involved, but excessive if the only suspicion was a minor expenses fiddle.

You should plan the *first step*, as you would for any other investigation. This would normally involve interviewing the subject and, assuming he has been identified with reasonable certainty, the informant.

## Interviewing the subject

Your approach to the subject will depend on the strength of the evidence and the fraud theory but in most cases it should be based either on blocking questions (see page 247 and 251), or on a low-key opening statement and then conducted along the lines laid down in Chapter 7. If his reaction tells you the allegations are likely to be true, you must press on to try to find the deep truth.

The greatest difficulties arise when you are not sure, one way or the other, about the accuracy of an allegation. In these cases, it is usually best to explain the allegations in detail and to ask the subject to cooperate fully, by making bank and other records available and to work with you to disprove them and to help you identify the informant.

*Innocent people usually fight to clear their names*

## Interviewing the informant

In many cases, the identity of the informant will become obvious and you should always try to interview him. Again your approach must be carefully planned and will depend on:

- the degree of certainty that he is the informant;
- the credibility of the information provided;
- his apparent motivation.

If you merely suspect that a person is the informant, you should still interview him but in a very circumspect way, using open questions about the area in which the subject works. You should not mention the subject's name unless he raises it first, nor should you show him the anonymous letter. If the person appears cooperative you may then move on to discussing the specifics of the allegation, but again avoiding the subject's name: his reaction should tell you whether or not he is the informant.

If you are reasonably certain that you have identified the informant you may take a more direct approach, but you must be careful not to put words in his mouth or slander the subject. Again your approach should be adapted to suit the circumstances. For example, if the information appears correct and the informant not motivated by malice you might take a low-key, empathetic approach from the outset, whereas if the allegations are false, you may treat the informant as a suspect and interview him accordingly with the objective of exposing and, in due course, punishing him.

In any event you should probe the information in depth, looking for supporting evidence and exploring other matters. If it emerges that the allegation is false and the informant is motivated by malice, consider obtaining a retraction in writing.

## Follow-up action

It is imperative that allegations are not left on the subject's personnel file unresolved, and in all cases a report on the investigation should be prepared. Other closure action is essential and can be determined on the matrix below (Table 9.5).

**Table 9.5**   Likely closure actions

| Motivation of the informant | Evidence supporting the allegation and worst case | | |
|---|---|---|---|
| | Accurate revealing malpractice | Accurate But not revealing malpractice | Inaccurate |
| Genuine | Investigation | Investigation | Close the file |
| Malicious | | Action against the informant | |
| Not identified | | Investigation | |

If the allegations are unfounded, the subject must be told and asked whether he wants the report retained in his personnel file and it is usually in his interest to do so.

## DESTROYED RECORDS

In 1995, allegations were made against an employee, investigated and proved to be untrue. However, the human resources manager at the time[18] destroyed the letters and investigations report on the basis that they were 'personal data' that should not be retained any longer than was absolutely necessary.

In 2001, the employee was being considered for promotion to a senior overseas position. A junior employee in human resources department submitted a note to the effect that: 'Suspicions had been raised about this employee some years ago, but there is nothing on file'. This spooked the senior line manager who was making the appointment and another employee was selected for promotion.

Cases such as this show that some of the data protection laws are counterproductive (see page 162).

# Elimination interviews

## BACKGROUND AND NATURE OF THE PROBLEM

There are occasions when a number of people *could* be responsible for a crime or some other problem: for example, cash may have gone missing from a cash register to which four or five people had access.

## OBJECTIVES

There are three main issues involved in elimination interviews:

- identify the guilty party and clear people who are wrongly suspected;
- obtain admissions and other evidence;
- make financial recoveries.

---

[18]   He moved on in 2000

To achieve these objectives, it is essential that the anxiety of the guilty party is increased so that he reveals himself and there are three ways of doing this.

## METHOD 1: ELIMINATION CHECKLIST

### Background and planning

You should obtain as much information as possible about the problem in question, and about any similar incidents, develop a fraud theory and prepare single-sheet summaries of any 'key points' which can be shown to the subjects at the appropriate time. You should also get as much background as possible on each of the potential suspects along the lines of Appendix 1.

### Preparing the checklist

Prepare a checklist on the lines of Table 9.6 below, tailored to the facts of the case concerned.[19]

Reformat the table on to sheets of A4 paper and prepare a clean copy for each interview.

**Table 9.6**   Potential elimination questions and profiled answers

| No. | Nature of question or statement | Indicative reaction | |
|---|---|---|---|
| | | Indicative of responsibility<br>Little detail<br>Lack of commitment<br>No volunteered information | Indicative of innocence<br>Detailed<br>Committed<br>Volunteered information |
| 1 | The opening statement | Anxious<br>Defensive body language<br>Appears threatened | Interested<br>Open body language<br>Relaxed |
| | Do you know why I have asked to see you? | Will usually prevaricate and say 'no' | Will usually know; he admits there is a problem |
| | Is there anything you want to ask me? | Unlikely to ask a question or asks one which is irrelevant | Asks a sensible question |
| 2 | Did you do it? | Prevarication<br>Not a clear binary answer | A committed 'no' |
| 3 | Have you discussed this case with your colleagues? | Prevarication | A committed 'yes' or 'no' |
| 4 | Have you had any contact with [names of people already interviewed] since I spoke to them? | Prevarication | A committed 'yes' or 'no' |
| 5 | If so, what did they say? | Prevarication<br>Unlikely to give detail | Likely to provide detail |
| 6 | Do you think the [actual losses] are deliberate and premeditated theft? | Prevarication or may minimize the seriousness of the case | May ask for clarification or a committed 'yes' |

---

[19]   The checklist should jump from topic to topic as shown

| No. | Nature of question or statement | Indicative reaction | |
|---|---|---|---|
| | | Indicative of responsibility<br>Little detail<br>Lack of commitment<br>No volunteered information | Indicative of innocence<br>Detailed<br>Committed<br>Volunteered information |
| 7 | Do you think there is any chance in this case that there could be an error? | Possibly | May ask for clarification or a committed 'no' |
| 8 | If we don't catch the [thief] do you think it will happen again? | Probably 'no' | Probably 'no idea' or 'yes' |
| 9 | List the names of possible suspects and say:' 'It has to be one of you, doesn't it? Who do you think is responsible?' | Unlikely to name anyone | May name someone |
| 10 | How would you react if we asked everyone who could have been involved to compensate us for the losses? | May consider | Unlikely to accept |
| 11 | Is there anyone you are sure did not do it? | May not name himself | Normally will name himself. 'I know I did not do it' |
| 12 | Where were you and what were you doing when this happened? | May produce an alibi too readily | More likely to seek clarification |
| 13 | How would you react if I told you a number of people believe you are responsible? | Defend or object | May seek clarification, or become genuinely angry May ask for the names of the people concerned |
| 14 | Show the subject the evidence ('key points') [List what it is]<br>Xxx<br>Xxx<br>Xxx<br>xxxx<br>and ask him detailed questions about it | Reactions indicating responsibility (see Chapter 4, page 102 onwards) | Reactions indicating innocence |
| 15 | Do you think the evidence points towards you? | May give an explanation | May seek clarification or become genuinely angry |
| 16 | Tell me why you could not have done it? | Possible objections such as 'because I would not be so foolish' | Probably a committed denial |

| No. | Nature of question or statement | Indicative reaction | |
|-----|----------------------------------|---------------------|---|
| | | Indicative of responsibility Little detail Lack of commitment No volunteered information | Indicative of innocence Detailed Committed Volunteered information |
| 17 | If you had been involved in this, how would you have done it? | May suggest a method May reveal information known only to the guilty person May make a stupid suggestion | Unlikely to consider the possibility |
| 18 | In forgery cases, ask the suspect to make 10 or 12 copies of the forged signature in writing | May make a poor attempt to copy the forged signatures | Likely to make a good attempt |
| 19 | Would you be prepared to give us access to your bank accounts to check this? | Probably 'yes' | Probably 'no' Possibly angry |
| 20 | How would you feel if we subsequently prove that what you have told me is untrue? | Prevarication | Committed response to the effect that you would be wrong |
| 21 | I have to tell you I think you did it | Pseudo-denial (see pages 98 and 235) or objection | Committed denial Genuine anger |
| 22 | Would you be prepared to take a polygraph test? | Prevarication Asks for clarification | A committed 'yes' or 'no' |
| 23 | Can we do it this afternoon? | Very unlikely and will give a reason for stalling | Probably a firm 'yes' or 'no' |
| 24 | If you were responsible for [xxx] would you admit it? | 'Yes' or 'what do you expect me to say?' | Probably not. Would depend |
| 25 | Why should I believe you? | More likely to make an objection such as 'Because I didn't have the keys' | 'Because I am telling the truth' |
| 26 | You look really worried about this. Has it been bothering you? | Without considering probably 'no' | Considers and then probably 'yes' |
| 27 | Would you like to change your explanation | Pause and may discuss the possibilities or say 'yes' | A firm 'no' |
| 28 | Do you have any other information that might help us identify the [thief]? | This is a purely informational question | |
| 29 | Do you think this interview has been fair? | Probably 'yes' | May be upset |

## Control interviews

You should interview two or three people, ideally of around the same age and rank as the potential suspects, using the approach set out below. Use their reactions as a baseline for evaluating the responses in the relevant interviews.

## INTERVIEWS WITH THE POTENTIAL SUSPECTS

## Invitation

Invite each potential suspect to an interview. If possible all of the interviews should be conducted simultaneously but where this is not possible, it is essential that subjects who have not been interviewed are prevented from speaking to those who have.

*Don't let the potential suspects compare notes*

## The opening statement

It is imperative that you do not allow the subject to interrupt at any point, by saying something along the lines: 'Please let me finish. We have to go through a set process which will get to the truth'.

You then make an opening statement.

---

*Example*: 'I am Bill Smith from internal audit. I am investigating a very serious case where [confidential company information has been passed to X, a competitor]. This theft could result in our losing a large contract in the Far East, to loss of jobs and other problems for everyone. The company will spare no time or expense in finding the truth and we have investigators working on this throughout the world. The top management of X is also very concerned and is cooperating fully. In fact, my colleagues are working with X as we speak.

We know the information was removed from the office in which you work and we hope to recover the original documentation, which we will have tested for fingerprints. We are also analysing telephone, Internet and computer records, expense statements and bank accounts. I am confident that we will find the person responsible.

There were only ten copies of this confidential report and we have recovered nine of them, so only the one is missing. We believe that the missing copy was taken from the office in which you work. There are only ten people who have access to that office and we are interviewing each of you to try to identify responsibility and to clear those who are not involved.

I am going to ask you some questions and note down your responses in one of two columns on this profile. Do not worry about what I am writing down. What I plan to do is go through the same process with everyone and then analyse the results. I promise you we will find the truth and put this very unfortunate problem behind us.'

---

You should adapt the opening statement to suit the case concerned and then pull out a clean copy of the checklist and use red (indicative of responsibility) and green (indicative of innocence) highlighter pens to mark the subject's reaction to the opening statement and then ask:

*'Is it possible that, by accident or otherwise, you released the copy that is now with X?'* (i.e. *'Did you do it?'*).

Again note down the response and continue with the remainder of the questions, marking the appropriate column in red or green as you proceed. If a response does not fit either column, put a small mark between them.

*Watch the subject and monitor his reaction*

Innocent people are much more likely to ask about the significance of the checklist and the coloured pens, whereas the guilty party will watch your every move, but is unlikely to say anything. If you are asked, play it low-key along the following lines:

*'This is a really brilliant method that enables us to clear people who are innocent. Now let's move on.'*

If the subject's reactions indicate that he is innocent (see Chapter 4) you should say so:

*'I am pleased to tell you, Bill, that it looks fairly certain that you are not responsible but I will probably have to see you again when we have moved forward with the investigation. Is that OK?'*

You should then spend a few additional minutes to see if he has any information that may assist you. Most innocent people usually do.

In most cases, if the fraud theory is correct and the guilty party is among those being interviewed, his responsibility will emerge and you should then raise the pavement possibly through a bridging statement or direct accusation.

## The bridging statement

The bridging statement might be along the following lines:

*'I have to tell you it appears that you were involved in this. How did it all start?'*

Depending on his reaction (for example, failure to deny, lack of commitment or feigned anger) you should move into Phase C and proceed as with any other tough interview (see Chapters 6 and 7).

## METHOD 2: THE FREESTYLE STORY

An alternative approach is to ask all potential suspects to a meeting and deliver an opening statement along the lines suggested above. They should then be asked to write down: 'Everything you know about the matter' and each one sent to a private room, where they cannot consult with each other, and allowed as much time as necessary. You should analyse their stories carefully and interview the person whose response is most indicative of guilt.

# METHOD 3: THE STRUCTURED CHECKLIST

You should consider designing a form specific to the case concerned, and issuing it to all of the people under suspicion and to three or four people you know are innocent.[20] Again you should deliver an opening statement along the lines of the example on page 373.

The purpose of the form is to:

- increase anxiety in the guilty party;
- identify responses that are indicative of guilt or innocence;
- use the form as a 'key point' in confronting the guilty party.

The form should be laid out carefully, so that it has the maximum visual and emotional impact and should consist of separate pages, each with marginal notes, boxes for official use and colour coding:

- an opening, setting out the background of the case and the purpose of the form.
- a release under the Data Protection Act along the following lines:

## DATA PROTECTION ACT

'I understand that the information I provide on this form may be classed as personal data under the Data Protection Act. I agree that this data may be used for the prevention and detection of crime and released to law enforcement and other agencies, to graphologists and forensic laboratories.

- If you do not agree to such a release please tick here .............................. ❑
- If you have put a tick in the box, please explain your concerns.'

- Questions covering the person's attitude such as:
  - Why did this happen?
  - Did you do it?
  - Do you think it will happen again?
  - If you had to investigate this case, where would you start?
  - Have you discussed this case with your colleagues?
  - If you were to do (the dishonesty suspected) how would you do it?
  - Would you do it by yourself or would you involve others?
  - Do you know anyone who has done this (the problem suspected)?
  - Is there anyone you know who could not have done this?
  - What should happen to people who do (the problem)?
  - Where were you when this (the problem) happened?
- Closing pages:
  - Would you like to change any of the information you have provided?
  - How did you feel when you were completing this form?
  - How do you think the person responsible would feel?
  - What would be your reaction if we found that the answers you have given are incorrect?

---

[20]  A sample form and worked example can be downloaded from www.cobasco.com.

- If all employees were asked to (repay or take a pay reduction) to cover these losses, how would you feel?
- Would you be prepared to take a lie detector test?
- Is there anything else you think might be relevant?

At the end of the last page, two horizontal lines should be drawn in the place normally used for entering a signature and date. However, no explanation should be given.

———————————————————    ———————————————————

Innocent people are more likely to use the lines to enter their signature and date, whereas the guilty party will leave them blank. Again, the subject whose guilt appears most likely should be interviewed along the lines of Chapter 7.

A structured checklist was used in a wire transfer fraud investigation, with interesting results:

## THE WIRE TRANSFER FRAUD

Around $10 million was transferred from a London bank by a fraudulent wire transfer instruction entered into a computer input queue: one or more of twenty employees had to be involved. Each was asked to write his or her explanation on a specially designed form. Although this was not exactly a freestyle document, it was designed to elicit freestyle explanations. One completed form stood out from the rest, because the author:

- Disputed that there was 'evidence' that the case was an inside job and presented a complex (and highly unconvincing, bordering on silly) case for responsibility being outside the bank.
- He responded to many questions with a question.
- He sought clarification of points that were obvious to all of his colleagues.
- He used the phrase 'to be absolutely honest' in reply to two questions.
- He used the phrases 'to the best of my recollection' and 'I don't really remember', when none of his colleagues had memory lapses.
- He used a number of discontinuity phrases (see pages 91, 107, 121 and 336) when accounting for his movements on the day in question.
- Many answers contained an unexplained change from past to present tense (when describing past events).
- He used generalizations ('I usually') and conditional phrases ('I would have gone to lunch') in explaining specific actions on the day, whereas none of his colleagues did the same.
- He consistently avoided using the pronoun 'I'.
- In response to the question 'How do you feel now that you have completed this form?', he responded with the word 'nothing' whereas all of his colleagues expressed a strong positive 'good' or bad 'angry that I am being accused' reaction.
- He admitted discussing the possibilities of fraud with others.
- In responding to the question: 'Should we believe your answers to the questions?' he responded: 'Yes, but you don't think someone would honestly omit [sic] to fraud' and continued: 'I've never done anything to prove I am dishonest'.
- For reasons best known to the bank, they disregarded the clues in this response and a few weeks later the man resigned and went to work in the US.

# Witnesses

## BACKGROUND AND OBJECTIVES

A 'witness' is any person who is able to provide information, possibly intelligence or evidence relating to a matter of concern such as:

- a person who saw a car accident;
- an accountant who can explain how the sales invoicing system operates;
- an interviewer who can say what a suspect admitted to him;
- a doctor who can explain the reasons why someone died.

There are three main problems with witnesses. The first is that a person may not wish to become involved, for reasons ranging from apathy to fear, and in the corporate fraud area, because he has been bribed or pressurized. The second problem is that some people genuinely cannot remember what happened and when they think they can, get it wrong. The third problem is that in high-profile cases, including frauds, witnesses come forward with false or malicious evidence to get their moment of glory or payment.

This section is concerned with getting reliable evidence from willing and unwilling witnesses in complex fraud cases and obtaining a written account of their evidence. This may be in the form of a Proof of Evidence, affidavit, statement or CJA statement (see Appendix 3) and is required by lawyers to assess the strength of their case, pre-trial, and to know what the witness is expected to say during it.

## COGNITIVE INTERVIEWING

In olden days, statements would be taken by police officers, lawyers, investigators or even accountants, based on simple question and answer interviews, which often contaminated the witness's memory or failed to produce accurate detail. The witness evidence in the assassination of President Kennedy illustrates the weaknesses.

*Witness evidence is vital*

Nowadays, more sophisticated methods are available, the most popular being 'cognitive interviewing'[21] (CI) which was invented in the US by Geiselman and Fisher.[22] CI is a little like NLP to the extent that the phrase is often bandied around but seldom defined: 'cognitive', much like 'initiative', 'issue' and 'fury', is a vogue word. The best explanation of what practitioners mean by CI is paraphrased from a paper by Brian R. Clifford and Amina Memon[23] as follows:

---

[21] Cognitive is defined as 'knowing, perceiving or conceiving as an act or faculty distinct from emotion or volition ... a notion, intuition, perception.'
[22] See R. Edward Geiselman and Ronald P. Fisher 1985, *Interviewing Victims and Witnesses of Crime*, National Institute of Justice, Washington, USA
[23] 'Analysing Witness Testimony', Brian R. Clifford and Amina Memon, Blackstone Press ISBN 1 85431 731 8

## WHAT IS CI?

The 'cognitive' components of CI draw upon two theoretical principles. First, that a memory retrieval cue is effective to the extent that there is an overlap between it and the information encoded in memory (see page 61), and that reinstatement of the original encoding context increases recall. Secondly, the multiple trace theory suggests that there are many ways in which memory can be cued and that if one cue fails, another may succeed.

For our own purposes we can define CI as: 'A structured, holistic process, based on an understanding of the brain's operation, in which a person's memory is stimulated by a combination of retrieval cues.'

There is no question that CI assists recall:

- for eye witnesses who can be compelled to assist;[24]
- who are not themselves under threat or maliciously motivated;
- in simple, single event cases.

Improvements in memory recall of between 35 and 46 per cent have been claimed,[25] and some academics suggest that CI is almost as effective as hypnosis. However, the basis on which measurements have been made are, at best, subjective and, more likely, suspect. Also, recent research[26] indicates that CI results in higher error rates, especially among young children and mentally handicapped witnesses, as a result of a process[27] in which pure memory is contaminated by what the witness, or someone else, has said before. So even in the applications for which it is recommended, CI has its limitations and is not a panacea.

Neither are conventional CI tools particularly relevant in serious fraud cases because, among other things:

- complex, multiple incidents are usually involved over extended periods of time in different locations;
- eye witness evidence is likely to be a small part of a much bigger picture (for example, the primary evidence in fraud cases is usually documentary, technical or verbal);
- even if he is not a participant, the witness may have personal reasons for not telling the truth (for example, he may want to hide his own poor performance).

The method proposed below advances CI into the fraud world to deal with witnesses who find it difficult to impart the truth because:

- of poor memory: as in conventional CI cases;
- of the complexity of the case;
- they are defending or improving their own positions;
- they are emotionally involved or fearful of the suspects or have been bribed by them;

---

[24]　e.g. police cases
[25]　These figures are virtually impossible to verify
[26]　Higham and Roberts 1996
[27]　Usually called 'reminiscence' or 'reiteration'

- they are not required to provide assistance and, on the contrary, may have a legal obligation of confidentiality to the suspects.

Since these days everything must have a title and an acronym, the process described below is called 'cognitive interviewing for fraud' (CIFF) and its objectives are to get accurate evidence from witnesses in the business world.

*CI is about enhancing recall.*
*CIFF recognizes other recall problems besides memory failure*

## THE CIFF METHOD

### Overview

CIFF can be viewed in a number of stages. As always, the most important are getting the background and effective planning.

*Inexperienced interviewers are too casual with witness interviews*

### Doing the background

The fraud theory and investigation plan (see pages 190–191) will usually result in the identification of people who are not themselves under suspicion, but who might be added to a list of potential witnesses in the categories shown in Table 9.7.

You should obtain as much background information as possible on all potential witnesses (see Appendix 1) and think about the evidence they might be able to give on the 'worst case', bearing in mind the factors in Table 9.6. You should also fully understand the case and its 'key points', having summaries and exhibits available to show to the witness at the appropriate time. If the witness has made previous statements on the matter, or other witnesses have, you should analyse these in a way that makes it easy to highlight the essential facts and discrepancies.

If you believe, for any of the reasons set out in Table 9.7, that the witness might be unwilling to assist, you should plan and rehearse persuasive arguments for delivery in the interview. The persuasion may be along the lines shown in Table 9.8.

Sometimes it may not be clear whether the person should be treated as a witness or a suspect. For example, you may have specific concerns or even an intuition that he is less than innocent. In such cases, you should interview him as a suspect using the techniques described in Chapters 6 and 7.

*Unless you are absolutely sure that the witness is innocent, interview him as a suspect*

You should consider the timing, sequence and location of interviews very carefully and unless you are absolutely sure[28] that a witness will not alert the suspect he should not be seen until after the first step (see pages 141 and 174).

---

[28]    Unless such an alert is part of the investigation plan to panic the suspects into action

**Table 9.7**   Willing and other witnesses

| Category A<br>Probably cooperative witnesses | Category B<br>Witnesses requiring persuasion |
|---|---|
| Position<br>An employee of the victim organization or an associated enterprise (such as its bank)<br>An expert witness | Position<br>A third party such as a customer or vendor, who is under no obligation to assist |
| Nature of case<br>Relating to a minor matter, such as an accident injury | Nature of case<br>Relating to a serious matter, such as a serious fraud |
| Type of evidence<br>Has formal evidence, such as explaining a process or producing records, supported by written or computer records | Type of evidence<br>Has sensitive or emotionally laden evidence against the suspect, such as what he did or said. Usually such evidence is not supported by formal, written records |
| Personal interests<br>Has nothing to hide | Personal interests<br>Wishes to hide poor performance or a personal ambition<br>Possibly malicious<br>Emotionally or financially involved with the suspects |
| Relationships<br>Has no relationship with (or often personal knowledge of) the suspect | Relationships<br>Is known to the suspect |
| Nature of suspects<br>Suspects are ordinary business people, citizens or employees | Nature of suspects<br>Suspects are violent criminals |

**Table 9.8**   Potential persuasive arguments

| Category B<br>Witnesses requiring persuasion | Possible persuasive arguments<br>You should make it clear that: |
|---|---|
| Position of the witness | |
| A third party such as a customer or vendor, who is under no obligation to assist, may refuse to do so | Persuasion<br>Failure to assist may result in the termination of all business relationships<br>You will invoke the audit clause in contracts<br>You will have no option but refer the case to the police<br>A witness summons may be issued that will compel the witness to attend court<br>Civil action will be started which will require the production of records |

| Category B<br>Witnesses requiring persuasion | Possible persuasive arguments<br>You should make it clear that: |
|---|---|
| **Nature of the case** | |
| Relating to a serious matter, such as a serious fraud | The witness will not be alone but will be supported by other witnesses, documentary and technical evidence. You must make it clear that the witness will be one of many |
| Type of evidence<br>Has sensitive or emotionally laden evidence against the suspect, such as what he did or said. Usually such evidence is not supported by formal, written records | |
| **Personal interests of the witness** | |
| Wishes to hide poor performance or a personal ambition | Rationalization: The reasons for any genuine mistakes and poor performance are understood and are not a problem providing they are openly admitted. Subject to legal advice and management approval you may give the witness immunity in relation to genuine mistakes |
| Emotionally or financially involved or has been compromised by the suspect | This is a very difficult situation and you must decide whether to treat the subject as a witness or suspect. Unless you have specific legal and management authority you must not give any witness immunity for his dishonesty[29] |
| Is known to the suspect | Persuasion<br>A witness summons may be issued, compelling him to attend |
| **Payment of a reward** | |
| The witness demands payment for giving his assistance | Again a dangerous area. Payment should only be made with specific legal and management approval. Also remember if the case goes to court, payments have to be disclosed to the opposing parties. This fact often exposes the witness to attack and reduces the credibility of his evidence |
| The witness demands immunity from prosecution | Unless you have specific legal and management authority you must not give any witness immunity for his dishonesty. If the case goes to court, the complete story has to be disclosed to the opposing party |
| **Nature of the suspects** | |
| Suspects are violent criminals<br>The potential witness has been threatened or pressurized, but does not appear to have acted dishonestly | Conduct the interview informally, promising the witness anonymity and total confidentiality and that his evidence will not be used overtly. Ultimately, cases of organized or violent crime should be reported to the police |

---

[29]  If you do so, it is likely to prejudice a fidelity insurance claim and lead to problems in court

## Principles

### General

All witness interviews should be conducted in private and should normally be non-confrontational, based on all of the rapport-building techniques described on pages 217–219 and an adult-to-adult transactional relationship. Important or complex interviews should be covertly tape-recorded. You must be careful not to reveal sensitive information, nor make derogatory comments about anyone, including the suspects. You should have all of the documents and other evidence you plan to discuss with the witness assembled in the way in which you plan to produce them as key points (see page 190).

> *Keep it at an unemotional level, but very professional*

In complex cases, the chances are that you will not be able to complete the interview and draft Proof of Evidence in one session. This does not matter, providing you:

- complete the freestyle version in one continuous session;
- get all documentary evidence from third party witnesses as soon as possible;
- make sure that any draft statements you prepare in the absence of the witness are subsequently agreed by him, line by line.

Thus you may arrange the detailed reporting phase, external stimulation sessions etc. on separate days and start completing and updating a draft Proof of Evidence after each one, rather than leaving it until the end.

### Monitoring and remaining aware

In every interview you should keep all of your senses switched on and monitor the subject's responses. However, in the early phases, you should not challenge anything that he says. Let the subject tell his story in a truly freestyle way and ideally do not take notes, other than simple bullet points[30] and Mind Maps. Actively listen to every word he says and evaluate his non-verbal communications.

> *Stay alert*

## The opening and freestyle story

As always, you should carefully plan and deliver an opening statement including:

- who you are;
- what you do;
- the reason for the interview and possible duration (always allow sufficient time);
- the structure of the interview;
- establish common objectives;
- emphasize confidentiality and security.

For example, in a simple case, with a witness you have evaluated as willing (Category A in Table 9.7), the opening might be as follows.

---

[30] And only then when the witness has paused

*Example*: 'I am Bill Jones from internal audit and I appreciate your seeing me. As you know, we are investigating a case of suspected fraud in accounts payable. I understand that you handle maintenance of the vendor master file and have worked for the company for the past five years. I would like your help in understanding how the system operates and any problems you have had. Our meeting, which is in total confidence, will take around an hour. In cases like this it is vital that we find the truth, so that we can all get on with our lives. So can you please tell me everything you know about x?'

Chances are the subject will ask for clarification and you should keep this to a minimum, so that you get a pure version.

*Example*: 'I don't know, Sam, you are the expert. Just go over it in any way you want. How it works, what you have seen going wrong, anything about the current case. Just let it all hang out.'

The witness's freestyle story is likely to contain the following elements:

- background or context applying to the story as a whole;
- clarification including his reasons for doing things, excuses and assumptions;
- emotions, including the way he felt throughout the time period concerned or in individual scenes;
- scene, topic or event detail.

In each of these aspects, the witness's recall is likely to be less than perfect, sometimes for reasons other than pure memory degradation. Try to identify the reasons why a witness is being less than open: is it a memory problem or something else?

## A CASE IN QUESTION

More than two million pounds were electronically transferred from the accounts payable system of a British company. Investigations, some five months later, indicated that standard settlement instructions hade been amended and false vendor files created. All of the documentation had been destroyed and there was absolutely no audit trail. However, investigations suggested that a temporary employee, called Robin Blind, appeared to be behind the scam. The problem was that his name and biographical details were false. Undercover investigation and intercepted communications established that employees working in accounts payable and in the wire transfer room were innocent and were totally devastated that they had reacted to instructions from Mr Blind without checking.

*Let the witness complete a freestyle story uninterrupted*

## Detailed reporting: CI tools and techniques

When the freestyle approach has been exhausted, move into the next phase and provide the subject with as many memory retrieval cues as you can. In an interview with an employee in the Robin Blind case, cues might be introduced as in Table 9.9.

Explain the process to the witness.

---

*Example*: 'We are going to try some memory retrieval techniques to see if we can dig more deeply. Some may seem a bit strange, but don't worry. I guarantee some of them will work and you may be surprised just how much detail we find.'

---

Then try the techniques in Table 9.9.

**Table 9.9**   Memory retrieval cues

| Memory retrieval cues<br>*Objective* | Example of your prompt |
|---|---|
| Context re-instatement<br>*Replicate the scene and circumstances when the witness encoded his memory* | Go back to the very start of that day and speak it out loud as though it were happening now in the present tense. 'Robin Blind is walking into my office … I am speaking on the telephone …' |
| Visualization<br>*Picture the scene*<br>*Draw diagrams*<br>*Get the witness to access his visual memory stores by getting his eyes to focus upwards* | Try to picture the scene. You were in your office. Let's do a Mind Map of all the things that were there when Robin walked in …<br>Did he touch anything?<br>What was odd about him?<br>How would you imagine his wife and family?<br>What sort of things do you think he likes doing?<br>What would his house look like?<br>I am going to play your role. I am sitting at the desk and you are Robin. Now go on |
| Change perspective<br>*Get a different view* | Just imagine you were Robin. What would you have noticed most in your office?<br>What would your secretary have seen? |
| Reverse or random sequence<br>*Break the chronological sequence* | Let's reverse things. Start from the moment Robin walked out of your office and let's go backwards |
| Humour (of the gallows variety)<br>*Cue the humour memory stores* | Imagine Robin at a fancy dress ball. What would he be dressed as?<br>Complete the sentence, Robin has had a bad day because … |
| Peripheral cues<br>*Trigger memory on dates, weather etc.* | Can you remember what was in the national papers that day? |
| Emotions, feelings and thoughts<br>*Cue the witness's emotional memory stores by looking downwards* | How did you feel when Robin asked you to sign the form?<br>What did you think was going on?<br>What did Robin smell like? |
| Non-happenings | What did Robin not do that he should have done?<br>Why didn't he ask you to go to his office? |

| Parallels | What did the incident most remind of you of? Have you ever seen anything like this before? Who did he sound like? Did he have squeaky shoes? |
|---|---|
| Holistic | Looking back, what are your most important thoughts on the case? On Robin? |
| Opinions and theories | Why do you think this happened? What exactly do you think happened? Do you think anyone else would have seen Robin? |
| Scene visit | Not appropriate in the Robin Blind case, but consider taking the witness to the scene |
| Names | Was it a long or short name? Did it begin with A, B, C etc.? What did it sound like? What would be your best guess? Why do you think that guess is not correct? |
| Repeated event | If Robin were to walk into your office tomorrow, what would you do differently? Why didn't that happen at the time? |

In practice, most of the cues will produce no result and expect that the witness may think you have lost the plot: don't worry, because some additional detail will emerge, often in areas neither you nor the witness expected.

## CONTINUING WITH ROBIN

Q: What date did Robin come to see you?
A: I am not sure.
Q: Was it this year or last?
A: Last.
Q: Winter or summer?
A: I can't remember.
Q: Did he come to your office?
A: Yes.
Q: Can you picture the scene?
A: More or less.
Q: Were you with anyone when he came in?
A: No, I was on the telephone.
Q: Can you remember who you were speaking to?
A: No, but I remember I was really pissed off and was shouting: it may have been my mother-in-law. [Laughs]
Q: Did Robin sit down while you finished your conversation?
A: No, he walked over to the window and stood there looking out: actually I thought he was looking over my shoulder.
Q: Was it day or night?
A: It was daylight.
Q: Sunny or overcast?
A: No, very sunny.
Q: So do you think it was summer?
A: Yes, because after he left [Pause], I walked into the park and fed the birds. It was the day before my wife's birthday.
Q: Which is when?
A: 4th June.
Q: So would your meeting with Robin have been on 3rd June?
A: Yes.

The witness's response to your prompting will tell you a great deal about him and his motivation. Usually people who don't want to recall, don't even think about the cues, whereas genuine people do.

*If the witness makes no effort to think about cues, he may have other reasons not to remember*

However, even if you conclude that the witness is being less than honest, do not challenge him at this stage, but press on.

## External stimulation

You should next produce exhibits, schedules and key points and ask for the witness's comments on them, using open and closed questions. Identify any discrepancies and seek clarification, again using memory retrieval clues.

*Press for detail.*
*Note discrepancies and the subject's reaction*

## Records retrieval and anything else?

### Principles and formal records

It is vital that you obtain copies of relevant documents and any other evidence in a witness's possession. For example, in a corruption case, you might want copies of the vendor's cash book, cancelled cheques etc. showing payments to a corrupt employee. If the witness refuses to produce these, you have a number of options based on your powers of persuasion.

Always consider obtaining personal and informal records such as:

- expense statements;
- image copies of the witness's computer;
- diaries;
- telephone call logs (including mobile telephone records).

## ROBIN BLIND

In this case, telephone call records confirmed the date of the meeting on 3 June at 11.34am, when the witness terminated a call to his mistress (just who can you trust?). More importantly, analysis of all telephone logs around that time showed a call from an internal conference room to a number which subsequently proved to be Robin Blind's home in the Channel Islands. He was traced through this and arrested.

*Effective investigation is all about detail*

In due course, you should analyse all records and make sure nothing has been missed and that they are consistent with the fraud theory.

*The little black book (almost like the white van)*

Innocent people on the edge of frauds often keep 'little black books' or private notes to protect their backsides if things go wrong. You should always ask about these.

---

*Example*: 'I have been involved in lots of cases like this and usually innocent people keep little notes, or bits of correspondence as insurance. What did you keep?'

---

## THE PA TO THE SALES DIRECTOR

A terrifying woman who was the PA to the sales director who had just been fired for fraud was asked: 'Jennifer, you are a very clever and prudent person and will have kept personal notes. Can we see these in confidence?' She subsequently produced diaries for the past five years that proved her boss's dishonesty beyond doubt.

*Try to get the little black book: someone will always have one*

## Interim summary

When all detail has been exhausted, you should prepare a summary of the witness's story. In a simple case, an annotated Mind Map or bullet point list may be sufficient. In more complex cases, you should consider drafting an outline Proof of Evidence or file note. Either way, you should have a list of:

- the people involved;
- the actions that took place;
- the objects involved;
- the conversations that occurred;
- other detail;
- emotions, thoughts and feelings.

You should then move on to the next stage.

## Detail on critical factors

You should again use memory retrieval cues to obtain detail on people, objects, actions and conversations etc. that form part of the witnesses' stories. You should cross-reference this detail with other evidence and resolve discrepancies.

## ROBIN BLIND

Various witnesses gave detailed descriptions of Robin Blind as shown in Table 9.10.

**Table 9.10**   Descriptions chart

| Factor | Description given by witnesses | | | |
| --- | --- | --- | --- | --- |
| | Witness 1 | Witness 2 | Witness 3 | Witness 4 |
| Age | 30 to 35 | 30 ish | Over 40 | 38 to 47 |
| Height | 5.7 | 5.9 | 5.10 | 5.975 |
| Weight | 150 lbs | 180 lbs | 180 | 189 |
| Hair | Brown/black | Brown | Brown | Tawny |
| Glasses | Rimless | No | No frames | YSL Type 52 |
| Reminds you of | Robin Day | Robin Day | No one | Plato |
| Sounds like | | | | |
| etc. | | | | |

Charts of this type help you to build up a picture of each of the important characters and objects in the witnesses' evidence. Someone, like Witness 4 in the above table, always seems to appear to have more precise information than others or provides significantly different recollections. Do not dismiss this: in every fraud theory, you are completing a jigsaw puzzle and if a piece does not fit, don't bash it into position. There is always an explanation and by identifying it, you could open up critical new lines of enquiry.[31]

*Deviations always open up new lines of enquiry*

You should continue with the same process on objects, actions etc. In most cases it is critical that you compile a detailed chronology of events that should be cross-referenced and annotated in tables summarizing the recollections of different witnesses (see Table 9.10 above).

## Challenging discrepancies and deception

You should not challenge discrepancies or suspected deception until you have covered everything that could be relevant and obtained and reviewed all documentary and other evidence. Then, your approach will depend on the circumstances and may range from low-key questions seeking clarification to direct confrontations on deception.

If your initial appraisal of the subject was wrong, you may decide to treat him as a suspect and to interview him along the lines of Chapters 6 and 7. The critical point is that you try to resolve all discrepancies, so that the final Proof of Evidence is as accurate as it can be.

---

[31]   In this case, witness 4 was a plonker!

## Homework

Finally, at the close of the interview or at overnight breaks in multiple interviews, you should thank the witness for his help (assuming he has given some) and neurolinguistically programme him to get his subconscious monkey working overnight.

---

*Example:* 'I am sure that when you get into bed tonight, your mind will race over the things we have missed. I know your wife will think you are barmy, but keep a pen and pad alongside your bed and when you wake up thinking about this, as you will, jot down anything that comes to mind. It always happens. I will do the same, so let's talk and compare notes at around 8.30 tomorrow. Is that OK?'

---

*Getting a witness to think overnight pays dividends*

## STATEMENTS AND PROOFS OF EVIDENCE

### The principles

A *Proof of Evidence* is a written account of what a witness can say in court and which may contain hearsay and other details not directly related to the facts in issue. The Proof of Evidence may support your case or destroy it. Either way, if it is relevant to the matters in issue, it must be fully documented.

> *Do not close your mind to anything.*
> *Don't reinforce prejudices*

Although in both criminal and civil proceedings in the United Kingdom, formal statements usually have to be disclosed to the opposing side, this is not always true of Proofs of Evidence, providing they are prefaced as follows:

---

**STRICTLY CONFIDENTIAL**

'This Proof of Evidence has been prepared for the legal advisers of X Ltd for information and in contemplation of legal proceedings relating to the matters referred to in it.'

---

This caveat should establish the privileged nature of the document. It is therefore much safer for inexperienced investigators to obtain Proofs of Evidence, rather than formal signed statements. However, the decision on whether or not anything has to be disclosed to the other side must be made by an experienced lawyer, so you must make sure that everything is drawn to his attention.

> *Failure to disclose is a mortal sin that can destroy even the best case*

### Preparing the final draft

You may draft the proof or statement in the presence of, and with the cooperation of the witness, although in larger cases this is seldom possible and you will have to prepare a number of drafts as you progress. The critical point is that the final version is not closed until every point and every discrepancy that could be relevant has been resolved. Documents and other exhibits referred to in the Proof of Evidence should be accurately cross-referenced and attached.[32] Normally, lawyers will use the Proof of Evidence for preparing a formal statement or affidavit and will also decide what has to be disclosed to the opposing party.

*Always keep your legal advisers fully informed.*
*Avoid surprises in court*

## Refusal to sign a proof

If a witness refuses to sign a Proof of Evidence, you should read the draft to him – word for word – and then ask him to check it himself. He should be asked if it is correct and, if not, any corrections or additions should be made and initialled even though he may refuse to sign the statement as a whole.

## Criminal Justice Act statements

When criminal proceedings are contemplated in the UK, witnesses may be asked to sign a *CJA statement*, bearing an endorsement under the Criminal Justice Act (CJA: see Appendix 3 and www.cobasco.com).

> 'This statement consisting of ... pages, each signed by me, is true to the best of my knowledge and belief, and I make it knowing that if it is tendered in evidence, I shall be liable to prosecution if I have wilfully stated in it anything which I know to be false or do not believe to be true.'

Statements of this type are sometimes invaluable because they can be introduced directly into evidence without the need for the witness to attend, but they should only be taken by experienced investigators and then under legal advice. They are particularly useful if you believe a witness may be lying. The statement can be drafted and the pavement raised by pointing out the seriousness of the perjury provisions. This has caused a dramatic change of direction by some deceptive witnesses.[33]

## UPDATING DOCUMENTATION

In complex cases, it is vital that you keep the fraud theory, chronology, investigations plan etc. up to date and that files are maintained and kept securely.

## ADVISING AND PREPARING THE WITNESS

Normally, lawyers will decide which witnesses will be called, but this can be a traumatic time for those who have helped you. You and your lawyers should make sure the witness is still prepared to give evidence and you should explain the process to him. You should again check the accuracy of his statement or Proof of Evidence with him and if there have been any

---

[32]   Usually in indexed binders
[33]   But you must keep the original draft and disclose it to your legal advisers

changes in the facts or in recollection, these should be recorded and drawn to the attention of your lawyers: preferably in writing.

There is no reason why you cannot accompany the witness to and from court. This has a two-way benefit. First, to make sure he does not lose his nerve and buzz off to the Canary Islands to avoid giving evidence. Second, he will appreciate your support.

Finally, when it is all over, it does no harm to drop a line of thanks to the witness for his help and, if the case has been stressful for his family, to buy his wife a nice bunch of flowers which you can describe on your expense statement as a 'rail fare'.[34]

## TAKING STATEMENTS FROM EXPERT WITNESSES

Normally witnesses can only testify to facts from their first-hand knowledge and cannot give hearsay evidence, nor can they express an opinion. The one exception to this rule arises in the case of *expert witnesses* who have a recognized expertise in a particular subject and who are allowed to express *an opinion* and advise the court generally. For example, a medical doctor may give an opinion as to the cause of death; an accountant can express an opinion about the reasons for a company's failure or the efficiency of its controls.

Before being called to give evidence, the expert witness must satisfy the trial judge that he is qualified by learning and experience to give an opinion within his field. Any statement taken from him should set out his qualifications in full and his past experience as an expert witness. It is absolutely vital that the background of an expert witness is checked out thoroughly and that any padding of his qualifications or experience is removed. It can be catastrophic if an expert witness is discredited in court: this sometimes happens.

Statements by expert witnesses will usually be taken under the guidance of lawyers, although the task of interviewing and obtaining a draft Proof of Evidence might be delegated to an investigator, auditor or manager.

Expert testimony is intended to inform and be helpful, and not simply to impress the court with the skill of the witness, nor to bamboozle the jury. The quality of expert testimony can be measured by its simplicity.

The objectives of simplicity and clarity can be achieved as follows:

- He should be given copies of anything that could be relevant in forming his opinion and especially anything that is unfavourable to your case.
- The expert should understand the case concerned and exactly what is required of him. Each question should be framed *in writing* and should deal with a single matter upon which an opinion is required.
- The conclusions that the expert is expected to reach should not be suggested to him. He must be free to make up his own mind.
- The expert should be given a realistic amount of time to study the facts and to form an opinion.
- The expert should provide an initial report, addressed to the company's lawyers, which should be read carefully and all ambiguities resolved.
- Technicalities, acronyms and abbreviations should be avoided.
- If the subject is complex, charts, diagrams, a glossary or working models should be used to assist in the understanding of his testimony.

---

[34] Just kidding to make sure you are still awake

- The draft Proof of Evidence should be submitted by the company's lawyers to two or three laymen who are not familiar with the case. They should be questioned on their understanding, and the Proof of Evidence revised if necessary.

The procedures outlined above should result in clear-cut and simple evidence, and not, as often happens, in technical gobbledegook which confuses the judge, jury and even other expert witnesses.

## Conclusions

The cunning plan is already flexible but you should adapt it to suit your personality and style. However you do it, getting to the deep truth is 95 per cent preparation and 5 per cent execution. You will find that the harder you work, the luckier you will become, especially at GOLF.

# 3 *In Court*

'I KNOW THE PARROT HAS CLAIMED THE FIFTH AMENDMENT, BUT I HAVE TO WARN YOU, CAPTAIN BLYTHE, THAT WHAT YOUR MONKEYS SAY MAY BE USED AGAINST YOU'

# **10** *Giving Evidence*

*A person who laughs in the face of adversity
has not understood the problem*

## Purpose

This chapter is to help if you are ever called to give evidence in criminal or civil proceedings, including employment tribunals. It contains two very important lessons:

- Litigation is always expensive and worrisome. The old saying, 'Before litigating, dig two graves', is true.
- You should understand that the reason you are required to give evidence is because your case left your opponents room for manoeuvre.

## The best solution

If you have *overwhelming evidence* that leads to a guilty plea or capitulation by the opposition, you:

- achieve the objectives of punishing or dealing with the offender and getting your money back;
- succeed in civil or criminal proceedings;
- establish a deterrent to others.

and remove the need to attend a court or tribunal. This is nearly always the best solution.

## Preparing the case

You should take the greatest possible care when preparing your statement, affidavit or Proof of Evidence and don't get carried away with enthusiasm or emotion in the heat of the moment. Remember you may have to justify every word – under hostile cross examination – so be sure.

Also tell your legal advisers everything that could be relevant and especially about evidence that could damage your case. If you don't make a full and proper disclosure to the opposing party, you could lose your case on this fact alone.

Also, although you may discuss your evidence with your colleagues, to refresh your memory and avoid mistakes, you must take the greatest care not to unfairly influence them or try and get them to say things they do not remember or do not know are true. Similarly, you must not be improperly influenced by others.

If you collude improperly, you and your colleagues could be at risk of criminal prosecution for perverting the course of justice. So take care, be fair, open and frank.

## The most likely venues

Criminal cases are held before magistrates in the lower courts or judges and juries in Crown Courts. Magistrates or juries decide guilt or innocence and give the benefit of any doubt to the accused. Thus cases have to be proved 'beyond reasonable doubt' and this is a very high standard.

In civil courts, the judges usually decide the outcome. In employment tribunals a panel consisting of a chairman (who is a qualified lawyer), and an employer's and employee's representative make decisions on the case as well as the compensation involved.

Both criminal and civil courts follow formal, if not ritualistic procedures with barristers usually wearing wigs and gowns. This can be unsettling for the inexperienced witness.

Employment tribunals are less formal, but nonetheless should be considered as courts of law and must be taken seriously. They have the powers to demand that information is produced and that witnesses attend and evidence is given on oath.

The chairmen are usually very astute, but because they have limited time, tend to dislike too much detail and become impatient with witnesses who wander off the point. Generally, they do not like allegations of fraud or dishonesty and can be adversely influenced by a witness who becomes emotional or difficult.

Thus in employment tribunals, you should focus on the key facts and stay emotionally detached.

## Background

The day will come when you, your colleagues or, heaven forbid, your lawyers[1] are called into court to give evidence. Although this is a terrorizing prospect, your ordeal can be made easier if you heed the following warnings. They are deliberately written in a very personal way, because at the time you will need to refer to them, the issues will indeed be very personal.

*Giving evidence is a very personal experience: much like torture*

Giving evidence is a great example of the saying 'What goes round, comes round' and you just have to accept it is your turn in the barrel. If you have done your job professionally and fairly, the pain about to be inflicted on you will be unpleasant but tolerable. If you have been unprofessional or unfair, this is the time when your ass is going to get severely kicked and it serves you right. We trust you will not be in this position, so your anxiety should be tolerable.

*Everything is easier to get into than to get out of*

---

[1] They usually just hate being in the witness box

# Prepare carefully

## CHECK YOUR PAPERS

Always prepare for court carefully. Know your statement, Proof of Evidence or affidavit, backwards, forwards and inside out and the exhibits to which they refer. Double check all schedules, calculations and conclusions you have made in your statement or which you might be required to comment on during your evidence. If you believe that a source of your information should be protected, or if you have some other problem, speak to the lawyer representing your side. You must also make sure that you have told him about every piece of evidence, intelligence or rumour so that he can decide what has to be disclosed to the other side. If something has not been disclosed that should have been, he will blame you. Remember, lawyers are very clever and never responsible for any failure.

Check your notes, and other records you may be allowed to refer to in the witness box to refresh your memory; make sure you can read and understand them.

---

### MAKING NOTES AT THE TIME

An investigator was asked in cross-examination: 'You have said that you wrote your notes at the time; that they were contemporaneous. Is that correct?' 'Yes,' replied the witness. 'And was the interview conducted at normal conversational speed?' Counsel asked and the witness agreed that this was the case.

'They are very neat and tidy, Mr Jones, aren't they?' 'Yes', replied the witness and then added a fatal piece of humour: 'Unlike lawyers and doctors, I have been trained to write nicely.' 'Very good, Mr Jones. I am now going to dictate a passage to you at normal conversational speed and I would like you to write down notes of everything I say.'

Within two minutes the witness was a blubbering wreck, because he could not keep pace with the dictation. The case was thrown out.

---

Also anticipate that your notes will be taken from you while you are in the witness box and scrutinized by opposing counsel and possibly a forensic document examiner acting on his behalf. This makes it imperative that they do not contain embarrassing things such as details of your Swiss bank accounts, notes about your neighbour's niece or golfing results.

*Experience is something you don't get until after you need it*

## GET IT IN YOUR DIARY

Make sure you have multiple reminders– in your diary, filofax, PDA and on the back of the fridge door – of the date and time you are required to attend court. If you forget to appear and instead buzz off to play golf with your pals, you will be in very serious trouble.

## THINK ABOUT THE QUESTIONS

Develop a fraud theory in reverse and think, if you were the defendant, how your evidence might be attacked. Consider the questions you might be asked and discuss them with your colleagues and, if he is willing, with your lawyer. If you have weak points or have made mistakes, be prepared to admit them and apologize if necessary. It is much better to make an open and contrite admission than to have the truth painfully dragged out of you in cross-examination.

*Plan ahead*

## CHECK OUT THE COURT

Familiarize yourself with the court, how to get there and how long the journey takes even when you have to stop every ten minutes for anxious lavatorial breaks. If you have not given evidence before, sit in on another trial[2] for a couple of hours before your big day. Watch and get the hang of things. It is pretty awesome; lawyers are clever and very smart.

# On the day

## APPEARANCE

On the day you are required to give evidence, arrive at court really early and make sure you dress sensibly. Your wife may tell you that you look wonderful in your yellow waistcoat, pink suspenders, Gucci sunglasses and Hush Puppies, but it is doubtful that the court will appreciate their sartorial elegance. Wear loose clothing and comfortable shoes, just in case you have to make a run for it. Also wear clothing that – unlike Tony Blair's – does not show how profusely you are sweating. Like fierce hunting dogs, lawyers smell fear and, if they see signs of your terror, it will just make matters worse.

If you wear dentures, a glass eye or a hairpiece, make sure they are firmly affixed. It will not be good for your credibility if in the heat of the moment an appendage becomes detached and the judge and jury (but, obviously, not the barristers) have to chase around trying to find it.

*Beware of your emblems*

If you are a member of the Surbiton Train Spotters' Club, however proud you might be of this rare distinction, don't wear the lapel badge, tie or cap. This is not impressive. All you will achieve is to mark yourself out as a plonker and thus damage your credibility before you even open your mouth. If you must have facial hair, make sure you do not look like a member of the Taliban and your court appearance may be the excuse you need to shave off your pencil-thin moustache. You always knew it made you look like a ballroom dancing teacher.

## WAITING TO BE CALLED

You can guarantee you will be kept waiting outside the court, possibly for hours if not days. Don't worry about this, it is all part of the softening up process. Do not read sensitive papers in public areas and be careful with your mobile telephone and laptop computer. Do not engage strangers in idle conversation because the delightful blonde sat next to you in the waiting room, who tells you she finds fat, old, grey-haired men an aphrodisiac, could be a plant by the oppos-

---

[2]   You will not be allowed to sit in on the trial in which you are a witness until after you have given evidence

ing side to get you into a compromising position. Believe it or not, this sometimes happens and what you tell her may be used against you when you are impaled in the witness box.

*Don't speak to anyone: pretend you are an accountant*

In fact, do not discuss your evidence or the case with anyone else waiting around the court and especially with a witness who has not completed his evidence and been released. A little paranoia does no one any harm, and waiting about makes matters worse. This is the time to read *this book* or have a nap: the two things are closely related as a NLP feedback loop.

While you are waiting, you will see barristers, solicitors, and even ordinary humans walking around, clutching papers and always looking either very happy or very anxious. It will help you if you try to picture the very impressive, robed and wigged figures as they would appear in real life: on the golf course or in the bath. This bit of NLP will help you set the right transactional relationship when you get into court. Although lawyers are very clever, they do have human tendencies, so don't be misled by their emblems which are a historical relic meant to increase your anxiety – as is the layout of the court. If you did not believe how important venue and emblems are in increasing anxiety, you are about to find out. Courts are nasty places, full of nasty people: much worse even than the Masonic lodge or bingo club.

## ENTERING THE COURT WITH PANACHE

Do not go into the court until your name is called. When this happens your legs will crumple and the past will flash before your eyes, so much so that you may wish you had heeded your mother's advice and, like your uncle Alf, become a butcher: but it's too late.

Make sure you pick up all of your belongings[3] – TURN OFF YOUR MOBILE TELEPHONE – and walk into court nice and slowly; don't panic. Take your time and grab some deep breaths. Wait to be spoken to and don't start off with a cheery 'Good morning, judge. I like your wig' or with some flippant remark to the defendant like 'Guilty bastard'. Neither will go down well. Also, if you are a Freemason, don't be tempted to give the secret gesticulations to members of the jury, the judge or anyone else. This will not be appreciated, especially if you outrank them. Stand still and wait until you are spoken to and take a few deep breaths, without overt panting or gasping.

*A closed mouth gathers no foot[4]*

## GIVING YOUR EVIDENCE IN CHIEF

You will be asked to take the oath or to make some other form of esoteric incantation, depending on your beliefs. Do this very carefully and remember that first impressions count; so that within seconds the judge, jury and counsel will have unconsciously categorized your emblems and formed an opinion of you. If you get off to a bad start or anyone senses any weakness, your ass will get kicked: that's a promise.

You will be asked your name and there is not much you can do about this, but it does have an effect on the way you are perceived, especially by the jury, which is made up of or-

---

[3]   Especially your spectacles, hearing aid and hairpiece
[4]   Based on 'A rolling stone gathers no moss'

dinary folk from Cheam and Islington. If your name is Peregrin Anstruther Tarquin Jocelyn Maltravers-Blythe, you might want to abbreviate it a bit. On the other hand, if your name is Richard Head, you should avoid shortening your first name, even though your wife says she likes it a lot. If you served in the armed forces and reached a commissioned rank, don't say you are 'Major Jones' or 'Field Brigadier Nonkins'. Similarly, don't append your educational qualifications to the end of your name, such as 'Dick Head, BA, MA, PhD'. Unquestionably, you and your mum are proud of your achievements, but most people won't give a damn, but will mark you down as a plonker.

### In court, you must appear ordinary

In normal circumstances you will be led through your evidence by counsel representing your side, but don't be thrown if as soon as you enter the witness box, opposing counsel jumps up and makes an objection. This is usually because the opposition's case is hopeless and his only hope is to argue some esoteric legal point. The judge may ask the jury to leave while the fine legal point is being considered. Don't worry and just stand there, look around the court, and answer any questions you are asked. This is the time for you to watch the lawyers closely and you will discover that many are more nervous than you. If fact the only person who is really cool is the judge.

If all goes well and under normal circumstances, you will then be asked questions by counsel representing your side. This is called your 'evidence in chief'. Your counsel should be friendly, or superficially so, and he may smile from time to time, nod his head and give you positive non-verbal feedback. Don't relax, because if things go wrong, he will drop you like a hot potato. Remember, lawyers are very clever, intelligent and smart and that you are a guest in their world. If a scapegoat has to be found, lawyers close ranks and turn on you or some other poor bugger who is not a lawyer. It does not matter who he is, how old, or how innocent; his only qualification is that he is not a member of the legal profession.

### A good turn never goes unpunished

Direct all of your answers to the judge and try to establish eye contact with him and members of the jury from time to time, but don't glare or wink. Keep your answers simple. Most honest witnesses genuinely want to assist the court and thus volunteer things they think could be helpful. Don't do this, just answer the questions you have been asked, preferably with a binary 'yes' or 'no'. Remember, lawyers don't necessarily want to hear the truth but just want their questions answered.

If – at any point – you are not certain of a fact, ask the judge if you can refresh your memory from your notes. Under no circumstances should you guess or try to crack a joke. Humour, especially, will backfire on you, although you must always laugh at the judge's humour.

Counsel for the other side may continue to jump up and down and make objections to your evidence. This is a good sign, unless he has a gerbil in his underpants in which case it means nothing. When you have finished your evidence in chief, wait in the witness box and whatever you do, don't look smug because the ambush is just around the corner. Never forget that lawyers are clever and the older they are the cleverer they become.

### The bodies of lawyers deteriorate much faster than their brains

## CROSS-EXAMINATION

The big problem comes with cross-examination by opposing counsel and, if there are a lot of defendants, each one will have a personal ogre who will attack you. It is one of life's great truths that opposing lawyers always appear bigger, better, cleverer and more determined than yours, but don't worry. They are all very smart: you are fodder for their cannons – they are the hunters and you the huntee. Just accept this and adopt the transactional role of an adaptive child and you may just survive.

Opposing counsel will ask you lots of dreadful questions, try to trip you up, and make you appear an incompetent idiot or much worse. Remember this is his job and he will be doing his best, but it's no worse than being grilled by your wife when she caught you chatting up your neighbour's niece with the little black dress and legs to die for.[5] Just remain calm and don't take it personally and remember when you get home your dog will still love you. Tell the truth and if you have made a mistake admit it and, if necessary, apologize. Lawyers are not used to apologies and your candour will impress them if only for the microseconds before they kick your ass.

Don't argue the case or matters of law – you are not an advocate; appear impartial and concede points genuinely in favour of the defendant whom, deep down, you know is a loathsome lowlife who pulls the legs off spiders and picks his nose. Just stick to the facts, remain emotionally detached and *never look* at the defendant because, if you do, he will have a face like thunder and this could unbalance you.

Occasionally, counsel will make mistakes and if this happens don't laugh because if you do, he will get you later. Lawyers are very clever and have long memories.

### THE HEARTBEAT

An unusually uppity lawyer was cross-examining a coroner about a man's death:

Lawyer: So, Mr Jones, you signed the death certificate without taking his pulse or temperature?
Coroner: Yes.
Lawyer: Did you listen for a heartbeat?
Coroner: No.
Lawyer: So when you signed the death certificate you did none of the things your professional training would require you to do, did you?
Coroner: Well, let me put it this way. The man's brain was sitting in a jar on my desk, but for all I know, he could have been out there somewhere practising law.

When opposing counsel sits down, you remain standing. Don't move.

## RE-EXAMINATION

Next you may be re-examined by counsel for your side. You can tell how badly you have been dented in the cross-examination by the number of questions he asks and the way he avoids eye contact. If there are a lot of questions, you can assume you have not been impressive. Don't worry: that's life, and lawyers are very brainy.

---

[5]   If you have forgotten, please see page 55

Finally, you may be asked questions by the judge. These are really important and take care as judges are cleverer than anyone else and they have unlimited power to kick ass. Simply tell the truth.

## BREAKS IN THE CASE

You can almost guarantee that you will not complete your evidence in one session and will have to worry through a lunch, overnight or some other adjournment. George Carman QC – perhaps the leading advocate and cross-examiner of his generation – used to love this, if not contrive it. He used to say, 'It will give the witness time to worry' and he was right.

Don't speak to anyone during breaks in your evidence. Politely ignore and avoid eye contact with members of the jury and the defendant if you happen to bump into them in the pub, bingo hall or lodge. Just get out of their space as quickly as you can and pretend you haven't seen them.

During longer breaks – however tempting it might appear at the time – don't console yourself by a prolonged session in the pub. Keep off the juice overnight and arrive at court the next day nice, fresh and preferably celibate. Tell your spouse you have a migraine and get a good night's sleep; if that's at all possible. If you just cannot doze off, start reading this book and that will do the trick, because NLP feedback loops are wonderful things.

## LEAVING THE WITNESS BOX

Don't try to leave the witness box until the judge says you can. He may or may not thank you, depending on how well you have performed. Pick up your stuff, glance confidently towards the jury and walk slowly away, taking care not to fall over or faint. If it is possible, sit down at the back of the court and wait until the next adjournment. Most witnesses leave the court after completing their evidence and this is a big mistake because in the animal kingdom – which is where you are – this is interpreted as desertion of territory and a cowardly flight response. So stand your ground and look occasionally towards the jury, but again avoid eye contact and Masonic signs.

## THE OPPONENT'S EVIDENCE

At the close of the prosecution or claimant's case, evidence will be called for the defence, including witnesses, experts, other defendants and even the malodorous villain himself may be brazen enough to take the stand. Last time you saw him he was six foot nine tall, with muscles like Popeye, a dark Benidorm tan, pencil-thin moustache and oozing with jewellery and fancy feet. In court he will present himself as a fragile old gentleman, about to pop his clogs and in whose mouth butter would not melt, so don't be taken by surprise. This is life.

If you have the time, sit in court while defence evidence is being given, but don't glare at the witnesses even though they may be telling dreadful lies and poking holes in your brilliant case. From time to time you can nod your head in disagreement, put your hand over your mouth, or affect a sickly smirk, but don't overdo the acting. Just sit back and wait, because your counsel will be able to cross-examine them and this is where the fun should start. If you discover that any of the witnesses are telling lies, try to get a message to your counsel, but don't keep bobbing up and down like a gerbil on minor points. Chances are, in any case, he will ignore you. Lawyers, like waiters, are trained to be deaf and blind when it suits their purpose: they are very clever.

## THE SUMMING-UP

Eventually, at the close of the defence case and submissions, the judge will sum up the evidence and this will reveal just how clever he really is. You may have thought he was an old codger who was asleep for most of the time, but now you will discover he has a mind as sharp as a razor and the recall of an elephant. Keep your eye on the jury during the summing-up but again don't nod, wink or make Masonic signs. Just watch and try to look really confident.

It always seems to be the case, whichever side you support, that the judge's summing-up is against you. Don't worry because it is much like watching the England football team on television to the extent that the action is always worse than the result.

## THE DELIBERATIONS

When the judge has finished, he will send the members of the jury out to consider the evidence and the court will adjourn to wait for the result. This is a bad time for everyone, so just relax. Many jurors, who have boring lives in Cheam or Islington, will see their noble calling as a chance to stay overnight in a fancy hotel, all expenses paid while they 'deliberate'. This is especially likely if one or more of the members has sexual aspirations towards one or more of his or her colleagues because it is a great excuse for a serious amount of rogering, at the state's expense. Don't worry about this: it is life.

After what will appear a lifetime's wait, the court will reconvene and the jury will amble in. It's strange, but jury members always look sheepish and have their heads down, especially if they have had boozy nights 'deliberating' in a luxury hotel. When the verdict is announced, grip your seat really hard and don't leap in the air and shout, but just accept it and remember this is justice.

If subsequently you happen to bump into a member of the jury, don't ask him anything about the case or the nights in the expensive hotel. Just acknowledge him and walk away because what happened in the jury room is secret: what happened in the hotel is even more of a secret, so don't even think about it.

# After the event

Chances are at the end of it all, you will leave court, feeling drained and with acutely hurt feelings because unfair allegations have been made against you. Even when you know you have carried out your work honestly, professionally and to the best of your ability, you will still get pulped.

Exceptionally, you might get commended by the judge. Don't wallow in false pride because commendations are but temporary aberrations in the miserable lives of witnesses.

Because of such systemic pulping, witnesses and others involved in investigations might wonder whether the whole episode and especially the torment in court was worthwhile. The answer is overwhelmingly affirmative, because someone has to take a stand against bad people. Besides that if there were no witnesses, there would be no lawyers and where would we be then?

As ordinary folk we are in the firing line and if any human wants an easy life he should become a lawyer or politician or, if he is clever enough, a judge: now that is a really good job. True the pay is not great but the perks, such as unrestricted ability to kick ass and having your jokes always laughed at definitely are.

Finally, remember that courts are the lawyers' hunting ground and that witnesses are their next meal. Lawyers always win, whatever the outcome. But every dog has its day and that's why this chapter has been just a little bit rude to lawyers.

*Witnesses are to lawyers what plankton is to whales*

## Learning the lessons

In the days and weeks after the case you will have time to reflect on your experience and, if you are a senior manager, you may conclude that you never want to see a court again. This is understandable, but please think. You have two courses. The first is to opt out, let crooks and ne'er-do-wells escape by not prosecuting them: this is a poor decision that will only make your organization's fraud and other problems worse. The second is to accept that the only reason you were called to give evidence was because your case gave the bad guys the chance to squirm. *This is the real lesson.*

If you can build an overwhelming case that leaves your opponents with no room for manoeuvre, you can prevail, leading them to plead guilty or capitulate. In this way, you avoid having to attend as a witness, save money, time and still succeed. You can do this by:

- having a fraud policy and contingency plan which sets out precisely how you will react when fraud is suspected, how the case will be investigated and by whom;
- having professional investigators work with you, who are expert interviewers and who can find the whole truth before going to court.

Lastly, and most importantly, you must have the best, most blood-curdling litigation lawyers on your side. If they are good, their reaction may be that you don't need investigators, but please think about this. Good investigators work with lawyers to produce overwhelming evidence before the matter gets to court. This saves time, aggravation and, of course, legal fees.

In major cases, your contingency plan (this can be downloaded from www.cobasco.com) should ensure that a senior line manager (who was not responsible for the area in which the loss occurred) is put in charge of a project team including lawyers and investigators. He can decide upon the relative merits of their arguments and, of course, if the lawyers and investigators still cannot agree, take the decision *to fire the lawyers!*

## Conclusions

The one thing most witnesses agree upon is that the experience in the court or tribunal was not the happiest of their lives. Chances are, if the investigation had been conducted properly, the need to be called as a witness could have been avoided. This is the ultimate lesson.

'PLEASE MAKE UP YOUR MIND, YOUR HONOUR. DO YOU WANT
THE TRUTH, THE WHOLE TRUTH OR NOTHING BUT THE TRUTH?
REMEMBER I AM AN ACCOUNTANT'

# **11** *Golf and the Cunning Plan*

*Never network with an idiot.*
*He will drag you down to his level and then beat you through experience*

## Now you know

God created golf, but the Devil spoiled its perfection by letting women and Japanese tourists find out about it. Sex, free dinners at Langan's and other ephemeral pleasures, the hard-wiring of the brain, Darwin and Freud, divisions between the conscious and subconscious, memory and imagination and all that other stuff evolved so that people could play golf. Wars, rebellions and terrorism are caused not by the reasons widely believed but simply because the combatants have been denied access to God's verdant links and deprived of Scotty Cameron putters. In a thousand years' time we will all look like Tiger Woods and be perfect golfing machines. People who don't play golf will be atrophied to be reborn as gerbils. This is what it's all about.

*Darwin said 'The survival of the Titleist',[1] not as widely believed 'the fittest'*

Now you know the truth. Golf is *the* meaning of life: an exemplar of the triumph of good over evil: providing, of course, the opponent does not cheat – and this happens a lot.

*Golf and business both bring out the worst in people*

Because of golf's deep meaning, it would be a sinful omission not to explain how the cunning plan applies and, if you have not understood how it works, the great game should provide the memory retrieval cues for a complete understanding. That is why this chapter has been included, so if you are not a golfer, just concentrate on the by-lines and the memory retrieval cues, which are shown in italics. If you are a golfer (bless!) visualize the golfing scenes and the cunning plan will be encoded in your memory forever for all situations in which deception may be at work.

*You can learn a lot from golf*

## Determine your objectives

As always, you first have to decide upon your objectives. If you are playing against your boss or an important client, your objective will be to lose, whereas you will almost certainly want

---

[1]  Who make Scotty Cameron putters

to humiliate subordinates and vendors. Too many people engage in a skirmish without deciding on their objectives.

*Determine your objectives*

In fact, if you want to create really enduring rapport with someone, you need to draw or 'halve' the match. You can do this by getting ahead and cunningly losing the last couple of holes. Your opponent will feel really good and bond with you. Sharing any tight, emotional competition is rapport building and this is true with both golf and interviewing.

*Create rapport*

Losing at golf is easy, if not instinctive, and made easier by applying the reverse of the techniques explained later, so we will assume you always want to win. Unless you play with yourself (and this to be avoided, because it makes your hands hairy) you will always have one or more opponents. Many will be younger, fitter and more skilled than you, as in all walks of life, and some will cheat badly. Nevertheless you can beat most people, most of the time and thereby make enough money to buy a second or third copy of this book.

*Never underestimate your opponent*

# Get the background

The second step of the cunning plan is to know everything possible about your opponent and what makes him tick. Ideally you should only play against people who are less athletic, older, dumber and not as rich as you. Thus you should concentrate on golf societies associated with Masonic lodges or pubs, the Law Society, Japanese tourism, Women's Institutes and old people's homes.

You can safely play these people and never lose. You are also in no danger playing anyone in Florida or Cornwall. However, never play the Irish or Scots, especially for money. The simple reason is that the former are fantastic golfers and the latter never pay up.

*Know everything about your opponent*

If you have no choice but to play against capable opponents, your chances of success are clearly reduced, but you can still win.

*Understand your opponent's weak points*

If you don't already know, find out which club or golfing society the potential opponent belongs to, telephone the secretary and confirm his handicap. Believe it or not, some people cheat on this point and claim a high handicap so you have to give them lots of strokes and then they beat you. A person who falsifies his handicap is the lowest form of life and if you believe someone has tried this you should report him to the Serious Fraud Office.

*Never be astonished that the police are not interested in your complaints.*
*Many are too busy playing golf*

As you know, you must always analyse the background of the case or 'matters in issue' and in golfing terms, this means knowing the course backwards. We will return to this point later.

# Deception theory

As always, you should work out what the opponent has done or is likely to do: perhaps he has a cunning plan of his own. So think about his objectives and how he might achieve them both honestly and dishonestly. Maybe he is a subordinate or vendor and is so ignorant that he does not understand the unwritten protocol and will actually try and beat you. Just what is he up to? Why did he ask you to play? What are his ulterior motives? Are you walking into a trap?

*A little paranoia does no harm*

# Resolution plan and specific planning

## BASIC STUFF

In golf these two steps can be rolled into one and they are very important. If the opponent is an orang-utang who hits the ball miles further than you, arrange to play him from the front tees on a short course with lots of bunkers, water and rough. If he pitty-pats the ball like a big fairy,[2] get him off the championship tees on a really long course and preferably on a wet, windy day. If he wears a hairpiece, the windier the day the better. If he suffers from hay fever, play him on a hot sunny day or if he is arthritic choose a cold winter's morning. Games with opponents who have dodgy eyesight should be played in the late evening, preferably in the rain.

*Get the basics right*

If your opponent works nights or has a young baby, fix the game for 6.30 am or earlier and phone him around 2.00 am to make sure he has not forgotten.

*Timing and venue are important*

If your opponent likes alcohol, arrange to meet him for lunch before the game and try and get him pickled, while remaining abstemious yourself. By getting to the bar first you can tip the steward to serve you straight tonics while your opponent thinks you are hitting the gin. It is a great advantage if you can arrive on the first tee stone cold sober and your opponent legless and disorientated.

*Plan to get immediate control*

---

[2]   This is a golfing technical term

## PLANNING ANXIETY INDUCING SCHEMES

### The principle
You should plan to get your opponent to defeat himself, through brain thrashing, anxiety and all that other good stuff. Like every other situation where deception is at work, you have to bring him to the pivotal point where he internalizes and loses all confidence in his ability to succeed. This is easy, but at the end of it all, you have to allow him to save face and this can be more difficult.

*Let the opponent defeat himself through his own anxiety.*
*Get him to the pivotal point*

### Silly gamesmanship
You should never stoop to the silly gamesmanship used by unintelligent wretches, such as coughing at the top of an opponent's back swing, secretly kicking his ball into the rough, childish verbals or claiming to have a handicap of 28 when you are really plus four. Any idiot can do that and the cunning plan is much more subtle and, of course, fair.

*Play it fair*

### Fear bad: anxiety good
We trust you have recognized the difference between fear and anxiety. The former is in relation to a specific external threat, such as, 'watch the motorway on the right. A member was killed on that last week looking for his ball', or 'if you sink that putt, I will cancel our purchase order', and increasing fear is a cheap trick that you should never use. Anxiety, on the other hand, is internally generated in the subject's brain and results from an accumulation of small, often subtle, worries. Causing an opponent to raise his level of anxiety to the point where he defeats himself is a legitimate tactic.

*Anxiety is legitimate: fear is not*

### Six key points
Good planning is essential and you should use six key points to increase your opponent's anxiety during the match. For example, if he is a right hemisphere, gregarious, arty type who likes to chat a lot, find out whether he walks around the course or takes a buggy. Whichever he prefers, plan to do the opposite, so that the only time you will have to speak to him is on tees and greens, making him lonely and anxious. The perfect game is with you on a buggy and the opponent walking. You can then motor-on quickly between shots and rush him. This will make him both anxious and knackered. On the other hand if you know he normally uses a buggy, you should plan to walk as slowly as you can and hold him up.

The objective of your planning is to upset your opponent's tempo, rhythm and confidence and if, on the day, you can be so unhurried that you have to let through a four-ball of Japanese ladies or, better still, a group of German travel agents playing in a seven ball, so much the better. Remember your objective is to win: not to enjoy the game.

*Pacing is very important*

## Introduce an ogre

Think about paying for a very elderly caddie who looks as though he is just about to pop his clogs; most courses have one or two hanging around. You can normally find them sleeping in cardboard boxes under the bushes or resting in the warmth of a pile of grass cuttings or manure. Most are retired investigators. You can then blame the geriatric caddy for your slow play and the malodorous smells.

*In serious exchanges appoint an ogre, so that you can stay neutral*

## Relentlessly professional

If your opponent is a boring left hemisphere type, plan to flood him with verbals: tell him jokes and show him photographs of all your grandchildren, explaining their measles, vaccinations or bowel movements in microscopic[3] detail and do so at every opportunity. Better still, plan to talk about prostate operations and show him your scars. Rabbit on about gout or some sickening medical condition; go on and on about it and keep his mind off the game.

*To increase anxiety you must keep up the pressure*

## Other ploys

If you know your opponent is umbilically connected to his mobile telephone, get the number and brief a colleague to telephone him every five minutes during your match, but to hang up before he has time to respond. If you want to be really sly, find out the area in which his mistress (or one of them) lives, and get your colleague to dial from a call box with the same area code. If this does not worry him, nothing else will, but as always, there are exceptions.

### GOLFERS ARE FUNNY

In a very important four ball match on New Year's Day, an elderly investigator was playing with a senior lawyer who throughout the first nine holes appeared a bit out of breath and flushed. At the tenth tee the lawyer said: 'Excuse me, old chap, but I have to make a quick call to my girlfriend.' After an animated mobile telephone conversation from behind a bush and an extended pee – both things happening at the same time – the lawyer returned. 'I am sorry about that,' he said, 'last night, I left my wife of 30 years and ran off with my girlfriend. She is playing in the ladies' competition at Wentworth today and I just wanted to make sure she is okay with her new putter.'

Try to find out what is happening in the opponent's business life and especially any problems he has.

For example, if you know that his company has just been raided by the Information Commissioner, plan to mention her or his name when he is facing a difficult downhill putt. 'Oh, by the way, Stan, did I hear you are going to jail?' The putting green is the one exception to the 'no verbals' rule.

*Plan how you will raise the pavement and increase anxiety*

---

[3]   It would be taking it too far to show him a sample, but photographs are allowed

## PLAN YOUR OWN APPROACH

### Equipment

All golf clubs have numbers on them to indicate how far and how high each one should hit the ball. The lower the number, the further and lower the ball should travel and for most golfers (except ladies and German travel agents) clubs called woods go further than irons. You are allowed up to 14 clubs in your bag at any time. The critical club is the putter and if you can get the opponent to lose confidence in his, so much the better. You can do this early in the match by having a practice putt with it. All you have to do is hit the ball really hard off the green and into a bunker and say something like 'Holy shit!'

*Use a bit of disinformation and keep the opponent guessing*

But getting back to planning. You should have all of your clubs renumbered so that your one iron is labelled as a three, down to your eight iron which you have marked as a wedge. You have your nine iron, wedge and sand wedge labelled as wedge a, b and c. Any metalworker will make these changes for you. These modifications have a two-way benefit. The first is that it will appear that with the equivalent iron you are hitting the ball much further than your opponent. This will drive him into a frenzy and he will try and smash his ball to death, resulting in loss of composure, loss of rhythm, loss of all balls, dreadful anxiety and loss of the match. The second benefit is that if your opponent watches what club you are hitting and copies you (or more usually takes one or two less to show off), he will always end up in the lake or the bunker short of the green.

*Make the opponent overstretch himself*

Always use the most modern clubs and balls. If you have less than 10 drivers and 23 putters in your garage you are not a serious golfer, so maybe this chapter is not for you. Try to make your state of the art clubs appear as old and scruffy as possible, while not diminishing their playing characteristics. You can do this by scraping the paint off the head and shaft, but make sure the grips are good and the striking face clean. You can also rebrand your clubs. For example, if you have a full set of new Callaways with gold shafts, why not stick 'Woolworths' transfers over them?

*Have a few surprises up your sleeve*

## PLAN EMBLEMS AND TRANSACTIONAL ROLES

You have to decide what transactional role you plan to adopt, but to win you have to be a critical parent and the opponent an adaptive child. Despite the fact that golfers are partial to asinine clothing, you should dress sensibly, so don't wear your purple flares or yellow Hush Puppies. Appear professional, with really clean, tidy and well pressed attire. All black is a great choice because it will remind your opponent of death and undertakers. All of this should put you in the right transactional role.

*Watch your emblems and transactional role*

# Rehearsal

Again, rehearsal is important and you should know the course backwards and have your strategy clear in your mind. If you want to be a little more devious than normal, play a practice round, by yourself or with your neighbour's niece[4] late in the evening before your big match in the morning, or in the morning for a match in the afternoon. If you have a hideous slice and find one, two or even 18 holes particularly difficult, you may hide a few balls (of the type and number you will use in the match) more or less in the areas where your bad shots are likely to land. Then, in the match, if you do hit a horror shot miles into the trees, you can find your pre-arranged ball, more or less on the same line, but in a place where you can play it.

This is a theoretical scheme and might even be classed by the ignorant as cheating. But it does emphasize the importance of good planning before the big day.

*Planning is critical and practice makes perfect*

Anyway, plan how you will play every hole and make sure you do so within your capabilities. For example, if you know you cannot reach the 300 yard, over the water, par three with one shot, plan a safety route or play on a day when the water is frozen over and you know your scuffed shot will bounce off the ice onto the green.

*Don't try anything fancy*

# Execution: on the day

## THE OPENING

If you have planned effectively, the match should be a cinch. As soon as you meet, consciously examine your opponent's emblems and especially his equipment.

> If he has a one iron in his bag (Lee Trevino said that not even God with lightning could strike a one iron) watch out. Be even more careful if he is carrying three or four different wedges: this tells you he is a serious golfer. If he is using hard, solid core balls (such as Pinnacles or Top Flights) you can assume he is a distance freak and therefore no danger. If he is using soft balata balls, but has a high handicap, you know you are in for a tough game. Think about calling in sick and hope to fight on another day.

*Don't be rushed. Take action only when you know you can win*

If the opponent has really top quality kit, pull a club from his bag, take a practice swing and hit the ground with such venom that a divot the size of a garage door smacks into his golf trolley or over his purple flares. Apologise profusely and then say something along the lines:

> 'Shit, these clubs are really heavy. How on earth can you use them?'

---

[4]   Don't forget page 55. This is a memory retrieval cue

*Get the opponent to lose confidence in his position.*

You might also try the dodge with his putter, referred to earlier, but don't do both because the opponent will smell a rat.

*Be a little bit subtle*

The usual dialogue on the first tee, like all openings, is key and you must get immediate control. Forget all that usual adult-to-adult stuff because you want to get into the role of a critical parent as quickly as possible and stay there until your opponent has conceded defeat.

## SELF-DEPRECATION

If your opponent makes self-deprecating remarks like 'I never hit my first tee shot very well' you must ignore him or respond quietly as a critical parent. 'I don't know why that should be. Have you been hitting the bottle, or what?' Whatever you do, don't sympathise with him: let him sweat.

There is always one really dangerous aspect and that is betting on the match.

## BETTING

If you have much more money than the opponent, try to make a bet that will hurt him, not you. 'What we playing for, Stan, five grand?' If this is half his annual salary and one percent of yours, you have seriously raised the pavement for him but not for you. If the situation is reversed and he says: 'Let's play for five grand', which after all is a childish boastful thing to do, respond as a critical parent: 'I don't play for money: that's a sure way to destroy a friendship/business relationship. If you must, I'll play for 50 pence or a Mars Bar.'

*The person with the most to lose, will*

Lots of golfers are quite nervous before the game and rabbit on about when they played with Tiger Woods last week in Cheam, how well they scored, or how they beat their boss into a pulp.

The reason for this garrulousness, besides overcoming nerves, is to impress you and usually what they say is an embellishment of the truth, which they don't expect to be challenged. So listen carefully and pick on something where the opponent may have over-egged the cake and say something like:

'Are you sure that's true, Stan? You could not have played in Cheam with Tiger Woods last week, because he was ill in bed, in Florida.'
  Stan: 'I didn't mean I played with Tiger himself. What I said was that I played with a taxi driver who looked like Tiger Woods.'
  'Oh,' you say, 'I thought you were bullshitting.'

If you catch him in a small lie, three things will be achieved. The first is that he will be more careful in the future. Secondly, he is moved towards the role of an adaptive child and thirdly you have deprived him of the anxiety-relieving balm obtained through rampant rabbiting.

*Challenge deception*

## PLAYING YOUR OWN GAME

You must neuro-linguistically progamme yourself to play positively. This is easy if you have rehearsed properly. Don't just aim vaguely down the middle of the fairway or at the green but concentrate on hitting on the line of a specific leg of a specific spider on a specific branch of a specific tree 300 yards away, or whatever, but always slightly further away than you actually want the ball to land.

*Make sure you don't fall short of your target*

Golf is easy if you commit to hitting on the right line and really focus. If you are a bit nervous, take a few deep breaths, concentrate on the opponent and consciously take on board his non-verbal communications. If you focus on his nerves, yours will disappear.

*If you feel anxious, concentrate deeply*

Programme yourself to ignore bunkers, water, rough and all that stuff and think positively, concentrating on microscopic targets. But if you hit a bad shot, don't worry: that's life and you can quickly recover by glaring at your opponent. The art is not to make the same mistake twice and never, ever, laugh at yourself or make self-deprecating proclamations. Pretend you are a Buddhist or someone else, possibly a lawyer or an accountant, with massive inner serenity.

*Success is all about commitment*

To get back to the evil of putting ... have you noticed that when you are on holiday in Benidorm and your wife says, 'How about a go on the crazy putting green?' she always wins, sinking monster putts from flower beds, up trees and from old ladies' hats. Serious golfers know that putting is really tough and another intervention by the Devil, who reduced the diameter of the hole from God's design of 12 feet to 2 centimetres. That's the way it is and you just have to live with it but you can NLP yourself to routinely sink any putt of under 40 feet.

> The way you do this is to talk to the ball and tell her that she really wants desperately go down the hole: that there are cream muffins with jam down there and a branch of Harrods. If you can get the ball on your side: job done.

*NLP is a vital tool*

## CHALLENGE DECEPTION

If you discover your opponent cheating, you must immediately let him know you have noticed with a direct confrontation:

'I am sure you scored an eleven there, Stan, not a three.' If he argues, get to the detail: 'You had a drive into the lake, you know the one that killed a duck, played a provisional, so that's three off the tee, then you had two air shots when you fell over into the ditch, hit your sixth into the bramble bush where that young couple were sunbathing in the nude, got out with your seventh and then had four stabs[5] with your putter. Isn't that right?'

*When in doubt, press for more detail*

If your opponent admits the truth, press home your advantage:

'And come to think about it, Stan, on the previous hole, where you said you had a four, you had a 27. Let's go back over it … I don't know what's worse, your golf or your adding up. And you're supposed to be an accountant? Who do you work for? ENRON?'

*The liar is vulnerable when he has had to admit a lie.*
*He is pushed into the role of an adaptive child*

The opponent may stoop to sneaky gamesmanship like dropping his club or farting when you are poised to the hit the ball. If he tries this, don't laugh – as most people do – because it will encourage him to do it again and, worse still, puts you in the role of an adaptive child. So cut him dead with a subtle rebuttal such as:

'If you do that again, Stan, you will get this driver up your ass.'

This elegant critical parent response supports the role you want to reinforce.

*Use phrases that reinforce your intended transactional role*

## PUTTING MONKEYS ON HIS BACK AND NVC

You can increase your opponent's anxiety in lots of ways and you should apply those you have planned. In addition, remember that non-verbal communication is very effective and in golf should be focused on getting the opponent to lose confidence in his swing.

So as soon as he hits a bad shot, do a grossly distorted mime (GDM) of his swing. If he swings in an upright plane, exaggerate this into a dreadful flying left elbow. If he swings in a flat plane, mimic it with a swing that decapitates all the daisies within a 30 foot circle. Repeat GDMs from time to time until he asks the magic question: 'I don't swing like that do I?' Now you have him, the seeds have been sown and you respond: 'Well, I did think you were swinging a bit on the flat side, yes.' He will now start making corrections and defeat is only moments away.

---

[5]   Note the embedded command (see pages 51–52 and 219)

*Use non-verbal communication to your advantage: people react to it*

Alternatively, after your opponent's bad shots:

> Say nothing, but just grunt or put your hand over your mouth or, better still, your eyes. In fact you can go for the eye covering non-verbal from time to time when your opponent is about to hit. The second option is to say: 'Good shot'. This will really upset him and he is likely to respond: 'No, it bloody well wasn't.' You can then be really cruel: 'Well, I thought it was one of your better ones.' If he becomes angry, his chips are up.

*Anger results in the opponent making more mistakes*

You also have a great opportunity to increase both anxiety and frustration every time your opponent carves his ball into the jungle or into Mrs Arbuthnott's flowerbed of prize geraniums:

> Start looking around 50 yards short of where the ball actually landed. The opponent will say: 'It was much longer than that'. 'I don't think it was,' you reply sincerely, 'I think you topped it.' If the opponent walks back in your direction you know you have him.[6]

*Frustration leads to anxiety*

From time to time, walk up to his ball when it is lying perfectly in the fairway, take off your glasses, crouch down on your hands and knees and look carefully at the little round object but say nothing. He is going to ask:

> 'What's up?'
> You reply: 'Nothing, I thought you might be in a divot, but you're not.'

This will set his mind racing and to be certain he does not hit the top of the ball – in what he is now convinced is a divot – he will take an almighty smack and duff it into the bushes. You should not overdo this ploy and ten or twelve times in an eighteen hole match is quite enough.

## THE PIVOTAL POINT AND TURN

If your cunning plan works you will reach the point where your opponent's head drops, his body shrivels and he says something like:

> 'I don't know what's gone wrong today. I normally play much better than this. Maybe you were right and my clubs are too heavy.' [This is a classic case of loss of confidence.]

---

6   Some readers may feel this is a bit sneaky, but it's the opponent's own fault. The idea is to hit fairways and greens

Until you have won, whatever you do, don't sympathise but increase anxiety and pile on the pressure: you have to get him to the pivotal point.

> 'Yes, you are playing badly. Have you been hitting the bottle again, or what?'

Keep this up, show no sympathy but remain polite, and he will soon become a nurturing child and ask:

> 'Can you see what I am doing wrong?'

Under no circumstances, until you have won, should you give your opponent any advice, because, if you do, he is likely to recuperate and win. You should simply say something like:

> 'I can't see what's up, Stan, but I think it must be your new clubs or too much gin at lunchtime.'

Work carefully on the turning until you have won. Then you must become really nice.

*No good deed goes unpunished*

## POST TURN EVENTS

Once you have won the match, hopefully with eight holes left to play, you should reinforce the role of a nurturing parent, so that future relationships with the opponent will not be damaged. After all, you will probably want to play this duffer again, so you must leave him feeling good about himself:

> 'You had some really bad luck, Stan, especially with that duck and the couple in the bush. You've got a great swing: just not your day, eh? It happens to all of us. Don't worry about it. Fancy another game next Thursday? Maybe if we had five grand on it, you would play much better?'

You can then suggest a small bet on the bye[7] and let him win. This always makes bad golfers feel good because they foolishly rationalize that there is still hope.

*Let the opponent know not all has been lost and that there is a future*

## THE DEEP TRUTH

After the match, there is not a lot of deep golfing truth you need to expose, except to get paid your winnings and possibly buy his new golf clubs for a song. However, you should never miss

---

[7] *These are the holes remaining after the match has been lost*

an opportunity and now you are in the bar and firmly in the role of a nurturing parent and the opponent is a confirmed adaptive child, he is defenceless. Now might be the time to raise anything in a wider sense that has been worrying you (i.e. the 'worst case'):

> 'Stan, you know that last invoice you sent us, it was way over the top, wasn't it. How about cutting it by half?'

*The deep truth comes when you are a nurturing parent and the subject is an adaptive child*

There is no question that losing at golf is a deeply depressing experience that you should avoid, unless you are playing against your chairman, the Information Commissioner or a customer. By following our advice, 'failure' should not be in your lexicon.

# Conclusions

You will note that even in the most important interactions, succeeding is 90 per cent planning and 10 per cent execution. That is the bottom line of the cunning plan.

*Concentrate on achieving your objectives and you will*

# **1** *Suspects Checklist*

| Stage | Page | Action | OK |
|---|---|---|---|
| Investigation planning | 176 | **MAINTAIN ABSOLUTE CONFIDENTIALITY**<br>Do not tell anyone who does not need to know<br>Protect the rights of honest people wrongly under suspicion<br>Assume that everything you do and do not do will be scrutinized by a court<br>Do nothing that might compromise your position<br>Take no action unless it conforms with your objectives and is part of the investigations plan<br>Remember that most investigations are compromised within 2 hours of discovery<br>Plan to catch the suspects by surprise as part of the FIRST STEP (see below) | |
| | | **Assume the suspicions are true and probably worse than you currently know. This is the safe course** | |
| | 192 | **Determine the objectives of the investigation**<br>To get money back<br>To expose and punish the offenders<br>To clear innocent people<br>Other | |
| | 193 | **Obtain the necessary authority to act (if you do not already have it)** | |
| Legal framework | 143 | **Understand the legal framework**<br>Criminal proceedings: and whether or not a caution has to be administered<br>Civil law: and possible channels of discovery of documents<br>Human rights<br>Investigatory powers<br>Proportionality<br>Interception of communications<br>Other investigative methods and resources<br>Internal disciplinary procedures | |

| Stage | Page | Action | OK |
|---|---|---|---|
| Case analysis | 144<br>148 | **Understand the weight of evidence necessary to achieve your objectives**<br>Criminal prosecution: beyond reasonable doubt<br>Civil action: balance of probabilities<br>*Ex parte* orders: arguable case | |
| External reporting | 178 | **Decide whether you will advise the police, when and by whom**<br>If criminal prosecution is an objective, advise the police as soon as possible<br>Agree the objectives and methods of investigation | |
| | 177 | **Decide on when you will advise regulatory agencies and by whom**<br>Remember you may be under an obligation to advise regulators without delay<br>Failure to report promptly may result in penalties | |
| | 177 | **Decide on when and how you will advise your external auditors, but do not employ them to conduct the investigation (simply because this may result in a conflict of interest)** | |
| | 177 | **Decide on whether you will advise your fidelity insurers and when**<br>You do not have to advise insurers of mere suspicions<br>Advising insurers too soon may compromise the investigation | |
| Fraud theory | 190 | **Develop a fraud theory and write down the *precise mechanics* of the worst case**<br>Identify who may be involved<br>List the evidence you have<br>Consider other potential methods of fraud<br>List the evidence that should be available and how you can obtain it<br>List details of potential witnesses<br>Consider what plausible excuses the suspects may offer and how these can be disproved by blocking actions or some other method<br>*Keep this theory under review as the investigation moves forward* | |
| | 190 | **Start to compile an EXCEL or Case Map (see www.casemap.com) chronology of events, showing every action relating to the case. Keep this updated as the investigation continues** | |

| Stage | Page | Action | OK |
|-------|------|--------|-----|
| Investigations plan | 191 | **Write down an investigations plan for all of the suspects: obtaining critical evidence**<br>How can critical evidence be obtained? Prepare lists showing how evidence you don't currently have can be obtained<br>If you can do so without alerting the suspects, secure vital internal records such as telephone logs and expenses statements<br>Consider having important evidence forensically examined<br>Personal computers<br>Electronic address books etc<br>**Resources and management**<br>What resources are necessary?<br>Who will direct the investigation? (This should be a senior line manager not responsible for the operations concerned. Investigators, lawyers and managers involved in the operations concerned should not control the investigation)<br>Consider retaining external advisers, but qualify them carefully | |
| | 188 | **Actions to improve your chances of success**<br>Consider monitoring the suspect's internal telephone (but make sure it is legal and 'proportionate' to do so)<br>Analyse telephone call records<br>Consider searching the suspect's work area, desks and files<br>Under legal advice, consider setting traps to catch the suspects in the act | |
| | 175 | **Planning the first step**<br>Decide when you will take the FIRST STEP that will catch the criminals by surprise<br>Determine the order in which suspects and witnesses will be interviewed<br>Identify other actions that must take place as part of the FIRST STEP | |
| Legal advice | 15 | Obtain top-level legal advice on the investigations plan<br>This is especially important in large-scale investigations | |
| Background | 178 | Fully **research the background** of each potential suspect and witness<br>Work, personal and other history<br>Maiden names of his wife and married names of daughters<br>Covertly inspect his home: look for cash improvements<br>Check company registration records | |
| | 187 | Obtain evidence of **minor breaches** by suspects and witnesses<br>Expense claims frauds<br>Misuse of discretion<br>Other<br>Arrange this so that it can be presented in interviews | |

| Stage | Page | Action | OK |
|-------|------|--------|-----|
| Interview planning | 197 | Determine whether a confession is important<br>If the evidence is already conclusive, you may decide to conduct a low-key formal interview, simply to give the suspect the opportunity to explain | |
| | 212 | Decide when, where and by whom each interview will be conducted<br>Assign suitably qualified investigators to each interview<br>Assign and brief interpreters | |
| | 205 | Consider how the evidence will be presented in each interview<br>Summarize evidence in easily understood schedules<br>Translate all important exhibits<br>Decide whether to display the evidence or hold it back until the suspect has given a false explanation<br>Consider enlarging important documents for display<br>Consider preparing bulky evidential files or labelling filing cabinets<br>Arrange the evidence professionally in the order in which it will be presented in interviews<br>Select the best pieces of evidence you have (the 'key points') and enhance their impact<br>Enclose in exhibit bags<br>Enlarge<br>Enclose in bulky files<br>Summarize on schedules | |
| | 200 | Consider how and when the suspects will be invited to attend interviews:<br>Give the minimum advance warning<br>Try to catch them in a dishonest act<br>Do not deter them from attending | |
| Arrange the interview room | 207 | Prepare the interview room(s)<br>Lay out the room carefully<br>Ask a colleague to give you his first impressions of the room<br>Make sure the room is clear of distractions and audio interference<br>Check and replay recording equipment | |
| Record of the interview | 209 | Decide how and by whom a record of the interview will be maintained<br>Is covert tape-recording allowed?<br>Don't make detailed notes at the time | |

| Stage | Page | Action | OK |
|---|---|---|---|
| Detailed interview planning | 201 | Decide on your opening approach<br>Introductory statement<br>Blocking questions<br>Direct confrontation<br>Probing approach | |
| | 201 and 202 | Write down and rehearse your introductory statement and decide how you will progress depending on the suspect's reaction | |
| | 230 and 262 | Determine how many topics you will cover and in what order<br>Base these around the 'key points'<br>Make sure you have documentary or visual evidence of each one<br>Produce these in conjunction with questions | |
| | 225 | Determine the questions you will ask and statements you will make to increase the suspect's anxiety to the point where he loses his confidence to continue with deception. Pay particular attention to visually reinforcing important questions with the production of exhibits | |
| | 249 | Decide how you will phrase soft and direct accusations and deal with lies (see page 236) | |
| | 256 | Decide how and where you might use enticement questions | |
| | 275 | Decide how you will phrase rationalization statements | |
| | 243 | Decide how you will deal with fishing questions | |
| | 281 | Decide how you will handle the pivotal point and the first admissions | |
| | 283 | Decide how you will close the interview | |
| Rehearsal | 222 | Rehearse the interview with interpreters and corroborating witnesses<br>Brief the interpreter on the tactics<br>Brief the corroborating witness to remain silent<br>Also carry out a rehearsal with you taking the role of the suspect<br>Refine your approach | |

| Stage | Page | Action | OK |
|-------|------|--------|-----|
| Interview | | Conduct the interview according to the plan<br>If the suspect continues to lie, force him into detail and indefensible positions | |
| | 222 | Close the interview<br>Agree future meetings and action | |
| | 282 | Agree the record of the interview with the suspect<br>Oral summary<br>Copy of tape recording<br>Joint notes<br>Admissions repeated before an independent witness<br>Statement | |
| Follow-up | 285 | Update the fraud theory and investigations plan | |

# **2** *Elimination Questionnaire*

This appendix is explained on pages 369 to 376.

COBASCO

# CONFIDENTIAL

## ELIMINATION QUESTIONNAIRE

### *Not to be copied without approval*

**DATA PROTECTION ACT**

Some of the information you are asked to provide on this form may be classified as "sensitive personal data" under the above act. We will handle such data in confidence. However, if you have any objection to our using this data for the prevention and detection of crime, by passing it to the Police or other official agencies, please tick the box below.

I do not want the information I have provided on this form released to any outside agency  ☐

# CONFIDENTIAL
## *In Contemplation of Legal Proceedings*

All innocent employees will be be **shocked** to hear that on 12th December 1999, over $20 million was stolen from the bank. It has left a **cloud** over everyone which can only be removed by the identification of the people **responsible.**

We have retained Cobasco Group Limited a **top firm of investigators,** which has **successfully** handled many cases of this type before and we are confident that the facts will emerge.

This form is part of Cobasco's **elimination process** and  we **urge** you to read the following instructions before attempting to complete it:

1    Every **word** you write on this form is important and has a **significance**

2    You are **not permitted** to copy the form either before of after you have completed it

3    Please complete the form in INK and BLOCK CAPITALS

4    This is not a DRAFT, so before you start to write please **think carefully** about your answers

5    If you want to alter an answer, please do NOT CROSS ANYTHING OUT, but write your amendments on page 7. These will be carefully considered

6    If there is not enough space for you to write an answer, please continue on  **lined** paper

7    If you have any questions about the form, please complete as much as you can and **explain** your **uncertainties** on Page 7. An **investigator** will contact you.

| | |
|---|---|
| **YOUR FULL NAME** | |
| **JOB TITLE** | |
| **LOCATION** | |
| **FULL TIME: PART TIME** | |
| **TELEPHONE NUMBER** | |
| **MOBILE NUMBER** | |
| **DATE YOU JOINED BANK** | |
| **SUPERVISOR'S NAME** | |
| **AGENCY NAME** | |

## CONFIDENTIAL

*Every word is important and this is not a draft. Please give as much detail as you consider necessary*

We know that false instructions were put into the FX system on 12th December 1999 with the result that $20 million was paid away to an account in Germany and then withdrawn in cash.  Please tell us all you know about this and why.

PLEASE LEAVE
THIS
SPACE BLANK

| T | D | O |
|---|---|---|
| LD | QNA | QWC |
| Loc | NATA | |
| | | |

| Route to: | | |
|---|---|---|
| | | |
| | | |
| | | |

# CONFIDENTIAL

P

*Every word is important and this is not a draft. Please give as much detail as you consider necessary*

If your were asked to conduct an investigation into this case, what would you do and why?

Who would you interview first?

**PLEASE LEAVE THIS SPACE BLANK**

| T | D | O |
|---|---|---|
| LD | QNA | QWC |
| Loc | NATA | |
| | | |

| Route to: | | |
|---|---|---|
| | | |
| | | |
| | | |

# CONFIDENTIAL

*Every word is important and this is not a draft. Please give as much detail as you consider necessary*

Who do you suspect of being responsible and why?

Do you think the fraud involves someone in the bank?

PLEASE LEAVE
THIS
SPACE BLANK

| T | D | O |
|-----|-----|-----|
| LD | QNA | QWC |
| Loc | NATA | |
| | | |

| Route to: | |
|-----|-----|
| | |
| | |
| | |

## CONFIDENTIAL

*Every word is important and this is not a draft. Please give as much detail as you consider necessary*

Please list the six most important causes of this problem

PLEASE LEAVE
THIS
SPACE BLANK

| T | D | O |
|---|---|---|
| LD | QNA | QWC |
| LOC | NATA | |
| | | |

| Route to: | |
|---|---|
| | |
| | |
| | |

*Every word is important and this is not a draft. Please give as much detail as you consider necessary*

If we don't catch the people responsible, do you think it will happen again and why?

PLEASE LEAVE
THIS
SPACE BLANK

| T | D | O |
|---|---|---|
| LD | QNA | QWC |
| Loc | NATA | |
| | | |

| Route to: |
|---|
| |
| |
| |

# CONFIDENTIAL

*Every word is important and this is not a draft. Please give as much detail as you consider necessary*

Please describe everything you did on 12th December 1999 and give details of any thing that appeared unusual

PLEASE LEAVE
THIS
SPACE BLANK

| T | D | O |
|---|-----|-----|
| LD | QNA | QWC |
| LOC | NATA | |
| | | |

| Route to: |
|---|

# CONFIDENTIAL

*Every word is important and this is not a draft. Please give as much detail as you consider necessary*

Please read through your answers and make sure they are complete and correct. If you would like to make any alterations or further explanations, please enter them below

**PLEASE LEAVE THIS SPACE BLANK**

| T | D | O |
|---|---|---|
| LD | QNA | QWC |
| LOC | NATA | |
| | | |

| Route to: | | |
|---|---|---|
| | | |
| | | |
| | | |

## CONFIDENTIAL

*Every word is important and this is not a draft. Please give as much detail as you consider necessary*

### Please carefully answer the following questions

1    Do you know who prepared the false instructions?

2    WERE YOU IN ANYWAY INVOLVED?

3    Have you ever discussed stealing money from the bank?

4    Do you know who handled the instructions?

5    What else do you know about this?

PLEASE LEAVE
THIS
SPACE BLANK

| T | D | O |
|------|------|------|
| LD | QNA | QWC |
| LOC | NATA | |
| | | |

| Route to: | |
|---|---|
| | |
| | |
| | |

*Please continue on the following page*

*Every word is important and this is not a draft. Please give as much detail as you consider necessary*

*Continued from previous page*

**PLEASE LEAVE
THIS
SPACE BLANK**

| T | D | O |
|---|---|---|
| LD | QNA | QWC |
| LOC | NATA | |
| | | |

| Route to: | | |
|---|---|---|
| | | |
| | | |
| | | |

# CONFIDENTIAL

*Every word is important and this is not a draft. Please give as much detail as you consider necessary*

> We know that cases such as this are unpleasant for everyone involved. Please help us for the future by answering the following questions.

1    How do you feel about this form?

**PLEASE LEAVE THIS SPACE BLANK**

2    Should we believe YOUR answers to the questions?

3    Why?

4    How would you feel if we asked you to attend a polygraph (Lie detector) test?

4    What would your explanation be if our investigations revealed that your answers were not true?

5    While filling out this form, what were your emotions?

6    Were you afraid of filling out this form?

| T | D | O |
|---|---|---|
| LD | QNA | QWC |
| LOC | NATA | |

7    Who have you discussed this case with?

8    How accurate do you believe your answers are? *(Please tick box)*

| Not Sure | | | | | | Totally |
|---|---|---|---|---|---|---|
| | | | | | | |

| Route to: |
|---|
| |
| |
| |

# 3 *CIA Witness Statement Form*

# WITNESS STATEMENT
### (CJ Act 1967, s9 MC Act 1980 s102; MC Rules 1981 r 70)

**Statement of:**.....................................................................................................................................................

**Age if Under 18**        *(if over 18 insert "Over 18")*        **Occupation**.............................................

This statement (consisting of        page(s) each signed by me) is true to the best of my knowledge and belief and I make it knowing that, if it is tendered in evidence, I shall be liable to prosecution if I have wilfully stated in it anything which I know to be false or do not believe to be true.

Signed        ............................................................ Dated................................................

Signature................................................ Signature witnessed

# WITNESS STATEMENT
*(CJ Act 1967, s9 MC Act 1980 s102; MC Rules 1981 r 70)*

Signature............................................... Signature witnessed

# WITNESS STATEMENT
## *ADDITIONAL INFORMATION*

## IDENTIFICATION AND ADDRESSES

| SURNAME | FIRST AND OTHER NAMES |
|---|---|
| MAIDEN NAME | MOTHER'S MAIDEN NAME |
| DATE OF BIRTH | PLACE OF BIRTH |

| HOME ADDRESS |
|---|
| |

| HOME TELEPHONE NUMBER | MOBILE TELEPHONE NUMBER |
|---|---|

| NAME OF EMPLOYER |
|---|

| ADDRESS OF EMPLOYER |
|---|
| |

| OCCUPATION |
|---|

| WORK TELEPHONE NUMBER | WORK FAX NUMBER |
|---|---|

| OTHER CONTACT POINTS |
|---|
| |

## DETAILS OF STATEMENT

| STATEMENT TAKEN BY | |
|---|---|
| STATEMENT TAKEN AT | TIMES FROM AND TO |
| NAMES OF WITNESS | |
| TELEPHONE NUMBER OF WITNESS | MOBILE TELEPHONE NUMBER |

## AVAILABILITY

| |
|---|
| |
| |
| |
| |
| |

# 4 *RIPA Analysis*

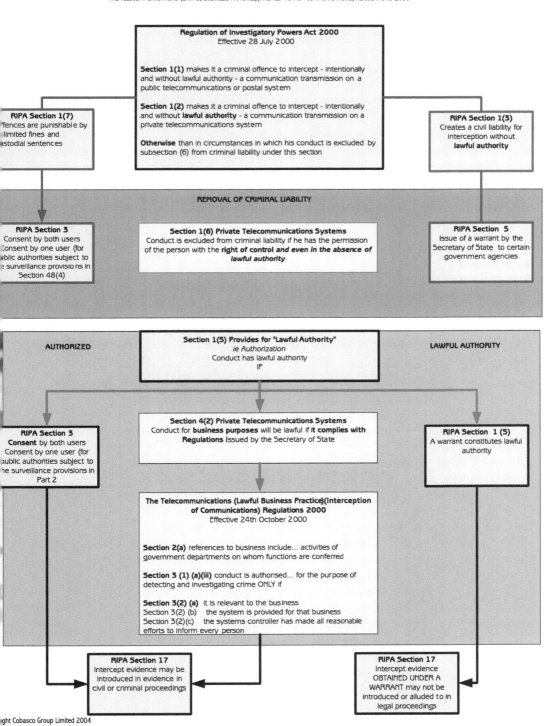

**REGULATION OF INVESTIGATORY POWERS ACT 2000**
*and*
*THE TELECOMMUNICATIONS (LAWFUL BUSINESS PRACTICE)(INTERCEPTION OF COMMUNICATIONS) REGULATIONS 2000*

**Regulation of Investigatory Powers Act 2000**
Effective 28 July 2000

**Section 1(1)** makes it a criminal offence to intercept - intentionally and without lawful authority - a communication transmission on a public telecommunications or postal system

**Section 1(2)** makes it a criminal offence to intercept - intentionally and without **lawful authority** - a communication transmission on a private telecommunications system

**Otherwise** than in circumstances in which his conduct is excluded by subsection (6) from criminal liability under this section

**RIPA Section 1(7)**
ffences are punishable by limited fines and stodial sentences

**RIPA Section 1(3)**
Creates a civil liability for interception without **lawful authority**

**REMOVAL OF CRIMINAL LIABILITY**

**RIPA Section 3**
Consent by both users
Consent by one user (for ublic authorities subject to e surveillance provisions in Section 48(4)

**Section 1(6) Private Telecommunications Systems**
Conduct is excluded from criminal liability if he has the permission of the person with the **right of control** *and even in the absence of lawful authority*

**RIPA Section 5**
Issue of a warrant by the Secretary of State to certain government agencies

**AUTHORIZED**

**Section 1(5) Provides for "Lawful Authority"**
*ie Authorization*
Conduct has lawful authority
IF

**LAWFUL AUTHORITY**

**RIPA Section 3**
**Consent** by both users
Consent by one user (for public authorities subject to he surveillance provisions in Part 2

**Section 4(2) Private Telecommunications Systems**
Conduct for **business purposes** will be lawful if **it complies with Regulations** issued by the Secretary of State

**RIPA Section 1 (5)**
A warrant constitutes lawful authority

**The Telecommunications (Lawful Business Practice)(Interception of Communications) Regulations 2000**
Effective 24th October 2000

**Section 2(a)** references to business include... activities of government departments on whom functions are conferred

**Section 3 (1) (a)(iii)** conduct is authorised... for the purpose of detecting and investigating crime ONLY if

**Section 3(2) (a)** it is relevant to the business
Section 3(2) (b)   the system is provided for that business
Section 3(2)(c)   the systems controller has made all reasonable efforts to inform every person

**RIPA Section 17**
Intercept evidence may be introduced in evidence in civil or criminal proceedings

**RIPA Section 17**
Intercept evidence OBTAINED UNDER A WARRANT may not be introduced or alluded to in legal proceedings

# Index